BURDENS OF HISTORY

ANTOINETTE BURTON

BURDENS
OF HISTORY

BRITISH FEMINISTS, INDIAN WOMEN,

AND IMPERIAL CULTURE, 1865–1915

THE UNIVERSITY OF NORTH CAROLINA PRESS | CHAPEL HILL & LONDON

The paper in this book meets the guidelines for permanence and
durability of the Committee on Production Guidelines for Book
Longevity of the Council on Library Resources.

Library of Congress Cataloging-in-Publication Data
Burton, Antoinette M., 1961–
Burdens of history : British feminists, Indian women, and imperial
culture, 1865–1915 / Antoinette Burton.
p.   cm.
Includes bibliographical references and index.
ISBN 0-8078-2161-6 (alk. paper).—ISBN 0-8078-4471-3
(pbk. : alk. paper)
1. Feminism—Great Britain—History. 2. Feminists—Great Britain—
Attitudes—History. 3. Women—India—History. 4. Imperialism—
History. I. Title.
HQ1593.B87   1994
305.42'0941—dc20   94-5722
CIP

cloth   06 05 04 03 02   5 4 3 2 1
paper   06 05 04   6 5 4

Parts of Chapters 1 and 4 appeared in "The White Woman's Burden:
British Feminists and 'The Indian Woman,' 1865–1915," *Women's
Studies International Forum* 13, no. 4 (1990): 295–308.

A shorter version of Chapter 6 appeared as "The Feminist Quest for
Identity: British Imperial Suffragism and 'Global Sisterhood,' 1900–
1915," *Journal of Women's History* 3, no. 2 (Fall 1991): 46–81.

Contents

Acknowledgments

My gratitude for the support and sustenance I have received over the years is as heartfelt as it is longstanding. To those who first nurtured me at the Agnes Irwin School, especially George Barnett, Eleanor Cederstrom, Evelyn Dohan, Lucy Knauer, and R. Patricia Trickey, I owe perhaps the most overdue acknowledgment. Thanks to Emmet Larkin for supervising a thesis that ranged far from his beloved Ireland; to Barney Cohn and Peter Marshall for their unfailing interest and their "colonial" and "imperial" perspectives; to Jim Grossman for his concern and dedication; and to Nupur Chaudhuri and Peg Strobel for their generosity toward me. Thanks also go to Rani Fedson for giving me shelter when I was in need of it; to Joan Anderson for offering me a "home away from home"; and to Michele Scheinkman, for keeping safe all of the personal history I've deposited in her.

Feminist communities at the University of Chicago, at Indiana State University, and at The Johns Hopkins University have proven invaluable to me as I conceived, wrestled with, wrote, and reworked this book. I have appreciated the opportunity to present my work in both the Feminist Theory Workshop and the Gender and Cross-Cultural Feminisms Workshop at Chicago and at a variety of research and public-speaking forums sponsored by the Department of History and the Women's Studies Program at ISU. This project has also profited from the input of members of the Imperial History seminar at the Institute of Historical Research and the

Institute for Commonwealth Studies, London, as well as from comments by Angela Woollacott and participants at the Women's Studies Program seminar series at Case Western Reserve University.

Thanks to David Doughan, Susan Cross, and the Fawcett Library for creating yet another home away from home, and to Veronica Perkins and Pam Upton for helping me in the last stages. Lewis Bateman has been not just an ideal editor but an enthusiastic supporter all along the way. Anna and Charles Denchfield generously gave me a room, good cheer, and lively company, all of which make "No. 17" worth coming back to. I would also like to acknowledge the financial assistance of the Fulbright Association, the Chicago branch of the English-Speaking Union, the University of Chicago, and Indiana State University, without which various stages of this enterprise would have been impossible.

Colleagues near and far read both parts and the whole of this manuscript while it was in process, and I would like to acknowledge them here: Emary Aronson, Leora Auslander, Karin Badt, Dan Beaver, Frank Biletz, Catherine Candy, Nupur Chaudhuri, Scott Clark, Gary Daily, Susan Dehler, Chandra de Silva, Geraldine Forbes, Dan Gordon, Darlene Hantzis, Steve Johnstone, Penny Kanner, Mike Kugler, Philippa Levine, Laura Mayhall, Arvid Perez, Barbara Ramusack, George Robb, Hannah Rosen, Deb Rossum, Sudipta Sen, Tom Steiger, and Peg Strobel. I have also profited over the years from conversations with Padma Anagol-McGinn, Cynthia Enloe, Janaki Nair, and Mrinalini Sinha and from correspondence with Claire Hirshfield, Katherine Kelly, and Leila J. Rupp. I am particularly grateful to Leora Auslander—who came into my life at a critical moment and whose support and friendship have never flagged; to Darlene Hantzis—who taught me, among many other things, how to practice feminist theories in daily life; to Philippa Levine—who never fails to nurture me intellectually and otherwise or to remind me what day it is; and to Barbara Ramusack—who has been from the start both a generous mentor and a cherished friend. Gary Daily and Chandra de Silva are, each in his own way, invaluable feminist friends whose good humor and intellectual camaraderie have become essential.

Thanks are due as well to a host of friends whose love and affection have kept me going in some difficult times. Among these are Layla Ahsan, Allison August, Cindy Bell, Chris Cannon, Hope Flammer, Dina Franch, Russell Galer, David Goodman, Kairen Griffiths, Maureen Harp, Karla Hershey, Alex Hoehn-Saric, Hilary Houghton, Candace Kean, Ann Klotz, Yi-Qing Liu, Nancy Mahon, Audrey Matkins, Julie Rogers, Carol Scherer, Nayan Shah, Michael Scott, and Michael Sohn. Students from and friends

in Terre Haute—especially Deb Drummond, Jasen Gibbons, Cheryl Gies-
ler, Kathy Hackelman, Suzanne Hobbs, Ann Malloy, Chris Malloy, Lee
Reberger, Tara Ross, and Pat Shavloske—opened up new worlds to me, for
which I will long be appreciative. My friendship with Steve Johnstone has
sustained me through thick and thin; without him, Hyde Park and much
else would have gotten the best of me. For Emie Aronson's inimitable
friendship I am also profoundly grateful. Deb Rossum and Hannah Rosen
are, together, the very heart and soul of my "imagined community." They
know, I hope, how much of this is theirs. And from those first Fulbright
days, George Robb has been there, sensible shoes or no: thanks to him for
"keeping the faith." Whether from Philadelphia or Paris, Monica Burton
has been ever supportive. To Vicki Burton I owe an immeasurable debt,
and so an even greater thanks, for always being there. Paul Arroyo, for his
part, hopefully understands all the ways in which he is the one.

And, finally, so much is due to my mother and my father, who have been
and remain the sine qua non. In different but equally powerful ways, both of
them have shown me the value of telling stories and the importance of
understanding history. The Ferrari sisters and the men who married them
know, I trust, how much I owe them. Nor is the memory of Isabella E.
Burton or that of her beloved Harry forgotten. To my maternal grand-
parents, who gave me the world and taught me the meaning of uncondi-
tional love, this book is in turn lovingly dedicated.

It is one of the great advantages of being a woman

that one can pass even a very fine negress without

wishing to make an Englishwoman of her.

—Virginia Woolf, *A Room of One's Own* (1928)

BURDENS OF HISTORY

1

The Politics of Recovery

HISTORICIZING IMPERIAL FEMINISM,

1865–1915

Organized feminism in Britain emerged in the context of Victorian and Edwardian imperialism. Historically speaking, arguments for British women's emancipation were produced, made public, and contested during a period in which Britain experienced the confidence born of apparent geopolitical supremacy as well as the anxieties brought on by challenges to imperial permanence and stability. Although historians of women and feminist historians have been concerned with what Adrienne Rich calls "the politics of location" in the work of reconceptualizing traditional history, Western feminism's historically imperial location has not been the subject of comprehensive historical inquiry, except insofar as the origins of "international sisterhood" are concerned.[1] This is true, despite the imperial discourses that leading British feminists utilized, the world-civilizing significance they attached to their role in national political culture, and the frequent invocation of non-Western and especially of Indian women as subjects in need of salvation by their British feminist "sisters." Relocating

British feminist ideologies in their imperial context and problematizing Western feminists' historical relationships to imperial culture at home are, therefore, the chief concerns of this book.

As historical phenomena, feminism and imperialism might at first glance be considered an unlikely match. In the course of working on this project, I discovered that, to other people, these two terms suggested Virginia Woolf—presumably because of her rejection of the terms of Englishness, her fierce attacks on Kipling's imperialism, and her claims to be a citizen of the world.[2] The combination "women and India" was also typically taken to signify lady missionaries or colonial memsahibs. Such ready equivalencies reflect both gender stereotyping in the narratives of imperial history and the lack of attention paid to the domestic culture of imperialism in which nineteenth-century middle-class British feminism came into its own. Although some of Woolf's "quarrel[s] with patriarchy and imperialism"[3] are echoed here, what is primarily at issue is not British feminists' opposition to empire, but their collaboration in its ideological work. And while the role of women as cultural and religious missionaries is certainly addressed, my emphasis is on the secular work of emancipation, frequently undertaken in the name of Indian women, which was the main concern of British feminists during this period. That the languages of imperialism—articulating as they did the parameters of cultural superiority, political trusteeship, and sheer Englishness—should have been among the most readily available to women involved in various aspects of the British women's movement from the Victorian period onward is not particularly surprising. Evidence of empire was to be found everywhere in Western culture from the nineteenth century onward. There were few who disagreed with its values, even if they questioned the efficiency of its agents or the effectiveness of its agencies.[4] The vocabulary of Victorian social reform and philanthropy at home was, moreover, steeped in racial metaphors and civilizing tropes, to which the emerging discourses of social Darwinism and institutional anthropology added their share.[5] The geopolitical context for all of this was an expanding empire and an expansive, if at times slightly anxious, confidence in Britain's cultural superiority. These are, indeed, among the hallmarks of Victorian culture, historically speaking—though admittedly they have not traditionally been seen as constituents of domestic political or social reform culture.[6] A quick chronological sketch therefore provides the immediate historical context for what Valerie Amos and Pratibha Parmar have called "imperial feminism."[7]

The beginnings of the organized British women's movement at mid-century coincided with the apogee of British imperial preeminence.[8] In meeting to discuss the "disabilities of the female sex" and, by the mid-1860s, to generate suffrage petitions to the House of Commons, the ladies of Langham Place and the founding members of the London Women's Suffrage Society were laying claim to the same benefits of citizenship that Lord Palmerston enshrined in his famous "civis Romanus sum" paean to British imperial hegemony.[9] Although she never called herself a feminist, after the Crimean War Florence Nightingale nonetheless became a symbol in the public mind of what one female's emancipation could do for Britain's imperial interests, and feminists claimed her as one of their own until World War I and beyond.[10] As Greater Britain became a formal empire, British women's movements achieved many of their goals: university education for women, municipal suffrage, marriage-law reform, and the abolition of the Contagious Diseases Acts. The "scramble" for Africa and the ongoing struggle for women's rights occurred virtually at the same time. Significantly, British feminists noted the coincidence and exploited it in order to advance arguments for what many believed to be the most fundamental right of all: women's suffrage. This was partly in response to the invective against women's suffrage that prominent imperial statesmen like Lords Cromer and Curzon hurled at women activists, but it was not simply a reflex action. Feminists and particularly suffrage advocates had their own traditions of imperial rhetoric long before the formation of the Anti-Suffrage League in 1908—traditions that they routinely invoked to ally women's political emancipation with the health and well-being of the British Empire.

The Boer War debacle and the eugenic concerns that followed in its wake undoubtedly shaped the terms of the imperial feminist Cause. The war itself disturbed feminists, albeit for different reasons. While Josephine Butler raged against the injustices done to "the native races" in South Africa, Millicent Garrett Fawcett defended the British government's war camps; meanwhile, woman as savior of the nation, the race, and the empire was a common theme in female emancipation arguments before and especially after 1900.[11] With the emergence of international feminist institutions like the International Woman Suffrage Alliance and the International Council of Women in the pre–World War I period, British women figured in British feminist rhetoric as the saviors of the entire world of women as well. As Sarah Amos put it, "We are struggling not just for English women alone, but for all the women, degraded, miserable, unheard of, for whose life and happiness England has daily to answer to God."[12] The persistence of rhetoric about "global sisterhood," together with what Deborah Gorham calls the "sacral" character attributed to international feminism in the late twentieth century,[13] has obscured the historically imperial context out of which "international" female solidarity was initially imagined and has continued to be unproblematically reproduced by some. As Chandra Mohanty has written, such notions of universal sisterhood are "predicated on the erasure of the history and the effects of contemporary imperialism." Behind the project of historicizing imperial feminism lies the problem of how and why the modern British women's movement produced a universal female "we" that continues to haunt and, ironically, to fragment feminists worldwide.[14]

By 1915 the war between Germany and England threatened to undermine what appeared to be feminist unity and British imperial predominance; both were to survive the peace, though not without short- and long-term damages. Victorian feminism thus came of age in a self-consciously imperial culture, during an extended historical moment when the British Empire was believed to be at its height and, subsequently, feared to be on the wane.[15] Its development was not just "consolidated during a period of popular imperialism," though anxieties about empire shaped the terms of feminist debate inexorably.[16] Imperial culture at home provided the ground for feminism's organizational resurgence after the decline of antislavery reform, while imperial anxiety furnished one of the bases for middle-class British feminism's appeals to the state in the aftermath of the Boer War. The fact of empire shaped the lives and identities of those who participated in the women's movement, making it a constituent part of modern British feminist identities.

Given the longevity of many in the first generation of women suffragists, there were some who, like Fawcett and Eleanor Rathbone, witnessed the onset of British imperial decline over the course of their own lifetimes.[17] Those born into the second and third generations had to have been aware of the tenuousness of British imperial supremacy after 1918, despite the fact that Britain emerged a victor from the European war. The role of Indian soldiers in defending the imperial nation during the Great War and the claims that colonial nationalists believed it lent to their own quest for self-government—not to mention the riots in Britain and at Amristar in 1919—signified to many that the old imperial policies and attitudes were increasingly outmoded.[18] Like feminism, imperialism after World War I was not what it had been in the nineteenth century, even while, as Brian Harrison and others have begun to argue, the break between 1918 and what came before is not perhaps as definitive as it once seemed.[19] In spite of these vicissitudes, and of course because of them, empire, from its mid-Victorian glories through its prewar crises of confidence, must be counted among the influences shaping the feminist discourses and self-images of these first generations of emancipationists. And because they enlisted empire and its values so passionately and so articulately in their arguments for female emancipation, British feminists must also be counted among the shapers of imperial rhetoric and imperial ideologies in this period.

Feminists working for reform in the political, social, and cultural arenas of late Victorian Britain demonstrated their allegiances to the imperial nation-state and revealed their imperial mentalities in a variety of ways. Although this tendency has not been critically examined by historians of British feminism, arguments for female emancipation were articulated in patriotic, and at times remarkably nationalistic, terms. Whether the cause was votes for women, the opening up of university education, or the repeal of the Contagious Diseases Acts, feminists of all persuasions viewed Britain's national political traditions and its traditional political culture as an irresistible justification for their claims upon the state.

Conversely, their exclusions and oppression were considered violations of their great heritage. "What is it, after all," Emmeline Pethick-Lawrence asked in 1908, "that British women asked of a British Government [?]" Her response followed: "Nothing more than that constitutional rights should be given to women who were British born subjects of the Crown. . . . It was neither a strange nor a new demand, and meant only the restitution of those ancient rights which had been stolen from them in 1832."[20] Victorian feminists traced their political disenfranchisement all the way back to Magna Carta, with Chrystal Macmillan calling for an equivalent Woman's Charter to redress the balance in the twentieth century.[21] While a few historians have disclaimed the nationalist rhetoric of Victorian and Edwardian suffrage women, others tend to view it simply as a product of war patriotism confined largely to the pronouncements of Christabel and Emmeline Pankhurst.[22] In fact, British feminists worked consistently to identify themselves with the national interest and their cause with the future prosperity of the nation-state. Practically the entire corpus of female emancipation argument depended on these kinds of associations; they were not, in other words, either erratic or uncommon. As this book works to illustrate, British feminists produced them across a variety of genres throughout the nineteenth century and down to the symbolic end of the Victorian period, the Great War.

A word is necessary here on the terms "English" and "British" and the significance of their relationships. They were often used interchangeably in the period under consideration and some modern British historians have tended to reproduce this elision.[23] While the women's movement was a British phenomenon, encompassing activists from England, Ireland, Scotland, and Wales, it often, as we shall see, privileged "Englishness" as its core value and attributed the so-called best qualities of the Anglo-Saxon race to it. As Graham Dawson has noted, this maneuver marked "the hegemony of England within the United Kingdom"—a hegemony that some English feminists accepted unquestioningly and that at times brought them into conflict with some of their Irish and Scotch sisters.[24] Feminist pride in Englishness was not necessarily crude or vulgar, and it was not perhaps exactly equivalent to the expressions of jingoism commonly found in music hall productions and other forms of popular culture in the late Victorian period. Of Englishness and its characteristics, for example, Ray Strachey told Fawcett rather genteelly in the 1930s: "I've always thought it was one of the solidly good things in the world."[25] Her gentility notwithstanding, Strachey and those feminist women who, like her, grew up with a keen appreciation for British imperial greatness, *did* pronounce their loyalty to things English and did commit the women's movement in Britain to what they believed to be the best characteristics of the "national culture." Compelling Britain to live up to its own unique cultural—and, of course, to its nationally specific moral—attributes was one of the forces behind feminist ideology before the First World War. In an interesting combination of rhetorical skill and political canniness, British feminists argued that female emancipation was necessary not simply because it was just, but because it was nothing less than the embodiment of Britain's national self-interest and the fulfillment of its historical destiny.

Aligning the women's movement, and especially the suffrage campaign, with the fate of the nation meant, in the context of late-nineteenth-century Britain, identifying it with the future of the empire. In Victorian culture nation and empire were effectively one in the same: in historical as well as in symbolic terms, the national power of Britain was synonymous with the colonial power of Greater Britain.[26] As a symbol the nation had the power to conjure the empire; allegiances to them were concentric and mutually dependent. This symbiotic relationship between nation and empire was one on which feminists of the period capitalized in order to legitimate the women's movement as a world-historical force and an extension of Britain's worldwide civilizing mission. References to India, to the colonies, and to "our great worldwide empire" were legion in nineteenth-century emancipationist literature, demonstrating the ways in which empire was both a rather ordinary fact of life and an important point of reference, not just for feminists but for all Victorians. Among other things, empire provided British citizens with "a world view which was central to their perceptions of themselves." They understood it as something that set them apart from the rest of the world, and they accepted it as a testament to their national, cultural, and racial supremacy.[27] For feminists, the British Empire was evidence of the superiority of British national culture and, most important, of the obligations that British women were required to discharge—for the benefit of colonial peoples and, ultimately, for the good of the imperial nation itself. In pageantry, in rhetoric—indeed, in virtually all forms of ideological production—middle-class British feminists of the period invoked the glories of empire in order to ally their cause with its global power and its social mission. Critiques of imperialism were articulated, but usually on the grounds that empire "gravely slighted" its daughters. As one contributor to *Common Cause* complained in 1914, celebrations of Empire Day, like the empire itself, only recognized the kinds of imperial service "which are done to the sound of a drum." The fact that organizers of that year's Hyde Park festivities deliberately excluded girls from the parade was symbolic, in her view, of the sexism of the whole imperial enterprise. She echoed the sentiments of many British feminists when she called for a recognition of women's "heroism and discipline" in the imperial nation and asked that empire accord them "the honourable place which they justly claim."[28]

Claiming their place in the empire was—along with educational reform, suffrage campaigns, and battles against the sexual double standard—one of the priorities of liberal British feminists during the period under consideration. The quest for inclusion in the imperial state (an extension of the call for representation in the nation) was not, however, the full extent of their imperial ideology. Arguments for recognition as imperial citizens were predicated on the imagery of Indian women, whom British feminist writers depicted as helpless victims awaiting the representation of their plight and the redress of their condition at the hands of their sisters in the metropole. Oriental womanhood as a trope for sexual difference, primitive society, and colonial backwardness was certainly not limited to British feminist writing. British official concern about the practice of suttee had been part of colonial discourse practically since the Battle of Plassy (1757); rhetoric about Indian women's condition, which was equated with helplessness and backwardness, was no less crucial to notions of British cultural superiority and to rationales for the British imperial presence in India than the alleged effeminacy of the stereotypical "Oriental" male.[29] Indeed, in order to justify their own participation in the imperial nation-state, late-Victorian feminists drew on some of the same arguments about Indian family life and domestic practices that had been deployed by British men in the 1830s and 1840s in order to legitimate control over Indian men.[30] "Our heathen sisters in

India," "the benighted women of our Queen's vast empire"—this was also
the standard stuff of contemporary evangelical discourse, utilized equally by
male and female missionaries as evidence of the need for salvation and
reformist intervention.[31] Even English women not ostensibly concerned
with conversion (or with feminism, for that matter) used the zenana as
shorthand for Indian women's imprisonment—and, not incidentally, as
contrasting evidence of their own cultural superiority and female agency.[32]
"The Indian Woman," represented almost invariably as a helpless, degraded
victim of religious custom and uncivilized cultural practices, signified a
burden for whose sake many white women left Britain and devoted their
lives in the empire. Contemporary Indian women, who were far from the
passive creatures of custom and zenana imprisonment, were active in social
and political reform both in India and in the British Isles. Some, like Pandita
Ramabai, Cornelia Sorabji, and Rukhmabai, traveled to Britain in search of
further education and philanthropic support; others, like Mrs. P. L. Roy,
were part of a more permanent Indian community in Britain concerned
with reform and charity work.[33] Their public activities notwithstanding,
images of an enslaved Oriental womanhood were the common possessions
of Victorian social reformers and exercised much of the rhetorical force
behind humanitarian narratives of the Victorian period.[34]

Feminist writers from the 1860s onward used what they and their contemporaries viewed as Indian women's plight as an incentive for British
women to work in the empire and as proof of British women's contributions to the imperial civilizing mission. "Have you leisure? Have you
strength?" Josephine Butler asked those interested in the reform of prostitution in India in 1887. "If so . . . there is a career open, a wide field
extending to many parts of the world, a far-off cry of distress waiting for
response."[35] British women who, like Butler, championed the cause of India
and its women gave a high profile to the condition of "Oriental womanhood." Although remembered chiefly for her work in the Crimea, Florence
Nightingale wrote persuasively about "our stewardship in India" and believed its health and welfare to be "a home issue . . . a vital and moral
question."[36] Mary Carpenter's visits to India in the 1860s and 1870s and the
emphasis she gave to the importance of Indian female education were also
crucial in "opening up" the colonies as a field for British women's social
reform, especially given the premium she placed on the opportunities that
India provided for women training as professional teachers in Britain.[37]
There were also many feminist women who became interested in India
either through family connections or religious curiosity or, like Mary Carpenter and Josephine Butler, because they had met the Indian reformers

Rammohun Roy, Keshub Sen, and Behramji Malabari during their visits to England.[38] Anna Gore-Langton, Frances Power Cobbe, Annie Besant, Henrietta Muller, Mary Scharlieb, Eva McLaren, Josephine Butler, Millicent Garrett Fawcett, Arabella Shore, Margaret Cousins, Emmeline Pethick-Lawrence, and Eleanor Rathbone are just a few feminist luminaries who wrote about or encouraged reform on behalf of Indian women. By virtue of the organizations that they headed and to which they were affiliated and sympathetic, the cause of Indian women was not limited to the interests of a handful of prominent women, but was taken up in one form or another by the broad spectrum of women's groups, affecting the whole British women's movement. The Victorian feminist press, which retailed the activities of a wide variety of female reform and feminist organizations, effectively broadcast the cause of Indian women to the feminist reading public throughout the nineteenth and early twentieth centuries, showcasing the imperial activities of British women and, most significant, the ways in which they were devoting themselves "to the glorious and blessed work of raising their Eastern sisters to fill that place in society for which the Creator has destined them!"[39]

British feminism was, as its historians have been at pains to elucidate, by no means monolithic. Its fragmentations, multiple constituencies, and various trajectories require us to talk about the women's movement as plural and to identify the ideologies that it produced as "feminisms." And although the focus of this book is chiefly on bourgeois women and middle-class organizations, they are not the whole story of feminist theory and practice in this period.[40] The same is true of women's suffrage.[41] Votes for women may have been something of a unifier, even across class, in the Edwardian period, but feminist organizations developed, splintered off from each other, and required hard and fast loyalties that could divide feminist women in painful and lifelong ways.[42] And yet most if not all middle-class feminist groups in the period 1865–1915 identified themselves with the cause of Indian women and, through it, with the civilizing mission of the empire itself. Concern for Indian women was not limited to women's suffrage groups, as the minutes of the National Union of Women Workers and the proceedings of the Moral Reform Union testify.[43] It was of interest to a wide range of Victorian activist women, some of whom have been viewed as feminists and some of whom were not. In light of the tensions between the National Union of Women Workers and suffragists over the issue of votes for women, the cause of Indian womanhood apparently unified British women reformers in cases where even (and especially) the vote could not.[44] And, finally, the attention that both *Votes for Women* and

Common Cause (the official organ of the constitutional suffragists) gave to Indian women in the first fifteen years of the new century lends plausibility to Sandra Holton's claim that constitutionalists and militants were not as ideologically heterogeneous as traditional historiography has suggested.[45] The images of Indian women that virtually all women's organizations deployed furnished them with a shared imperial identity and united them in a cause that they believed was at once greater than and identical to their own—whether their particular issue was suffrage, repeal, social purity, or a combination thereof. Reform causes at home and the plight of Indian women were believed to be intimately related, for many contemporary feminists were convinced that work on behalf of Indian women helped to demolish the case against female emancipation. As Mary Carpenter put it in 1868, "The devoted work of multitudes of Englishwomen in that great continent, shows what our sex can do."[46]

If Indian women, as imagined by British feminists, were used as an argument for white women's social-imperial usefulness, they were believed to constitute additionally a special political burden for British women and, more particularly, for British feminist women. An apparently unrepresented colonial clientele, they served as evidence of the need for British women's formal political participation in the imperial nation. In part, what British women depicted as Indian women's suffering ratified their own claims on the imperial state. Child marriage, the treatment of widows, the practice of suttee, and the prison of the zenana represented the typical catalog of woes that feminists enumerated as "the condition of Indian women." "If it were only for our responsibilities in India," Helena Swanwick told the readers of *Common Cause*, "we women must not rest until we have the vote."[47] This was the essence of the white feminist burden, premised among other things on the expectation that British women's emancipation would relieve Indian women's suffering and "uplift" their condition. One suffragist, Hester Gray, actually identified women's suffrage as the equivalent of "the white woman's burden" and linked the passage of a women's suffrage bill in Parliament to the redress of wrongs experienced by "the less privileged women of the East."[48] For Gray and others, this linkage was implicit in their belief that the parliamentary franchise would empower British women to reform a whole host of social evils—both at home and in the empire—and it consequently motivated their commitment to women's suffrage as the centerpiece of female emancipation.[49]

In the hands of suffrage women, the condition of the Indian female population made votes for British women an imperial necessity and, in fact, the sine qua non of the empire's continued prosperity. They were on quite safe and well-established cultural ground here, for it was more or less axiomatic in the Victorian period that the condition of women was the index of any civilization. Hence the continued oppression of British women through political exclusion threatened, they argued, the very premises of superior civilization upon which the whole justification for empire was founded. Indian women's status added fuel to the fire, since it was generally agreed upon among feminists that child marriage, Indian mothers' ignorance, and the persistence of zenana life were at the root of Indian cultural decay.[50] One did not have to be a missionary with personal experience in India in this period to conclude that "the maternal influence has been one of the chief hindrances" to progress there.[51] Although some feminist women, like Henrietta Muller, subscribed to the view that Indian civilizations had experienced a golden age, during which women had been queens and educated mothers, Indian women's responsibility for the degradation of Indian home life was practically an article of faith among Victorian feminists.[52] This did not necessarily entail blaming Indian women—in fact, it threw the burden of responsibility back on British women. It was also, of course, a useful explanatory device for Britain's imperial presence (India is conquered because it is a fallen civilization) and a rationale for Britain's civilizing mission (India needs British influence in order to progress). Such presumptions were, needless to say, lying around Victorian culture, and although they were not in any sense invented by British feminists, they were readily appropriated by them.

It is a testament to the warped logic of European imperialism that improvements in Indian women's lives should have been desired partly as evidence of what Britain was doing for India—proof in deed as well as in word of why the British Empire was regarded as the best civilizing force in the world. British feminists participated in and helped to legitimize this imperial logic when they claimed that not just Indian women's uplift but also British women's role in it was a project of the utmost importance to the future of the empire. British feminists arguably imagined the Western women's movement as something of a commodity—one of the products of a superior civilization that Britain exported for the benefit of its colonized people. As Hester Gray saw it, political emancipation would "release for action in the distant parts of the Empire, the kind of public servant so urgently needed," presumably because she anticipated that voting women would have a greater political impact than they in fact have had.[53] Suffrage thus became necessary in the minds of many in order to take advantage of the pool of female personnel available for service in the empire, a pool that feminist agitation since the 1860s had helped to create and for the benefit of which the feminist press continually advertised colonial reform work. The plight of Indian women proved fertile ground for two of the principal causes undertaken by the British women's movement: women's employment opportunities and women's suffrage. Their advocates suggested that while the women's movement was crucial to the maintenance of the British Empire, empire was equally crucial to the realization of British feminists' aspirations and objectives.[54]

There is little doubt that middle-class British feminists of the period viewed feminism itself as an agent of imperial progress, and their capacity to represent Indian women in turn as a signifier of imperial citizenship. Students of the British women's movement and of Victorian social reform will recognize these formulations as variations on a theme common among domestic female social reformers of the period: women, by virtue of their caretaking functions and their role as transmitters of culture, were responsible for the uplift and improvement of the national body politic. It was an argument that helped to justify women's activity in the public sphere and that could lead, in some cases though not in all, to national suffrage activity and feminist commitment as well.[55] Both middle-class feminism and female reform ideology dictated the existence of dependent clients on whom to confer aid, comfort, and (hopefully) the status of having been saved. What Judith Walkowitz calls the "custodial" aspect of female domestic reform was reproduced in Victorian feminist practice; in many ways the two have proven difficult to distinguish, as debates over what constitutes feminism, historically speaking, attest.[56] The equation of colonial natives with effeminacy, of Eastern women with primitiveness, and of both women and natives with children in Victorian political and cultural discourse indicates a slippage between the redeemable at home and in the empire that was not exclusive to British feminists.[57] While it may be going too far to say, as Brian Harrison does, that feminist reformers exaggerated the present suffering of the unenfranchised, they certainly exploited its pathos in order to dramatize the gains they believed to be possible through emancipation, both in terms of their representations of Indian women and the poor—their domestic clientele—in the United Kingdom.[58]

The extent to which social relations in the empire were an extension of the social at home is an important question and deserves its own study. Leonore Davidoff, Catherine Hall, and Mary Poovey have all pointed to the relationship of gender and class constructions to national-imperial identities, and this project suggests some of the ways in which middle-class feminism helped to shape those identifications too.[59] What concerns me here are the elisions that feminists in Britain made, and indeed insisted upon, between national improvement and imperial health and the claims to imperial authority as white women that they thereby felt empowered to make. These were used expressly to fortify their demand for participation in the councils of what was, especially after the Boer War, conceived of by contemporaries as the "imperial nation." Claims about women's imperial entitlement, and the invocations of cultural and racial superiority that accompanied them, were more than a nuance of modern British feminist argument. Like contemporary class and gender systems, imperialism was a framework out of which feminist ideologies operated and through which the women's movement articulated many of its assumptions. The sense of mission that middle-class British feminists felt toward Indian women cannot, of course, be divorced from the evangelical Christian enthusiasm that informed mainstream Victorian feminism. But it is not entirely identical with it either. Feminists cultivated the civilizing responsibility and its attendant imperial identity as their own modern womanly and secular burden. For many if not for all, the vote was its corollary. It represented the conferring of formal political power in the imperial nation-state, which, they argued, was really just an affirmation of the socioeconomic influence and especially the moral authority that they already exercised in the body politic. In this sense they drew on a long liberal political tradition that saw suffrage as an adjunct to power in the state that had already been secured.[60] The dialectic of already "in" but manifestly "out" was a point of frustration and, as Philippa Levine has suggested, a source of creative tension for feminists until the war, if not beyond.[61] Belief in, allegiance to, and identification with empire and its mission was an important way of combating the frustrations and resolving some of the tensions of a suffrage campaign that, by 1900, was nearly half a century old. From the point of view of many active in the British women's movement, empire was an integral and a strategic part of the "woman question" and could not therefore be separated from it.

In articulating the kinds of imperial claims that I have described, British feminists were undoubtedly responding to the powerful invective of the antisuffrage lobby, which attacked votes for women on the grounds that as women, they were unfit to exercise political power in the imperial nation. As Lord Curzon proclaimed in 1912, "For the discharge of great responsibilities in the dependencies of the Empire in distant parts you want the qualities not of the feminine but of the masculine mind."[62] Arguments from physical force—which is to say, those predicated on women's biological weakness—originated in reaction to the emergence of an organized feminist movement in the 1860s; they were buttressed by Victorian medicine and science and remained a mainstay of twentieth-century Anti ideology.[63] The chief grounds for women's exclusion was their alleged inability to take up arms in defense of the imperial nation: "That women should direct the military policy of the country if they cannot share the dangers of war or help to defend the State," wrote Goldwin Smith, "would seem by no means the dictate of justice."[64] Such rationales for women's exclusion from Parliament were produced by men and women alike. The novelist Mary Augusta Ward was only one of the most prominent of many women who opposed women's suffrage on the grounds that imperial politics was the sphere of men.[65] The idea of women ruling India was something that Smith—no friend to women's suffrage—confessed he could not even begin to imagine.[66] Brian Harrison and Lisa Tickner have both examined the ways in which the Antis exploited contemporary fears of imperial degeneration and imperial instability by pathologizing feminism and its advocates, especially in the early twentieth century.[67] The fact that the Anti-Suffrage League was headed by a former imperial viceroy—George Nathaniel Curzon, "a most superior person," as he was memorialized in *Balliol Rhymes*—who did not hesitate to dramatize what he believed to be the sheer ridiculousness of votes for women in an imperial nation such as Britain certainly helped to produce an intensified imperial rhetoric among feminists and especially among suffrage workers after 1908. There was also a deep-seated fear that imperial stability would be endangered if women got the vote; native races would revolt, taking it as a sign of imperial failure. Sir Almroth Wright, notorious for his arguments about women's emotional unfitness for public life, believed that the passage of women's suffrage would signify a failure of imperial nerve: "There cannot be two opinions to the question that a virile and imperial race will not brook any attempt at forcible control by women."[68] For many Britons this may have been an alarming prospect, but it was a source of amusement too. "Will they go and fight the Turks or the Russians?" asked one speaker at a women's suffrage debate in Scotland in the 1870s. The audience burst into laughter, as audiences tended to do when anti-suffrage discussions were publicly entertained.[69] For many the question of votes for women was so outrageous that it became easily reducible to comedy—if not farce.[70]

Satire, caricature, and ridicule had been typical responses to arguments for female emancipation at least since the eighteenth century, when jokes and obscene ballads like *The Lady's Choice of a New Standing Member* were used to mock proponents of women's rights and of course to frustrate rational argumentation on the subject.[71] Lord Curzon continued in that vein when he called women suffragists "female howling dervishes" and rebutted arguments for political enfranchisement with anecdotes designed to deride and humiliate its advocates.[72] Twentieth-century suffrage workers, for their part, found a humor of their own. Though even the staunchest suffrage women were angry and frustrated at the ridicule and the contempt, they were not naive about the fears underlying men's reactions to the vote and were not above lampooning the quintessential Englishman. Cartoons were a staple of the suffrage press and frequently held the Antis up to ridicule. In 1909 *Votes for Women* reprinted a cartoon from an American newspaper in which an Englishman was confronted by four men—Irish, Boer, African, and Chinese—and one suffragette. "Each of the first four he is seen attacking with ferocious courage," the caption read. "The Suffragette, however, is his fifth and most frightening problem, and from her he is seen running away!"[73] A more common response was the determination to have the last word. One feminist retort to Kipling's poem "Female of the Species" (in which women are supposedly "more deadly than the male") was an alternative version, "The Mother of the Man." The author reminded Kipling that without motherhood, there was no race, imperial or otherwise.[74] And in fact the racial motherhood argument was most commonly invoked to counter the Antis' insistence on "physical aptitude as a necessity of citizenship."[75] The point was not to deny their own feminist claims but to own up to them proudly—and however improbably. That embodiment of the rational feminist, Millicent Garrett Fawcett, is reported to have quipped, in response to Kipling's claim that women were the deadliest of the species: "That's me."[76]

These were not of course the sum of Edwardian women's responses to Curzon and his sympathizers. Arguments for the imperial significance of "national" work were common currency in feminist writing. Mrs. St. Clair Stobart, commander in chief of the Women's Convoy Corps, told a *Votes for Women* audience that "I have always felt that unless women can be of service in spheres of work that are national and imperial, [they are] not worthy of a place in national and imperial parliaments."[77] The National Union of Women's Suffrage Societies, led by Fawcett, argued that subject races were inspired by the Great White Queen and would not therefore resent British women's political enfranchisement.[78] Suffrage sympathizers also pointed to the success with which enfranchised women in New Zealand and Australia participated in politics, in order to disprove the prophesied disaster of imperial collapse. J. Malcolm Mitchell went so far as to canvass colonial statesmen in these white-settler dominions on their opinions about suffrage women. What he found was a consensus that "in matters of defence and Imperial concerns they have proved themselves as far-seeing and discriminating as men."[79] During the decade before the war the suffrage press and its auxiliaries ran article after article on women's work in the empire, the condition of Indian women, and the need to "think imperially"—all in an effort to counter the Antis' culturally powerful insistence that women's suffrage foreshadowed the end of the imperial race and, not incidentally, to reassure critics that the women's movement was pledged to both imperial values and the longevity of the empire.[80]

It would be a mistake, however, to attribute British feminists' imperial ideologies exclusively or even primarily to the imperial weight and stature that Curzon and, through him, the Antis gave to arguments against women's suffrage in the twentieth century. To do so presumes that feminists were merely reactive and ignores the considerable impact that reform work for Indian women, especially Josephine Butler's Indian repeal campaign (Chapter 5), had on the shaping of British feminists' imperial identities before 1900. It would suggest too that arguments about the imperial dimension of suffrage were new in the Edwardian period, when in fact they had underpinned opposition to female emancipation at least from the 1880s. Suffragists reassured the public more than once in the mainstream Victorian periodical press that enfranchised women did not plan to hijack foreign policy, become soldiers, or, as some critics feared, "set Hindoostan on fire."[81] Perhaps most important, privileging the Antis downplays the agency that British feminists exercised and the responsibility they claimed for determining what empire and citizenship should be during the period 1865–1915. As an examination of female emancipation writing demonstrates (Chapters 3 and 4), Edwardian feminists were not inventing imperialized rhetoric merely to combat Curzon's accusations that if women's suffrage were granted, Britain would have to "put up the shutters of the Empire."[82] Rather, they were drawing on a tradition of feminist argumentation, developed over the course of the Victorian period, which challenged the traditional equation of suffrage and public work with masculinity, on the one hand, and women with the primitive, the inhuman, the antipolitical, on the other hand. British women *were* the Other in Victorian culture. The quest for national subjectivity—to be a subject, in the formal political sense—involved identifying feminists and feminism with the nation and, in this historical context, with the empire. For middle-class British feminists it meant arguing not for the radicalness of their claims but for the basic Britishness of women's rights. As they strove to identify themselves with the Self of the nation, one of their chief concerns was to persuade their opponents of their cultural loyalties and reassure them of their attachment to the values of the national-imperial culture. Obtaining formal citizenship did not mean, as one feminist put it, that every woman would stand for Parliament or would want three husbands, "as in Thibet."[83] Feminists argued that they were indisputably English in their political philosophies (if not always in their tactics), morally responsible with regard to their social obligations, and above all imperially mindful of Britain's world-civilizing mission.

When in the process they created a colonialized female Other on whose passivity and disenfranchisement their claims for imperial representation largely relied, they did so partly as a pledge of loyalty to the imperial status quo. Female emancipation would not herald the end of the empire but, as many prominent suffrage women argued strenuously in the Victorian and Edwardian periods, would signify a more feminine and hence (in their view) a more ethical kind of imperial rule. In a sense this was not so much a feminization of empire as it was a refiguration of imperial power, symbolized in part by British women representing the cause of their Indian sisters in the imperial Parliament, as well as by the general moral uplift that women voters would give to national public life.[84] Although this was a hope chiefly articulated by suffragists, it was also part of Josephine Butler's imperial rhetoric after 1886. By virtue of the respect she commanded and personal prestige she lent to the cause of Indian women, the conviction that women were the purifiers of empire became the common possession of many Victorian women activists in the 1890s and after. Images of a dependent Indian womanhood were crucial to this kind of ideological work. Like reform on behalf of the nation's poor, women's philanthropic investment in Indian women was invoked as evidence of British women's public authority and of their fitness for citizenship in the imperial nation-state. Without their visible dependence on British feminist reform efforts (whether those were suffrage, education, or repeal), the case for female emancipation in the imperial nation would have been severely weakened, and with it, much of the rationale behind the claim of the women's movement to be a civilizing agent in the world.

It is important to understand exactly what was at stake here in order to fully appreciate the significance of British feminists' preoccupation with imperial authority and with Indian women as their special imperial burden. For if British women were considered the Other in Victorian gender ideology, British *feminists* were subject even more severely to that characterization. Whether it meant critiquing Rousseau's "fanciful kind of half-being," Walpole's "hyena in petticoats," or Burke's Marie Antoinette, British feminist writers had always had to engage their opponents in discussions about the basic humanity of women.[85] The humanity of feminist women was even

more in doubt. Women were, to paraphrase Christina Crosby, the unpoliti-
cal Other of politics, and when they claimed equality with men, they quickly
became the un-English Other of national political discourse.[86] In the Victorian period, suffrage seekers were accused of being too French on the one
hand and too American on the other. In either case, the call for female
emancipation was construed as a cultural betrayal, a violation of their
Englishness. "For my own part I confess," wrote Goldwin Smith, "that
rather than see English women become like some of the public women of
America, I would see them turn black."[87]

Fawcett's response is telling: she accused Smith of having "lost his touch
upon English politics and the English tone of approaching the question." It
was one of the principles of Victorian suffrage ideology that women wanted
the vote "on the same terms as men" and that they expected to receive it in
good time. Such had been, as Fawcett was fond of saying, the historically
"national habit" of suffrage reform in Britain.[88] Some suffrage women
would later run out of patience, choosing revolutionary tactics over faith in
the inevitabilities of liberal politics, if not of Whig history, and militancy can
certainly be read as a rejection of habitual national intransigence. Regardless of their strategies, however, *all* feminist women were targeted as unwomanly, and female emancipation as sterilizing and "un-sexing."[89] The
fact that Goldwin Smith would have preferred them to be black rather than
to be feminists suggests the range of Otherness with which feminism might
be associated.[90] Images of Indian women were a useful rejoinder to arguments that British feminists were unwomanly, desexed, and wholly unnatural. As representations of women of color have done for white women
in other contexts, Indian women, retailed throughout feminist writing as
foils to the progress of Western imperial women, undoubtedly did much to
humanize feminism.[91] The "white woman's burden" and the woman-to-
woman caretaking functions that British feminists exercised on behalf of
Indian women rendered them traditionally feminine and helped to neutral-
ize powerful arguments about the monstrous, antisocial nature of the wom-
en's movement that opponents of women's suffrage were apt to mobilize in
order to devastate the legitimacy of the Cause.

"Votes for women," which many Britons believed was absurd and even
laughable, gained respectability as well as the seriousness of imperial necessity through the representations of Indian women—and of their imperial
British sisters—which British feminists deployed throughout emancipationist literature. While images of Indian women served as humanizing
influences, however, they were ultimately intended as evidence of British
feminists' imperial capacities and their imperial authority. In a post-

Enlightenment liberal framework, representation was extended only to those who could be acknowledged as subjects; and where political subject-hood was by definition masculine, subjectivity itself functioned by asserting authority over Others.[92] In Victorian and Edwardian Britain, national-imperial subjectivity required nothing less.[93] Indian women, imagined as colonialized and dependent on British feminists for the representation of their cause, were evidence of the kind of conquering power that was required of those who sought admission as full citizens in the imperial nation-state. And the pledges that feminists made to oversee the condition of Indian women in the empire were one way of proving that they were ready, if not to take up arms, then certainly to defend the nation-state from corruption from within. The trope of the colonized female Other was, in an important sense, one of the major political effects of British imperial suffragism. In historical terms, middle-class liberal feminism was one of the manifestations of British cultural hegemony as well as one of the technologies of British imperial power.[94]

The project of historicizing imperial feminism that this book begins to undertake can itself be located at the intersection of several recent historiographical trends. Traditional imperial history, which wrestled with the core-periphery model down to the 1980s, has begun to question some of the polarities and the exclusions that have structured its practice from the nineteenth century onward.[95] Most notable among its assumptions has been the idea that imperialism was historically a phenomenon "out there," at one remove from the mother country, and the clearly related conviction that empire was historically "no place for a white woman."[96] The work of John Mackenzie and others has redirected the focus of empire to the domestic cultural scene, while Helen Callaway, Leslie Flemming, Claudia Knapman, and Margaret Strobel have all effectively challenged the misapprehension that empire was built in "a fit of absence of wives" or, for that matter, of women.[97] Empire was, for better or for worse, no less imperial for being domestic.[98] Although problematic in a variety of significant ways, Ronald Hyam's work is evidence of how seriously these critiques, while often misunderstood, have shaken the foundational presumptions of establishment imperial history.[99] And even British historians primarily concerned with traditionally domestic social movements, cultural paradigms, and gender discourses have begun to remark on the impact of empire on British national identities in the Victorian period.[100] Whereas empire had been seen as largely irrelevant to the project of British history, it is being

increasingly recognized as one of the bases of Englishness, if not Britishness, historically conceived.[101]

Distinctions between British history and imperial history, no less than
arguments about the masculinity of the colonial empire, have been produced at discrete historical moments.[102] Challenges to them in an era of
postcoloniality are no less historically situated, in part because "the colonial
past is by no means over and done with."[103] Until relatively recently, these
challenges were fashioned in quite different quarters of the academy. While
not necessarily in agreement over historical methodologies or even priorities, subaltern studies on the one hand and feminist history on the other
have asked whether such analytical concerns don't all belong in the same
field of debate.[104] Kumkum Sangari and Sudesh Vaid's collection *Recasting
Women: Essays in Colonial History* represents an impressive attempt to create
a new historiographical space for this kind of analysis—not only because it
argues for the interrelatedness of gender, class, feminist, colonial, and
metropolitan systems of hegemony, but because its authors insist on the
role of historiography itself in shaping fields of knowledge through which
such hegemonies have operated.[105] The fact that British feminists historically linked what were conventionally "domestic" political and social concerns to imperial ones both reshapes and complicates the fields of imperial-
colonial history that are currently being reconstituted. For in addition to the
women who ventured "out there," this book suggests that many feminists
who never left the British Isles collaborated in the imperial enterprise—a
historical phenomenon that gives "armchair imperialism" a whole new
dimension. That they used the imperial status quo as a constituent of—
rather than allowing it to function solely as an obstacle to—their claims to
equality and political representation was not, moreover, a political strategy
unique to them. Their use of Indian women as a site upon which to claim
their fitness for citizenship parallels similar maneuvers on the part of Indian
nationalist men, who claimed self-representation on the basis of their
commitment to improving the status of Indian women during this same
period.[106] British feminists' imperial concerns indicate that the trope of
Indian womanhood, as well as feminism and gender itself, had constitutive
power in the shaping of nationalist ideologies and imperialist discourses
during the period under consideration. And they testify to the influence
that Western *feminists*, in addition to Western *women*, possessed and exercised in order to promote "the cultural aspects of imperialism through
their gender roles as caretakers and 'civilizers.' "[107]

Maintaining a distinction between "women" and "feminists" is, needless
to say, crucial to this project. It was also, significantly, of concern to many

British activist women in the period 1865–1915 who did not want their reform work to be confused with feminist (which they largely defined as national suffrage) activity.[108] Their refusal of a feminist identity—and its acceptance by a number of men in the Victorian and Edwardian periods— suggests, in addition to the particularities of their own historical experiences, the inessentializableness of feminist politics. With Chandra Mohanty and Linda Gordon I take it as my premise that there is no natural or necessary connection between being female and being a feminist. The first is a socially, politically, and culturally produced set of identities and experiences; the second is, additionally, an ideological and political choice.[109] Those who have chosen—and who choose—the label "feminist" are generally opposed to traditional gender mores, though they do not necessarily see gender as part of the structural matrix of class, ethnicity, sexuality, and age; nor are their strategies for intervention the same. Now, as then, there exists a multitude of feminisms. Middle-class British feminism during the period under examination produced a gender ideology that challenged in significant ways the basis on which women were excluded from power, but not all of the structures through which political power itself was constituted in an imperial political landscape. In this sense the feminists who figure here help us to understand "how the category of 'women,' the subject of feminism, is produced and restrained by the very structures of power through which emancipation is sought."[110] They also contribute to an understanding of how imperial ideologies have been gendered and how gender ideologies have been culturally marked under certain historical conditions—a set of topics with which historians and cultural critics are increasingly concerned.[111] If, as Sangari and Vaid claim, defining gender is crucial to the formation of dominant ideologies, British feminism is an important historical example of how even an oppositional politics can inscribe hegemonies in its ideological practices. As Linda Gordon has written, "less powerful" does not always mean "powerless."[112] Feminist gender ideology—along with the imperial burden that its advocates inscribed in the women's movement—had a cultural appeal that was powerful enough to shape the "ideological encounter between England and India" and, some have argued, to continue to shape that encounter today.[113]

It is not a question of assessing blame or even of expecting feminists of the past to have been able to transcend the imaginative or ideological limitations of their own historical experiences.[114] It is, rather, part of the work of interdisciplinary feminist theory, which insists on scrutinizing the workings of power and, because of this, requires an examination of "the burden of history which every production is immersed in"—feminisms and their histories included.[115] Since the institutionalization of women's studies and women's history in the North American academy in the 1970s, an enormous literature has been generated about the feminist past in Britain, Europe, and the United States. For the most part, this "feminist past" has referred to nineteenth-century Western women's movements. Increasingly, the history of the second wave is beginning to be narrativized and the ethnocentrism of traditional feminist history addressed.[116] Despite the veritable explosion of work on women missionaries, white women travel writers, and the cooperations of race, class, and gender systems in European culture, however, the imperialist context of Western feminists' history has gone virtually unrecognized, except in the American scene. There, thanks to the work of Angela Davis, Rosalind Terborg-Penn, Ellen Dubois, and others, consideration of the racialist attitudes prevalent in the American women's suffrage movement is now a fairly conventional aspect of narratives of American feminism.[117] But despite the call issued by Amos and Parmar almost ten years ago for an examination of imperialist ideas in British women's movements, even those authors contesting what have become traditional narratives of or approaches to British feminism have not addressed its historically imperial frame.[118] This study is intended as an intervention in the historiography of the Western European feminist past in order to begin to account for the impact of imperial culture on historically feminist movements and to suggest its significance for feminist history and feminist politics in the present.

This kind of intervention could not have been conceptualized—or made necessary—without the ongoing work of critical theorists across a variety of disciplines who have insisted on the operations of cultural imperialism in contemporary Western feminist ideologies and practices. Until very recently, in historical terms, the category of "woman" was used by Western feminists as shorthand for middle-class, white, Anglo-Saxon, or Western women. Thanks in large measure to the work of feminists of color, white middle-class Euro-American feminist women have been called to account for racism in the contemporary women's movement—what Chela Sandoval calls "the Medusa within."[119] Accountability is an ongoing, difficult process; like all theoretical processes, it requires a relentless auto-critique. As Trinh T. Minh-ha has written, theory is threatening, "for it can upset rooted ideologies by exposing the mechanisms of their own workings."[120] For feminists, who have long used theory as a tool for exposing the mechanisms of patriarchy, being theoretical means confronting "the constitutive powers of their own feminist claims" and being self-critical about "the totalizing gestures of feminism" itself.[121] During an extended historical moment when critical theorists—and especially feminist theorists—are looking to ground their claims historically, we need to be careful about what narratives of "the feminist past" we rely on. We need to be rigorously critical of the histories of feminism—those cheery, triumphalist narratives—which we may be tempted to claim as the foundation for our theoretical critiques.[122] This is no easy task. Given the hostile political and cultural climates in which various feminist movements have developed and persisted, it is perhaps understandable that, as Sangari and Vaid note, "women's studies and feminist movements feel impelled to construct a positive and inspirational history." But as they warn, "If feminism is to be different, it must acknowledge the ideological and problematical significance of its own past."[123] Rematerializing the historically imperialist traditions of Euro-American feminism confronts the historical racism of middle-class Western feminism, especially where racism itself is defined as a failure to recognize the mechanisms by which racist ideologies are produced, historically as well as contemporaneously.[124] It helps to continue the process of interrogating the basis of feminist history and, with it, the very bases of feminist questioning itself.[125]

Although making women and their histories visible (again) has been one of the founding acts of women's history and feminist history, simply recovering the Western feminist imperial past is not sufficient in and of itself for a number of reasons. First, one does not "find" or "uncover" history. As Christina Crosby insists, one "commits historical acts"—in which case the act of writing history is a performance, a production, a process.[126] Historicizing imperial feminism must be seen as an ongoing process—part of the shifting ground that bell hooks and others have insisted is at the root of all feminist politics and, finally, all cultural productions.[127] This book, which renarrativizes the British feminist past, is not an effort to write a new story, but acts as a narrative intent on questioning and "rearranging relationships with old stories."[128] I do not oppose in order to eliminate, as Trinh Minh-ha says; nor do I wish, in historicizing the orientalism of modern British feminism, to define other feminist historians and scholars as Other.[129] I would, rather, emphasize that the writing of history is a site for the renegotiation of meanings—which, as feminist theorists have argued, all kinds of ideological production must necessarily be.[130]

Second, it is one of the premises of feminist epistemology (and, of course, of feminist history) that meanings are not fixed but are historically contingent and historically produced. From this flows the equally historical claim that feminism, like the term "women" itself, can "create an illusory unity"—for it is not only the experience of being a feminist but the specific

historical meanings attached to it that are of significance.[131] Among the
meanings that feminists attached to the women's movement in Britain was
its imperial purpose and its world-colonizing capacity. Coming to terms
with those meanings, and with the reconceptualization of the feminist past
that they require, is an inescapable part of the self-critical consciousness
that authorizes feminist practice, historical or otherwise, in the late twentieth century. We can hope that recovering the imperial feminist past will
not be an isolated gesture, but will sustain the continual critical reconsideration of the political and theoretical concerns in which a variety of scholars
are currently engaged. With any luck it will also help to remap the land-
scapes within which historians of Britain, of women, of feminism, and of
empire configure their projects.

Finally, and most important, rematerializing Western feminism's imperial
history means taking responsibility for its legacies to and relationships with
the present. However crucial the struggle for change may be, there are
times when Eveline Marius's plea has a certain appeal to it:

So we know about slavery
We write about it
We sing about it
So we know about slavery, so we unearth our history alright . . . what
    next,
When do we draw the line and say, to the best of our ability
Come let's make modern history.[132]

It is tempting to see history, as British historians have tended to see empire,
as something "out there," separate from everyday life and from the politics
of contemporary struggle. And yet if feminist movements are to be genuinely historically grounded, they cannot "draw the line." They must be
truly and continually accountable to their pasts; they must be willing to
enter into dialogue with them; and they must acknowledge the historicity of
the present.[133] Feminism must produce a discourse that interrogates its
own histories, particularly if it aspires to be something more than politics as
usual.[134] The cost of doing feminist history is undoubtedly high.[135] It means
letting go of the historically bound conviction that we inhabit a world that is
at some safe distance from the past and that we are not responsible for our
relationship to it. Women—and feminists—have been and remain implicated in "the process of history and contemporary imperialism" equally.[136]
This is not to deny feminists' agency or to suggest that their good intentions were historically insignificant. In a field like imperial history, where

"women as active participants can barely be conceived of,"[137] underlining feminists' appropriation of empire for their own purposes is crucial to understanding "what women did" during this particular historical period. But it is also important not to conflate agency with resistance.[138] In the case of the British feminists examined here, at any rate, it is clear that they operated in a historically imperial context that was determinant, if not fully determining, of their actions and that, while they resisted patriarchy, they were complicitous with much of British imperial enterprise. In order to make the kind of modern history that Marius envisions, we cannot hope to understand feminist consciousness and feminist identities in a vacuum. They must be read in terms of the variety of historical contexts in which they were and are forged, and against the cultural and political settings that produced them.[139] We must therefore be attentive to the kinds of complex and often contradictory historical legacies in whose shadow we think, work, and strategize for change—and from which we may derive part of our own feminist identities.

This book does not claim to be a comprehensive examination of what must eventually prove to be the complex relationships between feminism and imperialism. It is necessarily exploratory, partial, and inconclusive in any traditional sense of the word. As it was being written, and indeed as it is being read, work continues to be produced on gender and colonialism, feminism and imperialism, white women, colonial men, indigenous women, British imperial statesmen, India, South Africa, "the dominions," and the British Raj. "Empire" as a revived historical topic is proving a rich and fertile field for an entire generation of scholars, all of whom are presumably cognizant of the conditions of postcoloniality that make this work possible.[140] Because I labor in this postcolonial economy—in a set of historically imperial locations, under the persistent signs of North American white academic privilege—and because feminist historical work requires it, I wish to outline the parameters of this study and its limitations as I recognize them. I hope what follows will not be taken as any kind of disclaimer but rather as an enactment of the politics of my own location with regard to this project.

First, some definitions. I have chosen to consider "feminist" in this period those women and men who believed that women's biological inferiority was socially constructed and who worked to free women from the restrictions that prohibited them from gaining access to education, formal political participation, and other rights to which men were then entitled.

Although I might not use such terms to describe all feminists today, they are basically historically valid.[141] The debate over who called themselves feminists and who did not is of little significance here, except insofar as British women's fitness for national-imperial (as opposed to local government) service—a criterion that could divide Antis from suffragists—is concerned. Of greater importance perhaps is the distinction I make between British women working for female emancipation at home and those who were undoubtedly feminists but were not active in domestic campaigns in Britain. Hence Annie Besant, whose connections to feminism and India are well known, does not figure in this volume. She was not in Britain permanently after 1895, and although she was lionized by British feminist communities at home, she "did not play a significant leadership role in British feminism."[142] The same might also be said for Margaret Cousins and Margaret Noble, though their ties with British suffrage organizations were stronger than Besant's. However, since their contributions to imperial feminism occurred mostly after the war, they are not dealt with here.[143] While these women were clearly feminists, there are others who, despite their interest in Indian women, were not considered for this study. Hence I do not discuss either Lady Dufferin, whose association for female medical aid to Indian women was the centerpiece of colonial philanthropic work into the twentieth century, or Elizabeth Adelaide Manning, under whose guidance the National Indian Association was also influential in colonial reform circles. Their concerns about Indian women's emancipation were certainly no less motivated by cultural imperialism than those of the feminists whom I have chosen to examine. They were not, however, primarily active in work for British women's emancipation, although they may have been sympathetic to the cause.[144]

This might seem to be a replication of the home-India split that British feminists themselves worked to eradicate. In fact the merging of national and imperial concerns was a rhetorical strategy that, despite its considerable ideological effects, was not much manifest in British feminist practice. Women's suffrage organizations and other sociopolitical female reform groups that championed the cause of Indian women did not as a rule undertake the kinds of colonial reform that they called for. Their periodicals advertised zenana teaching opportunities as well as the meetings and scholarships on behalf of Indian women sponsored by groups like the Dufferin Fund or the National Indian Association, and there was occasionally an overlapping of personnel. But they did not go to India or take up reform there as an extension of domestic sociopolitical activity. Individual women might get personally involved and even contribute money: Millicent

Fawcett took an interest in child marriage and Indian women's education; the Muller-McLaren families sponsored Indian women students in Britain.[145] The kind of support that feminist organizations gave to those women working for Indian women's reform was by no means negligible: the advertisement that the feminist press gave it alone enabled connections between political reform groups and social reformers at home and abroad, the ramifications of which, except in the international temperance scene, have yet to be evaluated.[146] But even the Ladies' National Association, which worked for the repeal of the Contagious Diseases Acts in the colonies and was arguably the most closely involved in the lives of Indian women in India, maintained a kind of division of labor: it did the work of repeal, but it did not get involved in supporting any actual reform work in India until just before the war. And, as should be clear by now, most British feminist women interested in India never went there, at least not before World War I. Despite their insistence on the need for Indian women's "uplift," British feminists working at home prioritized their own needs, principally because they believed that improvements in the condition of Indian women were contingent on their own enfranchisement. It is quite possible that their relative lack of involvement with real Indian women and their unfamiliarity with colonial conditions in situ account in some measure for the cultural imperialism of their feminism—though as Barbara Ramusack's work on Eleanor Rathbone has demonstrated, personal experience could not alone offset their imperial attitudes toward Indian feminists who were their contemporaries.[147] Future research on the work of British feminist women in India and on British women's social reform work for India will help to contextualize imperial feminist attitudes in Britain.

Given the level of reform activity on behalf of Indian women in late Victorian Britain and after, why focus on British feminist discourses? Imperial feminism is a historical problem with many dimensions and as many possible approaches. Biographical sketches about feminist women involved in the empire might serve the purpose just as well; an excavation of individual feminists' involvement with Indian reform is needed; analyses of the party political activities of feminists with regard to Home Rule and Unionism would also be instructive. I have chosen the discursive tack because I share Margaret Strobel's conviction that ideologies were as important as the troops that colonized territories, as the bureaucratic structures that carried out the daily work of imperial rule, and as the policymakers in the India Office who issued memoranda and guided imperial statesmen on how best to keep the imperial enterprise afloat.[148] The public rhetoric of imperial feminism provided one of the ideological contexts (if not the only one) within which all colonial reform by women was carried out from the mid-nineteenth century onward—whether it was from the top down or through grassroots social reform movements, whether it was undertaken in India or in Britain.[149] "New" women who, like Mary Kingsley or Augusta Ward, did not call themselves feminist ran the risk of being labeled one, and not in a complimentary way, simply because they were active in the public sphere. For women who were interested (in colonial) reform this was even more true, since they took as their "public space" the empire itself. Significantly, this was the line that divided feminists from many Anti women.[150] One can only imagine what outrage Antis like Ward and Violet Markham must have felt when in 1912 they were accused by Cromer of being "extremists" for supporting a prosuffrage woman for local government in West Marleybone. While Ward held out as an Anti until the end, firmly believing that empire was a male preserve, Violet capitulated to suffragism eventually because she saw that women's work in the local, as opposed to the national-imperial, arena was not sufficient for the realization of social reform goals.[151] The cause of imperial reform was thus made persuasive to some unlikely people, in no small measure because of British feminism's rhetorical insistence on it. Even Beatrice Webb, another pillar of the Anti position, ultimately justified her conversion to women's suffrage using familiarly feminist, if slightly underdeveloped, arguments about imperial rule.[152]

Evangelism, class consciousness, institutional anthropology, and antisuffragism were some of the other discourses that shaped domestic imperial culture and its reformist impulses in the decades between 1865 and 1915. Interestingly, mainstream British feminist rhetoric either mediated or transformed each of those for its own purposes. Examining the ways in which feminism produced a colonized female Other across a variety of its public discourses demonstrates that British feminism's imperial concerns were not idiosyncratic, but permeated the whole fabric of feminist ideology and, indeed, that British feminists' identity *as feminists* depended upon convictions about the cultural, political, and racial superiority of all Britons. The work of feminist reform, whether for India or for "home," occurred in relationship to, and at times in tension with, this ideological frame. Perhaps most significantly, this approach suggests that imperialism was not just a cultural mindset in the Victorian and Edwardian periods, but additionally one of the metanarratives of liberal social reform, shaping the ideologies of oppositional groups as well as of official policy. The dependence of British feminist discourse on a degraded Indian womanhood means, at the very least, that the "political pluralism and humane values" that were constituents of "the national self-image by the late Victorian period," and to which contemporary feminists adhered, were profoundly influenced by the values of imperialism as well.[153] Obviously, the ideological forces behind imperial feminism were not sufficient to win votes for women before the war, any more than were arguments from custom, from democracy, from Whig tradition, or from social evolution—all of which British feminists employed against an intransigent political establishment from the 1850s onward. These failures do not make British imperial feminism any less historically significant; to the contrary. The contemporary cultural attitudes British feminists embodied and the discourses they borrowed from in the service of their own ends indicate how thoroughly British the modern women's movement was, and tell us much that is invaluable about British culture and politics before World War I. Histories of feminism, like those of the empire, belong in the same field as the rest of British history, and neither is properly a "separate sphere" of historiographical debate.

Why India? It was certainly not the sum total of Britain's colonial empire, nor was it the only focus of feminist concern. British suffrage women were international in their connections and paid particular attention to the progress of votes for women and black men's suffrage in the white-settler colonies.[154] What's more, Irish politics and Home Rule—colonial issues closer to home—figured in feminist periodicals, emancipationist pamphlets, and women's suffrage debates. As Cliona Murphy's work on the women's suffrage movement in Ireland testifies, Irish women in the twentieth century experienced their English sisters as culturally imperialist with regard to Irish feminism, which some Irish believed they wanted to colonize for their own organizational purposes.[155] National unity and national political culture were something of a fiction in the United Kingdom of the late nineteenth and early twentieth centuries, especially at certain political moments and over certain political issues, most notably Home Rule for Ireland. Regional pride and national loyalties could not always be contained by English feminists' attempts to create a "British women's movement," though, again, the cause of empire could be a unifier when the collective national spirit showed signs of strain.[156] If British feminists felt a special responsibility toward Indian women, however, it was because India had always been important to British imperial confidence. After the Mutiny of 1857 this was even more true. Rebellion on the part of native troops deepened British distrust of Indians while at the same time heightening the conviction that the British presence alone could bring progress to India. As the century drew to a close and Britain felt its imperial status threatened by outside competitors (not to mention by the growth of Indian nationalism),

India became the linchpin of empire, as well as the symbolic responsibility upon which Britain's success or failure as an imperial power would be judged. More so than with South Africa, Australia, or Ireland, feminists who claimed an imperial role for themselves fixed on India as the barometer by which British imperial might would rise or fall. The contemporary associations between India and the fate of imperial power meant that their pledge to save Indian women was easily extrapolated into the argument that the goal of British feminism was to save the faltering empire itself.

While images of a colonized Indian womanhood were the linchpin of British imperial feminism, this book is not about contemporary Indian women, except insofar as they were imagined by British feminists and manipulated as types in the service of Western feminist strategy. There were many Indian women in this era whose lives and life work contradicted the stereotypes deployed by British feminists, and some of them were familiar figures in British feminist and female reform circles. There were notable female social reformers traveling to Britain: both Pandita Ramabai and Rukhmabai lived for a time in England in the late 1880s, and a variety of other Indian women came and went between India and the British Isles in the 1865–1915 period.[157] Many Indian women were also active in the Indian National Congress movement and in women's suffrage in India both before and after the First World War. Even before Gandhi's emphasis on *satyagraha* and women's role in civil disobedience, Indian women took to the streets to protest colonial rule and the policies of the Anglo-Indian colonial state.[158] And, as is clear from a variety of encounters between Western feminists and Indian women on British soil, Indian feminists could and did subvert the version of international sisterhood that their British imperial sisters attempted to foist on them. The representations that British feminists created of passive Indian women were inherently unstable and were contradicted by the actions, and in some cases by the very presence, of the Indian women whom it was their intention to depict as part of the sisterhood of women across the world. To imagine Indian women as silenced hinges not so much on the assumption that British women had the power to render them mute as it does on the dubious contention that any record of their actions, either contemporary or historical, has the power to make them speak.[159]

"The Indian woman" and the variety of images attendant upon this characterization was thus largely the invention of middle-class British feminists in an imperial culture. As a trope it did not necessarily bear a relationship to the experiences of contemporary Indian women, though it is important not to overlook the fact that patriarchy, class systems, and religious fundamentalism adversely affected women's lives in India as they did else-where during this period. The trope also undoubtedly functioned as the standard against which many Indian feminists who encountered British reformers and imperial personnel were measured, and in that sense it cannot be disregarded as simply incidental to the histories of Indian women. It was certainly used as a signifier of historical truth, and not just by Western feminists. "The Indian woman"—the female gendered, colonized body—was "the discourse terrain, the playing fields" on which Indian men and British feminist women each imagined their own liberation and politi-cal self-representation in "imperial Britain."[160] In these contexts Indian women were rarely if ever featured as capable of self-representation. They were interpreted as the guarantors of traditional values in nationalist dis-course and as security for the imperial status quo in Western feminist rhetoric. It was, in short, their deployment by imperial Britons, male and female, that permitted the "speaking for" that was one of the prerequisites of political subjectivity in British imperial culture.[161]

How Indian women seeking "emancipation" fashioned their own sub-jectivities is a different, though not an entirely unrelated, story, and I make few claims about it here. Like Euro-American feminists in this period, Indian feminist women utilized both a periodical press and the languages of nationalism to seek recognition of their claims to equality and to authority in the public sphere. The historical context of Indian nationalism itself involved them in opposition to the British Empire and, in some cases, to British feminists as well.[162] Indian feminism was not derivative of European women's movements, even while historically there are some important parallels, especially in terms of class composition and reliance on the ideol-ogy of motherhood as the grounds for political citizenship.[163] And there were some instances of feminist cooperation in spite of the imperial-colonial power dynamics, such as the relationships between Margaret Cousins and Kamaladevi Chattopadhyay and Cousins and Muthulakshmi Reddy. Significantly perhaps, these flourished much later than 1915.[164] Indian feminists undoubtedly appreciated the imperial context in which the struggles for national liberation and female emancipation were being waged, and they were keenly aware of the imperial attitudes of which British feminist women were capable. As one anonymous contributor—apparently an Indian woman—wrote in the feminist press in the late 1880s, if Indian women were to give an account of their own condition, it would be a very different story.[165] In the nineteenth century such sensibilities drove Rama-bai out of England to seek support for her reform projects in America; after the vote for British women was obtained, they generated tensions between

Indian women and the British female M.P.'s now representing them.[166] In
Ramabai's case, and perhaps in that of others, resistance to British women's
imperialist gestures was arguably a spur to individual self-consciousness, if
not feminist identity. This is not to say that empire created feminism or that
without imperialism colonial women, or British women for that matter,
would have been less feminist or incapable of feminist consciousness. It is
fair to say, however, that empire helped to shape the conditions under
which imperial and colonial women articulated their claims for equality and
citizenship, both differently and similarly, in the modern world.[167] This is
not simply because it was the geopolitical reality in the context of which
feminisms emerged across cultures, but because empire itself carried gender, class, and ultimately political valences that all feminists engaged with in
their struggle over the terms of power.

   I am, finally, acutely aware of the dangers of reinscribing the kinds of
colonial discourses that are being subjected to critical examination here. As
bell hooks reminds us, white feminists have a history of centralizing themselves in order to marginalize the Other, and this project, by examining just
such a maneuver in a discrete historical context, runs the risk of reproduc-
ing the imperialist effects that it hopes to critique.[168] Studies of orientalism
need not be orientalist, just as "a study of the formation of masculinity need
not display complicity with patriarchal discourses" and, indeed, as studies
of women need not necessarily be feminist.[169] Even the best feminist
historical intentions are, however, subject to the cultural and historical
locations in which they are produced. I am as conscious of some of the ways
in which this project is itself constituted by my position as a historian inside
the North American academy as I am unconscious of others. I recognize
too the "real authoritative position" I occupy. Historians, like the poets of
Adrienne Rich's "North America Time," "never stood a chance of standing
outside history"—or outside the geopolitical frameworks that constitute,
without fully determining, them.[170] Feminism has historically recognized
writing and rewriting as necessary to the creation of consciousness and to
the future of feminism itself. Hence the issues raised here mark the beginning of conversations about the histories of imperial feminism and their
ramifications rather than the end.[171] These are the terms on which all
histories should be negotiated. If nothing else, historicizing imperial feminism will enable those who so choose to use the past to interrogate the
locations from which they speak, write, and do the work of feminism's—
and feminist—histories.

2

Woman in the Nation

FEMINISM, RACE, AND EMPIRE IN

THE "NATIONAL" CULTURE

Although it is often taken to be synonymous with votes for women, the "woman question" in nineteenth-century Britain was as much about the public exercise of women's moral authority as it was about the battle over political rights.[1] Attention to suffrage campaigns has, until quite recently, obscured not only the importance of other (nonsuffrage) social reform projects taken up by women, but also the significance of late Victorian feminist definitions of female public authority and of the ways in which feminist writers constituted the "national" body politic.[2] Throughout feminist discourse the public and the national were held to be synonymous; citizenship was participation in and a sense of belonging to the nation; and the vote was the public and political exercise of national but traditionally privatized female authority. "Why are we out?" asked Charlotte Despard, leader of the Women's Freedom League, rhetorically in 1910. "Because we are citizens; because we belong to the nation ... because the business of the nation is our business."[3]

The quest for a recognition—and, in light of the socioeconomic changes brought on by industrialization, a recalibration—of women's moral authority in the nation was not limited to conventionally "feminist" reformers. Jane Lewis has suggested that the traditional divide between suffragists and antisuffrage women turns out to have been based on differences of degree rather than kind when it came to the question of action in the public domain. Many of those who were outspoken against votes for women articulated certain traditionally feminist ideas about women's authority in the public sphere. Where they parted from suffragists was on what constituted "the public," *not* on whether women should exercise power *in public*. And even these were not permanent rifts.[4] As Dorothy Thompson has noted, whether they were working for suffrage, more general social reforms, or, as in the case of someone like Augusta Ward, women's right to participate in local, "domestic" politics, what Victorian women wanted was inclusion in the nation-state on the basis of their moral authority as women. And, as I shall argue in this chapter, it was a nation that they, like their contemporaries, could not conceive of except as an *imperial* nation-state. Indian women—transformed in feminist discourse into the right and proper colonial clientele of British women—helped to ratify the public space as imperial and to justify British women's right to participation in it.

The conviction that nation and empire were crucially joined was typical of both imperial apologia and popular perceptions in this period. Significantly, it served the interests of suffragists and their opponents equally. Feminists were not the only ones in Victorian culture to insist that women's responsibility for the nation meant women's responsibility for the race and hence for the empire itself; it functioned as an argument both for and against the vote. This was especially the case after 1908, when Lords Cromer and Curzon, official statesmen of empire, helped to found the Anti-Suffrage League, whose platform was premised on the related notions that women must be barred from the vote because they were incapable of defending the imperial nation, and that women's suffrage would be the beginning of the end of British imperial supremacy, not to mention British imperial prestige. Given contemporary conflations of empire and nation—and contemporary anxieties about racial and imperial decline—feminists' interpretation of women's public role as a necessarily imperial one was a logical (and, of course, a shrewd and deliberate) extension of the "national" suffrage argument. It might even be argued that by insisting on these national-imperial connections, British feminists did little more than transform popular cultural mores into one of the most culturally predictable justifications for women's suffrage to be advanced in the prewar period.

The fact that feminists' imperial claims proved to be among the most heatedly challenged and apparently untenable arguments advanced in favor of suffrage in British culture between 1865 and 1915 suggests that equations between woman and nation, on the one hand, and woman and imperial duty on the other, were by no means self-evident—at least not when they were linked explicitly to demands for *parliamentary* political authority. In fact, feminists' identification with the imperial nation-state was a complex process that simultaneously challenged and reaffirmed traditional notions of the nation and the empire, their relationships to one another, and the relation of middle-class British women in turn to them both. It involved not simply the construction of Indian and a variety of non-Western women as Other, but also the invention of new, "feminist" narratives of national history and, as we shall see in the following chapter, distinctively feminized narratives of cultural progress. At work throughout these discursive formations was the conviction that Britain's national character, its national institutions, and its national culture were, by virtue of being British, the most progressive and most civilized in the world. Support for Britain's imperial mission across the globe followed naturally enough. The fact that Western women were considered the inferior sex in the superior race meant that there was a lot at stake in feminists' quest to identify themselves and their cause with British national-imperial enthusiasm, politics, and glory. Primarily it worked to undermine the Victorian construction of woman as Other by identifying her with the Self of nation and empire. Not incidentally, it was instrumental in making possible—and even necessary—British feminists' construction of non-Western females as a recognizably non-British Other as well.

NATION, RACE, AND EMPIRE IN LATE VICTORIAN ENGLAND

Although Victorians imagined nation and empire concentrically, it has not, until very recently, been the practice of British historians to talk explicitly about the relationship between imperialism and nationalist discourses—or vice versa—during this period. What Shula Marks calls "the distorting insularity" surrounding notions of national identity in Britain is partly responsible for the absence of these kinds of conversations.[5] The Tory government's proposals for a national school curriculum in the 1980s prompted a reassessment of the ways in which British nationhood was "built up" through the empire, most notably in the three volumes on patriotism produced by the History Workshop under the editorship of

Raphael Samuel.[6] Much work remains to be done on the ways in which empire was (and is) constitutive of national identities "at home" as well as on the impact of colonial nationalisms, in turn, on them.[7] A more challenging problem still than recognizing the fact of English nationalism in the nineteenth century—the term itself, we are told, still "sounds odd to many ears"[8]—is to take seriously its implications for understanding late Victorian history and historiography. The emergence and consolidation of "new" national states in Europe in the nineteenth century, combined with the conviction that modern state-formation in the British Isles dates from the sixteenth century, can give the impression that nineteenth-century English nation-building was, if not a contradiction in terms, then a fait accompli by the 1850s. In the first part of the century, "British nationalism and imperialism reached maturity at the same moment," largely as a response to the changing balance of "national" powers in Europe itself.[9] Given the serious challenges posed to Britain's geopolitical preeminence after the 1870s by rival industrializing nations, it seems likely that national institutions—no less than national identities—in Great Britain were involved in a continuous process of self-definition and self-justification down to World War I (and, of course, beyond).[10] Despite historians' traditional neglect of these connections, national and imperial identities were codependent because "at the core of empires nations were continuing to emerge," to define and to distinguish themselves from other national states in terms, among other things, of their national versions of imperialism.[11]

In the late nineteenth century "the Nation"—which could be conceived of as English or British or both—was the impetus behind much of the imperial enterprise, "both as mentality and material reality."[12] Perhaps because it appears to be so obvious, this requires further elaboration. Convictions of superiority that underpinned the British imperial ethos were deeply rooted in national pride. The industrial revolution and the ensuing developments—urban centers, mass production, an extensive and sophisticated infrastructure—gave Britain the lead over other industrializing nations until the 1870s. Even after the onset of competition from European and American rivals, economic power and military might continued to give Britain the leading edge well into the twentieth century. In addition to proving Britain's inherent superiority, the continued prosperity of the nation was routinely invoked to promote the maintenance of imperial rule. Despite their often radically different approaches to empire, prime ministers from Disraeli through Roseberry described and defended official imperial policy in terms of "the national interest." This privileging of nation put liberal politicians in particular at odds with the internationalist strain inherent in Cobdenite radicalism—an internationalism both Chamberlain and Roseberry were ultimately to reject in favor of a social imperialism that professed to put the interests of the nation first.[13] The increasing vulnerability of Britain's industrial superiority after the 1870s gave national concerns such a compelling urgency that by the end of the century imperial activities were being justified in terms of national stability and "national efficiency."[14] Empire was defined as national in its purpose as well as nationally profitable in its result. Imperial ideology thus contained a cult of nation that made Britain and its citizens at home of primary concern in the ostensibly "external" imperial enterprise.

National feeling and national pride permeated other late Victorian notions of superiority and cannot be separated from them. Convictions of racial supremacy, the most familiar rationale for British imperial rule, were inescapably national in their origins. The "race" that possessed the genius for conquering, colonizing, and otherwise civilizing was not just any race. It was English-speaking, Anglo-Saxon, and unequivocally British—a term that itself "derives [and derived] its legitimacy from the expansion of the nation-state."[15] Relationships between the designations "British" and "English," not to mention the differences among the political and "national" cultures invoked by them, have historically been contested and remain so today.[16] That the British Isles contained peoples whom the dominant English frequently categorized as other "races" could go conveniently unnoticed in Victorian discourse, despite the fact that the empire was becoming increasingly settled by emigrants from the Celtic fringe.[17] In any event, the imperial mission was described in terms that were at once inclusive of all contemporary "Britons" and exclusive of most other Westerners.[18] The virtues that flowed from the British character were typically held to be good government, economic prosperity, and social order, which translated more or less into indirect rule, education, and health provisions. Such evidence of "civilization" was quite recent in the British experience, but it was believed to have a long and specifically British history nonetheless. As Paul Rich explains it, "British parliamentary liberties were a product of Anglo-Saxon tribal institutions which had been carried down through the centuries and underlay the British imperial mission to spread freedom and justice to other, more backward parts of the world."[19] The imperial impulse, no less than racial character, was thus distinctively (and, given the diversity of Greater Britain, somewhat fictively) national.

Rich also argues that with the Boer War, racialist discourse became less national and Anglo-Saxon and more "imperial."[20] There is no question that a generalized crisis in imperial confidence after 1900 shifted the terms of the debate away from racial toward more cultural explanations for imperial rule and, in time, toward the possibility of self-government. But as Thane and Mackay argue, "race" and "nation" were used interchangeably into the 1900s, and even Rich admits that "the cult of Anglo-Saxonism lived on in the public mind" into the twentieth century.[21] Clearly race here signified cultural identity and heritage, and racial superiority the supremacy of nationally specific cultural values. "National character" was thought to demand the subjugation of "lesser races" well into the twentieth century.[22] Racial superiority, like imperial ideology itself, depended on and nurtured the cult of Britishness that continued to justify British imperial rule on grounds that were expressly national—even when such rule was being modified in the direction of political cooperation rather than unilateral dominance. Thus could Lord Lugard write of the "dual mandate" arrangement in Nigeria in 1922: "We hold these countries because it is the genius of our race to colonise, to trade and to govern. The task which England is engaged in the tropics . . . has become part of her tradition, and she has ever given her best in the cause of liberty and civilisation." That Britons should bring "the torch of culture and progress" to Africa "while ministering to the material needs of our own civilization" seemed to Lugard nothing less than the right and proper balance of national self-interest and imperial civilizing mission.[23]

The sense of moral superiority for which the Victorians are so notorious was inexorably shaped by the same national preoccupations. While it is difficult to reduce to a single explanation, the unflagging conviction of British moral superiority in the nineteenth century was significantly informed by the leadership of Britain in the abolition of the slave trade. As James Walvin has pointed out,

> Ignoring the fact that for almost two decades the British had been the western world's pre-eminent slave trader, emancipation allowed the British to congratulate themselves on their moral superiority in having ended slavery. Not only that, but the survival of slavery—in the USA, in South America, Africa and elsewhere—provided the British with a perfect illustration of their own moral superiority. What made the British feel superior was not the military facts of empire or the undeniable evidence of industrial and economic power, but that superior morality which, in the case of slavery, provided so distinguishing a difference between Britain and the rest of the world.[24]

Critical to Walvin's assessment—and indeed, to Victorians' assessments of themselves—is the very notion of a "national" morality and its dependence on other, inferior nations for its ascendant place in a normative hierarchy.[25] British moral superiority, like its racial counterpart, justified the imposition of Britishness on others. Walvin argues that the evangelical campaign against slavery enabled Britain "to hawk its moral superiority around the world and to insist that others—Europeans as well as native peoples— should accord to the standards of the new found morality."[26] As Benjamin Kidd wrote in 1898, "If our civilization has any right to be [in Africa] at all, it is because it represents higher ideals of humanity, a higher type of social order."[27] With the moral benefits of British imperialism construed as national in nature, empire itself came to represent the highest expression of the *nation's* collective virtues.

And, finally, the civilizing mission was regularly ascribed to national character, often in specifically religious terms: "The British race may safely be called a missionary race. The command to go and teach all nations is one that the British people have, whether rightly or wrongly, regarded as specially laid upon themselves."[28] Conversion was just one dimension of the larger civilizing project, which became increasingly secular after the 1870s. Lord Roseberry, for his part, called the British Empire "the greatest secular agency for good known to the world."[29] Regardless of its secularization, it never ceased to be conceived of as a fundamentally British vocation. According to Chamberlain, "In carrying out this work of civilisation we are fulfilling what I believe to be our national mission."[30] By the turn of the century, there were critics of the nation-oriented impulse motivating British imperialism, most notably in the person of J. A. Hobson. His treatise on imperialism, published in 1902, contained a chapter entitled "Imperialism and the Lower Races," in which he rejected the intervention of governments in colonial territories solely on the grounds of national interest. In Hobson's view, the "moral defence" of imperialism rested on two premises: that empire advanced civilization and that it promoted the good of colonial peoples. Dealing an effective blow to claims of British disinterestedness in colonial territories, Hobson suggested that moral imperialism was a contradiction in terms because economic gain would always be the first object of colonizing nations. As a result, "the claim of a 'trust' is nothing less than an impudent act of self-assertion."[31]

Hobson's critique had little impact on the steady development of a nationally oriented social imperialism during the first decade of the twentieth century.[32] Labour's support of the Liberal party cannot be solely attributed to the government's imperial policies (especially given Keir Hardie's sympathies with Indian nationalism), but the organized working classes responded favorably to the Liberals' equation of national prosperity with imperial stability.[33] Imperialism effectively combined "national purpose" with "high moral content" to produce, if not class conciliation, then at least relatively peaceful class coexistence.[34] To cynical—and class-conscious—observers like Cecil Rhodes, it appeared that imperialism functioned as nothing less than a deterrent to all-out civil war.[35] However qualified by socialist internationalism or punctuated by labor opposition in the years before the war, the unification of diverse class interests in and through the imperial enterprise reflects the power of empire's national appeal.

This appeal was not limited to the arena of high politics, but permeated many aspects of national life. John Mackenzie argues that imperialism was a "core ideology" in modern Britain precisely because what had been "an essentially middle-class ethos was transferred to the other social classes through the potent media of printing, photography, spectacle and pageant."[36] Convictions of racial and moral superiority were to be found throughout popular culture, which was practically imperialized in the late nineteenth and early twentieth centuries.[37] Although, for example, the impact of the jingoism and patriotic enthusiasm common to late Victorian and Edwardian music halls could vary according to the location and the class composition of their audiences, empire remained eminently marketable across class throughout the period 1870–1914.[38] As in their official variety, expressions of popular imperial sentiment were components of a larger sense of national superiority in which "the domestic 'under classes' could become imperial 'over-classes'" by virtue of their essential Britishness.[39] This Britishness, with its associations of historical progress and civilization, produced a national-imperial ideology that justified empire as the provision of British commodities—whether they be capitalism, Christianity, or, tellingly, feminism—to "the dark places of the earth." To be British meant to be superior in all regards; such superiority was fundamental to national identity. And, by virtue of the national mission connected to that superiority, to be British meant to be intrinsically imperial as well. Indeed, it was the knowledge that Britons were "an imperial people" that made them "conscious of their collective existence as such."[40] Those seeking inclusion in the imperial nation-state were at pains to demonstrate their Britishness, which is to say, their imperial capacities. In practical as well as in ideological terms these were prerequisites for "national" citizenship.

Clearly, then, the future of the nation lay at the heart of British imperial enthusiasms down to World War I. Empire was "a means of moral self-elevation"—an undertaking that, despite its external thrust, had a fundamentally self-reflexive purpose. In its own way, empire helped to create and sustain national self-consciousness across class divisions, across internal ethnocultural particularities, and in the face of apparent economic decline. It became a symbolic site, a means of imagining and sustaining the idea of a vital, righteous, and self-preserving national unity in an extended historical moment when national fortunes were feared to be spiraling downward.[41] For despite its various political and cultural guises, the premium placed on the nation-in-the-empire remained a constant throughout the period 1865 – 1915, even while and perhaps in part because Britain experienced the beginnings of a decline in its global fortunes. Mackenzie believes that with the emergence of an accelerated popular imperialism in the late 1890s came an emphasis on empire "as a means of arresting *national* decline."[42] This evaluation, along with the repeated defense of national interests offered by Victorian imperialists themselves, would seem to indicate that the nation was the symbolic, as well as the material, motor of imperial purpose. What needed preserving in this era of imperial instability—especially after the Boer War—was not primarily the empire, or even its colonial peoples, but first and foremost the nation itself. The preservation of empire, to which British feminists pledged themselves and their Cause, appeared to be instrumental to the survival and the future of "the national culture" as a viable domestic and global political entity.

WOMAN AS SAVIOR

If, as Evelyn Higginbotham claims, "we know far too little about women's perceptions of nationalism," British feminist rhetoric provides important historical evidence of the role that national consciousness played in the shaping of both imperial feminism and Western feminist ideologies about citizenship.[43] Like many of their contemporaries, Victorian feminist thinkers prioritized the nation and its needs in their arguments for the emancipation of British women. In fact, they made "British womanhood" central to the continued moral regeneration of the national body politic—a claim with increasing appeal as Britain's national-imperial security appeared to be under threat by the early twentieth century. Again, like many other reformers of the Victorian period, they believed that women acted as moral agents in national life. As historians of the British women's movement have argued for almost two decades, feminists borrowed heavily from Victorian domestic ideology when they made women's moral superiority one of the chief justifications for female emancipation. This often involved an approach to political equality based on women's differences, their special "female" qualities. Millicent Garrett Fawcett put it most succinctly when she wrote, "We do not advocate the representation of women because there is no difference between men and women; but rather because of the difference between them. We want women's special experience as women, their special knowledge of the home and home wants, of child life and the conditions conducive to the formation of character to be brought to bear on legislation."[44] The instinctive morality of women was linked to their maternal functions, or, rather, to their maternal potential, since Victorian feminists, many of whom remained single, did not believe that the exercise of women's special moral qualities depended exclusively on biological motherhood.[45] Moral superiority inhered in woman qua woman. Sexual difference thus implied more than just different social functions flowing from different genders. In keeping with Victorian sexual ideology, femaleness in feminist terms meant not inferiority, but a moral superiority that justified participation in the political sphere. In the hands of Victorian feminists, this superiority dictated a moral ordering of the sexes, with women at the top of the hierarchy. This is not to say that feminists did not wish to cooperate with men either in working for social reform or in the national political arena.[46] But in the context of Victorian feminist gender ideology, women were believed to be the morally superior sex.[47]

The historical phenomenon of a "feminist gender ideology" may appear to be redundant, oxymoronic, or, most likely, self-evident. In any event it is crucial to remember that "gender is *produced* as well as uncovered in feminist discourse."[48] As conceptualized by nineteenth-century feminists, women were not only inherently more moral than men; they were also the vessels through which the moral improvement of society could be achieved. Femaleness thus dictated a saving role for women in feminist thinking. It was a role that, both historically and culturally, resonated with Christian evangelical principles and that could and often did embed womanist claims in a separate sphere of ideology.[49] Sarah Lewis, for example, had this to say about "woman's mission" in 1839: "That the sex, characterised by such noble moral development, is destined to exercise no unimportant influence on the political and social condition of mankind, we must all believe. . . . We claim for [women] no less an office than that of instruments (under God) for the regeneration of the world. . . . That [woman] will best accomplish this mission while moving in the sphere which God and nature appointed, and not by quitting that sphere for another, it is the object of these pages to prove."[50] Although most departed from Lewis by arguing that the public domain was woman's "appointed" sphere, Victorian feminists nonetheless relied heavily on Christian principles to justify the notion of female moral superiority and, not surprisingly, linked the two together to affirm the special righteousness of the British civilizing mission. Lewis, for example, claimed that Christianity was the first and only religion that "brought to light the true value of women," and British feminists echoed her sentiments in later writings, attributing the emancipation of Western women to the triumph of Christian principles.[51] Not all feminists condemned Eastern religious traditions, though the political salvation of non-Western women was linked both explicitly and implicitly to the extent of their Christian conversion. In a general sense, the idea of British women's superiority was reinforced by invoking Christianity as a religion superior itself in part because of the special place it accorded to women.[52]

Christianity and, more specifically, the Christian commitments of British women, contributed not just to emancipation ideology but to justifications for women's emancipationist activity as well. Early feminists' reliance on religion to validate a public role for women is evident in the antislavery activities of the 1830s and in the campaign against the Contagious Diseases Acts from the 1860s onward. Scripture was invoked not only to protest the injustices of black slavery and regulated prostitution, but also to legitimate the public work of women fighting to redress those social problems.[53] Feminist argument in the pre–World War I period never completely lost touch with its religious roots. Indeed, Martha Vicinus has remarked at length on the Christian symbolism of the body invoked in the early twentieth century by radical suffragettes in their rhetoric and in their protest activities.[54] For many feminists, a better feminist world meant a more spiritual, more Christian one. And yet feminists' call for moral improvement, for all that it depended on Christian validation, was in many respects a secular project, with the moral elevation of British social and political life as its objective. Armed with Christian legitimacy, feminists authorized a redemptive role for women in public work as well as within the private domain of the family. In doing so they did more than redefine separate spherism. They transformed women's moral superiority from a domestic responsibility into a public trust, providing gender with a national moral function linked explicitly to the public sphere that it had not previously possessed. In contrast to opponents of parliamentary women's suffrage, many of whom were not averse to women's public activity in school boards or in philanthropic work, they defined the arena of the "public" to mean national, as distinct from local or domestic, politics.

This connection between female moral superiority and the progress of Britain as a nation was one that feminists strove to make explicit. The obstacles to achieving parliamentary suffrage in the nineteenth century and the sheer radicalism of feminists' call for "female emancipation" made the attempts of early feminist reformers to improve British politics and society necessarily localized and small-scale. Philippa Levine reminds us that while women's suffrage was repeatedly deferred in Parliament until 1900, women achieved the local franchise in 1869, which enabled them to sit on local school boards, and by 1889 they had received the London municipal franchise, which put them in positions of considerable metropolitan power.[55] Jessie Boucherett, chronicling the progress of the women's movement in 1870, expressed similar sentiments about the quality of small victories.[56] At the same time, Victorian feminists never ceased to petition Parliament for legislative redress, to conceive of the women's movement in national terms, or to seek female emancipation for the sake of the nation. The first organized suffrage societies, although regionally based, were united under the title National Society of Women's Suffrage. The unifying "National" remained, despite a variety of rifts and fissures in the 1870s.[57] When Millicent Garrett Fawcett took the lead in combining all existing suffrage societies under one umbrella organization in 1897, it was called the National Union of Women's Suffrage Societies.[58] Similarly, Josephine Butler's repeal organization was the Ladies' National Association; and even though its commitment to strictly feminist principles came under fire in the 1890s, the central society for rescue work was also the National Vigilance Association. Finally, the first issues of *Votes for Women* indicate that the Pankhursts' Women's Social and Political Union was initially called the National Women's Social and Political Union, suggesting the identification by even radical suffragettes of their particular variety of "the Cause" with national unity and the national good.[59]

The above examples point to a desire on the part of both the first feminists and of feminists in the early stages of their collective activism to name themselves and their organizations as national in scope and in constituency—even while one of the greatest strengths of the women's movement was its regional branch activity. Female emancipation was, as the *Englishwomen's Review* editorialized in 1881, essential to the "increase of national strength"; suffrage organizations were "national in character"; and the feminist press was national in its audiences.[60] Feminist rhetoric insisted that women's responsibility for the nation, once proven, was not static: the moral superiority of femaleness guaranteed that when granted equal rights, women would uplift the nation in the political as well as the private sphere. Prominent in suffrage argument was the contention that the participation of women would raise the moral tone of the political process. As one suffragist put it, female emancipation was rooted in women's "moral purpose." "I believe that the typical virtues of woman—truth and tenderness—

may hallow even the franchise!"[61] This was in part a strategic response to the accusation by opponents that exposure to the rough and tumble of the hustings would "blunt [women's] special moral qualities." It also reflected feminists' conviction that votes for women meant "the infusion into political life of those higher moral and spiritual influences which it is the mission of women to diffuse in family and social life," enabling them to elevate the character "of the nation at large."[62] For Victorian feminists, the public sphere was national by virtue of its being political and social; the vote was a "national question" and a "national privilege."[63] Even women's presence in higher education would, according to Fawcett, strengthen "the national position" of the universities.[64] In this sense, women's public responsibilities were harnessed to national welfare, linking women and, more important, female emancipation in the public sphere to Britain's continued moral progress as a nation.

That national progress depended on women's redemptive authority in the public sphere Victorian feminists were in little doubt. As I have suggested, they borrowed much of their rhetoric about women's national saving role from contemporary female reform ideology. What defined and motivated female reformers was a body of clients who were in need of salvation: the poor, the sick, the aged, the unemployed, the prostitutes.[65] Reform activity, dubbed "rescue work" by contemporaries, was contingent on the idea that woman's mission was to protect the weak. If emancipated, "women might use it to claim justice, the only sure defense of the weak, not for herself but for all who are oppressed and downtrodden in the struggle for life; to strengthen the right which ought to be might, against the might which asserts itself right. Is this not women's work?"[66] The protective impulse dominates Victorian female reform ideology, running through charity work, poor-law relief, and campaigns against prostitution. Middle-class women's moral authority, much like imperial authority, relied on the existence of a dependent class whose moral redemption was as important as their material needs. Feminists interpreted protection as moral authority over Britain's dispossessed, thus transforming the human capital of the poor into the symbolic nation that British women were responsible for saving. In feminist argument, women's work was considered to be inherently redemptive not just of individuals but, taken as whole, of the nation at large. Feminist writers relied heavily on this interpretation, arguing that decades of female social reform were evidence that women had long been prepared to assume national responsibility.[67] In this way feminists constructed women as the subjects rather than as the object—or the potential Other—of national concern.[68]

In a political culture where the figure of Britannia was a prime signifier of the nation, feminists' arguments about the British woman's contributions to and sacrifices for the national body politic affirmed the equation of her selfhood with the national interest, not to mention with an already gendered "feminine" nation. Feminists exploited Britannia and related imagery, especially in the twentieth-century suffrage campaign, where she came to embody the collectivity of British womanhood seeking entrance at the doors of Parliament and, more generally, in the councils of the nation. Feminists' reliance on gendered female national types facilitated comparisons between all non-British women and the British female, not to mention a sense of superiority rooted in apparently recognizable "national differences." Feminist periodical literature in the pre-1900 period was rife with articles on "the American woman," the "jolly" Russian girl, Brazilian womanhood. While genuinely interested in the condition of women's lives in other cultures, feminist writers tended to inscribe national peculiarities in the womanhood of various national cultures. This was mostly, though not always, to show off the advantages possessed by a woman with a British birthright.[69] The latter was personified in one Edwardian suffrage journal as a feisty Jane Bull. In an article called "John Bull and His Daughters" for the *Women's Franchise* in 1909, Euphemia Johnson reminded "the Bully" that women who wanted the vote "are your own flesh and blood, with capacities of love and freedom inherited from yourself." Jane's British blood and her heritage of liberty were enough to distinguish her from almost any other nation's womanhood.[70] Used traditionally as "the symbol of the good English housewife, frugal, modest and hospitable,"[71] this feminist Jane was John Bull's daughter rather than his wife. As the embodiment of British womanhood (and the biological inheritor of John Bull's genetic Britishness), she was a compelling argument for political equality—one that played on British notions of fair play, liberty, and racial entitlement. Jane was a less common and certainly a less idealized representative of British women's national self-interest than Britannia, but they both worked to identify British women's cause with that of the nation—to differentiate British women on national grounds from other women of the world and to point out that they were already at the sacred center of the national culture.[72]

The leap from nation to race was evidently an unself-conscious one for Victorian feminist writers. They were well aware of Britain's empire and often expressed pride in belonging to a nation with worldwide possessions—which could be referred to variously as "our great Oriental empire" or "our magnificent colonies." For Mary Carpenter, Josephine Butler, and other female social reformers, it was, as we shall see, considered nothing less

than the natural ground for the practice of British women's philanthropy—
for feminism in action. In that sense it provided relief from the constraints
on women's reform activities at home and proof of colonial women's
dependence on the good will and services of British women, as well as a
source of collective national pride. At times imperial pride made its way into
emancipationist debate. Jessie Craigen, a Scottish feminist speaking to a
crowd of women suffragists in Manchester in 1880, told her listeners that "at
Westminster . . . the clock of empire strikes; every time it sounds it marks an
epoch in the history of nations, and far and wide, to the ends of the earth,
men hold their breath and listen for the voice of England pealing out in
power from Westminster."[73] At other moments, the success of British
imperial rule itself was invoked as evidence that women could ably participate in the public sphere. "The sex which furnished a sovereign for the
British empire," wrote Lydia Becker, "could not be unfit to exercise political
power."[74] Feminists on occasion referred to the public realm into which
they sought inclusion as not only national but imperial as well. Mrs. Henry
David Pochin, for example, complained that equal rights were denied "to
the numerically larger section of the subjects of the Empire."[75] Suffrage was
envisioned by one writer as "a beginning of new duties and new work, new
responsibilities and new life, not to women alone but to England and her
Dependencies." It was considered by another to be the right and fitting
reward for those "who live in the greatest and freest Empire which the
world has ever seen."[76] Explicit references to empire are not as common as
those to nation (at least not before the twentieth century), but feminists
could allude to Britain's imperial power without ever directly mentioning
empire per se. "How much power does our country possess," exclaimed
Mary Carpenter, reflecting on India, ". . . [for] disseminating wise and good
principles over the world!"[77] Such allusions also arose in the context of
arguments about equality between men and women. Pochin pointed out
that "it would be hard indeed to show why the political and civil rights of
one sex should be considered of more importance than those of the other.
To both was committed the dominion of the world."[78] "Veritas," the author
of a pamphlet entitled "What Is Women's Suffrage? and Why Do Women
Want It?" made explicit the connection between "the dominion of the
world" and Britain's status as a world empire. Let "woman" ask for the vote,
she exhorted, "because she is a Christian, with a moral duty to perform
towards the ignorant and perverted; let her ask for it because she is a citizen
of the great nation whose power is as wide as the whole earth, and whose
duties are commensurate with that power, and because she is bound to help,
not only the material prosperity, but the moral growth of her fellow cit-

izens."[79] For Victorian feminists, women's moral influence was "commensurate" not just with national political responsibility but with the imperial duties to which Britain was committed. As Mrs. Duncan McLaren put it to a public meeting in St. George's Hall in 1875, "The agitations which have of late years been carried by moral suasion have opened the eyes of women to their just claims to share in the moral government of the world."[80] Authority over Indian women and tutelage of their emancipation was the "natural" next step from this claim to worldwide moral government.

There was little disagreement among feminists, then, that the work of emancipated British women would double "the mental and moral forces of the world."[81] For them, as British women, the entire globe was their purview. They considered their authority over its salvation to be as much a national as a gender prerogative, proceeding as it did from their status as British women. The authority of motherhood transformed this quest for governance in the national-imperial arena into racial necessity. For like many of their contemporaries, British feminists conceived of women's relationship to the nation not just in political and social but also in racial terms. When feminists spoke of British women's national responsibility, they did so frequently, and fervently, by emphasizing their racial responsibility as mothers. Historians of the British women's movement have generally failed to take the racial dimension of female emancipation into account, and when they have, it has sometimes been in the interests of distancing "feminism proper" from racial rhetoric and racialist ideology.[82] While it is true that here too race signified cultural heritage, it had an inescapably biological implication as well. Racial motherhood meant quite

 literally the preservation of the race, of the species—of civilization itself.

If feminist argument was preoccupied with race preservation, racial purity, and racial motherhood, this was in part because it had to be. One of the most damaging attacks made against the case for female emancipation was that it would enervate the race. Suffrage opponents like Frederic Harrison were convinced that with women out of the home, the care and feeding of England's children (and by extension, the whole Anglo-Saxon race) would be neglected and the nation would eventually collapse from within. Feminists responded with assurances that not all women would necessarily choose public life and that those who did would not neglect their domestic duties.[83] But they did not hesitate to claim their responsibility as racial mothers as a compelling argument for female emancipation. Throughout feminist literature runs the theme that women were the mothers of the race, that they possessed as much if not more racial responsibility as men and so deserved equal power in "the councils of the nation."[84]

These arguments were legion, and they were mostly variations on a basic theme: as mothers women were "race creators"; the greatness of the race was attributable to the role mothers played; racial concerns were "instinctively" maternal. Although the term "maternal imperialism" was coined in the late twentieth century,[85] Victorian feminists' arguments for inclusion based on their maternal responsibilities certainly resonated with culturally encoded tropes for British power both at home ("the mother of all parliaments") and in the empire (the "mother country"). It was a resonance not lost on contemporary suffragists, many of whom believed that British women's maternal qualities entitled them to be the worldwide leaders of the women's movement as well.[86]

It is worth underlining that the invocation of racial motherhood, like feminists' identification with empire writ large, was of enormous strategic importance in the case for female emancipation. Feminists were able to utilize the accepted Victorian reverence for the sacredness of motherhood and raise it to the level of national and racial duty. Thus maternity, a heretofore private domestic function, acquired a set of significances that transcended the merely public. Racial responsibility was interpreted as the highest form of national responsibility. By appropriating it in the name of female emancipation, Victorian feminists committed British women and the women's movement to the service of Britain's national racial ideals. In the process, they also made racial stability dependent on women's access to the public-national-imperial sphere. For when women were disqualified from equal rights by virtue of their sex, wrote Lydia Becker, "the welfare of the race suffers accordingly."[87] Along these same lines, "L.S.," a Victorian feminist pamphlet writer, claimed that the opponent of female emancipation "ignorantly insists on stunting woman" and that votes for women, if granted, "would in time revolutionize the whole race."[88]

In the climate of late Victorian and early Edwardian Britain, feminists' emphasis on women's racial responsibility had a particular urgency. The cyclical depression of the 1870s began a crisis of British confidence that centered around fears of racial deterioration and national decline. The "condition of England" question dominated debates on Victorian social problems, and concerns about the erosion of national racial strength were exacerbated at the end of the century by evidence of the British failure in South Africa; this failure was attributed to the fact that the troops recruited for the Boer War had been of inferior racial stock. Finally, the eugenics movement at the turn of the century lent scientific credibility to racial anxieties and emphasized the crucial role that healthy mothers played in guaranteeing the strength of Britain's future citizens.[89] Early-twentieth-century feminists played to Britain's racial crisis, often with warnings about what a failure to emancipate women would do for Britain's racial strength. *Common Cause* called suffrage "The Eugenic Vote," thus linking women's suffrage with race preservation; contributors to the *Vote* emphasized race as a female instinct, predicting an acceleration of national decline and "race suicide" if women were not emancipated.[90] In feminist rhetoric women, long assumed to be the moral guardians of the nation, became the saviors of the race at a time when British racial supremacy was thought to be at stake. As Maude Diver phrased it in 1909, "Woman is the lever, the infallible lever, whereby sunken nations are upraised."[91] She might well have substituted "feminist" for "woman," since by the 1910s suffrage seekers of all stripes were arguing that the women's movement, by institutionalizing female values in the national political arena, was one means of saving Britain from national and racial crisis. The result was that British feminists dictated a saving role for feminism as well as for women in the present and the immediate future. Emmeline Pethick-Lawrence was not alone when she proclaimed from the pages of *Votes for Women* that women were "the race-builders" and hence could better deal with the racial crisis than men.[92] It was a conviction that cut across suffrage divisions and party lines, drawing constitutionalists and militants into some of the very same kinds of racialized arguments about the need for suffrage at a time when they were, if not deeply divided, then certainly at odds in terms of political strategy.[93] Racial and imperial concerns thus functioned to bridge the salient divisions among women suffragists and their organizations, anticipating what feminists hoped would be a similarly unifying effect on the political nation as a whole.

The linkage between motherhood and race was not an exclusively feminist formulation in the late Victorian period. As Anna Davin has argued, women were induced—by the state, by eugenists, by doctors, and by all manner of social reformers—to bear responsibility for racial strength and racial purity.[94] It should be clear that, in contrast to those whom Davin cites as manipulators of the rhetoric of imperial motherhood, feminists utilized the burden of their particularly gendered responsibility to claim a specifically *female* authority in *imperial* government as well. Under feminist auspices women's guardianship of the race was not a separate or private function, in the sense that it was not limited to the domestic sphere of child-rearing. As with femaleness, the moral responsibilities inherent in motherhood legitimized, if not required, women's participation in national political affairs. Responsibility, in other words, had its privileges, and feminists argued that the racial responsibilities incumbent upon women authorized full equality in the public sphere—whether it be municipal or parliamentary politics. Trading on the relationships between the national body politic and the imperial body politic, feminists argued for not just full equality but inclusion in the nation in its *fullest*—that is, most imperial—sense. Precisely because racial stability and national progress were considered to be fundamentally imperial concerns in Victorian cultural discourses, feminists could, by emphasizing their contributions to both, assume imperial responsibilities on behalf of British women and the British women's movement. Feminist writers believed that women's special qualifications as national mothers and homemakers automatically gave women an imperial role: such was the symbolic function of "the home, which is the nursery of national life, and the reproduction of which across the seas will always be the ideal of Imperialism."[95] Arguments about racial motherhood provided a political entree into the imperial nation even as they worked to justify female emancipation in it. Immersed in these discourses of feminist imperial authority, British women were readily able to imagine Indian women as the deserving (because colonial and apparently unemancipated) objects of their imperial patronage.

Attention to the intensification of racial-imperial language in feminist rhetoric in the twentieth century should not obscure the ways in which invocations of the nation per se continued to mark arguments for female emancipation and women's suffrage in particular. Charlotte Despard's emphasis on the role of "woman in the nation" was echoed by suffrage pamphlet writers, feminist periodical contributors, and, as we shall see shortly, women trying their hand at feminist historical narratives in the late nineteenth and early twentieth centuries.[96] Arguments for emancipation were arguments for national subjectivity, and they grew out of claims about the relationship of women's authority—as women, as mothers—to the national body politic. "We belong to the nation as we belong to the family," wrote Despard, "and in truth, the nation is only the larger family, because the business carried on by the House of Commons is our business, concerning us and our children quite as intimately as it concerns the men." For many, the intimacy of the family unit suggested not only the intimacy of the national parliament, but a similarly intimate relationship between the peoples of the empire and the mother country as well. And arguments about the fate of the race and that of civilization itself were never far behind. For Despard the coincidence of cultural disintegration and women's self-consciousness in the early twentieth century meant that it was "the nation whose destinies [women] must help to mould." Like many of her feminist contemporaries, she believed that one way of doing this was for women "to bear and rear a fine and healthy race, capable of holding its own *in the world.*"[97] Women's "national" function was routinely transformed into a national duty and, finally, into a justification for inclusion in Britain's world-wide government.

In addition to the relationship of nation to race and of race and nation to empire, what is significant here is the ways in which "race" could, as Barbara Fields has suggested, be used to mean "nation." The term "race" itself was, moreover, given the power to evoke communities that were "imaginary" but nonetheless ideologically powerful.[98] For British feminists, the imagined community was the collectivity of British women who, in their view, already constituted the nation and the empire. Like other groups excluded from the centers of national political power during this period, feminists invented themselves as a nation, using the power of race to conjure up national identities and to legitimate their claims to national political power and imperial authority.

THE NARRATIVES OF BRITISH
FEMINIST HISTORY

The work of late Victorian and Edwardian feminist historians was crucial in legitimizing these claims to imperial moral authority and national political power, providing evidence as it did of the long and respectable tradition of British women's activity in public life and their long-standing role in fostering the health of the race. Few historians of women today would take issue with the argument that the recovery of women's historical experiences and of their historically excluded voices is one of the most important grounds of feminist struggle.[99] Victorian feminists recognized the political importance of history and, in anticipation of later feminist historians, intervened to rewrite it so that it reflected more accurately what they believed to be the historical precedents of their own emancipationist claims. Feminist narratives of the nation not only privileged British women as moral agents of national imperial regeneration; they also reassured their audiences that they were not by virtue of their claims either unpatriotic or un-British, but rather part of the liberal Whig march toward greater democracy that had come to define English civilization and the English civilizing mission by the end of the nineteenth century. By "writing women back" into the collective British past, they registered their claims as historically, and hence as legitimately, political in the imperial present.[100]

Early feminist periodicals featured a number of articles on the origins of Anglo-Saxon culture, the effects of the Norman invasion, and life in ancient

Britain. The purpose of these pieces was to trace the origins of female equality to the first stages of British history. Feminists were eager to prove that from earliest times British women had been accorded respect and equality; one author, quoting Tacitus, remarked how he had commented "with surprise upon the superior morals of a barbarian nation" and had attributed it to "national character."[101] Feminist writers often invoked Boadicea as the first British heroine, emphasizing her efforts to encourage citizens to rebel against the Romans and "to be knit together as one family against all foreign invasion."[102] In addition to establishing a line of historical foremothers, accounts of the achievements of British women of the distant past linked women's work to the foundations of the nation and made feminist claims appear to be long-standing rights needing to be restored.[103] Feminists routinely reminded their reading public that after Magna Carta many noblewomen had participated in local politics and demonstrated their fitness for political life.[104] After citing four abbesses summoned to Parliament under the reign of Henry III, Lydia Becker remarked, "Women have, and always have had, coeval rights with men in regard to local franchise; they have a share in the foundations, and they have a right to a corresponding share in the superstructure that has been reared upon it."[105] Such examples were intended to prove that female emancipation was bound up with the basic political culture of Britain and that to demand women's political equality was to affirm and even restore British tradition rather than overturn it.

The festivities organized by suffrage workers to celebrate the 700th anniversary of Magna Carta in June 1915 are emblematic of the ways in which British suffrage women cultivated a sense of continuity with the ancient national past. Preparations had been in the works since May of the previous year. The pageant, the procession, and the pilgrimage to Runnymede that had been planned had to be canceled because of the war, but celebrations were carried on in Caxton Hall, the site of so much feminist activity since the 1860s. The events were organized primarily by the Women's Freedom League, and the main speaker was Helena Normanton, whose essay "Magna Carta and Women" had been published in the May issue of the *Englishwoman,* a feminist periodical affiliated with the National Union of Women's Suffrage Societies.[106] Normanton sketched the origins of Magna Carta, emphasizing that in it was to be found the source of English women's national rights. As "the legal basis for the enfranchisement of Englishwomen," she declared, "it is everything to us."[107] The use of symbolic traditions to argue for the ancient English origins of women's suffrage was especially shrewd here, linking female emancipation with the best emblem of British national identity at a moment of national wartime crisis. As constructed by feminists, women's equality was represented as both historically and culturally British and served as a continual reminder of Britain's historical commitment to political equality between the sexes—even, and especially, when the nation-state was at war with a rival European empire.

Underlying these arguments was the conviction that British traditions were the most durable, that British forms of government were the best, and that British culture was capable of producing the highest form of male-female relations. Feminists often expressed such convictions in racial terms. Charlotte Carmichael Stopes began her account of British women's "historical privilege" by citing "the racial character of our ancestors. They reverenced women."[108] Helen Blackburn was even more explicit. In her history of the women's suffrage movement, published in 1902, she attributed the early equality of women in Britain not just to racial character but to Anglo-Saxon superiority above "all the Indo-Germanic races." She acknowledged that many early systems of jurisprudence "looked upon women as under the guardianship of men" but that the Anglo-Saxon idea of protection "was modified by their preference for life in separate independent homesteads, rather than in wall-begirt cities—thus whereas the early Roman law construed protection as complete absorption of the will and possessions of the wife, the Saxon law constructed it as ensuring to women their share of personal independence."[109] For Blackburn, the privileged legal status of women, as well as the whole constitutional system, derived from Anglo-Saxon racial characteristics and, she implied, from the progressive nature of Anglo-Saxon civilization. Unlike the Celts or the Normans, the earliest Britons were said to have treated their wives as "helpmeets" and protected their property under the law. "It is therefore part of the continuity of historical development that the movement toward recognising the public duties of women should have made the most progress amongst the English-speaking race, the founders of the constitutional form of government."[110] Such sentiments also appeared in parliamentary debates on women's suffrage: "All that is best in our modern industrial system, in our representative government . . . partakes of the primal characteristic of the Anglo-Saxon race."[111] That England was the birthplace of modern representative government was accepted as an irrefutable historical fact among British feminist writers. "Why," asked Fawcett with regard to votes for women, "should she not continue to lead as she has led before?"[112]

Convictions like these would be invoked by Christabel Pankhurst and others later in the early twentieth century in support of the argument that British women should "lead the way" toward a suffrage victory, ahead of other national suffrage movements in Europe.[113] Given the long-standing exclusion of women from the political nation, however, feminists could hardly be complacent about British women's "historical privilege." Jessie Boucherett, for her part, vacillated between boasting of women's progress in the preceding two decades and lamenting how little power they had actually had over the past five centuries.[114] Feminist historians of the period strove to downplay the "long ebb" by cataloging the little-known abbesses, duchesses, and freewomen who had voted in borough elections, owned property, and generally enjoyed some measure of equality in earlier times. Both Blackburn's *Women's Suffrage* and Stopes's *British Freewomen* reconstructed a "golden age" of female participation in British political life that proved very useful to feminists who liked to argue that female emancipation was really just the recovery of lost rights implicit in the constitution—instead of a radical innovation, as their opponents were wont to claim.[115] The utility of such histories in an imperial culture was straightforward enough. They pointed to the existing limits of current national-imperial subjectivity while providing precedent for women's inclusion in the imperial nation-state. As accounts of women in French history did for French feminists, they sought to hold male leaders accountable to the historical traditions that they used to justify their own political practices and to legitimate feminist political action "through symbolic appeals to historical memory."[116] Feminists' insistence on the inherent superiority of British politics and culture was not unreflected chauvinism. They depended on it to associate female emancipation with pure "Britishness" and to identify it with the achievements of a *historically* national-imperial culture.

Feminist efforts to identify their work with that of courageous women in the national past took a variety of forms. As Lisa Tickner has ably shown, the spectacle of visual imagery and of elaborate pageantry proved a powerful medium in which to make suffrage arguments.[117] History itself was an argument in these settings, and its enactments reveal much of the sense of historical drama that many feminist women experienced as they worked for female emancipation.[118] Cicely Hamilton, with the help of Edith Craig—the daughter of the famous stage actress Ellen Terry—organized a Pageant of Great Women, which was performed at suffrage gatherings and throughout the country in the early twentieth century. The pageant featured "Learned Women," "Artists," "Saintly Women," "Heroic Women," "Rulers," and "Warriors" who, while not limited to British women, portrayed the likes of

Florence Nightingale, Alice of Dunbar, and Joan of Arc in costume. Here were the great traditions of female activism performed and made manifest to feminists around the country working for national-imperial citizenship.

Significantly, pageants like the one in London in June 1911 could also reveal the rifts and fissures just below the surface of a collectively re-imagined "British" history—not to mention the fault lines in an equally fictive "national" culture and, more to the point, in the "national" women's movement. Some members of the Women's Freedom League had already taken issue with the designation "English" as applied to the women's movement because it appeared to slight the women of Scotland, Ireland, and Wales. This had generated quite a stir in the pages of the *Women's Franchise* in 1909, with Charlotte Despard trying to calm tempers and reassure readers about the unity of British women's struggle against patriarchy and class oppression.[119] The debate was taken up again in *Common Cause* when in 1911 Nellie M. Hunter objected to the fact that the Women's Suffrage Procession had been misnamed the March of England's Women:

> Some of us have been rudely awakened and have realised the fact that though we may have the temerity to include ourselves among the nation's women the NUWSS denies our right to any such position. Were there no Irish women, no Colonial women, no Scottish women present? England is certainly the 'predominant partner,' but a pre-dominant partner who arrogantly slights and ignores his junior partners . . . does not make for peace and consolidation. Some of us in the North think that 'England's' is not a happy title to apply to the body of representative women who assembled.[120]

Although there was some consensus on the narratives of British women's role in national history, the "national" rubric of Britishness was not always able to contain the differences of the present. Significantly, Scottish and Irish suffrage workers also dressed up as "historical figures" in their own national-patriotic marches and public pageants in the early twentieth century. As Leah Leneman has remarked, however, a distinctly Scottish pride did not necessarily preclude a more collective racial sensibility. Said one observer of a mass meeting of Scottish feminists on the Calton Hill in Edinburgh in 1910, "Scottish men and women cannot fail to see that the fight in favor of freedom is a contentious one, and that women are carrying on today the old battle of Scotland, the glory of the race."[121]

When suffrage women dressed themselves elaborately in the historical garb of each figure in order to reenact the lives of famous British women, they testified to their belief in the persuasive power of a feminist version of

British history, whatever its form, for their own emergent feminist consciousness. It was a principled rejection of what Frances Power Cobbe called the theory of "woman as Adjective" in favor of "woman as Noun"— the subject of action and, in this instance, an agent of British history itself.[122] Contemporary commentaries suggest too that participants understood what late-twentieth-century feminists and other critical theorists have described as the performative dimension of resistance.[123] They perceived, in other words, that they were themselves enacting, producing, and contesting British history by fighting for emancipation. They were not the only ones taking to the boards to perform political resistance. Indian women living in Britain engaged in similar contestations, as illustrated by their reenactment of the love story of Siva at the Court Theatre in 1912 as a benefit for Indian female education.[124] Even when they were too modest or too self-effacing to deny their own individual contributions, British women could be quite clear on the role played by their collective actions. As Alice Colinge remarked of the women's suffrage march in 1910, "All the women made history that particular day, but me."[125] Women, who were traditionally represented as outside culture and outside history, were not simply restored here, but were claimed as makers of their own historical destinies. Mobilizing a version of British history that accounted for the participation of women was a way of refusing the historical associations between manliness and subjectivity—between male citizenship and men's capacity to represent women—which was one of the bases of British political culture.

The function of this newly "feminized" British history was, in addition to its nontraditional content, its radical forms of expression, and even its consciousness-raising function, quite conservative of British traditions as well. Although its purpose was to "challenge the inequalities concealed in the vision of a 'common' nationhood,"[126] this was not the full extent of its effect. For rather than causing feminists to discover the roots of women's oppression in Britain's past, the task of historical revision gave them an opportunity to locate their movement in the long march of British national progress. Feminist history functioned as an updated, more inclusive version of British history and, in the process, identified the women's movement with what was great (and, finally, superior) about British political culture. To unearth great protofeminists in the past became a way of paying tribute to British cultural and political greatness as well as a self-conscious exercise in national patriotism. This is not to deny that revisionist feminist history challenged the exclusiveness of the British political tradition, for such a critique was clearly at the heart of the performance of "great women" of the past. The various historical pageants even questioned the central claim of

British national identity before World War I: the conviction that the British political system had marched inexorably toward democracy since the early modern period.[127] As one official program phrased it, such performances were intended to demonstrate "the great political power held by women in the past history of these Isles, the last vestige of which was lost with the vote in 1832 when the Reform Bill was passed."[128] The Reform Bill of 1832, which pluralized the British electorate in significant ways, had made masculinity an explicit test of citizenship by framing the qualification for voting in terms of "male suffrage." While feminists performed their objection to this exclusion, however, they did not reject or even question the conviction of sociopolitical evolution that defined and sustained ideologies of *British* democracy and citizenship. Appropriating the discourse of traditional Whig history, they argued that 1832 had interrupted the great march of British national progress that the movement for women's suffrage inherently embodied.[129] Arguments for female emancipation relied on the same sense of national historical progress that had underwritten accounts of Britain's history since Magna Carta. Feminists of the period claimed, in other words, that the Cause was not just more faithful to the ideals of the British political tradition than the current system itself, but in fact that it *better* embodied those ideals—and in so doing they pledged themselves to the advancement of British superiority and cultural greatness.

In this sense Victorian feminist historiography did not act as a counternarrative but rather served as a strand or dimension of the traditional narrative of Whig history. It was a narrative that certainly lent support to, if not justification for, the civilizing mission of British imperialism. Indian and other Oriental women, who often appeared in the pageants or "bazaars," as suffrage performances were sometimes called, could be designated as "Women of the Past," while European women were women of "The Present" or simply "The Future."[130] And where they appeared as part of the Pageant of Great Women, they could be read as impostors of "womanly" (i.e., British) womanhood. According to one pageant program, the Ranee of Jhansi (who was featured in the pageant and who died leading Indian troops in battle against the British during the Indian Mutiny in 1857), represented "the best man on the other side."[131] These kinds of representations, along with the convictions of Anglo-Saxon racial superiority in feminists' histories, created an understanding of England as the nation "in which reform is a 'sacred business' and empire the civilizing advance of history itself."[132] British feminists produced women as historical subjects, but one of the effects of their national historical agency was an Oriental womanhood that was apparently less progressed and not ready for the present state of social evolution, let alone for the future. Like much emancipationist argument, the new British history fashioned by feminists of the period called for public recognition of their authority—through political representation—in the imperial nation-state based on British women's allegiances to and solidarity with the racial, national, and politically imperial aims of a historically British culture. It was a strategy that did not question the imperial status quo in the present, except insofar as it excluded British women. *Darwin*

The languages used to create the new feminist history testifies again to the power of race to invent national communities in the past that could serve the political needs of those same communities as they were emerging in the present. Cicely Hamilton wrote some lines for Ellen Terry to speak in her pageant performance of Nance Oldfield, the eighteenth-century English actress—lines that were a tribute not just to Terry's influence on the English-speaking stage but, as Sheila Stowell observes, to the "palpable connection between past achievement and a living present."[133] Such performances also demonstrate the power of liberal feminist history-writing both to articulate oppositional political identities and to identify with a progressive, individualist historical worldview. "Woman in the nation" was, feminists argued, an achievement both historically British and ripe with historical evidence about the superiority of Britain's cultural and political traditions. Given the crises in imperial confidence of which they were acutely aware in their own time period, it was no doubt their hope that British women's history would be persuasive of the *historical* as well as the cultural and political necessity of granting British women emancipation. In their view the very future of imperial Britain, and of its uninterrupted progressive march, depended on it.

WOMAN, NATION, AND BRITISH
FEMINIST IDENTITY

As imagined by Victorian and Edwardian feminists, "woman" was the moral guardian of the nation, the guarantor of British racial stability and the means of national-imperial redemption. These functions, as we have seen, derived from the moral superiority and the national role feminists claimed for women, from the elisions made between nation and empire and both Victorian culture and feminist rhetoric, and from the power that feminists gave to traditions of national and racial duty to signify imperial authority for "the British-born woman."[134] The invention of an imperial female authority was essential to emancipationist success because, in political and cultural terms, the British state was a self-proclaimed masculine preserve—made masculine by the fact of empire and kept masculine by the "fact" that women could not raise arms to defend it. "Citizens" were, properly, men who had the physical capacity to take up arms in protection of the state in order to preserve its future stability. As Linda Kerber has written in another context, this was an "antique definition of the citizen, a definition as old as the Roman republic."[135] As such, it was in keeping with Britain's view of itself as a successor to, and improvement on, Roman imperial greatness— and it was frequently invoked by Antis, many of whom were also imperial apologists. British feminists insisted that, by virtue of racial motherhood, traditional definitions of imperial citizenship had to be renegotiated. This argument was somewhat weakened by the paradox of the "woman in the nation" concept itself: for as we have seen, feminist writers argued that women were de facto citizens in the nation, that they inhabited the very sacred center of the national culture already, even while they demanded inclusion in the nation from which, in traditional parliamentary political terms, they were obviously excluded.[136] More persuasive was a related argument, namely that the imperial nation-state could not be considered an exclusively masculine preserve because women were and had historically always been essential to its health, welfare, and future progress. By depict-ing women, and more specifically feminists, as the saviors of the nation and empire at a time of apparent imperial crisis, feminists made themselves as women indispensable to the very future of the national-imperial enterprise. Although feminists' imperial identity ultimately depended on colonial women and expressed itself in a sense of responsibility for the uplift of Indian women, its first point of reference was not Britain's colonial subjects but the imperial nation-state itself.

The redemption of colonial peoples was considered to be instrumental to the survival of the nation-in-the-empire, and this may be counted as one reason British feminists adopted Indian women as objects of feminist salvation. Woman-in-the-(British)-nation was clearly the savior of the im-perial nation as a whole. Woman-in-the-nation was also, as Maude Diver observed, the uplifter of *any* nation; targeting Indian women was therefore a culturally appropriate method for woman-in the-(imperial)-nation to save civilization by uplifting woman-in-the-(colonial)-nation.[137] Taking respon-sibility for Indian women was at once a fulfillment of imperial duty and proof of imperial citizenship. Significantly for the development of an impe-rially minded feminism, this harmonized well with the basic assumptions of the late-nineteenth-century British imperial mission. Uprisings and unrest in various localities of the empire had, by the end of the 1860s, signaled a shift in justification for British rule away from moral force toward military might. But the notion of moral responsibility (later, "trusteeship") remained at the core of British imperial ideology.[138] Not just in India but throughout Britain's colonial possessions indigenous peoples were seen as being in need of improvement and "civilizing." Even when a non-Western culture was recognized as having elements of civilization, as in India, "heathen" religion and apparently underdeveloped political and social organization made it an object of reform and uplift. Both feminism and imperialism were motivated by a redemptive impulse based on a sense of moral superiority and national responsibility. It is hardly surprising that feminists identified themselves willingly and proudly with the British civilizing enterprise, so closely were its ideological dynamics related to their own.

Any apparent parallels between feminist and imperial rationales, however, belie the fundamentally complex relationship between the two ideologies. In historical terms they shared an ethic of moral responsibility and translated that responsibility into authority over dependent clients—for imperialists it was colonial peoples, for feminists it was those whom they identified as the poor, the downtrodden, the socially redeemable—both at home and, as this book argues, in the empire. The extent to which feminism borrowed its vocabulary of moral uplift and redemption from imperial ideology (or the reverse) seems a less compelling question than the problem of how and to what extent these discourses were interdependent and cooperative in the production of ideas about British citizenship and, indeed, about Britishness itself in this period. Such ideas were gendered even as they were culturally marked. Gender ideologies structured both feminist and imperial ideologies, both of which simultaneously intervened to define what constituted masculinity and femininity, not to mention what defined Jane and John Bull. That this occurred within feminist discourses as well as outside them testifies to the discursive agency of late Victorian feminist women as well as to the cultural context in which they operated. They were not "intellectually impermeable, existing apart from the society around them." Nor could they "ignore outside forces and fight their cause in a vacuum."[139] Most significant is the ideological capital feminists made out of empire and its contemporary historical condition in their arguments for female emancipation. The crisis in confidence that Britain experienced in the three decades before the First World War enabled feminists to seize a critical historical moment and use it to their advantage in fashioning a feminist identification with race, nation, and empire. The instability of the period allowed them not only to identify with nation and empire at this critical juncture but also to attempt to reshape national and imperial identities along more "feminine," not to mention "feminist," lines. Feminist polemicists, as we have seen, agreed that to be British meant to be nationally superior and imperially responsible. What they tried to argue was that it meant to be feminist as well—to champion female emancipation as part of the British national-imperial heritage.

3

Female Emancipation
and the Other Woman

Victorian feminists' admiration for empire and their identification with its racial and cultural ideals shaped a nineteenth-century women's movement with recognizably imperial concerns and sympathies. Although a fully developed imperial feminist rhetoric did not emerge until the early twentieth century, British feminists exhibited an imperial worldview from the 1860s onward. For in addition to privileging the role of British women in the national-imperial enterprise, Victorian and Edwardian feminist writers relied on images of Eastern, and especially *Indian*, women to bolster a variety of arguments about female emancipation.[1] Descriptions of "Oriental" women as prisoners of the harem, suffocated by religious custom and at the mercy of brutish husbands, frequently interrupted the narrative of emancipationist arguments, serving as brief but apparently graphic "proof" of women's fate in cultures where female emancipation went unrecognized. Feminist writers who constructed arguments about the need for female emancipation built them around the specter of a passive and enslaved Indian womanhood. As a result, a colonial female Other was one of the

conceptual foundations of Victorian feminist thinking. What this suggests, among other things, is that British feminism is part of Western European orientalist traditions—traditions in which identity "relies on the concept of an essential, authentic core" and the search for identity itself is "a process of elimination of all that is considered [O]ther."[2]

Historians of British feminism may be surprised by this contention. Conventional historical wisdom tends to parrot nineteenth-century British feminist argument, which claimed to derive female emancipation from British traditions of liberty and representation.[3] One of the more recent studies of the British women's movement goes so far as to challenge even the hallowed distinction between constitutional suffragists and militant suffragettes; this, together with the shared rhetoric of racial concern between the two groups, suggests that British feminism was more unified than divided by traditional loyalties and domestically "British" values.[4] Indeed, there appears to be little overt indication that British feminists thought about "Oriental" women or used them in any comprehensive way in their arguments for female emancipation. In the Women's Source Library series, edited by Dale Spender and Candida Ann Lacey, for example, hundreds of women's suffrage and feminist pamphlets have been collected in dense and handsome volumes, making feminist argument—a heretofore neglected aspect of "the Cause"—accessible to scholars. Not a single title in the almost one dozen volumes mentions women of the East either by name or by allusion. All the pamphlets reproduced appear to be geared toward the domestic feminist struggle, as the following selections indicate: "Reasons for the Enfranchisement of Women," "The Political Disabilities of Women," "The Legislation of Female Slavery in England."[5] From all appearances, then, the case for female emancipation had a limited horizon, confining itself to British social and political traditions and to the British parliamentary system.

As Elizabeth Spelman has remarked in another context, however, the apparent invisibility of "the Indian woman" is itself a product of her embeddedness in British feminist discourse.[6] Precisely because notions of "the Orient" and assumptions about the racial and cultural superiority of non-Western peoples were among the self-evident cultural facts in imperial Victorian culture, images of "Oriental womanhood" were deeply rooted in feminist writing.[7] One of the purposes of this chapter is to show how often women of the East cropped up in emancipationist writings as examples of a variety of womanhood that feminists dismissed out of hand as unacceptable in a civilized society. Whether feminists used her to delineate their own superiority or to prove the universality of women's oppression, they invoked a degraded female Other to persuade audiences that the Western, and specifically the British, women's movement was part of the march of Western civilization. The case for British women's emancipation in all its complexity therefore depended on images of an enslaved "Oriental" womanhood. As in the writings of other, nonfeminist English women during this period, British feminists' use of the symbolic Indian woman was "profoundly ideological."[8] In feminist usage, she worked specifically to substantiate the moral authority that feminists claimed for themselves in the public-national-imperial sphere.

Although drawing attention to these allusions is crucial to the work of understanding British feminism's imperial context and its orientalist bases, simply making the "Other woman" visible again is not sufficient for conceptualizing imperial feminist ideologies in Britain. "The Indian woman" was a recurrent theme in feminist literature, and referencing her was more than a stylistic preference or even an "intermittent polemic."[9] It was something like a "narrative habit" for Victorian feminist writers—a rhetorical and explanatory device that structured much of the argument for female emancipation.[10] It functioned to authorize British feminists and their movement as agents of the continued progress of civilization—and implicitly, of empire—in the West. Late-nineteenth-century British emancipation argument was akin to what Thomas Lacquer has called "humanitarian narratives"—narratives that describe a particular kind of suffering and that do not simply offer "the means for its relief" but, finally, create "a moral imperative to undertake ameliorative action."[11] The pathos of feminist narratives about Indian women—whom they depicted as helpless, unemancipated, and trapped in zenana existence—made the body of the Eastern female the object of humanitarian concern and, as we shall see in the next chapter, a pretext for feminist imperial intervention.[12] But the intended subjects in emancipationist polemic were British women themselves, whose exclusion from the political realm on the basis of sex put them in danger of being compared with "uncivilized" Eastern women. The "immediate action" required was, therefore, not the liberation of suffering Eastern female populations but rather the emancipation of British women. The rescue of British women from barbarity for the sake of continued national-imperial progress lay at the very heart of feminist argument and allied the Cause with the larger late Victorian ethos of humanitarian—and civilizing—reform. What this chapter suggests is that invocations of Indian women and their non-Western counterparts served to underline the essential Britishness of female emancipation and, by extension, to legitimate it as a progressive Victorian reform movement. Indian women were, in short, instrumental to the project of proving the indisputable role of female emancipation in advancing the cause of "civilization."

EMANCIPATIONIST ARGUMENT AND THE
OTHER WOMAN

Women of the East appeared in a variety of forms in feminist literature, ranging from specific "national" types to generic Asian or "Oriental" females. Egyptian and Persian women figured occasionally in feminist writing, but the women of India and Turkey were by far the most common.[13] Often Eastern women were identified as such solely by their religious beliefs, which were typically Hindu or Moslem, and sometimes Buddhist, as in the case of Burmese women. With few exceptions, Eastern women figured in feminists' imagination as prisoners of religious law and custom.[14] Early writers willing to exonerate Turkish men for the condition of Turkish women, for example, blamed instead the "deplorable constitution of the Mussulman family," which they interpreted as requiring wives and mothers to be domestic drudges and harem inhabitants.[15] And although Mary Carpenter emphasized the potential of Indian women for self-improvement through education, her account of her six months in India in 1868 conveyed the impression that many Indian women needed to be freed from the confines of the "dreary walls" of the zenana, deprived by their countrymen "of those who might have called out their highest powers, and to whose pure enjoyments they might have imparted the highest zest."[16] Disdain for the harem became an essential part of feminist emancipationist argument. Seclusion was thought to be the equivalent of degradation, and harem life "dull and vacuous to the last degree.[17] The harem was an object of fascination for feminists partly because it was accessible only to women, but also because it was the site of what to them constituted "Oriental" female imprisonment. As one of the tropes of the Orient and a female segregated space, it was as intriguing to Western feminists as it was to female travelers and male observers, if not more so.[18] In some instances feminist commentators acknowledged that Eastern women could enjoy certain freedoms— "The ladies of Constantinople are not contented with contemplating the world through the bars of their casements, they walk in the town, in the bazaars, everywhere they please"—and could even exercise domestic political power. But the overall impression given was that most were "closely immured all their lives."[19] "Think," Gertrude Torrey exhorted her readers, "of the life of the caged odalisque, robbed of all her womanly rights and even of her reason and her soul."[20]

Indian women, though described from time to time as partly emancipated thanks to British-inspired educational improvements, were chiefly depicted as trapped in the "sunless, airless" zenana existence or, alternately, in early marriage and enforced widowhood.[21] The campaign against Indian child marriage is often associated with Eleanor Rathbone, longtime suffragist and M.P. in the 1930s, but it had a history as a British feminist issue from the 1890s, when B. M. Malabari appealed to feminist societies to take up the cause of their Indian sisters.[22] Millicent Garrett Fawcett was one who responded to his call by writing several passionate articles for mainstream periodicals in which she pleaded the case against "infant marriage" and defended the right of Rukhmabai (who had been the subject of a much-publicized child marriage case in India) to reject her husband's marital claims.[23] References to helpless child-wives punctuated feminist writings as examples of the victimization of Indian women at an early age.[24] Indeed, although Fawcett praised Rukhmabai's refusal "to ratify a marriage to which she had never been a consenting party," she ended her 1890 essay in *Contemporary Review* by asking the viceroy "to protect little Indian girls from the pernicious custom of infant marriage."[25] Over time, feminists began to acknowledge the achievements of their Eastern "sisters" and to applaud the development of what they identified as a women's movement among Asian women.[26] Writing in *Votes for Women* in 1911, Ella Wheeler Wilcox could rejoice that at last the harem was coming to an end.[27] But even in the early twentieth century feminists could still be heard lamenting that Eastern women seemed incapable of attaining or understanding personal freedom. Lillian Hay-Cooper attributed this to the Eastern "social system," whose harem seclusion prevented women from developing any sense of freedom or "the meaning of life."[28] The zenana was, as Janaki Nair has demonstrated, subject to a variety of meanings in British women's private and public discourses from the early nineteenth to the mid-twentieth century: it was construed as a site of conversion, secular reform, female power, and Eastern backwardness.[29] Like other women writing about the East, feminists brought the zenana—along with child marriage and enforced widowhood—before their reading public, often as the totality of Eastern women's experiences and as the totality of their identity as women. Even when tempered by what contemporary feminists considered to be compassion, the harem was understood to serve as shorthand for Eastern slavery and female oppression—and it was always used as an argument for the necessity of female emancipation for British women.[30]

In feminist periodical literature, a great deal of attention was paid to individual Indian women, such as the celebrated nationalist-feminist activist and poet Sarojini Naidu, the social reformer Pandita Ramabai, and Rukhmabai, who later became a medical doctor. As the next chapter illustrates, Eastern wives, widows, and mothers were popular features in feminist journals, where the great diversity of the female Other was made apparent to feminist readers. In contrast, feminists writing more polemical, specifically emancipationist pieces rarely if ever referred to Indian women who were active in the contemporary feminist scene. Unlike articles in feminist periodicals, emancipationist essays were not topical; moreover, they rarely utilized an *ad feminam* approach to the "woman question." Rather, they were part of a long-standing tradition of feminist argumentation that relied self-consciously on abstract reasoning and moral suasion to persuade opponents that the case for female emancipation was the logical product of British political and cultural tradition.[31] Feminist essay and pamphlet writers relied on Indian women to serve their emancipationist arguments, but they tended to reduce them to the one-dimensional category of "Oriental" or "primitive" womanhood. As she appeared within the structure of arguments for female emancipation, the female Other was not just helpless and degraded. In contrast to the particularities attached to the British feminist woman, she often lacked national-cultural specificity, and her passivity was utilized to represent the condition of "Woman" in all non-Western societies.[32]

The assumed helplessness of Eastern women was frequently invoked in arguments for British women's emancipation in the nineteenth century. Harriet Taylor's essay "Enfranchisement of Women," first published in 1851, was certainly not the earliest feminist text in English to mention women of the East, but it was one of the most influential essays for female emancipation in the nineteenth century, and its use of "Oriental" women in relationship to Western women's struggle for freedom is revealing.[33] In the course of her argument that female emancipation was indicative of the progress of modern civilization, Taylor pointed to primitive societies, where she claimed women did most of the physical work. She cited the "savage" Australian and the American Indian as uncivilized men who coerced their women into doing the "hard bodily labour." "In a state somewhat more advanced, as in Asia," she continued, "women were and are the slaves of men for the purposes of sensuality." Taylor admitted that in Europe there had evolved a milder domination, "the "sedulous inculcation of the mind," which bound women to men by feelings of obligation and duty. In contrast to Asian women, however, she noted that European women had recognized their oppression and were now demanding full equality, owing to their "present state of civilization."[34]

Several pages later Taylor returned to the condition of Eastern women in order to contest the popular argument that most English women did not really want emancipation.

> Supposing the fact to be true in the fullest extent ever asserted, if it proves that European women ought to remain as they are, it proves exactly the same with respect to Asiatic women; for they, too, instead of murmuring at their seclusion, and at the restraint imposed upon them, pride themselves on it, and are astonished at the effrontery of women who receive visits from male acquaintances, and are seen on the streets unveiled. Habits of submission make men as well as women servile-minded.[35]

Taylor's intended meaning is somewhat ambiguous. Whether she meant to say that, like Asian women, some English women were in fact unaware of their own enslavement or that detractors wrongly equated English women and Asian women, the whole passage turns on her representation of Eastern females as secluded, "servile-minded," and compliant. A few lines later Taylor suggested that the submission of Eastern women was an indication of their lack of appetite for freedom: "The vast population of Asia do not desire or value, probably would not accept, political liberty, nor the savages of the forest, civilization." It was custom, she insisted, that "hardens human beings, by deadening the part of their nature which would resist [oppression]." The argument from custom was popular among Victorian feminists, and it had some potentially radical implications for feminist ideas about social and political change, as we shall see shortly. Taylor, for her part, claimed that women do not prefer submission, nor is it part of their natures—although the natural capacity for Asian women to resist would seem to be too deadened by the habits of custom to afford them much hope of self-liberation in her presentation.

The appearance of "Asiatic" women in Taylor's argument is brief, taking up no more than a total of seven or eight lines. Despite the casual nature of the reference, it served an important function by invoking and then rejecting Oriental women as examples of what ostensibly unemancipated "looked like." Women of the East often surfaced like this in arguments for female emancipation in the nineteenth century. Commenting on the "progressive improvement in the condition of women" over the centuries, for example, Millicent Garrett Fawcett reminded her audience in 1872 that "among savage races women have little better lives than beasts of burden.

In India a widow is sometimes compelled to sacrifice her own life at the death of her husband. In the semi-civilizations of the East we know that women are principally valued as inmates of the Seraglio."[36] Mabel Sharman Crawford, in her contribution to a pamphlet called "Opinions of Women on Women's Suffrage" in 1879, complained that the opponents of female emancipation had yet to learn from the negative example of the East, which taught that "if the physical health of woman is admittedly impaired by confinement within a limited space, her mental health also suffers through legislative disabilities; and that it is unfair to deprive her . . . of political liberty, as in the Oriental mode, to shut her up within four walls."[37] The victims of this "Oriental mode" included, but were not limited to, Indian women; their collective impact, in turn, was considered to be monumental. Sidney Smith, a member of the London Liberal Association and a committed suffragist, pleaded for the enfranchisement of women by emphasizing the negative effects of early marriage and harem existence on Indian women. According to this line of reasoning, failure to enfranchise women would lead to the decline of Western civilization. "What has ruined Turkey and every eastern country," Smith asked, "but leaving the culture of each rising generation of the governing classes to the sultanas and female slaves of the seraglio and the harem?"[38]

As in Smith's speech, references to Indian or Eastern women were often fleeting, sandwiched into lengthy arguments about the rightful place of emancipated women in Western civilization. One anonymous pamphleteer, reflecting on the second reading of a women's suffrage bill in 1898, called the event "one of a series of facts which reveal an unmistakable movement amongst the women of all English-speaking countries . . . [in] the Victorian Era." After six pages of detailing women's suffrage as the logical outgrowth of Anglo-Saxon culture, the writer claimed that without it the ideal of male-female companionship would be seriously threatened. "What the loss of [this ideal] may ultimately involve, is only too clearly and sadly revealed to us in the secluded twilight lives of our Indian sisters, closed within Zenana walls, to the undoing of the moral and physical fiber of the people."[39] The characteristically Victorian sentimentality of these kinds of allusions should not obscure their ideological function: conjured up as helpless creatures, Indian women were more than symbols of a non-British womanhood to be pitied. They were used as material evidence of what might happen to the physical vitality of a race when women were prohibited from exercising political freedom.

Not all feminists agreed that Eastern women were completely powerless within the confines of the zenana. Emily Pfeiffer, recounting a conversation she had had with "an Oriental of high mark," agreed with his claim that "in India women are all powerful, even as they are here." "I believed and do believe him," she wrote.

> The women of India are nimble-witted and acute, or they were no match for their husbands and brothers; and, smooth and subtle as snakes, they fold the limbless strength of their degraded souls about every question, which appeals with sufficient force to their passions or interest. Held by men in a condition of abject subjection, deprived by jealous superstition of all moral-self-support, the Nemesis of the virtues which have been killed within them appears in the characters of craft and subtlety which they *print upon the race*.[40]

This is a celebration of female empowerment in spite of subjection, but Indian women emerge from it in some of the most exaggerated stereotypes of "the Oriental character." They are compared to snakes and are said to be responsible for the "craftiness" of the race. What's more, although cognizant of the power they wield within zenana walls, Pfeiffer still depicts them as enslaved. Their "abject subjection" accounts for their "degraded souls" and the impossibility of "moral self-support" or freedom. Pfeiffer concludes by explaining that, while acknowledging the limits on Western women's freedom, she would not equate their condition "with that of their cruelly crippled sisters in the East." The specific reasons for their presumably superior status are evidently understood without being adduced; they are as much the common possessions of imperial culture, and of feminist imperial understanding, as Indian women themselves. Even more important, Pfeiffer claims that "the illustration they have furnished me has been used only to give point to the argument" that all obstacles to the exercise of human freedom should be removed. Indian women are used here as a negative example expressly to fortify the argument for British female emancipation. Perhaps most tellingly, the symbolic economy of racial motherhood is inverted, contrasting Indian woman as destroyers, rather than the saviors, of Indian society and culture. What is at stake in the comparison is not just Indian women, but the whole social fabric of colonial India. Indian women's regenerative power, which was central to Indian nationalist and even to some Indian feminist claims in this same period, is clearly overshadowed in Pfeiffer's piece by the service rendered by images of Eastern female powerlessness to the cause of Western female emancipation.[41]

As they appeared in most feminist polemic, Eastern women were not markedly different from European male interpretations of "Oriental womanhood." Contrasts between Eastern and Western womanhood and concern about reproductive practices and sexual norms were standard fare in Victorian public discourse on the East. The Reverend Edward Storrow's *The Eastern Lily Gathered* (1852) typifies the male missionary view, emphasizing the superior position of women in Christianity and the degrading customs of early child marriage and widowhood imposed by both Hinduism and Islam. Storrow confessed that he could not "have intercourse" (by which he presumably meant social interaction) with "respectable Indian ladies," but he generalized nonetheless about "Oriental" female sexuality, judging Moslem women to be the most polygamous and sensual.[42] Both he and the Reverend Alexander Duff, who worked for indigenous female education in India, used Indian women explicitly as evidence of Eastern women's "absolute subjection," warning English mothers to be grateful for their freedoms and the privileges of their faith.[43] Missionaries were also concerned about "nautch girls"—that is, women who danced at princely courts "and in the British imagination were most commonly associated with the Lucknow court of Awadh and the Indian states which survived after 1857."[44] The Christian Literature Society, for example, condemned them as prostitutes and claimed they were under the control of Hindu elders.[45] Secular male commentators writing on Indian women tended to focus on child marriage, especially in the 1890s and after. The debate, which centered around whether or not the British government should "meddle" with indigenous religious custom, provided the opportunity for observers like J. D. Rees to act as arbiters of the civilized nature of Indian cultural practices.[46] Max Muller, a prominent Indologist, chided critics of child marriage, admiring "the possibility of a pure attachment between children under the warmer skies of India."[47] Muller's interpretation was the exception rather than the rule, and, given the role he played in popularizing colonialist versions of the Hindu golden age, it was not without its own ideological preoccupations.[48] The general consensus among male observers was that Eastern women might exercise some indirect power, but that, "shut up from the light and air of heaven," they were to be pitied as prisoners of unenlightened religions and brutal social custom.[49]

That British feminist characterizations of Indian women should have resonated with more general stereotypes is not surprising, since feminist writers gleaned much of what they "knew" about Eastern women from these very sources. Missionary accounts were legion during the Victorian period, and many feminists, possessed of Christian enthusiasm themselves, embraced missionary men and women as both accepted authorities on the colonial "native" and as valuable instruments of England's imperial mission.[50] The Rees and Muller articles cited above appeared in *Nineteenth Century* and *Contemporary Review* and are only two of many on Indian topics that appeared in the mainstream Victorian periodicals—periodicals to which feminists like Millicent Garrett Fawcett, leader of the constitutional suffrage movement after 1897, contributed and which other activists may well have read.[51] As for Max Muller himself, he was frequently quoted in feminist magazines and was personally known to some members of the Women's Freedom League as well as to the editor of the *Woman's Penny Paper*, Henrietta B. Muller, which may account for feminists' apparent familiarity with and their use of certain narratives of the Aryan past.[52] Even if feminists did not encounter these specific sources, their own journalism indicated a familiarity with missionary work as well as a sympathy for the work of women evangelicals among Indian women.

What distinguished feminists' negative image-making was the narrative contrast they repeatedly established between Eastern female oppression and Western women's quest for freedom. Recurrent references to Eastern female slavery created an opposition not just between Eastern and Western women (that much was accomplished by the likes of Storrow and Duff), but between Eastern women and British *feminists*. It was a contrast that, by emphasizing Asian women as victims, privileged British feminists as agents of their own liberation. As we have seen, feminists depicted women of the East most often as trapped in the harem, emphasizing their lack of access to the public world. The public access evidently denied to Eastern women was among those rights which British feminists were claiming by seeking political equality, university education, and other opportunities for women. Women's rightful place in the public realm may seem at this distance like a fairly straightforward demand, but it signified a considerable challenge to Victorian convention. Millicent Garrett Fawcett, who used her husband's campaign hustings in the early 1870s to lecture publicly about women's suffrage, recalled much later how traumatic her public appearances had been. She was criticized in the House of Commons and the press, as well as by her mother-in-law, because "at the time it was an unheard of thing for women to speak on election platforms."[53] Depictions of Eastern women in the harem—with its connotations of imprisonment and female submission—furnished a didactic contrast. Such images served as exaggerated and threatening examples of the limits imposed on women's freedom in "uncivilized" countries. They also valorized the public sphere in Britain as civilized and "clean" compared with the dark, unhealthy interiors of Eastern women's domestic space as it was imagined and reproduced by feminist writers. British women's determination to bring about their own emancipation in the public sphere was, feminist writers suggested, an effort to avoid the fate of Indian women: it was an attempt to preserve the differences in cultural practice that signified Britain's superior status and guaranteed its maintenance.

As Edward Said has written, representations are never free-floating but are "put to use in the domestic economy" of society.[54] In the domestic economy of feminist imperial rhetoric, the fact that Indian or Turkish women were Eastern—hence "primitive"—made British feminists seem comparatively progressive and associated female independence and self-representation with an advanced state of society. The success of this comparison was contingent upon the imagined primitiveness of "Oriental" women. In keeping with the assumptions of British imperial culture, feminist writers considered Asian civilizations to be evidence of primitiveness in action, a means of understanding what savage society was like in the present day. Non-Western societies were evidence of the stages of human development, and Indians an example of "the savage races still in existence."[55] The distinction between Indian society and primitiveness was often blurred, if not completely elided. Ellis Ethelmer, noting the barbarous treatment of women in primitive societies of the past, advised that "somewhat as to these ancient conditions may be gathered from the position of women in India at the present day."[56] Or, as Lady Sybil Smith wrote in her "Woman and Evolution," in primitive times when physical force prevailed, woman "sank into a condition of complete subservience to man—she became his slave, his absolute possession, as we still see her among savage tribes and in most Oriental countries."[57] Women of the East appeared in feminist argument as throw-away examples—helpless victims whom feminist writers presumed to exist at the bottom of the evolutionary chain. This presumption functioned in two ways, perhaps the most obvious being that it imposed an accepted set of hierarchies on women of the world, dividing them into degraded and progressive, if not into colonial and imperial. More subtly, Victorian feminist writers enmeshed feminist argument in those hierarchies, thus establishing an ideological opposition between Western female emancipation and its apparent negative, Eastern female backwardness. Embodied as weak and helpless and the opposite of Western women, "Oriental womanhood" was at the base of feminist argument, acting as an important ideological and imaginative support to claims that British women's emancipation was part of Victorian social progress.

THE INTELLECTUAL ORIGINS OF
THE FEMINIST OTHER

The conceptual hierarchy of women that structured feminist narratives of emancipation had roots in the several traditions that produced the first generation of nineteenth-century British feminist thinkers. The two sources most often cited as the theoretical origins of modern European feminism, the enlightenment and evangelical Christianity, both invoked "savage" society as a point of comparison with Western development, and similar invocations made their way into early feminist writing, mainly in order to glorify the domestic achievements of Western women. Eighteenth-century feminist writers tended to refer to "the degraded condition of women in the savage state" as evidence that, with the onset of civilization, women's position improved—that is, they gained the responsibilities of home and the care of children. This comparative method, although containing the seed of cultural relativism, had perhaps a less tolerant Christian intent: "Comparison with other religions and civilizations was made to conform to the assumption that Christianity alone had raised woman to her destined and natural place, neither 'tyrannised nor impiously honoured.' "[58] Jane Rendall makes the insightful observation that the evidence of past and present societies, together with arguments about women's nature and "God's ordinances," contributed to the "ideological unity" of woman's domestic role in the early Victorian period.[59] As much needs to be made of how dependent that unity was on a hierarchal view of the world; attention to the equation with Western family forms and female roles with "nature" and "progress" is required as well. In addition to rational individualism and religious enthusiasm, the twin traditions of the enlightenment and Christianity bequeathed to feminism a Great Chain of Being that stratified the women of the world. It proved to be a chain into which feminist theorists easily slotted "Oriental," primitive women at the opposite end of the descending scale from themselves.

Feminists writing in the eighteenth century had viewed reason and Christianity both as the hallmarks of civilization and of Englishness, and so perhaps not surprisingly they too relied to some degree on references to non-Western women and non-Western societies in building their arguments for female emancipation.[60] Moira Ferguson has recently shown the ways in which slavery and the colonial slave trade figured prominently in Mary Wollstonecraft's arguments—as they did in the writings of many British women before the Victorian period, when the points of reference were primarily Afro-Caribbean.[61] Joyce Zonana takes this argument one

step further not simply by excavating the "Eastern" references in Wollstonecraft's writings, but by expressly naming her feminist discourse as
"orientalist." In a maneuver that foreshadows the rhetorical strategies
of nineteenth-century feminists, Wollstonecraft and other pre-Victorian
women writers used images of Eastern women's slavery so that they "displace[d] the source of patriarchal oppression onto 'Oriental'" society and
so that they might "define their project as the removal of Eastern elements
from Western life."[62]

I would not take issue with these characterizations except tentatively to
draw some distinctions between eighteenth- and nineteenth-century us-
ages. First among such distinctions is geographical specificity. When Wollstonecraft did refer to Eastern women as "exotics," she did not necessarily
name their locations. Rarely, if ever, were they Indian or even more generally Asian; and when they were not Afro-Caribbean, they appear to have
been most often Turkish.[63] Given the geopolitical relationship of the Otto-
mans with Western Europe down to the eighteenth-century on the one
hand and the centrality of India in the nineteenth-century British imagination on the other, the fact that British feminists of different historical
moments should have correspondingly variable "female Others" is not
especially surprising, though it certainly bears further scrutiny than I am
prepared to undertake here.[64] Second, Wollstonecraft's work, particularly
"A Vindication of the Rights of Woman" (1792), emphasized Islam almost
exclusively as the source of corruption and degradation for non-Western
women. While Victorian feminist writers were not uncritical of Islamic
practices, it was Hinduism that primarily concerned them, at least in the
Indian context.[65] Orientalist scholarship and missionary discourses, together with the institutionalization of English language and literature studies, virtually guaranteed the Victorian equation of Hindu religious practices
with moral, intellectual, and cultural deficiency.[66] And, finally, invocations
of the seraglio served slightly different functions for Victorian feminists
than they had for their foremothers. With Wollstonecraft, the seraglio was
used didactically in the same way that later feminists would employ it: to
contrast Eastern women's idleness with Western women's assertiveness and
their involvement in "the serious business of life." Significantly, however, it
was represented as a source of "languor" and pleasure—but not explicitly of
evil or imprisonment, as in Victorian feminist polemic.[67] Lady Mary Wortley Montagu, writing from Constantinople in the mid-eighteenth century,
believed the harem women she observed in Turkey to be more free than
English women. She did so perversely, as Katharine Rogers argues, "to
bring into question the remarkable liberty that English women were sup-

posed to enjoy," but also in order to underline Western women's lack of
progress and not necessarily Eastern women's degradation.[68] In the context
of nineteenth-century imperialism, the contrasts were more organized and
more sharply drawn between English *feminists* and non-Western *women,* in
part because the former were conscious of writing from inside an organized
feminist movement. And while Turkish women functioned as an important
feminist Other in their own right into the twentieth century, in the Victorian period feminists specified India most frequently to evoke what they
considered to be the primitiveness and slavery of women's conditions
outside the West. The fact of empire, and of India's apparent embodiment
of it, heightened Victorian feminists' belief in a global Great Chain of Being
and made the indigenous women of the colonial empire the most easily
imaginable as less advanced versions of their Western feminist sisters.[69]

The British antislavery movement has not always been given sufficient
weight in the intellectual biography of modern British feminism, though
recent historiographical attention to the role of its female adherents is
beginning to change the landscape. The work of Moira Ferguson, Clare
Midgley, and Vron Ware have illustrated the ways in which antislavery
discourse exercised no less a formative influence on nineteenth-century
feminist consciousness than evangelism or rationalism, from both of which
it derived its impetus.[70] Many mid-century feminists received their first taste
of organizational reform in antislavery societies, which, like the early wom-
en's movement, began in the northern counties of England.[71] What Josephine Butler's repeal movement against the Contagious Diseases Acts did
for suffragists between 1870 and 1886, antislavery agitation did for women
reformers in the era before organized women's suffrage societies: it gave
them the experience of campaigning for a just and moral cause, taught them
antiparliamentary strategies, and immersed them in a collective woman-
based effort that ultimately contributed to the abolition of slavery in 1833.[72]

Most significant for feminist thinking and writing, the antislavery movement created a vocabulary of slavery versus emancipation through which
feminists quickly learned to articulate the dimensions of their own oppression. References to slavery were commonplace in feminist literature from
the mid-Victorian period onward, with parallels inevitably drawn between
the disabilities of color and those of sex. Harriet Taylor declared in 1851
that sex was "a distinction as accidental as that of colour, and fully irrelevant
to all questions of government." She viewed the enfranchisement of
women as part of the progress of a world that had "but just begun to cast off
injustice. It is only now getting rid of negro slavery."[73] Slavery in the Greco-
Roman world was also referenced, most notably in Elizabeth Martyn's 1894

pamphlet, "The Case of the Helots,"—which substitutes the word "helot" for "woman" throughout in an attempt to depict the condition of women as interchangeable with that of ancient slaves.[74] And feminist rhetoric surrounding campaigns against female prostitution (called the white slave trade in the twentieth century) was deliberately evocative of the abolitionist crusades, thus testifying to the power of the slave image well beyond the memory of the first generation of suffragists.[75] For Marion Holmes the history of antislavery made the whole question votes for women cut and dried: "In a word, the difference between the voter and the nonvoter is the difference between bondage and freedom."[76]

As did white American feminists like Angelina Grimké, British feminists "used the terms of the female antislavery emblem" after abolition had been achieved in order to underline the continuity of purpose between their own political movement and antislavery. It was, as Jean Fagan Yellin has written about the American context, a way of reinscribing one powerful—and successful—emancipatory discourse onto another.[77] Arabella Shore, citing the participation of women in the fight against the slave trade, claimed it was "won by the same process that we are now pursuing, steady peaceful constitutional effort." She was confident that the subjection of women "will, like other barbarisms, melt away into the darkness of the past."[78] The success of abolitionism was also invoked as inspiration when women's suffrage seemed impossible.[79] What emerges from feminist writing is a strong sense of national pride about the abolition of the black slave trade, not only because women participated in the British abolitionist effort but also because the condition of slavery was retrograde, evidence of an uncivilized society. Feminists emphasized slavery as a thing of the past, as unworthy of a modern nation, and, by the Victorian period, as something beyond which Britain had progressed. Its abolition was, for them as for other Victorian commentators, proof that Britain led the civilized world. Putting an end to slavery was an achievement that, along with the abolition of suttee in India, feminists heralded as the mark of true civilization.[80]

Feminist pride was necessarily tempered by the recognition that women in England still suffered like slaves at the hands of the law. One pamphleteer recalled that in Elizabethan times Britons could proudly claim that "the air of England is too pure for a slave to breathe." And yet "the right in this land of ours of a human being to personal freedom has never been questioned, except in the case of an English wife."[81] Charlotte Despard reminded her readers that, in the words of their national anthem, "Britons shall never be slaves," though she warned that it could not be sung with gusto until

"Britons shall never be masters" of their women equally applied.[82] The political slavery of British women was an effective metaphor for forcing the opposition to admit that female emancipation, like the abolition of the slave trade, was the prerequisite of a civilized society. Together with rational individualism and evangelism, the antislavery ethos was part of a feminist tradition that encouraged feminist theorists to construct their arguments in terms of slavery and backwardness versus emancipation and progress. Slave metaphors had of course been a staple of feminist argument virtually since the seventeenth century.[83] In the context of Victorian imperialism, this tradition enabled British feminists to identify with Indian women's enslavement in the harem, even while it allowed them to articulate, however unself-consciously, "a feminist consciousness that was race-specific."[84] It also permitted them to see Indian women as creatures whose colonial status simultaneously explained their slavery and required British feminist reform and "uplift." And, finally, it allowed them to make women whom they perceived to be enthralled the objects of their pity and concern, and simultaneously to maintain themselves as the chief subjects of emancipationist argument.

There was a final influence on feminist thinking that generally goes unrecognized but that subtly shaped arguments for female emancipation— the developing field of Victorian anthropology. Darwinian theory was all-pervasive after mid-century, and the coincidence of the emerging women's movement with the beginning of institutionalized anthropology in the 1860s must in part account for the incorporation of social evolutionism into the case for women's rights.[85] For the feminist dichotomy between primitive Eastern women and advanced Western women was not simply an alternative interpretation of primitive culture. It was part of a larger social evolutionary worldview that tended to pervade discussions of female emancipation, primarily in response to the contention that women's physical weakness precluded them from political participation. Feminist writers drew especially on the work of Sir Henry Maine, who used modern marriage and relationships between the sexes as evidence in his arguments about progressive social evolution.[86]

Women writing in favor of female emancipation argued that what characterized civil society was its movement away from brute strength as an organizing principle toward the recognition that moral, not physical, force should be the basis of government. "I have always thought," wrote Arabella Shore in 1877, "that government was designed to *supersede* physical force, that civilization meant the reign of law instead of that of brute-strength.

Public opinion, moral restrictions, mental power and organization, make up now the forces on which government rests, compared to which bodily force is simply nothing. This would be going back to savagedom, indeed."[87]

Throughout feminist pamphlet literature, writers vacillated between declaring that, on the one hand, physical force was a thing of the past and wryly remarking, on the other, that for all its progress Britain was still in danger of predicating its political system on physical force by virtue of excluding women. And yet the relative historical newness of society based on moral rather than physical force was uppermost in the minds of more than one feminist writer. Harriet Taylor, for example, wrote, "Until very lately, the rule of physical strength was the general law of human affairs. Throughout history, the nations, races, classes, which found themselves the strongest, either in muscles or in riches, or in military discipline, have conquered and held in subjection the rest."[88] The author of an editorial for the *Englishwoman's Journal* agreed, suggesting that "many illustrations will at once present themselves to the mind of the reader in confirmation of the fact that the domination of physical force was the law of the human race until a relatively recent period."[89] This was social evolutionism in a more or less Darwinian form, albeit one that ignored the physical force involved in Britain's acquisition and maintenance of imperial possessions. As an explanatory device for Britain's own cultural superiority, it was embraced by feminist theorists no less readily than by other social reformers of the late nineteenth century who sought not simply "a solid, historical, evolutionary justification for the role of women in their own culture" but the means by which to identify their particular causes with Britain's evolutionary progress as well.[90]

Feminists not only accepted a social evolutionary narrative as an explanation for modern forms of government; it was crucial to their argument for female emancipation in the political realm as well. Helen Blackburn, an early suffrage theorist, summarized the feminist viewpoint on the subject in an 1878 suffrage pamphlet:

> In the rudest forms of social life the will of the strong man dominates, overawes the mass into a chaotic sort of obedience, rough and uncouth in its forms and customs, step by step experience develops laws which tone down these customs and . . . then . . . interposes an ever broadening barrier between the brute force in the community and the motives impelling action. . . . Let us make our laws . . . confidently, for if we know it is possible for men to fall back to the lower type, we also know that it is in their hands to advance to the higher ideal, and bring

about a time when it shall as little enter into the heart of civilized man
to return to the rule of the strongest fist, as to return to the habits of
the brute tearing and rending its prey.[91]

Modern society's barbarisms against women notwithstanding, most feminists presumed, like Blackburn, that with the help of women's suffrage,
civilization would continue to advance to "the higher ideal." "Is not the
extension of the suffrage to women a step," Millicent Garrett Fawcett
asked, "in the direction of increasing civilization? Will it not bring about a
retreat of the forces of savagery and barbarism?"[92] Emancipationist writers
staked their feminist argument on a linear-ascendant view of progress in
which female slavery was the symbol of primitive culture and women's
emancipation was among the highest expressions of civilization. In this
sense, they fashioned their own feminized narratives of cultural progress—
narratives predicated on the assumption that female emancipation was the
world-historical as well as the culturally specific necessity for society's
survival and its continued progressive evolution.

There was a tendency among Victorian feminists to conceive of the
women's movement itself as one of the most highly evolved products of a
civilized society. John Stuart Mill, champion of women's equality and a
feminist theorist in his own right, argued that feminism was a progressive
movement whose time had come. He told a group of suffragists in 1871,

We live at a period of human development, when the just claims of
large numbers cannot be permanently resisted. The whole movement
of modern society, from the middle ages until now, greatly accelerated
in the present century, points in the direction of the political enfranchisement of women. Their exclusion is the last remnant of the old
bad state of society—the regimen of privileges and disabilities. . . . The
whole spirit of the times is against predetermining by law that one set
of people shall be allowed by birth to have or do what another set shall
not by any amount of exertion or superiority of ability be allowed to
obtain.[93]

This long view of female emancipation was shared by other feminists.
Some used the language of Darwinian science and anthropology to ally the
woman's movement with evolutionary trends. Jane Hume Clapperton, responding to an antisuffrage petition signed by a number of prominent
Victorian women in 1889, titled her article "An Evolutionist's Reply."
Among her rebuttals was the argument that "the irresistible forces of
unconscious evolution are carrying us forward in a perfectly definite direc-

tion." For women, that direction was "towards the goal of her complete development, her physical, mental and moral maturity—till, on a plane of high civilization, she moves side by side with man in what further progress the material conditions of happy life render possible. Woman can no longer be man's plaything or doll, his domestic tyrant and mistress, his legal chattel and slave."[94] While Clapperton did not specify the women's movement as evolutionary, others did. Thus was feminism itself considered to be part of the narrative of cultural progress, a progressive organism in the evolutionary body politic. One contributor to *Shafts* (subtitled *A Paper for Women and the Working Class*), who called herself "Libra," argued that "the Women's Movement is really an evolutionary force" that would right the inequalities in the marriage relation and throughout society.[95] For others, the women's movement in the twentieth century was part of the "spiritual evolution" of modernity. According to Brian Harrison, for Fawcett the suffrage movement was "something of a religion, and she saw women's emancipation as steadily spreading, like Christianity in the third century."[96] Charlotte Despard, leader of the Women's Freedom League and a practicing theosophist, claimed a messianic status for the process of female emancipation: as an evolutionary force it did not stand alone but "with other movements of the time is preparing for that 'one far off divine event to which the whole creation moves.'"[97] Assumptions of cultural superiority, combined with a shared sense of feminism as progress, made feminists perceive the British movement for female emancipation as one of the highest expressions of Western evolutionary development. Eastern women, who were manifestly primitive in British feminist representations, provided proof of what Western women and especially British feminists had evolved *away from*.

Despite their reliance on women of the East to fortify their arguments for female emancipation (and because of it), British feminists were in fact less concerned with the Other woman per se than they were in articulating a positive image of the women's movement. In this sense they participated in and reproduced in feminist rhetoric some of the same orientalist-imperialist dynamics that marked mainstream political and scientific discourses in the Victorian period.[98] Feminist writers constructed the female Other negatively and then dismissed her in favor of a model of womanhood that was most often white, Western, and British. Like Spivak's Rani of Sirmur, she appeared in cultural production only when needed.[99] The Other woman acted as a foil against which feminists could exhibit their role as agents of civilization, their commitment to racial motherhood, and, especially, their essential Britishness. As with feminist discourses around the idea of the nation, the chief function of the Other woman was to throw into relief those special qualities of the British feminist that not only bound her to the race and the empire but made her the highest and most civilized national female type, the very embodiment of social progress and progressive civilization.

Progress was one of the defining tropes of Victorian culture, and it was so commonly used in nineteenth-century discourse that in feminist and non-feminist writing alike it almost seems incidental to the arguments at hand, part of the conventional literary style of the period.[100] If, as Peter Bowler has suggested, the Victorians invented progress to impose upon history "the sense of order that they craved," Victorian feminists too created meanings around progress to promote specific scripts for women in society.[101] From its earliest stages the women's movement claimed that women's special virtue was their capacity for civilizing human society—for keeping it on track in humanity's progressive march into the future. Whether because of maternal influence or religious persuasion, Sarah Lewis claimed, for example, that it was "women who directed the savage passions and brute force of men to an unselfish aim, the defense of the weak, and added to courage . . . humanity."[102] Twenty years later, in 1862, Frances Power Cobbe expressed her belief that women would be able to "carry forward the common progress of the human race."[103] The rhetoric of progress was applicable but not limited to votes for women; it was used to justify all aspects of women's reform activities as evidence of the historical necessity of female emancipation. Elizabeth Blackwell, arguing for medicine as a profession for women, claimed that "every advance in social progress removes us more and more from instinct . . . compelling us to guard against the sacrifice of our physical or moral nature while pursuing the ends of civilisation."[104] Woman's "progressive character" and her superior moral attributes made her the civilizer not only of the home but of the public domain as well. The link between women and progress, on the one hand, and women and civilization, on the other, was made early and often by feminists, chiefly to counter the opposition's fear that female emancipation foretold "the end of the human race."[105] Henrietta Muller's declaration that "the intelligence and status of the women of a country are a measure of its civilization" was practically axiomatic in feminist writing.[106] Lydia Becker and Alice Scatcherd articulated the conviction of many of their feminist contemporaries when they claimed, "Hitherto every advance that has been made in the elevation of women from a servile and subject condition has tended to the benefit of the people among whom it has taken place; and the degree of civilization to which a nation has attained corresponds to the degree in which the condition of its women has been raised."[107]

More often than not, feminists presented the equation between woman and civilization with images of primitive society or the threat of social disintegration lurking not far behind. Maude Diver's choice of phrase is instructive here: "Woman is the lever, the only infallible lever, whereby *sunken* nations are upraised."[108] In other instances the contrast of the female Other was explicitly invoked. "It has become little short of an accepted fact that the manner in which women are treated by any race or society is not only a testament or thermometer of their civilisation," wrote a contributor to the *Englishwoman's Review* in 1877, "but also is in itself a cause of their progress or degradation." Following this assessment was a paragraph about enslaved Turkish women as evidence of the imminent collapse of Turkish civilization.[109] Even while championing progress, feminists were acutely conscious of the possibility of regression; to a large degree, the impetus for progress depended on it. The Eastern woman, represented as evidence of non-Western cultures in decay, was by no means an unusual figure; she was in fact, as John McBratney has observed, "the chief sign of the Indian [and, I would add, of India] as 'other.' "[110] In the Victorian feminist context she acted additionally as something of a scare tactic, underscoring the vital connection between female emancipation and the continued advance of Western civilization and suggesting the dire consequences for Britain's future if emancipation were denied or, perhaps more pointedly, indefinitely deferred, as suffrage bills repeatedly were in the House of Commons in the latter part of the nineteenth century.

The female Other also heightened feminists' consciousness of British women's racial responsibility. Like the term "progress," references to race in nineteenth-century feminist literature are so frequent that historians appear to have interpreted them as convention, if they remark on them at all. As Mariana Valverde has noted, the term "race" had a variety of meanings in feminist discourse.[111] It might be used to distinguish among European nationalities, to link English-speaking peoples as diverse as Americans and white South Africans, or to denote a group of religious believers.[112] Lucy Bland has suggested that "race" should be read primarily as "humanity," as, for example, in Harriet Martineau's advocacy of "a race of enlightened mothers" or in the claim of the National Union of Women's Suffrage Societies that the women's suffrage movement was "the Cause of the Whole Race."[113] And yet feminists' use of race, while perhaps intended to suggest a universal model for humanity, invariably resonated with assumptions about Anglo-Saxon supremacy. References to the Anglo-Saxon race were not merely descriptive; the qualities associated with it were linked to notions of inherent superiority that were accepted as givens in Victorian culture. In an era when the conviction that Britain was the governing race constituted the rationale for imperial conquest and settlement—and when, as we have seen, feminists themselves relied on the British imperial connotations of race to guarantee their claims for women's suffrage—the implications of racialist language for the construction of a feminist Other cannot be discounted. Feminist writers were, as I have demonstrated, quite explicit about their racial priorities, with racial motherhood a commonplace in feminist discourse. Frances Swiney's *The Awakening of Woman* (first edition, 1899) is perhaps the most unabashed elaboration of racial feminism in the late Victorian period. Subtitled *Women's Part in Evolution,* it applied "the evolutionary ideals of social and racial progress" to the ideology of women's special role.[114]

Swiney's association of women, and more specifically mothers, with the future of the race was a standard feminist cry. But the reasons she gave elaborated on the usual racial motherhood formula that feminists subscribed to. According to Swiney, the race was to be entrusted to women because they possessed more racial pride than men; unlike their male counterparts, they did not "descend to union" with members of other races. Speaking of white women, Swiney wrote:

> As slaves, or prisoners of war, as victims of enforced marriage, they have been constrained to bear children to hated masters; but left to their own inclinations, inherent racial pride has led them to form connections with men of their own race or of higher nationality than themselves. The Aryan woman, happily, has never stooped to the sexual degradation of the Aryan man; and it is to the influence of the white woman in the future, that we must look for the enforcement of that high and pure morality, which will restrain the conquering white man from becoming the progenitor of racial crossing with a lower and degraded type, dangerous to the social and ethical advancement, in the lands that come under his sway.[115]

In this scheme, there were rankings within the womanhood of the world, roughly correlated to the racial and imperial hierarchies that divided the world into the conquering and the conquered. In Swiney's view the Anglo-Saxon woman had reached the height of women's social evolutionary development, evidenced, she noted, by the fact that the empire was headed by the "Great White Queen." At the base of this evolutionary pyramid was the Other woman. Swiney explained that "under the combined influence of a long development of political, aesthetic and moral civilization, the Anglo-Saxon woman has happily attained a position far in advance of her sisters of other nationalities." She compared the status of women in Britain to that of her French, Belgian, German, and Russian sisters and found all of them relatively lacking. Behind Western women came Turkish, Persian, and, finally, Indian women. Though admitting that the Persians had better divorce laws than many Western countries, she stressed Indian infanticide, suttee, and lack of female education. Swiney envisioned the "Woman's Era" as one in which "racial and national antipathies" would subside, but for now "the Anglo-Saxon woman leads the van."[116]

Swiney's piece might be dismissed as whimsical and even untypical, in its mystical enthusiasm, of rational feminist argumentation.[117] The fact that she had been raised in colonial India may also have influenced her thinking.[118] Her attitudes cannot, however, be easily dismissed: she was the president of the Cheltenham branch of the National Union of Women's Suffrage Societies and not a negligible activist in the women's suffrage movement. Her assumption that the Anglo-Saxon woman was the highest racial model underlay much of the rhetoric of the early Edwardian suffrage movement, which was as imperial in its assumptions as it was in its intent.[119] The specter of enslaved Eastern womanhood remained at the heart of feminist insistence on racial motherhood, for it was by contrast with the slave mothers of the East that Swiney's Anglo-Saxon model derived its full symbolic power. In effect, the flip side of the free-woman-as-progress idea was the decline of societies where women were oppressed. As Henrietta Muller succinctly put it after detailing the demise of Egyptian civilization, "You cannot be free if your mothers are slaves."[120] The relationship between enslaved motherhood and the decay of civilization preoccupied feminists working to secure women's legal rights in this period. Writing in defense of a women's suffrage in the late 1880s, Millicent Fawcett warned that "great men do not spring from feeble mothers."[121] Charlotte Despard, in her pamphlet "Woman in the Nation," summarized the feminist position as follows:

> We do not forget that nations have fallen into decadence, and finally into decay, through the enslavement of their women. Slave-mothers in Rome, in South America, in India, were factors no doubt, in that absence of virility which gave these nations as a prey to their conquerors. To bear and rear a fine and healthy race, capable of holding its own in the world, we must have women of healthy mind and body— women vigorous and pure and independent, and this we can only hope for when women are free.[122]

Feminist writers often attributed the fall of Rome and the decline of ancient Greece to the low status of their women. But it was Eastern cultures past and present that bore the brunt of their criticism, particularly because of the connections feminists insisted upon between women and *racial* stability. Lady Sybil Smith, remarking that "woman's whole destiny, according to Eastern eyes, is to be a breeding machine and an instrument to man's pleasure and profit," speculated that such women might in fact be happy with their condition. "Whether she is the best possible mother for the rising generation of a progressive race is another matter."[123] For feminists, the enslavement of Eastern women accounted for the apparent physical, moral, and spiritual weakness of the "lower races"—a collective weakness that explained, if not justified, their colonization. The specter of degraded Eastern woman and the degenerate children she produced provided feminists with sinister evidence of what the Anglo-Saxon race—and perhaps the imperial nation—might become if female emancipation in Britain were prohibited indefinitely. Such fears were prominent concerns among British feminists, especially after the Boer War, when a falling birth rate was widely viewed of the "signs of decadence in our nation." At stake was "maternal energy," which one concerned suffrage woman claimed "alone can give an imperial future to our race."[124]

At the same time that the varieties of female Other worked to solidify the image of British feminists as the embodiment of civilization and the saviors of their race, they helped to signify the essential Englishness of their cause. Some feminists perceived the parallels between the subjection of Eastern and Western women and did not hesitate to point them out. In 1879 Louisa Bigg presented a paper entitled "Should the Parliamentary Franchise Be Granted to Women Householders?" at a conference in the Council Chamber at Luton. Addressing herself to the contention that women should stay at home and darn socks rather than demand the franchise in any form, Bigg made the following heated reply:

> Let her darn the stockings by all means, but let her think while she darns. An Eastern traveler, struck with the unbearable tedium and monotony of life in the Harem, asked a native gentleman whether he should like to be treated as he treated his wives who were shut up in their dreary prison from one year's end to another. "Oh, no," he answered, "I am a man." It is this spirit which dictated the Suttee, which prompted the Mahomedan spirit to deny that woman has a soul, and which bids the Englishwoman stay at home and darn the stockings.[125]

Bigg's point was that opponents of female emancipation expected women to stay at home, shut up in the house—though English women would not, significantly, be as idle as the harem inhabitants. English manliness might, it is hinted at, be persuaded to rankle at the comparison between Western women and Eastern women (or, even more persuasively, between Western and Eastern men) and hence advocate women's suffrage. A sense of national pride is similarly appealed to by another suffrage writer, who described the Ladies' Gallery in the House of Commons, where women were consigned to watch the proceedings, as the equivalent of a purdah curtain.[126] Other feminist writers interpreted the relationship between English women and Eastern females as one of sharp contrast, not comparison. Mrs. Grey seemed to find the very idea of comparison absurd. Writing in 1870 in response to opponents' claims that women could not vote because it required them to be seen in public, she replied, "Softly, ladies. Surely we are in England, not in Turkey. It is of Englishwomen we are speaking, not of the secluded inhabitants of an Oriental zenana, and it seems strange to hear that English women are afraid of mingling in crowds and public places."[127] Helen Taylor's pamphlet, "The Claim of Englishwomen to the Suffrage Constitutionally Considered," laid out the Englishness of the case for female emancipation for fifteen pages, stressing throughout that English women only sought from English men inclusion into a political system characterized by its inherently English promise of representation. She concluded her argument with the observation that "it is too late to be afraid of letting Englishwomen share in the life of Englishmen. We cannot shut up our women in harems, and devote them to the cultivation of their beauty and of their children. We have most of us long ago acknowledged that a perfect woman is 'Not too bright and good / For human nature's daily food.' "[128]

From time to time in emancipationist literature, feminists expressed more commonality with English men than with the Eastern female. Some suffrage writers like Arabella Shore took Taylor's tack, arguing for women's suffrage as "a right which English *men* have set themselves steadily to acquire."[129] Women's rights could also be expressed as a challenge to male prohibition and, more particularly, a defiance of the exclusivity of English men's racial-imperial preserve. "I want the vote," said Maud Arncliffe-Sennett, "because Lord Curzon says 'it is the imperishable heritage of the human race' and therefore it belongs to me."[130] Racial bonds—in the sense of cultural ties and historical traditions—could transcend the gender difference between English feminists and English men: at times emancipationists identified and sought comparisons more readily with men of their own race than with non-Western women. As Arabella Shore reminded her readers, "Englishwomen are of the same race as English men, and partake of the same strong national character. . . . Magna Carta is not likely to be repealed by the female descendants of those who won it for us."[131] In view of their opponents' accusations that the women's movement threatened the very bases of English civilization, one of Victorian feminists' greatest challenge was to persuade critics that women's emancipation, whether strictly political or more diffusely social, would not entail a cultural—or a sexual—revolution. When Mrs. Arthur Lyttleton denied that "the suffrage means that every woman will try for a seat in Parliament, or that it will lead to . . . every woman having three husbands, as in Thibet," she pledged the cause of female emancipation to English civilization, as symbolized by monogamy and marital respectability.[132] These were considered the hallmarks of civilized society and of Britain's role as leader of the cultural vanguard worldwide.[133] Comments like Lyttleton's are rare enough, since feminist writers emphasized Eastern women's passivity rather than their agency and alluded even more rarely to the impact that emancipation might have on British women's sexual freedoms. But here as elsewhere non-Western women are used as evidence of what British women would *not* become if emancipated. To be sure, Victorian feminists did not always require the presence of a female Other to evoke their commitment to the cultural and political practices that they agreed underpinned Britain's achievements and its status around the globe. Arabella Shore, defending women's suffrage against claims that women voters would vote "as a class," declared that when that happened, "England would be no longer England."[134] And yet the presence of female Others in feminist argument cannot be ignored. Their invocation and simultaneous rejection by feminists as any kind of model for womanhood acted as an important symbolic reassurance of Victorian feminists' cultural loyalties and not simply of their contrasting Britishness. In any given argument the female Other worked to consolidate identification of the women's movement with Britain's culturally progressive stature and to assure opponents and supporters alike that feminism itself was worthy of the best traditions of the imperial nation-state.

FEMINIST CULTURAL CRITICISM AND THE CONSTRAINTS OF IMPERIAL IDENTITY

The cultural contrast implicit in the very idea of "civilization" is, as George Stocking has written, "as old as civilization itself."[135] The fact that feminists used the terms of anthropological tradition and imperial culture to justify female emancipation did not necessarily mean, however, that they were naive about what male-dominated British society considered cultural progress or that they were incapable of generating trenchant cultural criticism. For although British feminists placed themselves and their movement in the cultural vanguard, feminist writers did not take their own superiority completely for granted. Ever mindful of their superior place on the evolutionary scale, British feminists were quick to note that the current condition of women in England still left a lot to be desired. "Many English writers have expatiated upon the great respect which women receive in England," wrote Anne Isabella Robertson in 1871, "and contrast this so-called respect with the bad treatment of women in other lands." But she warned, "Men who imagine that England is a free country . . . [should read the laws, which] bear a strong resemblance to the laws regulating serfs, to slaves, and to the peoples of conquered nations. . . . [They are] disgraceful to the age we live in, and which calls itself civilized."[136] Questioning the "so-called civilization" of Britain was a popular tack in Victorian emancipationist literature.[137] Many feminist writers stressed the legal subjection of women in England, echoing Robertson's vehement claim that, without female emancipation, Britain did not deserve to be called civilized. One author described the position of women in England as paradoxical, since it was "rising with modern civilization" at the same time that it remained "a modification of ancient barbarism."[138] What kept British women in a state of oppression was the variety of legal disabilities excluding them from the professions, the universities, and the vote. "In no country in the world is the legal position of a female so degraded, so barbarous or so cruel as [in England]," accused one anonymous feminist.[139] Another saw the "progress" made by the Englishwoman as nothing more than advancement "from her primitive condition of slavery to her present position of legal subjection."[140]

Feminists' rhetoric about the relative civilization of British society was more than a clever strategic maneuver, designed to shame opponents of female emancipation into admitting that the exclusion of women from the public sphere testified to the true barbarity of British civilization. It grew out of the conviction, fundamental to Victorian feminist ideology, that women's oppression was not fixed in nature but was the product of specific historical and cultural conditions that, like those in Victorian Britain, could be changed.[141] While debates about social constructionism are legion in late-twentieth-century feminist discourse, we are only just beginning to understand the ways in which feminists in the nineteenth century used cultural critiques in order to promote women's suffrage and other historically feminist causes.[142] The argument from custom was an important plank in the Victorian feminist program, at least from the 1860s, when it was promoted to counter objections from early opponents that women's domestic role was natural and God-given. Barbara Leigh Smith Bodichon, writing in 1866 on the objections to the enfranchisement of women, digressed briefly from her discussion of the legal qualifications for the vote to ask the following questions:

> If we contemplate women in the past, and in different countries, we find them acting in addition to their domestic part, all sorts of different *roles*. What was their *role* among the Jews and the Romans? What was it in early Christian churches? What is it in the colliery districts—at the courts of Victoria, and the Tuileries? We can conjure up thousands of pictures of women, performing different functions under varying conditions. They have done, and do, all sorts of work in all sorts of ways.[143]

The italic "roles" is Bodichon's and indicates her challenge to the notion that women's function was inscribed in nature. She used evidence from ancient and primitive societies to reaffirm her reading, as did other feminist contemporaries.[144]

Conventional Victorian notions of nature made it one of the great enemies of female emancipation. But the definitions of "woman's mission" that feminists derived from so-called primitive societies encouraged them to see the cultural specificity and the historical contingency of nature too. To wit, Arabella Shore in 1872:

> But one would like to know when it is so glibly said that Nature is opposed to this or that, what is meant by Nature. Is ancient usage or established convention, the law or custom of our country, training, social position, the speaker's own particular fancy or prejudice, or what? And when Nature has been defined, one would like to have defined what particular actions are, or are not, against that aforesaid Nature. It seems that for a woman to manage property, carry on a business, be a farmer . . . or member of a School Board, or even a Sovereign, is not against Nature, but to give a vote for a Member of Parliament is.[145]

Feminist writers tended to view woman as a pure form, a kind of *tabula rasa* whose moral nature was inherently superior to that of men but whose social roles were not determined except by the dictates of custom—whether political, social, or religious—and the historical moment by which they were shaped. "Is there anything in the past history of the world, which justifies the assertion that [women] must and will do certain things in the future?"

asked Bodichon. "I do not think there is."[146] Feminists applied this environmental view of woman's condition in specific terms to the history of women in Britain. Feminist historians Helen Blackburn and Charlotte Carmichael Stopes, for example, both advanced a degenerationist explanation of British women's history, arguing that the earliest Anglo-Saxon women had been the equals of their husbands.[147] Other feminist writers venerated Magna Carta, that great document of British national pride, as both the glory of the British political tradition *and* as the source of British women's historical privilege as citizens.[148] In Stopes's eyes the Saxons' "racial peculiarities" were clearly superiorities, diluted momentarily by the Norman invasion but persisting down to the present day.[149] "British freewomen's historical privilege" was construed by feminists as the product of the Anglo-Saxon cultural heritage that they were striving to recover and reinstitutionalize in late-nineteenth-century politics.

Historical accounts like Stopes's are prime examples of the cultural components of racial ideology, on the one hand, and of the racial dimensions of gender ideology, on the other.[150] But while these traditions were considered to be, as we have seen, a source of national-racial pride, they also enabled Victorian feminists to take a culturally deterministic view of the condition of women in other countries. Differences in national approaches to female emancipation greatly intrigued British feminists, who kept a watchful eye on the development of the women's movement around the world. German and French feminist activities were particularly scrutinized, with a view to recording British superiority in organization and principle.[151] Objections to female emancipation were also believed to be nationally specific as well. The *Woman's Herald* ran several articles in the autumn of 1892 on a pamphlet entitled "The Dangers of the Emancipation of Women" by a German Anti named Adele Crepaz. Her argument, which actually echoed many of the objections of English Antis to female emancipation—that it would destroy family life—was condemned by one critic as "thoroughly German" because of its excess of sentiment: "It is sentiment *ad nauseam*. . . . [Crepaz] taxes the resources of the German language, rich in sentiment beyond all other tongues, to describe the bliss of *Muttergluck*. . . . [F]rom her one might sum up the whole duty of German women briefly as follows:—'Marry, be a mother, become a Hausfrau, thank God, and die.' "[152] The only value attributed to Crepaz's piece was that "it gives interesting insight into the depths of sentimentalism of which a German woman is capable." Precisely because of its Germanness, the critic saw no reason to fear "that pamphlets of this kind from over the sea will carry much weight with English women, or will appeal very strongly to their tougher fibre and robuster independence." Another critic, who signed herself "Albion," agreed, declaring, "I am not able to see that it is good for a nation to let the women stand still while the men move forward. Before a nation can progress truly, men and women must keep step in the march, otherwise the women will simply act as a drag on the heels of progress."[153] British feminists, confident that their own movement was part of the march of progress, saw British methods as a lesson for other nations to admire and to imitate. Such an attitude made all other women, European or Asian, potential Others too.

And yet it was non-Western women who were most commonly invoked to prove the conditional nature of women's oppression. The degeneration-ist argument that feminist interpreters made about the history of British women was frequently applied to women of the East. If Indian women were enslaved and oppressed now, they argued, this did not reflect any kind of "natural" or permanent inferiority. Nor did it represent the true condi-tion of women under "Oriental" civilization. One offended reader of *Shafts* objected strenuously to the negative characterizations of Asian women as slaves and drudges. Pointing to the ancient civilizations of Egypt, she claimed that women were held in honor and esteem, ruled the nation-state, and were "just as eligible as man for initiation into the highest religious mysteries." The Indian woman of ancient times had unprecedented free-doms and even could leave her husband if she chose.[154] Henrietta Muller agreed, attributing this feminine power to the "ancient Vedic view of women," which regarded her as "Sakti," the "vital energy of the Human Race."[155] Discussions of Indian women's former glory usually provoked diatribes against modern Western society—"When one comes to compare the position of [Western] women today with that of ancient Hindu women, then assuredly one must arrive at the conclusion that our civilization is a civilization in name only"—but they could also lead feminists to blur the lines between "Eastern" and "Western" civilizations and to see the subjec-tion of women as the result of the decadence of *any* civilization.[156] This historical interpretation of Asian women allowed feminists to contrast the enslaved condition of contemporary Indian women with their previously powerful state, thus buttressing the argument that women's oppression was not a naturally dictated but a historically conditioned process, the product of all civilizations in decay. Their emphasis here was, needless to say, on India's past history, and it echoed contemporary official discourses that "acknowledged India's greatness but only in terms of her scriptural past."[157]

If Eastern women's oppression was historically conditioned, feminists suggested that it was socially and culturally determined too. Helen Blackburn, in a contribution to the *Englishwoman's Review*, explained the subservience of Eastern women as the product of customary practices. Taking eating rituals as her example, she explained that in "stationary China," custom proscribed men and women eating together; in India it was the laws of Manu that forbade husband and wife to eat together. "And, to make the descending scale . . . still more complete, the Tahitians, when first visited by missionaries, strictly prohibited a wife from partaking of the same kinds of food as her husband; moreover, 'sacred custom forbade that she should eat in the same place, or prepare her food at the same fire.' "[158] Blackburn's interpretation echoed Harriet Taylor's insistence, cited above, that Asiatic women were oppressed by their culture, not by nature. By using evidence from non-Western cultures, feminists effectively refuted the argument from nature as culture-bound itself. The female Other could, in other words, furnish evidence for the universality of women's oppression and the timelessness of the "woman question."[159]

Significantly, the very universalism of feminist ideology depended on the existence, or rather on the active construction of, an apparently less civilized female Other. In a very real sense, it was thanks to her omnipresence in Victorian feminist discourse that the argument from custom was so persuasive. In a postscript to an article on matriarchy and the Amazons, the editor of *Woman's Franchise* noted:

> We have great pleasure in printing the above article on the condition of women in primitive and early society. Without laying undue stress on the evidence of comparative history, we urge upon our readers the importance of such a study as a method of arriving at the underlying principles of our cause. Our opponents are only too willing to snatch at arguments from so-called "Laws of Nature," in default of valid objections, that it is pleasant to be able occasionally to "hoist them with their own petard."[160]

Without the Other woman, the feminist case against nature would have been substantially weakened and, with it, the postscript continued, "the underlying principles of the cause." As with all of the other invocations of non-Western women cited here, these feminized narratives of cultural progress were ultimately useful to feminists only insofar as they buttressed emancipationist argument. Like many of their Victorian contemporaries, British feminists were not interested in "the data of cultural variety" for its own sake but as the means by which they might effectively critique contemporary cultural and political forms—in their case, in the name of women's rights.[161]

The full potential for Victorian feminists' cultural critique was undercut not so much by their self-interest, which is predictable, or by their "narrative habit," which was potentially interruptible, or even by imperial culture per se, but ultimately by the requirements that Western European modernity made of those seeking to create new social and political identities for themselves. British feminists, who were undoubtedly in the process of inventing a modern women's movement and of substantiating their claims to national-imperial subjecthood, stood to inherit the same set of "modern" traditions as English male sociopolitical subjects. Feminism was produced in a post-Enlightenment era indelibly marked by Christian, liberal, and imperial ideologies—a political culture which held (and to a great extent still holds) that "the world is a complex but unified unity culminating in the west."[162] The women's movement was in many important regards an oppositional subculture, and feminists approached identity itself as the simultaneous identification with a Self and the production of an Other. Despite the ways in which it was a force for social and political change, Victorian feminist discourse reproduced many of the structural dynamics of power and authority that it sought to reform. The language of incorporation utilized by feminists in order to gain entrance into the imperial nation made political representation contingent on the demonstrable capacity to reform, to uplift, to civilize the body politic. The production of a feminist female Other was one consequence of how liberal political ideology developed in imperial culture at home. Among the effects of *feminist* political ideology in the Victorian period was a series of Other women—Others who have become, over time, "a trope of feminist discourse" itself.[163] Yet another lingering effect is the notion that the West is the future that non-Western societies will eventually encounter and that Western women are the prototypes into which all female Others will eventually evolve.[164] This particular narrative has become habitual for certain varieties of modern Western feminism, and as such it constitutes one of the most troubling and politically fragmenting legacies that the Victorians have bequeathed.

Thomas Lacquer warns that no narrative is independent of its audiences and that humanitarian narratives in particular depend for their efficacy on the specific historical and cultural circumstances in which they are read, understood, and acted upon.[165] There is no way of telling how many Victorian feminists read emancipationist pamphlets or, for that matter, how exactly they may have fashioned a set of imperial identities as a result. We can speculate that their recurrent images may have encouraged fledgling feminists who read the literature of female emancipation to conceive of the world of women in terms that correlated to already accepted colonial

hierarchies. What's more, the very image of an Indian womanhood corrupted by Indian culture and society enabled entire generations of British
feminists and social reformers to imagine Eastern women awaiting rescue
at the hands of their British feminist sisters. It also contributed to an
imperial feminist identity that, as we shall see, a variety of later feminist
writers articulated quite explicitly and well beyond the confines of pamphlet literature. Nor, finally, should the subtleties of their imperial assumptions blind us to the powerful contradictions Victorian feminists wrote into
their arguments for female emancipation. By constructing the Other
woman as helpless and degraded, British feminists could both express
solidarity with them as women *and,* in the imperial context, claim responsibility for them as their special British feminist burden. As the next chapters demonstrate, that imperial feminist burden was essential to British
feminist identity. Feminists' self-confidence in shouldering such a burden
derived in great measure from their capacity to use images of Indian
womanhood as rhetorical devices that could "nevertheless function as
historical truth."[166]

4

Reading Indian Women

FEMINIST PERIODICALS AND

IMPERIAL IDENTITY

The appearance of non-Western women in middle-class British feminist writing was not limited to emancipationist pamphlet literature. A wide variety of Victorian women writing for feminist periodicals demonstrated a keen interest in the condition of Eastern females, and especially that of "the Indian woman." News and information about Indian women filled the feminist journals of the period, appearing across a broad range of monthly and weekly magazines in Britain, both inside "Foreign News and Notes" columns and in articles especially dedicated to them.[1] Scores of features on the women of India and the East were presented didactically, as authoritative knowledge tempered and justified by feminine—and, most significantly, by *feminist*—understanding. Victorian feminist periodicals functioned as a critical site for the representation of Indian women by Western feminist interpreters and for their consumption by a far-flung feminist reading audience. British feminist self-images were continually created and experienced through reading, in contrast to images of Indian women, whose colonial status and colonialized images furnished an ongoing sense of imperial identification for feminist readers.[2] The Victorian feminist press thereby served as a forum in the emerging feminist community where British women's imperial relationship to Indian women could be exhibited and their authority over colonial womanhood could be imagined and exercised.

In contrast to emancipation pamphlets, which were limited-edition publications targeting very specific issues and a more limited readership, feminist journals deployed images of a female Other to a heterogeneous, geographically diverse audience of female readers. They were a fairly regular, subscription-based set of feminist spaces in which "the Indian woman" was made available for scrutiny by her Western feminist "sisters."[3] In its capacity as a mechanism for the dissemination of knowledge and the articulation of arguments for female emancipation, the Victorian feminist press was indeed "a powerful statement of political intent."[4] It constituted, I will argue, a powerful declaration of feminist imperial authority as well. For those who read the feminist periodical literature of the period learned who "the Indian Woman" was according to British feminists; needless to say, what British feminists "knew" about Indian women justified their colonial and subordinate role. This reservoir of knowledge allowed them to claim sympathy for and ultimately to exercise professionalized authority over Indian women—responses that were the logical consequence not simply of imperial ideology but of feminist reform passionately committed to imperial ideals. If, as B. S. Cohn has suggested, the conquest of India was a conquest of knowledge, feminist periodicals provided an important epistemological basis for British feminists' claims to imperial identity and female moral authority in the public-imperial sphere.[5] They encouraged generations of feminist readers to understand what it meant to be a British feminist in an imperial culture and to aspire to the glorious imperially minded causes of the British women's movement.

THE FEMINIST PERIODICAL:
IMPERIAL AUTHORITY AND IDENTITY

Feminist periodicals were a mid-nineteenth-century phenomenon whose role in shaping, rather than merely reflecting, the women's movement in Britain is only beginning to be recognized.[6] Female voices were not excluded from the mainstream quarterlies and monthlies. In fact, prominent women like Harriet Martineau and Millicent Garrett Fawcett were regular contributors to *Fortnightly Review, Contemporary Review,* and other periodicals, where they often put forth cogent feminist arguments to a wide, and probably largely male, audience. But there was a sense among feminists that women required their own journalistic space. Evelyn March-Philips, commenting in 1894 on the proliferation of women's journals in the nineteenth century, pointed out that "the views and interests of women are crowded out or receive scant attention in ordinary newspapers." Women's magazines were, in contrast, "systematic and recognized channels" for women to consult about matters of importance to themselves as women.[7] The founders of feminist periodicals created forums in their publications where an empowering kind of separate spherism could be experienced in practice, by women readers reading women's journalism. March-Philips recognized the production of this kind of a woman-oriented genre as "a significant token of [women's] vitality." It was also an important activity in feminist work toward building a distinctively female culture. In the estimation of Josephine Butler, the mainstream press "has forced us to create a literature of our own."[8]

The significance of feminist periodicals, and indeed of the feminist written word, as vehicles for establishing British feminist authority in the public sphere cannot be overemphasized. In the British context as in the American, the periodical press was critical to the transformation of women's organizations into formidable social movements; journals edited and published by sympathizers were a "rhetorical medium" that was fundamental to claims for emancipation in the Anglo-American feminist tradition.[9] They functioned, as Martha Solomon and others have elucidated, to establish women's shared identity outside of domestic duties (though journals were most likely read in the home), to promote consciousness among women readers who might not yet be fully conscious of their oppression, and to encourage women to view themselves as "competent, sensible, potentially important persons."[10] Geographical distance and emotional isolation were two of the many difficulties facing the Victorian feminist community, and subscription to feminist magazines could overcome the sense of alienation that suffrage workers and other female reformers experienced in their localities. The fact that many journals were produced in the metropole but covered the events and activities of regional branches helped to create the sense of a national network rooted in local contributions. Moreover, the frequency with which national periodicals reprinted articles from similar magazines around the world suggests a sense of internationalism among British feminists which produce a rhetoric about global sisterhood across a variety of women's organizations.[11] Like suffrage spectacle and other forms of public agitation, feminist periodicals worked to create viable

political communities and active citizens. As such, they were instrumental
in shaping feminist ideas about national citizenship and its responsibilities
in the social and political realm.[12]

For Victorian feminists striving to identify their cause with the public
good and with national need, the very production of a feminist journal was
a publicly political act—subversive of conventions that prevented women
from speaking in public.[13] For others seeking to promote their interests as
nationally distinctive—like the Irish women behind the publication of the
Irish Citizen, for example—a periodical could in certain circumstances become the public expression of cultural difference within the British wom-
en's movement.[14] Feminist periodicals in nineteenth-century Britain were,
additionally, arenas where feminist argument could be worked and reworked publicly. They provided an opportunity for feminists to hammer
out their theoretical claims in a public space.[15] It was a space that they
usually controlled financially as well as politically, though managing the
business of periodical publication proved a bane to more than one committed feminist in the Victorian period.[16] Control over the periodical space
was a means of female empowerment, and, as Chapter 6 illustrates, disputes
over the ownership of *Votes for Women* figured prominently in the divisions
between suffrage militants and constitutionalists in the early twentieth
century. The power that feminists invested in and attributed to their periodical press was not confined to the British suffrage movement. It was
influential enough to redefine the issues, to constitute membership, to
determine the direction that certain debates should take, to institutionalize
differences of opinion among feminists, and even to disrupt transnational
alliances among women reformers with a variety of different concerns. The
periodical genre was one of the most effective weapons in the feminist
arsenal precisely because it was used not as a passive showcase but rather as
an instrument of power and legitimacy.[17] For contemporary Western feminists it was virtually impossible, as Carrie Chapman Catt remarked, to
imagine the women's movement without it.[18]

Reading periodicals was, like reading itself, constitutive of certain historically and culturally specific identities.[19] For feminists in Victorian Britain
these were public leadership, national citizenship, and, above all, imperial
authority. The regular representation of Indian women in the feminist press
is an example of British feminists' bid for imperial identification—of their
belief that feminism must be seen as the truest expression of imperial values
because feminists were concerned with colonial women and hence with
imperial concerns. Their claims were aided by the privileges of imperial
rule, which permitted them to offer up Indian women as the "subjects" of

discussion while at the same time subjecting them to feminist scrutiny and interpretation and distancing them continually on the grounds of their Otherness. By representing them in this kind of textual space and making them the ostensible topic of ongoing debates about "womanliness," feminists objectified women of the East into types of their own making. Like all stereotypes, Indian women were "the primary point of subjectification" in British feminist imperial discourse: they were both the object of feminist inquiry and the means by which British women constructed a set of feminist self-images.[20] Discussions of Indian women in feminist papers rarely occurred without reference either to the superior condition of British women *or* to the responsibility of British women for saving their Indian sisters. What feminist writers told their audiences through their representations of Indian women was that colonial womanhood existed in an enslaved state for the purposes of British feminist imperial reform activity.[21] Indian women appeared, in other words, as a colonial clientele that defined and authorized British feminists' imperial saving role. The textualization of Indian women within the contained space of periodical literature was, to modify Lata Mani's terms, a precondition for feminist-imperial domination at the level of discursive meaning[22]—though it was not necessarily the final word on what Indian women were capable of. As in emancipationist argument, the chief purpose of this kind of textualization was to advance justifications for the compelling—and, finally, the imperial—necessity of British women's emancipation.

In an important sense, Indian women were not considered suitable material in and of themselves: they became proper texts, catechisms even, only as they were explained, modified, and put to feminist use. It is this didactic purpose behind feminists' representations of Indian women that was so important in shaping an imperial feminist identity. What the reading public viewed was nothing like the contemporary Indian woman, but rather a set of very particular constructions of colonial womanhood that British feminist interpreters created. British feminist periodicals thus quite literally became the mediators, the translators of certain versions of Indian women to a feminist audience throughout Britain and beyond. In the context of a feminist press whose chief aim was to address the lack of opportunities for British women's paid labor, this kind of mediation quickly became an advertisement for Indian women's special needs and for work opportunities open to British women in the empire.[23] Feminist periodicals routinely discussed Indian women's condition in terms of the new medical, educational, and other reform activities being taken up on their behalf by English women: they publicized the need for British women's professional services

at a historical moment when women were becoming professionalized at a
rapid rate, partly as the result of feminists' efforts to open up the universities to women. Not incidentally, the feminist press offered relief in the
empire for professional women—those "superfluous governesses," as
Mary Carpenter called them—who could not, for a variety of reasons, find
employment at home.[24] Readers of the Victorian feminist press were actively encouraged to shoulder the imperial burden for the sake of Indian
women and British imperial greatness, yes, but ultimately they were appealed to in the name of British women's livelihood. In this sense, feminist
imperial domination was not only textual and symbolic but material and
economic as well. And because it provided one of the forums for the
exercise of feminist imperial authority, the periodical press must be viewed
as part of the apparatus of feminist imperial power.[25]

Although the imperial power relationships envisaged and exercised by
British feminists over women of the East appears throughout feminist
periodical literature, the scope of this study does not permit an exhaustive
examination of the attention given to "the Oriental woman" by feminist
periodicals. In this chapter I have therefore chosen to examine one feminist
journal, the *Englishwoman's Review*, as one example of how this dynamic
worked in the feminist periodical genre. Despite the fact that the *Englishwoman's Review* had four different editors over the course of its publication,
"the Indian woman" who was presented in its pages remained virtually
unchanged over the years.[26] With few exceptions, she was presented as the
object of pity and rescue—as the female colonial subject in need of salvation by her British feminist "sisters." Such fixity is, Homi Bhabha reminds
us, the key to colonializing discourse, just as stereotypical representations
are "its major discursive strategy."[27] The *Englishwoman's Review* is not necessarily typical of Victorian feminist magazines, which were nothing if not
varied in their scope, readership, and longevity. But it does begin to illustrate the workings of feminist imperialism as shaped by British feminists'
writing and reading about Indian women.

THE *ENGLISHWOMAN'S REVIEW*
(1866–1910)

The *Englishwoman's Review* was among the very first Victorian feminist
periodicals and, as such, was an important product of the early women's
movement. It first editor, Jessie Boucherett, viewed it as a direct successor
to the feminist-run *Englishwoman's Journal* (1858–64), which had been
founded by Bessie Rayner Parkes and Barbara Leigh Smith Bodichon, two

early feminist reformers.[28] The format of the new magazine differed from
that of the old—on the whole, it featured fewer substantive articles and
served more as a "current awareness bulletin" for feminist activists—but
Boucherett intended it to influence public opinion on women's issues as its
predecessor had done.[29] During its first few years the *Englishwoman's Review*
had a slightly rocky run: it was briefly discontinued in 1869 and picked up
again in 1870, after which it ran without interruption until 1910.[30] Unfortunately, no circulation figures are available for the *Englishwoman's Review*. Its
immediate predecessor, the *Englishwoman's Journal*, had 1,000 subscribers at
the time of its demise in 1864, and it is possible that many of these readers
carried over to the new journal.[31] The fact that the *Englishwoman's Review* was
a flourishing concern for four decades suggests it was a successful periodical, without of course indicating the scope of its readership. Nor is it
possible to ascertain the price of the journal—though its size and its style
presumed both a high level of education and a willingness to pay for such
material, reflecting the middle-class composition of the early feminist community toward whom it was directed.[32]

Indian women were not the only women of the world who got coverage
in the *Englishwoman's Review*. Like many of its counterparts, it reported on
women across the globe as a matter of routine as well as of genuine interest.
Curiosity about women of other cultures had always been a motivating
purpose of feminist journalism. To understand why this was so, it is necessary to appreciate what a fundamentally nationalistic enterprise a periodical
like the *Englishwoman's Review* was. Boucherett, introducing the first reissue
of the magazine in January 1870, explained that it was to be an "accurate
record" of feminist work: "as in the log-book of a ship, the events that mark
our progress will be noted down."[33] Boucherett's confidence in the progress of the women's movement is revealing, for the function of the *Englishwoman's Review* was not to record stasis but to note the continuous growth
and ascendancy of feminism in English public life. On one hand, the speed
of feminist achievement required coverage in the press. "For five hundred
years no advance has been made in raising the position of women," she
observed, "but now the progress is rapid and . . . the good cause . . .
advance[s] with ever increasing velocity." On the other hand, gains were
made in such small increments (Oxford's extension of university exams to
girls and Edinburgh's acceptance of female medical students are two cited
by Boucherett for 1869) that the act of recording prevented these seemingly
"minor events" from being overlooked and made them real—to hardwork-
ing feminists themselves as much as in the eyes of "public opinion." It also
helped to concretize them for the British historical record. If, as Boucherett

felt sure they were, "the workers in the women's cause are making history," the *Englishwoman's Review* was writing history by recording their accomplishments.[34] By insisting on its history, British feminists sought to make the women's movement part of the nation's heritage. Their project, like feminist histories of the late nineteenth and early twentieth centuries, was grounded in love of and identification with nation. It legitimized feminism as indigenous to Britain and enabled them to claim it as a source of national pride. To keep an account of the women's movement in a forum like the *Englishwoman's Review* was thus a tribute to English national greatness as well as an exercise in British patriotism.

Victorian feminists' pride in nation had its corollary in curiosity about the national customs and characteristics of other countries. It was their confidence in British superiority that prompted their interest in how other nations evolved. Just as Britain's progress had been shaped by its unique history, so too "every nation had its special way of carrying on the work of intellectual and social progress, if such progress have any national vitality at all, and be not a blind copy of another form of civilisation."[35] The *Englishwoman's Review* promised from its beginning to be a "log-book" of "the progress of the women's movement abroad," and by mid-1870 it had instituted a regular column called "Foreign Notes and News," which covered the activities of European, Asian, Russian, South American, Far Eastern, and Australian women—the whole international scene. In addition to this column, which ran under a variety of names in every subsequent issue, longer articles frequently appeared on women of other lands, European feminist activities, and English women travelers. The *Englishwoman's Review* was worldly in a structured and concerted way that the *Englishwoman's Journal* had not been, and saw itself as a place where feminist workers could "become acquainted with what is being done for women in all directions."[36]

The occasional article on European women notwithstanding, the *Englishwoman's Review* was preoccupied with what one contributor characterized as "the status of women in uncivilised nations."[37] Central Africa, Turkey, Egypt, Tibet, China, Burma, and India all fell into this category, but the most attention by far was given to India and its women. Between 1868 and 1910 over thirty special features were devoted to some aspect of women and India, ranging from descriptions of Indian women's position in society and law to the progress of Indian medical education to accounts of accomplished Indian women. This is not counting the considerable space dedicated to Indian women in the "Foreign Notes and News" column, compared with one story each on Turkish women, a Tibetan doctor, and female emancipation in Egypt.[38] The activities of prominent English women like Mary Carpenter, whose first visit to India in 1867 sparked a widespread interest in Hindu female education, or Lady Dufferin, who initiated a fund for Indian female doctors in the 1880s, accounted in part for the quantity of material about Indian women published in the *Englishwoman's Review*. In its capacity as a "current events bulletin" of feminist doings, it made sense for the magazine to publish the foreign as well as the domestic causes of Victorian feminists. A not unrelated explanation was the continued popularity of colonial emigration as one outlet for the surplus female population. A piece like the one in the January 1888 issue, entitled "Opening for Women in the Colonies," advertised outright what articles about helpless Indian women implied—that is, the need for English women readers to offer their services to colonial peoples.[39] Thus the *Englishwoman's Review* acted as a clearinghouse of information on opportunities for English women in the empire, with Indian women commodified as a special and deserving object of feminist concern.

Feminists' construction of "the Indian woman" as a pretext for British women's intervention and social reform in the empire took place within the pages of periodicals like the *Englishwoman's Review*, where Indian, "Oriental," and "primitive" women were brought into debates on womanliness and civilization as feminists attempted to work out definitions of those terms and their relationship to them for themselves. Although non-Western women were most often portrayed as "downtrodden," "degraded," and "pitiful," their total oppression was not always a foregone conclusion. In much the same way that feminist historians could not ignore the unpleasant truths about the status of women throughout British history, feminists writing for the *Englishwoman's Review* could not help noticing that among some "uncivilised peoples" women appeared to enjoy what English women identified as great freedom and even great power. By their reckoning, for example, the women of Central Africa's Banyai tribe were savages; but "strange to say . . . their land is an elysium of women's rights."[40] Husband and wife were equal, "the women even do business on their own account," and there was no evidence of dowry or wife exchange. Feminist surprise at these kinds of "discoveries" was entirely self-interested and self-promoting. The more shocking the "realities" they presented to their public, the more they enhanced their own roles as purveyors of authentic knowledge about colonial, "subject" women. The debate about just how "uncivilised" women of India actually were, which raged over the years in the *Englishwoman's Review*, was a crucial means by which feminists' imperial status was experienced and affirmed. It did not arise incidentally but was set up and controlled by Western women interested primarily in colonial women for the unexplored fields of social reform and power they offered to Victorian women. Nor was it a dialogue: contemporary Indian women, many of whom were active on the English reform scene, were rarely if ever solicited to speak about their own condition or their own assessment of social issues in India, let alone about their own feminist consciousness. In the hands of British feminists Indian women became what Lata Mani argues they were in nineteenth-century male-dominated debates over tradition in India and Britain: the site on which "the moral challenges of colonial rule were confronted and negotiated."[41]

The terms of the Victorian feminist debate can be crudely divided into "positive" and negative views on Indian women. "Positive" assessments usually involved overthrowing stereotypes: some Indian women are educated, they often do move about freely, divorce can be obtained in cases of abuse.[42] In any case, "good" meant those characteristics that would guarantee Indian women's inclusion in the Western European mainstream.[43] Such revelations were accompanied by apologetic surprise: "the women of the far off East," remarked one commentator, "are not the hopeless, helpless victims we have long thought them."[44] Negative evaluations, which could be motivated by Christian antipathy, tended to repeat the stereotyped belief that "the condition of women among barbarous and non-Christian nations is invariably one of servitude and degradation."[45] Most frequently, however, competing views existed side by side. In her article "The Position of Women in India" (1868), Mrs. Bayle Bernard proposed just such a "singular contrast." She reviewed two books, Florence Marryatt's *Gup: Sketches of Indian Life and Character* and Mary Carpenter's two-volume *Six Months in India*. Bernard dismissed Marryatt's book as Anglo-Indian gossip with nothing good to say about Indians, quoting the author's opinion of the natives of Madras as proof: "I do not believe any stories of their honesty, fidelity or attachment to the service of their masters, to be applicable to them generally or to hold good except in individual cases, and those are very rare and far between. . . . Their characters may be summed up in a word: the men are cruel, crafty and indolent; the women are notoriously vicious."[46] According to Bernard, Mary Carpenter's account had no such "frivolous details" and its "comprehensive views and lucid statements" would be much more acceptable to the readers of the *Englishwoman's Review* since Carpenter did not depict India in "such dark colours" as Marryatt.

Having selected for her readers the version of Indian women she deemed more "positive," Bernard summarized Carpenter's account in terms that can hardly be considered flattering to Indian women. According to Bernard, the "lower classes" had no education and worked at menial, "unfeminine" jobs, while those in the harem were imprisoned and idle in the "sunless, airless" rooms all day long. In short, "the women of an Indian household are a constant source of bad influence," since they cannot bring up "healthy" children and invariably cling to superstition and idolatry. Bernard's article is full of pathos and pity for the Indian women whom Carpenter has brought to her attention:

> [T]hey must rise early and go late to bed, eat of the worst food, and act as servants and drudges to all the rest of the household. [The] rooms to which they are confined have, naturally, too an effect upon their health and spirits, and as they commonly become mothers at twelve and grandmothers at twenty-five they appear withered old women when they ought only to have reached their prime. Ordinarily be-trothed in infancy, should their *fiancé* die even before marriage has taken place, they are still looked on as widows, and widowhood is the culmination of female misery, for all in that state are condemned to the utmost neglect and privation, and must pass the rest of their lives in a sort of continual penance, utterly hopeless, since remarriage is strictly forbidden.[47]

Given this evidence, Bernard pointed out, "we can well imagine that every benevolent heart must be impressed." Just this sentimental effect is the overarching purpose of her piece. The "contrast" promised by the author between Marryatt and Carpenter was prevented by Bernard herself, who turned the debate into a choice for the readers between horror and compassion at the "sight" of Indian women. Marryatt and Carpenter were not competing, and neither were their "positive" and negative views of Indian women. Readers were being encouraged to struggle within themselves for the "correct"—and in this context, the proper *feminist*—attitude toward "Oriental womanhood." They were also being asked to begin to think of themselves as reformers capable of remedying the situation.[48] For Bernard argued that Indian women, though not savages, were yet uncivilized enough to warrant English women's help. She shared Carpenter's confidence that Indian women were educable and that their education is a task to which English women in and outside of India must address themselves: "Let them throw their hearts and souls into the work, and determine never to rest until they have raised their Eastern sisters to their own level; and then may the women of India at last attain a position honourable to themselves and to England, instead of, as is now so generally the case, filling one with feelings of sorrow and shame."[49] Bernard's concluding exhortation to the women of England underlined her self-interested attitude toward Indian women, who appear to be most valuable for the possibilities of charitable rescue and imperial pride they promised.[50] The self-interest motivating British women's reform work could not have been made much more explicit. "Such endeavors," Bernard reminded readers, "would scarcely be less beneficial to those who undertook [them] than to those for whom they were undertaken."[51]

Bernard's article was the first of many in the *Englishwoman's Review* that examined the lives of Indian women, including such features as "The Burmese Woman," "Women under Mahommedan Law," "Women Doctors in India," "Zenana Societies," and the like. Debates over the status of Indian women frequently centered around Hindu and Muslim law and their provisions for the treatment of women. The *Englishwoman's Review* discussed Hindu marriage law regularly in the late 1880s and after, mainly because of the publicity given in the national press to the case of Rukhmabai, a Hindu child-wife who contested her marriage and took her husband to court.[52] The editors were extremely sympathetic to Rukhmabai and called for the government to alter the law so that age of marriage for girls was fifteen instead of eleven. Feminists' attention to cases like Rukhmabai's was prompted by the view that child marriage was responsible for the low status of Indian women and by their related interest in Eastern religious law. This they used as a source of comparison with English civil law, which they privileged as a measure of English "civilization."[53] More than one contributor to the *Englishwoman's Review* argued that Islamic law was much more favorable to women than legal systems in the West and lamented the ethnocentrism of British jurists.[54] Victorian feminists' interest in the legal rights of Indian women grew out of their own battles for married women's property rights, child custody, and divorce law—all of which was the stuff of feminist activism in the 1870s and 1880s.[55] The relatively high legal status of Indian Muslim women offered hope, as well as a warning about the limits of Western freedom for women: "If we contrast the legal condition of Mahometan wives . . . with that of English wives, we shall not find the advantage of the side of that nation which has the greatest mental culture or the greatest political freedom."[56] Rukhmabai, for her part, became something of a cause célèbre among Victorian feminists. Through the auspices of an active suffragist, Eva McLaren, and a doctor who worked in India, Edith Pechey Phipson, she came to Britain in 1888 in order to study medicine. She attended at least one Women's Liberal Association meeting at Crewe and graduated from the London School of Medicine to become the medical officer in charge of a women's and children's hospital in Surat.[57] Her successful challenge to marriage laws in India earned her respect from contemporary British feminists, and she received praise in the feminist press as "the courageous girl who refused to live with her brutal and worthless husband."[58]

For women working in the early feminist movement, Rukhmabai was one case among many faceless others that the feminist press used to demonstrate the ways in which Indian women needed the help of British feminists in order to be rescued from the barbarity of native custom. The *Englishwoman's Review* in particular nurtured this perception by providing a space where English women's successes in the imperial setting could be exhibited and experienced vicariously. Articles on Mary Carpenter's work in India, Lady Dufferin's fund for Indian women doctors, and Annette Ackroyd Beveridge's school for Hindu girls are just a few of those items related to British women's work among Indian women that were featured in the periodical.[59] Some space was devoted to Mrs. Archibald Little's visit to China, and there was a piece entitled "A Lady Doctor in Afghanistan," but English women's Indian activities received the most publicity.[60] Indian women hardly ever appear in these kinds of articles, despite misleading headlines like "Women Doctors in India" or "The Education of Indian Women." More often than not, these turn out to be about what English women were doing to promote Indian women's medical training or general education.[61] Presumably such reportage was intended to draw the readers of the *Englishwoman's Review* into supporting charitable efforts on behalf of Indian women by enlisting their sympathy for the hard-working English women already converted and presenting imperial activities as just causes for feminist involvement. Inducements to imperial activism often came in the form of model women like Mary Carpenter, whose visits to Indian cities in the late 1860s and early 1870s were thought to have "opened up" India to feminist attention. Before her death in 1877 Carpenter and her work were frequently discussed in the *Englishwoman's Review*, either in book reviews, excerpts from her two volumes on India, or features promoting her plans for Hindu female education. Mary Carpenter was someone feminists could be especially proud of because she was a pioneer in educational reform at home (she founded the Ragged School Movement) who did not limit her feminist vision to home issues. Carpenter's twentieth-century biographers have tended to bracket her Indian visits as momentary distractions from her real concern for domestic reform, but feminists at the time felt that India was a cause "with which her name will be inseparably connected."[62] The *Englishwoman's Review* devoted fully half of Carpenter's obituary to her interest in Indian women, which was equated with the Ragged Schools as "two of the most important social works of our generation."[63]

In 1868 Mrs. Bayle Bernard had called Carpenter an "earnest philanthropist" as opposed to "a superficial woman of the world" like the novelist Florence Marryatt.[64] Insistence on this distinction was part of feminists' attempts to legitimize women's public work, to portray philanthropy and social reform as serious disciplines.[65] Women's reform work in the empire was certainly intended to be evidence of this, and, like nursing, women's contributions to the imperial cause helped legitimate their quest for entrance into the public sphere.[66] It also gave their observations the weight of firsthand experience and imperial authority. Carpenter's earnestness, along with her "gentle manners," "profound sympathy," and reform experience at home, all certified her to observe Indian women before she ever got to India. Once there, the readers of the *Englishwoman's Review* were encouraged to accept her observations as scientific fact, as the "regime of truth" about India.[67] Carpenter emerges from the pages of the *Englishwoman's Review* as a feminist role model and an imperial heroine. By holding her up as a pioneer in India, early feminists established imperial reform as a feminist virtue and an admirable component of feminist activity as a whole. No doubt too from reading her life they gathered what the terms of Indian social reform were in the late nineteenth century. For Carpenter believed that "the capabilities of Hindoo women are not inferior, under proper development, to their western sisters" and that, perhaps most important, "the natives work well under the English, if . . . they fully realize the superiority of the British character and yield to its guidance with willingness." Her story provided a lesson in the practicalities of imperial governance even as it produced a compelling narrative of female imperial heroism. From her, too, would-be imperial reformers got reassurance that their training would be useful in India. She encouraged British women living in India to get involved in Indian women's education and targeted "lady-students from the mother-country," with the explanation that "a large number of young persons do not find a sufficient demand for their labor in our over-stocked market, and we may hope to obtain some of those who could devote themselves to the work."[68]

The readers of the *Englishwoman's Review* were privy to a wide variety of reform efforts carried out by English women like Carpenter on behalf of their Indian sisters over the years. From time to time the journal featured reports of missionary activity such as the zenana societies, but the bulk of the news reported English secular efforts to improve Indian female education.[69] Annette Beveridge contributed a lengthy piece in 1876 on the Hindu Mahila Bidyalaya, a short-lived Indian-English cooperative experiment in Hindu girls' education in Bengal.[70] And just before her death Mary Carpenter, with the help of Lady Anna Gore-Langton, drew up a proposal for funding trained English "lady teachers" to be sent to India to preside over girls' schools in the cities Carpenter had visited.[71] Carpenter had concluded from her Indian travels that, while Indian women were eager to learn and in some instances had even been decently educated, what they really needed was well-educated and English-trained teachers to assure their continued progress. "The time seems therefore to have arrived," she wrote in her proposal, "when Englishwomen in England are especially called upon to help in this work, *by an associated effort*."[72] Although later efforts would stress the need for Indian women to undergo teacher training, the very first initiatives were chiefly concerned with what English women could do for their Indian "sisters." In the same issue that reviewed the Carpenter-Langton proposal, the *Englishwoman's Review* reported that "most of the lady Vice Presidents in India . . . have interested themselves warmly in the cause of female education." This was followed by a list of governors' wives and their contributions to native women's educational facilities all over India.[73] Feminists may well have been responding to the accusation that English women in India were nonentities who did little for and cared less about the territories of empire in which they lived.[74] Both Carpenter's scheme and the editor's pointed references were ways of demonstrating that English women accepted an active role in the imperial enterprise and were willing to assume responsibility for Britain's female colonial subjects.

Particularly in the area of education, feminists ended up enabling British women residents in India to participate more actively (and more intrusively) in the lives of Indian women and girls. The *Englishwoman's Review* reported in June 1879 that Indian female students were profiting greatly from the monies provided by the Mary Carpenter Scholarships founded for their benefit: "The Lady Mary Grenville writes as follows, 'I am glad to tell you that of the two girls receiving scholarships one is engaged in teaching needlework, and the other English to an infant class. I visited the School privately the other day, and also presided at the distribution of prizes to the girls who had made the most progress during the year. I was much pleased with the marked improvement in the appearance of the girls and in their progress in English . . . and also in the work done.' "[75] Communications like this one permitted feminists to note visible progress in their efforts to help Indian women and, in turn, allowed them to present their successes to the wider feminist public. As Nupur Chaudhuri has noted, it also enabled English women worlds apart to bond in a common imperial purpose and a shared imperial pride.[76]

Schemes for Indian women's reform brought British feminists at home together as well. In 1882 Dr. Frances Hoggan gave a lecture to the Moral Reform Union on the need for qualified women doctors in India. Hoggan herself had practiced in India; along with Edith Pechey Phipson and Mary Scharlieb, who had also worked in India, she lobbied tirelessly among British women's groups for the establishment of a fund to finance British women doctors in India.[77] The Women's Liberal Federation, the Moral Reform Union, the Social Science Association, and the Women's Emancipation Union all hosted speakers on this subject at one time or another in the 1880s, so British feminists of varying interests came together out of concern for this imperial issue.[78] As noted earlier, Lady Harriot Dufferin, wife of the Indian viceroy, established a Fund for Female Medical Aid in August 1885. Its activities, annual reports, and yearly meetings were faithfully reported by the *Englishwoman's Review* throughout the 1880s and 1890s.[79] The Dufferin Fund had close ties with the National Indian Association, initially founded by Mary Carpenter to promote Indian female education; the *Englishwoman's Review* relied on the association's journal for much of its information about India and its women during this period. Coverage of India was a significant chunk of the total copy of the *Englishwoman's Review* for close to twenty years, in part because feminists from so many different areas of the Victorian women's movement were drawn to Lady Dufferin's Fund and, by extension, to the cause of Indian women. Ironically, the magazine remains an important contemporary source about the Fund still available to historians. Such is the lingering effect of Victorian feminist periodicals: they have the capacity to help recover the very structures by which nineteenth-century British feminists exercised control over Indian women, and they provide the ground for a critical interpretation of the apparatus of feminist imperial power.

The Dufferin Fund had been created specifically to provide female medical aid to Indian women because social custom prevented them from being treated by male doctors. In the opinion of one contributor, it was only right and "civilised" that "women who prefer to be attended by a medical attendant of their own sex should have the facility of doing so."[80] British women doctors were the perfect solution to this problem. Indeed, when reading the *Englishwoman's Review* from about 1882 to the end of the 1890s, one is struck by how instrumental Indian women could be for the feminists concerned about them. The struggle for women's entrance into medicine had spearheaded the early Victorian feminist movement. Indian female patients provided a welcome outlet for qualified female doctors and even justified their access to the medical profession. Perhaps anticipating this interpretation, Frances Hoggan was eager to differentiate their interest in empire from that of English men, who, she claimed, see it "simply in the light of a convenient outlet for the surplus youth and energy of the educated classes in this country." English women, in contrast, viewed it "not as a source of income, of emolument of any kind, of titles, of social distinctions and of honours, but as a heavy responsibility laid upon us by our predecessors; one which we cannot shirk, but which we are bound to do our best to lighten for those who follow after us.[81] Hoggan recast what she perceived as crass masculine self-interest into the morally superior and uniquely feminine sense of responsibility, thereby valorizing the feminist commitment without changing what is a fundamentally imperialist purpose. This is all the more evident in her assumption that the British—"those who follow after us"—will always be in India.

Imperial attitudes like Hoggan's did not necessarily preclude respect for Indian women or a genuine desire to enable them to do things for themselves. In the years following the death of Mary Carpenter, many feminists recognized the importance of training native women as doctors and hospital assistants. Before the creation of the Dufferin Fund they raised money for this purpose; as for the fund itself, from the very beginning it disbursed money and offered scholarships to Indian women for training in both India and England.[82] Hoggan and others were committed to creating a professional medical corps for India. In her two-part article entitled "Medical Work for Women in India" for the *Englishwoman's Review* in April and May 1885, Hoggan lamented that "many people think that a lesser amount of knowledge and skill than are necessary for medical women in this country will suffice for India; indeed, some seem to think that experience of nursing, common sense and a little smattering of medical knowledge are enough to furnish forth medical women for India."[83] Having been in India, Hoggan claimed to be aware of cultural differences between Indian and English women and, without citing any specifics, she warned those hoping to take up medical work to be sensitive to such differences. Sympathy, in fact, was thought to be an essential ingredient for medical women heading out to India. In the words of two historians of women's Indian medical work, it was "the open sesame" to Indians' trust and confidence in English doctors.[84] "The mere scientific, well-trained doctor might be a professional," Hoggan warned, "but she would never be in India a social and moral success." As Hoggan foresaw it, Indian women could and would participate in their own redemption. Their intelligence was "beyond all doubt" and "the women of India must take this matter in hand themselves, and not be content to see it taken in hand for them." Hoggan's cooperative vision, despite its best intentions, was somewhat undercut by her assumption, cited above, that the British would always be in India. She believed that Indian women would eventually become doctors, but that time was in a distant and unspecified future. Until then it was mainly English women who would "prove . . . incontestably their value and efficiency in dealing with the native population, and their power of doing work in India which, without them, must remain undone."[85]

Just as significant as the feminists' claim to imperial authority over Indian women is the use to which they put them in the *Englishwoman's Review*. The journal offers some interesting evidence of cooperation between British women and Indians over the financing of Indian female medical aid. For example, Mancherjee Bhownaggree, his sister Avabai, and Mr. and Mrs. P. D. Cama are among several Indians who attended the annual prize-giving at the London School of Medicine for Women in June 1883, and it appears that they contributed to some of the scholarship funds for Indian girls.[86] The Camas also donated 10,000 rupees toward the foundation of a hospital for women and children in Bombay.[87] Events like these were covered in the column "Record of Events," usually under the subheading "London School of Medicine for Women." This choice of format highlighted the feminists' institutional affiliation, which might have been less obvious had the events been noted under "Foreign Notes and News," where most information on India otherwise appeared. It is also one of the rare occasions in which India was construed as a "home" issue in practice as well as in principle. Although they worked as individuals or at best in small groups, feminists for India saw and presented themselves as acting with the support of established organizations—as well as with the backing of members of the Indian and Home governments, since Anglo-Indian officials and M.P.'s are often listed as having attended these events. From reading the *Englishwoman's Review* it would be easy to assume that the London School of Medicine for Women—whose director was Elizabeth Garrett Anderson and which counted among its strongest supporters her suffragist sister Millicent Garrett Fawcett—was responsible for the origins and the achievements of the Indian female medical aid funds. In fact, many of the funds were initiated in India and owed as much of their impetus to Indians and Britons in India as to the feminists, if not more.[88]

Feminists were eager to demonstrate their solidarity with colonial philanthropy, so it is not surprising that in their journals they should have given special attention to their role in Indian efforts. This is part of the point: with British feminists' eagerness to publicize their own role, Indian women could become secondary if not virtually disappear from the scene. There are, consequently, few Indian women to be found here.[89] The magazine's coverage of the first annual report of the Jaffa Sulliman Dispensary in Bombay in February 1885 is worth quoting at length:

The temporary building used for the dispensary "was opened on July 7, 1884; nine patients presented themselves on that day, and by the end of the week the numbers had increased to such an extent that it was computed that the crowd asking for admission daily numbered over three hundred. It was therefore necessary, to avoid clamour and confusion, to restrict the number each morning to 100," and this regulation remained in force so long as Dr. Pechey was the sole acting medical officer. In November, however, she was joined by Dr. Charlotte Ellaby, and since then it has been possible to admit patients almost without restriction. The whole number of patients treated in the course of six months has been 2,818, of whom 1,961 were women and 857 children. The exact number of visits is not given, but it must have considerably exceeded 10,000, an amount of work that appears truly enormous to be laid, except for the last month, on one pair of shoulders. Such a fact as this may be worthy the consideration of those who think women physically unfit for the fatigues and responsibilities of medical practice. . . . It may be remembered that the foundation stone was laid by H.R.H. the Duke of Connaught during his visit to Bombay. The Viceroy and Lady Dufferin visited the Dispensary while at Bombay. The new dispensary building will give accommodation for four medical women, and thus double the present facilities. It is to be hoped that, with the encouragement given by those in authority, funds may be found before the new building is ready to justify the Committee in engaging the services of another lady, so that no patients need be turned away. If any doubt existed before as to the need of female medical attendance, the crowds that throng this dispensary every day, must have removed that doubt.[90]

Clearly the piece is not only about the dispensary. It is intended as proof of English women doctors' competence (stemming the tide of criticism that women were not "physically fit" for the work); of the Indian government's support for the project (the Dufferins' visit); and, of course, of the demonstrated need for British women to continue to make female medical aid possible. The pride exhibited in patient statistics is again an attempt to make scientific what was thought to be "soft" female charitable work. There is no question that Victorian women who wanted to be doctors had to fight deeply rooted cultural stereotypes about women's capacity and that those who wanted women doctors to work in imperial territories had to battle against more biases *and* the imperial male bureaucracy. No one could deny that these feminists wanted to do good. They also wanted to stake their claim in the imperial setting. The *Englishwoman's Review* was a place were they could present their claims and give themselves the credit that perhaps the larger culture would not award them. The periodical itself can be read as a terrain where feminist footholds were mapped and feminist reform strategized. It was certainly a space where the feminists' imperial profile could be delineated and appreciated.

The *Englishwoman's Review* did report on contemporary Indian women, though its subscribers would have had to read very carefully to find them. They appeared most often in the "India" section of the "Foreign Notes and News" column, sometimes at the head of the paragraph but more typically after news about English women in India. Almost always a subheading in this column that reads "Women Clerks" or "Medical Women in India" is about English women; Indian women are always denoted as such, or by the designation "native ladies." The Indian women reported on in "Foreign Notes and News" can be divided into two categories, one of which included wealthy maharanis who had given money to hospitals or helped found girls' schools.[91] Of these, the maharani of Surnomoze was recognized by the *Englishwoman's Review* when she received the Imperial Order of the Crown of India for her famine and other charitable work. The magazine noted that she was known as "the Burdett Coutts of India," a reference to the wealthy London Quaker philanthropist, Angela Burdett Coutts.[92] The other major group of Indian women covered in the news were students, mainly those attending Indian institutions. Virtually every issue of the periodical from the late 1870s onward contains some mention of Indian women who received scholarships, passed their exams, or became certified teachers. All of this news was presented in the "Foreign Notes and News" column. It was a condensed version (and in smaller print) of a similar section, which announced the educational achievements of English women on a regular basis. It would be an exaggeration to say that there was a sense of competition between English and Indian women, because even in their most generous moments Victorian feminists felt that Indian women had a long way to go before they "caught up" with their British sisters. But the editorship of the *Englishwoman's Review* wanted to mark "progress," and the similarity in the layout of the two educational columns implies at least a suggestion of comparison between English and Indian women. In any case, for readers of the *Englishwoman's Review*, many if not most of whom never went to India, these columns supplied a virtually uninterrupted stream of information about Indian women and their educational achievements for nearly half a century.

For all its imperial presumptions, the *Englishwoman's Review* does serve as a record of the achievements of some educated Indian women in the nineteenth and early twentieth centuries, albeit an imperfect one. Too often its editors were content to report that, for example, "fifteen native ladies" were attending the Campbell medical school in Calcutta in 1889 and that some of them were on eight-rupee scholarships.[93] The anonymity imposed on these women is telling and must in part be attributed to a cultural tendency to collapse Indians and "Others" together into an undifferentiated group. As has been mentioned, the *Englishwoman's Review* relied on the journal of the National Indian Association and other Indian newspapers for much of its Indian information, so if these sources did not break down such groups, the *Englishwoman's Review*, either from disinclination or lack of more information, did not either. Nonetheless, a number of Indian women are identified. The princess of Tangore endowed a Sanskrit school for women in the 1870s, and the maharani Rajrupkuar of Tejkan, in addition to financing female education, was the vice president of the Bengal branch of the National Indian Association until her death in 1885.[94] In January 1877 the *Englishwoman's Review* reported that Miss Radharini Lahiri and Mrs. Rajlukshmi Sen, both of whom were graduates of the Native Ladies' Normal School of the Brahmo Samaj in Calcutta, remained actively involved with their alma mater and that two other women, Mrs. Khantomony Dutt and Miss Mohini Kastogiri, were beginning to teach some of the lower-form classes there. In May of the same year the journal commented on the success of Miss Chundra Muhki Bosu in passing her entrance exams and announced that Misses Suvarnala Bosu and Sarala Das were preparing to sit for similar exams.[95] The columns of the late 1880s are dotted with one-liners on Indian "lady lecturers" and teachers, and in July 1886 a brief account appeared of a "lady zemindar" in East Bengal, Farzenmessa Choudranee, who "is distinguished by her liberality and her ability in business matters."[96] These women's successes were clearly at variance with the less than favorable stereotypes that British feminists produced elsewhere in the *Englishwoman's Review*, though they appeared in such small print that they may well have escaped the notice of all but the most dedicated readers. Given the large and growing Indian student population in London in the late nineteenth century and after, it is possible that Indian women living in Britain read these columns and derived some sense of their own achievement from them.[97] In any event, their regular appearance in the back pages of the journal testifies to the educational advances and public activity of Indian women in the late nineteenth century. They are themselves challenges to the "coherence and authenticity" of British feminism's female Others, revealing among other things "the artificiality of the 'truths' they purport to tell."[98]

There were other contemporary Indian women who contested British women's representations and hence destabilized the myth of the passive Indian woman. One of the most prominent and well-traveled Indian women of the late nineteenth century was Pandita Ramabai Sarasvati. Educated by her father in Sanskrit and philosophy, she was widowed at a young age and devoted her life to helping Hindu widows.[99] Her search for funds for her Hindu widows' home at Poona took her to both England and the United States, and she was one of the few Indian women whom Anglo-American feminists met personally on their own soil. Ramabai's career was followed closely in the columns of the *Englishwoman's Review*, which reprinted her testimony to the Indian government's Educational Commission in 1882, noted whenever she spoke in India or abroad, and kept its readers continually abreast of the progress of the Poona establishment.[100] There were also several articles devoted to her, like the one by Frances Willard (then president of the World Woman's Christian Temperance Union and a friend to many British feminists) in October 1888.[101] Among feminists there was a warm and unqualified admiration for Pandita Ramabai and her work. As an educated woman, a Christian convert, and a social worker dedicated to improving the condition of her sisters in India, she became a heroine for many and the embodiment of the "best" qualities of "Eastern womanhood." Unfortunately, feminists were not always comfortable with evidence of Indian "progress." Reporting on Ramabai's widows' home in 1905, the *Englishwoman's Review* commented that "it is good to read of a movement among the Hindus themselves to alleviate their lot, and to raise them from a position of degradation, to that of members of a society with useful work to perform in the world. A movement initiated and worked by their own people cannot, we should think . . . have a more lasting effect than one coming from without." The editor was quick to point out, however, that "it may be freely confessed that the outside movement probably prompted that from within and led the Hindus themselves to look into matters and to consider whether their customs were, as they thought, based entirely on the teachings of their faith."[102] Even when acknowledging and praising Indian achievement, Victorian feminists felt compelled to take credit for it themselves and to claim that they had actually been able to reveal to Hindus what was allegedly inherent in their religion but was stifled by their custom. As Mary Carpenter wrote of her visits to a variety of Indian-run educational institutions in India, "A change is gradually going on . . . through the sensible influence of British civilisation."[103] Criticism of native custom had the familiar ring of British superiority and moreover implied that Indian culture was in need of "cleaning up" by feminist reformers. It also helped establish British feminists as authorities on Indian culture, not to mention as the final arbiters of Indian women's "progress."

Reporting on the progress of Indian women—which was one of the main activities of the *Englishwoman's Review*—could only be problematic for British feminists, since the further Indian women "progressed," the less justification British women might find for exercising their influence in India. Thus the author of "The Education of Indian Women," which appeared in a January 1904 issue, was obliged to conclude:

> The retirement last year of Mrs. Brander, Senior Inspectress of Schools in the Madras Presidency, calls attention to the remarkable development of female education in India. We are told that in the early days there were learned Indian women, and probably there have been occasional instances of such throughout all the ages; but speaking generally, the education of women in India, as far as book-learning is concerned, has long been practically non-existent. . . . Though at present the movement is in its infancy, it appears to be possessed of considerable vitality.[104]

Indian women were caught in the circular argument of British imperial ideology: they need us to progress, they are making progress, we will remain until they've progressed, but they've never progressed sufficiently for us to say our time is up. Feminists trapped Indian women in their own version of this imperial "logic," in spite of evidence that they themselves gathered in the columns of the *Englishwoman's Review* that Indian women were being educated and contributing as women to the improvement of their own society. British feminists' quest for an imperial role—and for colonial clients—took priority over any conventionally "feminist" hopes they may have harbored for the independence of Indian women. The representation of "Indian womanhood" in forums like the *Englishwoman's Review* itself legitimated this priority because it enabled feminists to construct Indian women always as only half-formed feminists in the making.

Without a proper field to conquer, Indian women were in many ways only partly "women" themselves in British feminist terms. According to one contributor, the truly "womanly" woman turned her attention to empire, where "she will establish a more Christian code of morals, which will purify the dark places of her earth."[105] Hence Indian women's access to womanliness, and certainly to feminism, was blocked, except if they followed the kinds of examples offered by the *Englishwoman's Review* of British women's imperial activities—the likes of Mary Carpenter, Frances Hoggan, and Mrs. Brander. Conversion to Christianity was never an explicit requirement, but it remained an unwritten expectation for Indian women aspiring to social reform work along British lines. Admiration for Pandita Ramabai was certainly contingent on it.[106] And there were some who believed, with Helen Hanson, that suffrage "makes for practical Christianity."[107] It was not that British feminists did not believe Indian women to be capable of achieving freedom and equality or even, as we have seen, that they did not consider them likely to obtain these things themselves. But they were confident that custom and tradition in India had shaped them into habits "which years may not be able to eradicate."[108] The Victorian feminist press offered a set of lessons to British feminists about the nature of all women's work in an imperial culture: its purpose was to uplift, to purify, and to civilize—all this in the name of the Cause. Equally instructive was the fundamentally imperial understanding that the work of British women's emancipation would, should, *must* come first.

READING "THE INDIAN WOMAN"

The *Englishwoman's Review* was not the only feminist periodical to display Indian women for its readers' consumption during this period. As discussed in Chapter 6, several political suffrage organs devoted attention to "women of the East." Other journals, like the *Young Woman* (1892–1915) and *Womanhood* (1898–1907), devoted some space to English women and female missionaries in India and often featured Indian women incidentally.[109] The *Englishwoman*, which appeared just as the *Englishwoman's Review* was being phased out, continued the tradition of discussing Indian women and paid a great deal of attention to imperial affairs.[110] The *Women's Penny Paper* (later the *Woman's Herald*) ran for only a little over four years but produced volumes on Indian women. This was partly due to the interest of its first editor, Henrietta Muller, in India and things Indian.[111] Unlike the *Englishwoman's Review* (and virtually any other contemporary feminist journal), the *Women's Penny Paper* occasionally featured the activities of contemporary Indian women, often only briefly, but sometimes provided them a forum from which they could speak for themselves, through interviews or excerpts from their own writings.[112]

"The Indian woman" was made widely accessible to feminist readers in a variety of feminist periodicals, so by 1915 she was as common and as familiar a figure in feminist journalism as she was in Indian nationalist discourse. For Indian male reformers, as for British feminists, she was an object of concern and a signifier of India's future health and security, albeit for ostensibly different purposes.[113] Indian nationalists had been, since the days of Mary Carpenter, among those who mediated the condition of Indian women to Western feminists, and although by the twentieth century British feminists' representations were less dependent on male interpreters, there were some important links between Indian nationalist and feminist communities.[114] Feminist periodicals, for their part, normalized, domesticated, and brought Indian women "home" to British feminist audiences in a way that naturalized empire and made colonial women seem like "sisters under the skin." And yet the dynamics of the imperial family slated Indian women as daughters, subordinate to their British mothers, rather than as sisters, despite the rhetoric of sisterhood. British feminists' feeling of imperial responsibility for Indian women encouraged and even required this power relationship. In feminist ideology, as in imperialism, "the dark places of the earth" were considered British women's purview and its inhabitants their special burden. As it was represented by the feminist press, the condition of Indian women provided pathetic and compelling evidence for the imperial necessity of this particular maternal burden. That such images were both heterogeneous and basically uniform across most of the Victorian period bears out Meyda Yegenoglu's claim that "despite the polymorphous nature of the texts that constitute it," orientalism can establish "discursive unities," albeit those which are historically specific and theoretically unstable.[115]

In addition to being sites for the colonization of Indian women, their periodicals were places for feminists to design a position of power for themselves in an imperial family configuration of their own making. They were, more concretely, avenues through which British women could "discover" Indian women and formulate a role for themselves as imperial reformers. The kinds of advertisements that the *Englishwoman's Review* and other periodicals gave to social reform organizations and institutions in India suggest a link between feminist activism and imperial social reform that was monetary as well as political—though financial contributions tended to be idiosyncratic and, at least in the late nineteenth century, were not part of the concerted effort of Victorian feminist organizations. Economic support for Indian female education was largely an upper-class women's project, with Lady Dufferin, Lady Hardinge, and even the queen furnishing the funds along with an elitist cachet to colonial reform initiatives.[116] These reform efforts were not strictly feminist in that the women involved in such enterprises were not active in domestic work for women's rights. Their concern for Indian women grew out of their personal colonial connections; these were usually husbands involved with the Raj at quite high levels of government. Middle-class feminists at home talked and wrote a lot about Indian women, and through their periodical press they clearly helped other groups who were specifically concerned with the condition of contemporary Indian women to make connections with those in their readership who might be interested in working for them too. But they were not expressly concerned themselves with remedying the condition of Indian women, even while such an example proved useful to the domestic work of the women's movement. It was an interesting and fairly well-organized division of labor, one that replicated the division between imperial and home spheres that feminist discourse worked so hard to bridge.

There were of course exceptions to this pattern. Mary Carpenter, who made four successive trips to India, became a model of feminist imperial activism because she had attended to both home and colonial affairs. She was, according to her biographer Millicent Garrett Fawcett, "a true empire builder in the best sense of the word."[117] Fawcett herself was another exception, although her lifelong interest in India began because Henry Fawcett, her husband and an M.P., had been active in Indian affairs during his lifetime. Millicent Fawcett wrote occasionally on the subject of Indian women, though not, interestingly, for the feminist press but rather for mainstream Victorian periodicals. She befriended Cornelia Sorabji, the first Indian woman to pass the bar in Britain, and she led the deputation on education for Indian women to the secretary of state for India in 1915.[118] Such work was the product of many years' familiarity with the "problem" of Indian women—knowledge gleaned in part from the attention that their status received in the Victorian feminist press. Again, there is no doubt that Fawcett and others intended to "do good" on behalf of Indian women and that their concern, whether it manifested itself in words or in actions, was genuine. It was also motivated by a belief that the fate of Britain and its empire was bound up with the health and welfare of India's women. Saving women was part of the imperative of the civilizing mission; it grew out of the notion that women were the civilizers of any nation—their rescue "mark[ed] the moment when not only a civil but a good society is born out of domestic chaos."[119] The "good nation" was perhaps India, but it was most certainly also Britain itself, and by intervening to save Indian women, feminists again marked themselves as qualified—and heroic—British citizens. As Fawcett herself said, "There is no patriotic work more noble than saving such as these and making good citizens of them."[120] Although she was referring to Carpenter's work among the "ragged children" of northern England, she might well have been talking of Indian women. Given the conflation of Indian women with female children—daughters waiting for "the old mother," as Mary Carpenter was called in India—they were in fact close to being identical as objects of British women's moral authority and reformist intervention. Work on behalf of Indian women drew attention to British feminists as a national collectivity committed to imperial stability and to matters of "imperial importance" both "at home" and "over there."[121] Concern for Indian women was part of women's work to promote Britain's "true interest, and her elevation to a high position among the nations." Success in India, "that great continent," was nothing less than proof of "what our sex can do."[122]

Victorian feminist periodicals were instrumental to the production of these messages and to the working out of feminist imperial ideology in public. They were, in a very real sense, an expression of imperial culture in and of themselves. Like biscuit tins and cigarette cards and other ephemera coded with imperial signifiers, they were consumed "at home" (in Britain) and in the family home by women.[123] If, as Philippa Levine has suggested, readability was an indicator of circulation, news about Indian women and imperial issues may even have contributed to the longevity of the *Englishwoman's Review*, especially in the last years of the century as the crisis of confidence after the Boer War made imperial stability and racial concerns of paramount importance in Victorian culture.[124] British feminist subscribers would have been reading about "what their sex could do" for reassurance as much as for inspiration. In this sense the feminist press not only created but consolidated feminist identities at moments when they were shaken and in need of reinforcement. In the context of growing Anti rhetoric in the early twentieth century, journal reading may well have helped to combat feminists' negative self-concepts, shoring up their distinctively imperial arguments for women's suffrage in Britain.[125]

Of all its possible functions, the most important effect of the late-nineteenth-century women's press was undoubtedly to create a sense of community among Victorian feminists.[126] That this was a community pledged to imperial ideals there can be little doubt. I have isolated the *Englishwoman's Review* partly in order to underline the connections between feminism as a woman's movement, and feminism as a self-consciously nationalistic and imperialistic enterprise. The presence of "English" in its title, as in the titles of two other major feminist periodicals of the period 1865–1910, suggests feminists' sense of national-imperial identification, their determination to identify an English feminist audience, and their willingness to allow England to stand for Britain as the ultimate sign of imperial power and cultural hegemony. When Barbara Bodichon, writing for the predecessor of the *Englishwoman's Review* in 1863, interrupted her description of Algeria's physical beauty with "I must tell the 'ENGLISH WOMAN' something about the hospital at Marengo," it is not entirely clear whether she was addressing a real audience of English women, "the English woman" as a collectivity, or perhaps the journal itself as the personification of English women everywhere.[127] In the absence of a recognized female constituency, feminist periodicals themselves could stand for English women, or, at the very least, could serve as evidence that an English women's community existed. It was the kind of "imagined community" that simultaneously institutionalized a collective sovereign self and created an audience before whom that collectivity could represent itself and its "evolving identities."[128] The identification of Indian women as a client pool requiring English feminist tutelage justified British feminists' claims to be an essential part of the imperial nation and affirmed an imperial identity for feminist writers and readers that might be tried on, modified, or even rejected. As Chapter 6 indicates, it was an identity that fueled arguments for suffrage in the early twentieth century and was subscribed to by almost all feminists of the period. That editors and contributors to the feminist press intended their readers to constitute a separate, female audience closed the circle all the more tightly around the Indian women they proposed to represent, suggesting a protectiveness and an authoritarianism based on a presumption of knowledge that were, together, at the heart of British feminists' use of Indian women as political capital in the imperial nation-state.[129] The act of reading about Indian women—quite apart from the representations themselves—is an important component of their feminist imperialism because of the imperial authority it assumed and the feminist-imperial authority it legitimized. Whenever Indian women were represented, their images worked to challenge this authority and to resist the process of colonizing that was basic to British feminists' reform ideology. As a result, the feminist press was not necessarily completely successful in its operations, despite British feminists' determination to identify their concern for Indian women with what many of them believed to be the benevolent civilizing power of the "mother country."

The capacity of feminist journalism to create and sustain community identity lives on in the late twentieth century, when "the feminist press" in all its variety is one of the most powerful forces in the production of academic and mainstream feminist discourses.[130] Feminist periodicals, to a

great extent a form of feminist praxis inherited from Victorian feminists in
the Anglo-American tradition, are today believed to constitute not just
expressions of discrete feminist ideologies, but histories of the ideas of the
women's movement as well.[131] The proliferation of feminist journals, then
as now, is taken to be a sign of the vitality of women's movements and of the
emergence of a set of distinctively feminist academic voices.[132] In the last
half of the twentieth century feminist periodicals have also proven to be the
grounds on which a critical assessment of feminism's history is undertaken:
the vehicles through which modern feminists have sought to interrogate the
legacies of historically feminist movements. In the past decade, some feminist scholars have mounted a critical challenge to the presumptions of
feminists to "know" non-Western or nonwhite women and to claim from
that knowledge a universal sisterhood. Much of this debate in Britain has
occurred in the pages of the *Feminist Review,* which, as a late-twentieth-
century British feminist collective, seems an appropriate place for contesting the ethnocentric assumptions about womanhood originally promoted
in Victorian feminist periodical literature.[133] Where and how this newest
manifestation of the feminist press is produced and by whom it is read
continues to reflect the disjunction of resources globally and the persistence
with which imperial ideologies still frame the imagining of even resistant
sociopolitical identities. There is, however, an increasing consciousness
about feminism's imperial roots and the importance of its historically imperial locations. It remains to be seen whether the late-twentieth-century
feminist press can continue successfully to critique the mechanisms of its
own production and remain both mindful of and accountable for its own
relationship to the history of Western imperial feminisms.

5

The White Woman's Burden

JOSEPHINE BUTLER AND THE INDIAN CAMPAIGN,

1886–1915

As we have seen thus far, British feminists devoted a considerable amount of attention to "the Indian woman" in a variety of genres during the Victorian period.[1] She appeared throughout British feminist productions as a deserving object of feminist concern and as proof of the need for women's emancipation so that they could publicly exercise their moral authority in the imperial nation-state and help to guarantee its maintenance. Indian women also served as evidence of the need for social reform intervention in India—and not just for British feminists, as I have chosen to define them in this study. The work of missionary women, of concerned middle-class secular reformers, and of aristocratic women like Lady Dufferin was instrumental to the creation of an imperial reform culture in Britain, of which feminists—for our purposes, women active in the work of female emancipation in Britain—were a part. India had been the object of feminist reform interest beginning in the 1860s with Mary Carpenter's Indian visit and her subsequent promotion of Hindu female education.[2] Educational improvements for Indian women were an ongoing concern among reform women until World War I and beyond, as was the need for female medical aid.[3] Indeed, as I have suggested, these issues and the organizations that addressed them received attention throughout the feminist press during an extended historical moment when more and more women were being made available for work in the empire. Josephine Butler's crusade for the repeal of the Contagious Diseases Acts in India was the best organized and most prominent of feminist reform movements for Indian women in the late Victorian period. Although her domestic campaign (1869–86) has received much attention, its extension to empire has not been examined until recently, and even then, not in depth.[4] In this chapter, it will be treated as an example of how the rhetoric of imperial feminism could be combined with feminist reform in a colonial setting. Butler's crusade underscores the parameters of British feminist activity in India, the imperial attitudes that informed feminists' interest in Indian women, and, finally, both the conditions and the limits of middle-class British feminists' involvement in colonial reform.

In addition to analyzing what contemporaries often referred to as "the Indian campaign," I have two chief concerns here. First, I will explore the ways in which Indian women were represented throughout the Ladies' National Association's Indian crusade—in part because these were the kinds of representations that shaped the attitudes with which suffrage women and other late Victorian and Edwardian female reformers approached the "cause" of colonized women and enlisted it in the various campaigns for women's suffrage in Britain. As depicted in the repeal campaign literature, Indian women were made to exhibit many of the same characteristics that had been attributed to them by the Victorian feminist writers discussed so far. They were constructed as the helpless victims of state-regulated prostitution and as being in special need of protection by their British feminist "sisters"—not only because of regulation but because they were viewed as a subject race as well. The Christian feminism espoused by Butler posited Indian women as equals, yet ultimately she embraced an imperialized view of the world's women, with Indian women falling somewhere on the scale between the saints and "the noble friend of man, the dog."[5] In feminist activism as in feminist ideology this construction justified an imperial role for feminist reformers which gave late Victorian feminism a distinctively imperial mission. Although critical of the treatment of Indian women under imperial rule, Butler and her followers were not critics of empire per se. Like the Edwardian suffragists of the next chapter, they saw themselves as the reformers of an imperial ideal gone badly wrong.

If Indian prostitutes emerge from Butler's crusade as helpless victims in need of feminist salvation, the repealers themselves appear as the saviors of Indian women and the feminist watchdogs of empire as well.

I will also suggest that, in addition to providing a framework for much of the Edwardian suffrage campaign's imperial concerns, Butler's Indian crusade points to the complex relationship that British feminists had toward Indian women and toward the empire as a site of British feminist reform intervention. On the one hand, the Indian repeal campaign would appear to embody both the spirit and the practice of imperial feminism: as Butler and her fellow repealers argued, the plight of Indian women was their plight, India and Britain were part of the same "nation," and feminist calls for reform action in the colonial context represented a bridge between conventionally separate spheres of empire and home. On the other hand, the repeal crusaders, while calling for the rescue of Indian women, saw repeal itself—that is, the removal of governmental legislation that interfered with women's personal liberty—as the full extent of their contribution to the uplift of Indian women and the amelioration of their condition. As they were simultaneously doing in the pages of the *Englishwoman's Review*, those working for repeal in India imagined reform work on behalf of Indian women as distinct from their own "domestic," British-based political and social reform commitments. The Ladies' National Association, for example, did not support, either financially or in terms of personnel, any reform efforts in India until after 1910, when it contributed modestly to women's rescue homes in northern India. This was not because advocates of repeal and their associates were hypocritical with regard to their own rhetoric; it was not, in other words, because they did not believe that the health of India and that of Britain were bound up with one another. It had rather to do with the priority they assigned to their own emancipation in the imperial nation and the power that they presumed British women's enfranchisement would have to reform Indian women's lives once inclusion had been achieved. It had to do most of all with their unequivocal belief in the capacity of the empire to be an instrument of reform and in their equally tenacious belief that British women, qua women, could and would feminize and purify the imperial nation-state. It was in large measure because of Josephine Butler's leadership in the Indian campaign that British suffragists in the twentieth century took empire as their field and Indian women as the political clientele that justified women's suffrage and guaranteed that, once enfranchised, British women would contribute to the grandeur and the glory of what British feminists believed to be the greatest reform organization the world had ever seen—the empire itself.

THE INDIAN CRUSADE, 1886–1900

Butler's crusade on behalf of Indian women was the second phase of a domestic movement aimed at freeing prostitutes from the intervention of the British state. From its beginnings in 1869 until repeal in 1886, the campaign against the Contagious Diseases Acts was dedicated to the removal of laws regulating prostitution.[6] The acts were a series of measures legislated in the 1860s that authorized the detainment and medical examination of women designated by local authorities to be "common prostitutes." They were an exercise in social and sexual control that operated in port and garrison towns (like Plymouth and Southampton) where the incidence of venereal disease was feared to be high due to the influx of soldiers, sailors, and other transients. Butler and her coworkers, in both the predominantly male National Association and the Ladies' National Association, objected to the acts because they considered them to be a violation of personal liberty, a humiliation for the women obliged to submit to them, and, not least, an ineffective solution for reducing venereal disease or eliminating prostitution. Of course, the repealers hoped to eradicate prostitution: their method was moral suasion rather than state regulation, which they argued only promoted sexual vice by implying it was a necessity that had to be provided for. By insisting on an equal standard of sexual morality for men and women, Butler and the associations she led not only achieved repeal by act of Parliament, but in the process shaped considerably the sexual premises of feminist arguments for female emancipation.[7]

Meanwhile, regulation continued to flourish in other parts of the British Empire. India, Hong Kong, Fiji, Gibraltar, and the Straits Settlements were among the locations where prostitutes were examined regularly for venereal disease, typically in lock hospitals.[8] In India this was achieved through the Cantonments Act of 1864, which provided for regulation in military cantonments, and the Indian Contagious Diseases Act of 1868, which dealt principally with India's cities and seaports. Significantly, lock hospitals predated such legislation by decades. According to Ladies' National Association sources, the first Indian lock hospitals had been established in the Madras presidency as early as 1805. By 1809 nine out of seventeen hospitals had been shut down, on the basis of evidence showing that they did nothing to reduce the incidence of venereal disease among British troops.[9] For the next fifty years hospitals were opened and closed in Madras and Bengal, depending on the outbreak of disease and the persuasiveness of the argument that examination could actually control it.[10] In the late 1850s regular lock hospitals were reopened in India and by 1861 registration and inspection were made obligatory—two years in advance of the legislation at home. Despite the conclusion of several Army Sanitary Commissions over the decade 1874–84 that "the amount of venereal disease in the Indian army is irrespective of lock hospitals" and examinations, regulation persisted in India under the auspices of the Contagious Diseases Acts until 1888.[11]

It was not until repeal was secured at home in 1886, however, that the Ladies' National Association turned its full attention to empire. Although Butler herself had never been to India (nor was she ever to go), she had been aware of the effects of the Contagious Diseases Acts there as early as 1870, when Keshub Chandra Sen, leader of the Brahmo Samaj, wrote to her detailing the horrors Indian women suffered as a result of the compulsory medical examinations.[12] Butler mentioned the possibility of turning the LNA into an organization for the colonies in a letter to her friends the Priestman sisters in May 1886, and her imperial concerns were fueled by revelations in the ensuing months that in spite of repeal at home, the acts were still in effect in military cantonments throughout India.[13] Writing to them again from Switzerland in October 1886, she called for an LNA circular to be issued on the subject, declaring that "we must never give up til we have avenged the wrongs of Indian and Chinese women as well as others. . . . For twenty years Indian women have been oppressed and outraged . . . and by a *Christian* nation!"[14] From her point of view, the situation in India necessitated the continued existence of the LNA, which Butler urged be maintained as "a separate *woman's* organisation" for at least a year. As it turned out, unlike the men's National Association, which disbanded almost at once, the LNA—which was a predominantly, though not exclusively, middle-class organization—lived on with its local and regional networks virtually intact, justifying itself at least partly in imperial terms for the next thirty years.[15]

In addition to the LNA, of which she was honorary president until her death in 1906, Butler was involved in a second committee concerned with empire, the British Committee for the Abolition of the State Regulation of Vice in India and the Dominions.[16] This committee originated as the British branch of an international society known as the British, Continental, and General Federation, which had been founded by Butler and like-minded European repealers in 1875 and which had, as its name implies, been active in making regulation a cause that was "international" mainly in a Western European sense.[17] Repeal at home remained her principal goal, yet Butler was always keen on promoting an international movement. At times during the 1890s she chided her fellow workers that India was not the only place in the world where women were downtrodden.[18] If Europe was her true love, however, she felt India was her duty. By 1887 the British Committee was discussing a national campaign for the repeal of the Contagious Diseases Acts in India and organizing protest meetings in Exeter Hall, the site of LNA meetings for the previous twenty years.[19]

The executive members of the LNA and the British Committee worked closely together on the Indian question after 1887. Their membership overlapped, they had offices on the same premises, and they contributed to each other's publications and frequently held joint meetings to publicize conditions in the Indian cantonments.[20] Together they dispatched agents to India, submitted memorials to the Indian and home governments, published several journals and a steady stream of pamphlets, and organized meetings all over the British Isles. As Butler observed in 1893, "All Abolitionists . . . by this time are aware that the question of highest interest presented . . . [to them] is that of India."[21] This shared sense of purpose was due largely to the person of Butler herself, whose Indian interests carried with them the prestige of her personal reputation in addition to the support of this network of female reform organizations.

Butler's Indian crusade followed the model of the original "home" campaign, using the same tactics that had eventually brought success in Britain. This meant that the initiatives on behalf of Indian prostitutes were chiefly parliamentary and at first involved working for a House of Commons resolution that would compel the government of India to abide by the repeal statute passed at home. Several M.P.'s who had worked with the original repeal organizations continued to act as liaisons between Parliament and the LNA and the British Committee. These were Henry Wilson, Walter McLaren, James Stuart, and James Stansfeld, all of whom were Liberals and all of whom had been active participants in the movement for repeal at home and continued their involvement in the British Committee into the twentieth century.[22] Stuart was the first to raise the issue of colonial regulation in the House when he moved on July 20, 1886, for a return of the colonies and dependencies where the acts still operated.[23] The results of his inquiry, as well as of information provided by friends of repeal as to the situation in India, launched a full-scale parliamentary assault by repeal M.P.'s to pressure both the home and the Indian governments to abandon the acts.[24] Parliamentary tactics were supplemented by extraparliamentary activity in the form of "indignation meetings" all over the British Isles. The LNA and the British Committee drew up memorials and solicited missionary support for repeal as part of their lobbying action. The purpose of all this activity was to convince M.P.'s to support a full-scale repeal measure in the House. With the eighteen-year-old domestic campaign concluded, thousands of LNA workers might have been in danger of becoming redundant. The crusade for India rescued repealers from this fate and gave them a renewed imperial purpose.[25]

The impact of this agitation on government policy was minimal at first. The government of India admitted to Lord Cross, the secretary of state, that "some of the existing arrangements are open to objection," and Sir John Gorst, the undersecretary for India, assured members of the House in February 1888 that if repealers' accounts of medical examination proved true, the government would take action. But when subsequently pressed by Stuart with details of the harassment of women in the cantonments, Gorst stalled, repeating that the government was looking into it and professing ignorance about scientific and medical reports on the inefficiency of regulation in halting the spread of venereal disease.[26] Cross privately viewed the controversy as a "disagreeable subject" and the abolitionists as "fanatics."[27] The viceroy (Lord Dufferin), for his part, claimed, on the one hand, that the "rules and injunctions" had been issued with his knowledge or authority and, on the other, that the Cantonment Acts must continue to operate except in Madras and Bombay. Conciliating the repealers was not the issue. Indeed, Dufferin characterized them as "the raging sisterhood who are troubling our mental purity by their obscene correspondence" and as agitators "willing, apparently, if they had their way, to allow disease and death to be propagated wholesale throughout the British Army."[28]

The impasse was broken in May 1888 when London newspapers published a memorandum authorized by the commander in chief in India, Lord Roberts, which disclosed the true attitude of the military to the whole regulation question. Addressed to general officers of the divisions and districts by the quartermaster general, E. F. Chapman, it ran in part as follows:

> The treatment of venereal disease generally is a matter calling for special devotion on the part of the medical profession.
>
> To mitigate the evil now experienced, it is not only necessary to deal with the cases of troops in hospitals, but to arrange for a wider-spread effort which may reach the large centres of population, and in this view, His Excellency [the commander in chief] has suggested to the Government of India the desirability of establishing a Medical School from which native practitioners trained in the treatment of venereal diseases may be sent to the various towns throughout the country.
>
> It can no longer be regarded as derogatory to the medical profession to promote the careful treatment of men and women who are

suffering from diseases so injurious, and in mentioning the step which his Excellency has taken, he desires me to indicate the extreme importance . . . of medical officers being prepared to study and practice this particular branch of their professional work, under the assurance that their doing so must certainly result in the recognition of their officers.

Whether or not the Lock Hospital system be extended, it is possible to encourage in every cantonment, and in Sudder and Regimental bazaars, the treatment of those amongst the population who are suffering from venereal diseases. The bulk of women who practice the trade of prostitution are willing to subject themselves to examination by Dhais or by Medical Officers, if by their so doing they can be allowed to reside in regimental bazaars.

Where Lock hospitals are not kept up, it becomes necessary, under a regimental system, to arrange for the effective inspection of prostitutes attached to regimental bazaars, whether in cantonments or on the line of march.[29]

In addition to setting forth a policy of routine inspection to combat the putative spread of venereal disease, Chapman's memo underscored the central assumption of military officialdom: that prostitution was only a problem insofar as it had medical consequences—and that its treatment fell under the jurisdiction of doctors with the support of officers but did not require any more active role for the military. This stance put the LNA and the British Committee at odds with both the government of India and the military establishment, primarily because it privileged the health of the soldiers over that of the prostitutes but also because it failed to acknowledge prostitution as the moral evil that they so strenuously believed it was.[30]

It was the following clause, however, which most outraged repealers: "In the regimental bazaars it is necessary to have a sufficient number of women, to take care that they are sufficiently attractive, to provide them with proper houses, and above all to insist upon means of ablution being always available."[31] Even seasoned repeal workers were appalled by the crassness of the language and by the official sanction given to the active procurement of "attractive" women for the pleasure of soldiers. Writing to the LNA in March 1888 about documentation she had recently read about the condition of Indian women in the cantonments, Butler said: "Your hands would be torn and filled with burning indignation if you read them." Of orders similar to Chapman's circular, quickly dubbed "The Infamous Memorandum," she wrote, "Has anything ever been recorded worse of slave hunting in Africa?"[32]

If they were not already predisposed to do so, the circular led many repealers to see the military in India as evil tempters of innocent soldiers' virtue. Where the domestic repeal campaign had depicted the profligate aristocrat as the seducer of young working-class girls, the officer class became the object of moral condemnation in the Indian crusade.[33] Added to this was the fact that the circular had been issued in 1886 and had not come to light until two years later—during which time military officials and the government of India had been reassuring Parliament and repeal agitators that regulation was not operating in the Indian cantonments. Accusations of conspiracy flew, fanned by Butler herself, who viewed the Anglo-Indian military establishment as a bureaucratic canker on the body politic, defying Christian principles and thwarting democracy at home.[34]

The publicity given to the memo and the volume of questions put to the government about the Indian acts prompted Lord Cross to issue a dispatch condemning regulation, but the LNA and the British Committee were determined to settle for nothing less than official repeal, and they stepped up their meetings, petitions, and agitation. On June 5 a resolution was carried in the House of Commons on a motion from Walter McLaren recommending that the Indian acts be rescinded. In July the Indian Council at Simla voted for repeal on the grounds that regulation had "not had the anticipated result of extirpating disease." By September 5, 1888, the Repeal Act for India had received the assent of the governor-general.[35]

The fact that the regulation system had been abolished on the basis of its inefficiency rather than on its essential immorality did not diminish repealers' sense of accomplishment at their victory. The *Sentinel*, a Christian reform journal run by Alfred Dyer, placed the projected repeal triumph of 1888 with three other remarkable historical "'88s": the Armada, the French Revolution, and the Glorious Revolution.[36] Josephine Butler sat proudly and attentively in the Ladies' Gallery while the announcement was read in the House, reporting later with satisfaction that many gentlemen were heard to remark, "'What an extraordinarily purifying influence on this House of Commons your movement has had!'"[37]

Despite the official declaration of repeal, several species of "Cantonments Rules" continued to operate in India under the direction of army officials—rules that permitted brothels to operate within regimental lines and subjected Indian women to the now infamous compulsory examination. Repealers could not rest long on their laurels: by November they had evidence from missionaries in India that the regulation system was being maintained in various places all over the subcontinent. In locations like Rawal Pindi and Peshawar, for example, lock hospitals had been closed and registration discontinued only temporarily.[38] Throughout 1889 and 1890 reports poured into the offices of the British Committee and the LNA at Tothill Street of the persistence of the "old methods" in India.

Repeal workers had heard about the situation firsthand from one Captain Banon, who had been sent to India as an agent of the British Committee, but in the fall of 1891 the committee decided to send two women to observe cantonment life. Elizabeth Andrew and Katharine Bushnell were American reformers who belonged to the World Woman's Christian Temperance Union, the umbrella organization for international temperance societies. They had been visiting London and had become interested in Indian repeal while attending an LNA meeting in March 1891.[39] At the request of the British Committee and with the support of Josephine Butler and the LNA, they traveled to India in 1892 and published an account of their experiences in an English edition called *The Queen's Daughters in India* in 1898.[40] What they found distressed repealers at home, for in every military station they visited they discovered that regulation was rampant and that Indian women submitted rather than face expulsion from the cantonments.[41] Between their book and the extensive lecture tour of the British Isles they made upon their return, Bushnell and Andrew popularized the Indian cause among feminists and female reformers throughout the United Kingdom and provided the repeal crusade with much of its ammunition against the government for the next decade.

Bushnell's and Andrew's testimony before a House Departmental Committee on the Cantonment Acts in 1893 was part of the continued parliamentary action that repealers pursued against the government in an attempt to make the reality of regulation part of the public record. The committee, headed by Stansfeld and Wilson, interviewed Lord Roberts, who up until this time had denied the truth of Bushnell's and Andrew's observations. In the course of his interview Roberts was obliged to admit that the testimony of the Americans was accurate, and the majority report of the committee concluded by substantiating Bushnell's and Andrew's claims.[42]

As with repeal in India, this ended up being a victory without real impact on the life of Indian prostitutes. In 1895 the Legislative Council in India voted to amend the Cantonments Act so that it would prohibit all examination.[43] Without on-the-spot policing of the new rules, however, regulation continued in many areas. Soon thereafter, there was renewed alarm about the increase in venereal disease in the Indian army and a call from some quarters, mainly military, for the reintroduction of the acts. The movement for an official return to regulation in India was fueled throughout 1895 by similar measures in other parts of the British empire—namely in Guernsey, Auckland, and the Cape Colony. By 1896 reenactment looked imminent, as Lord George Hamilton (secretary of state for India, 1895–1903) appointed a departmental committee to examine the official statistics on venereal disease among British troops in India.[44]

The response of the repeal organizations was swift and unequivocal. Josephine Butler called for an "aggressive warlike spirit" among repealers, and a huge meeting was organized in Birmingham in November expressly to protest the return of the acts in India and the Continent.[45] The specter of revival brought many old LNA workers back into the fray: at the annual meeting in 1896 in the Westminster Town Hall "both the floor of the hall and the gallery were crowded to the utmost."[46] The British Committee was equally poised for action: India was now "the center of the fight."[47] As always, repealers worked hard to impress upon the government that regulation did not, statistically, reduce venereal disease. This was a long-standing repeal argument that by the 1890s could be persuasively demonstrated. Among the many pamphlets calling for vigilance against the government's intentions for revival was H. J. Wilson's *History of a Sanitary Failure*, which documented the relationship between regulation in India and the incidence of venereal disease among British troops, relying on the official statistics of the Army Sanitary Commission to uphold repealers' dogged claim that medical examination was not an effective solution to the problem of Indian prostitution.[48]

Motivating these empirical proofs was a more urgent concern: the fear that a change in official policy in India in favor of return to inspection meant the sure return of the Contagious Diseases Acts at home. Josephine Butler warned that events in India constituted the "first step" for bringing repeal home.[49] In a somewhat more elaborate metaphor, Stuart told the annual meeting of the LNA in 1896, "The water flows in from all sides. . . . We in England must either be militant in this matter to keep the tide off, or else the tide will come in upon us."[50] This essentially defensive posture can also be seen in the argument most commonly advanced for Indian repeal—that soldiers who had consorted with Indian women would return home physically diseased and morally corrupted.[51] Petitioners in one "mothers' memorial" for Indian repeal worried that the impact of the acts "cannot be confined to the Army, but must permeate the whole of our social life . . . [and] cannot leave unimpaired the sanctity or happiness of the English home.[52] From the perspective of these reformers the Indian act was as much a threat to the health of the home country as it was to the health of Indian women or even British soldiers in India, if not more so.

The threat of contagion and the real possibility of a revival of the Contagious Diseases Acts in England prompted the most enthusiastic collective effort among repeal groups since the initial campaign for India in 1887. The LNA and the British Committee both issued numerous circulars, petitioned M.P.'s, wrote letters to the *Times*, and garnered signatures for official protests against the reenactment of regulation in India.[53] This acceleration of repeal activity could not, however, forestall a shift in government policy toward a reconsideration of regulation. In April 1897 Lord George Hamilton issued a dispatch to the government of India recommending that certain unspecified "measures" be adopted for checking the spread of venereal diseases and suggesting that such diseases should be explicitly included under the Cantonment Rules of 1895.[54] Hamilton's dispatch produced an uproar in the repeal community. The *Shield*, which was revived as the journal of the British Committee in May, just one month after Hamilton's pronouncements, quoted Butler's warning that "the door is left wide open by the Government proposals for the easy and speedy re-introduction of the whole system of regulated vice in one form or another."[55] The Executive Committee of the LNA lost no time in sending a memorial in June to Lord Salisbury protesting regulation, followed in July by an LNA-wide memorial to Lord Hamilton with over 61,000 signatures.[56] Running through all of these reactions was the persistent and familiar repeal refrain: that regulation only served to legitimize sexual vice and that it produced "hygienic failure and moral depravation." A group of medical women, who petitioned Hamilton in 1898, also argued that the method for initiating inquiry as to whether a woman was diseased—accusation by a soldier of infecting him—was objectionable and illegal. These female petitioners, who practiced both in Britain and throughout the empire, included such luminaries as Elizabeth Blackwell, Agnes McLaren, Helen Wilson, and, significantly, Rukhmabai, who was then heading up the Morarkhai V. Hospital and Dispensary for Women and Children at Surat. While some were strictly practitioners, others had been involved in repeal and were clearly determined to contribute their professional expertise to substantiate the moral objections of the repealers to the regulation of prostitutes. Indeed, they concluded their memorial by opposing "any measures containing features of the old Contagious Diseases Acts, which were equally repugnant to our moral sense and to our scientific convictions."[57]

Despite this display of female professional solidarity, there was growing evidence of a breakdown in consensus within the women's movement about the evils of the regulation system in the wake of Hamilton's dispatch. Shortly after the release of the secretary of state's recommendations Lady

Isabel Somerset, president of the British Women's Temperance Association and a friend of many active repealer workers, wrote a lengthy letter to the *Times* suggesting a series of specific measures for dealing with prostitution in the cantonments. These included the registration and periodic examination of both prostitutes and soldiers,[58] with the added proviso of "severe penalty" for men who consorted with women not under the supervision of medical officials.[59] Although Somerset's concern for establishing an equal moral standard for men and women had always been at the cornerstone of repeal philosophy, Josephine Butler roundly condemned Somerset's letter as an endorsement of the regulation principle that she had been crusading against for over thirty years.[60] The *Shield* concurred, claiming that Somerset's ideas embodied "the most complete State Regulation of prostitution which we have ever seen described, in its baldest and most absolute form."[61]

The British Committee issued a heated reply to Somerset's proposals that affirmed its commitment to an equal sexual standard but rejected examination, whether of men or women, as degrading and brutalizing.[62] The repealers' response to Somerset may seem overanxious, but in fact it reflected their fears about the course of official policy in 1897: with the government pressing for the return of systematic regulation in India, the defection of a prominent leader like Lady Isabel could well appear to signal the decline of a unified antiregulation movement whose leaders were aging and whose energy required constant fanning. So dangerous did Butler consider Somerset's letter that she resigned her office as president of the Purity Department of the World Woman's Christian Temperance Union. She cited "the wavering or undecided" position of its leaders toward regulation as the reason for her resignation, and confided privately to Frances Willard that "I feel it necessary to emphasize my conviction in the matter by a public act of severance of our official relationship."[63]

The concern in repeal circles caused by both Hamilton's dispatch and Somerset's letter was somewhat offset by the publication in late summer of an order by Sir George White, now the commander in chief in India, on venereal diseases. Acknowledging that sexual vice was as much a moral question as a medical or military one, White's memo was hailed as a turning point in the Indian campaign since, at least in theory, it no longer pitted army officers against repeal activists and their agents. "Officers of the Army who confine their efforts to theoretical discussion on these points are not likely to do much practical good," wrote White in his General Order of 1897. "Regimental officers must not stand aloof as mere spectators, allowing the evil to take its course."[64] Although White's concern was as much about army efficiency as it was about morality, his willingness to address the army's responsibility in such matters as soldiers "consorting with loose women" represented an official recognition of the lines of argument that the LNA and the British Committee had been advancing since the beginning of repeal initiatives in India, and indeed since the very start of the domestic campaign in the 1860s.[65]

And yet among repeal workers there remained a sense of urgency and crisis that was not to abate even as the Indian campaign moved into its second decade. Hamilton's dispatch resulted in the Cantonments Acts and Regulations of 1897, which repealed the legislation of 1895, reinstated examination, and enforced the penalty of expulsion for all those refusing to submit.[66] The new laws made continued agitation all the more crucial: in Butler's estimation, they were startlingly similar in their formulation to the original Contagious Diseases Acts in England.[67] With this in mind, the British Committee and the LNA did not relent in their efforts to keep the "Indian scandal" prominently before the public. The *Shield* reported evidence of regulation in the cantonments and consistently refuted the alleged correlation between examination and diminished disease. Stuart and Wilson raised questions and sustained debate on India in the House, and the LNA and the British Committee continued to convene meetings, issue pamphlets, and condemn regulation routinely at both annual meetings and international conferences. The turn of the century marked the height of the Indian campaign, with no less than four repeal journals in operation (the *Sentinel*, the *Shield*, the *Stormbell*—an LNA publication, and the *Dawn*), three of which covered regulation in India or the British Empire. In Butler's assessment of the situation in 1898, "This danger is no less to-day than it was twenty or thirty years ago."[68]

JOSEPHINE BUTLER AND LATE
VICTORIAN IMPERIAL FEMINISM

As is clear from the account of repeal for India so far, it was Josephine Butler's special interest in the empire that gave direction to the repeal movement after 1886. Her commitment to India was part of her larger sense of Britain's responsibility for the peoples of its empire and, more specifically, the responsibility of British women for the health and welfare of colonial women. In spite of the fact that these concerns dominated her thoughts and her writing during the last twenty years of her life, historians of both the women's movement and of the repeal campaign have, as Vron Ware has recently noted, failed to take notice of her imperial attitudes or their relation to her feminist ideology.[69] Butler's biographers, if they look beyond the end of the domestic repeal campaign, tend to take Butler at her word when, at the death of her husband in 1890, she declared an end to active campaigning and repeal activity.[70] Her sporadic ill health in the 1890s, which is the subject of much of her correspondence during this decade, confirms the impression that she had retired from the scene by 1900. Moreover, most accounts of the two decades between repeal at home and her death in 1906 focus on her European interests: in addition to her affiliation with the Continental Abolitionist Federation, her sister lived in Switzerland and she spent a considerable amount of time traveling to and from the Continent.[71]

There is no doubt that Butler was concerned about regulation on the Continent and that she had to fight to get European news reported in repeal journals and to secure funds to send to European repeal workers. In 1892, for example, she wrote to the Priestman sisters, "You will see that I could not help writing in The Dawn an appeal for funds for the LNA. The Indian Committee now s[oaks] up everything, and the Indian repeal work is so important that it will become more difficult to get funds for any other branch. Yet we cannot desert our Continental friends."[72] And yet she maintained an active interest in the repeal agitation in India as well as in reform activities throughout the British Empire. In 1893 Butler made a point of stating that she had not withdrawn from the repeal cause.[73] This was in part because of the impact that the plight of Indian women made on her, which helps to explain why, although regulation in other parts of the empire and its dominions was an issue for many British repealers in this period (including Butler), India seems to have preoccupied her in the late 1880s. As she confided to friends in Bristol, what she heard and read of life in the cantonments in 1886 and after "made my blood boil again with quite youthful wrath."[74] Throughout the 1890s she wrote pamphlets, contributed to repeal journals, and corresponded with missionaries in India. Whenever there was a new crisis in the post-1886 crusade, she responded to it with her pen and her tireless reaffirmation of repeal principles.[75] At times Butler's imperial concerns and her insistence on Indian prostitution as the main focus of the campaign met with resistance from other repeal leaders, many of whom were just as interested in rescue work, the white slave trade, and social purity as they were in abolishing regulation.[76] This is not to suggest that there were not other British women active in and concerned with the Indian repeal cause or that Butler was isolated from other repeal activists— only that repeal, like suffrage, was the kind of issue from which other reform causes took off and to which a variety of reform organizations subscribed without necessarily making it their exclusive or even primary commitment.[77] Maintaining distinctions between repeal work and other kinds of reform intervention remained a priority for Butler, for whom the former always took priority and had in her eyes a prior claim, in terms of the historical narrative of late Victorian abolitionism.[78]

That India emerged as the special object of her imperial commitment and Indian women as those most urgently requiring British women's attention attests to the kinds of obligations that Butler felt the empire required of female reformers in the metropole. It is also evidence of the special place that Victorian feminists, like many of their contemporaries, accorded India in the British Empire: it was the linchpin of imperial security and the symbol of Britain's imperial strength and achievement in the world. In an important sense, the Indian imperial burden was a practical administrative one: repeal organizations focused initially on India to the exclusion of other imperial territories ostensibly because it was ruled from Westminster. When the British Committee of the British, Continental, and General Federation formed in late 1886, its members considered the fact that regulation operated throughout the British Empire and dominions—in the white settlements like South Africa and parts of Australia and New Zealand. But these were self-governing colonies, and the British Committee decided that the problem of regulation should be left up to the discretion of their respective governments.[79] In contrast, repealers considered India to be an extension of the home government and hence under its jurisdiction; similarly, the repeal movement was considered an extension of domestic reform to imperial soil. In her first Indian pamphlet Butler described the imperial crusade as "the revival and extension of the Abolitionist Cause" and referred to India as the "second chapter" of English repeal work.[80] For her, the implementation of repeal principles in India followed directly from the first parliamentary victory at home. She recommended that the LNA phrase its first Indian resolution so that it conveyed the idea that "it is logically necessary that the abolition carried out in England sh[oul]d be also carried out in India and the Colonies, and that it should be done without delay."[81] This is not to suggest that Butler or repealers for India were not concerned about the operation of the Contagious Diseases Acts elsewhere in the colonial dominions. But these were not considered to be extensions of the "home ground" in the same way that India was and hence not as likely to become, as we shall see, carriers of contagion back to the mother country. The burden of India was, if not greater, then certainly more symbolic than that of other colonial possessions.

In addition to administrative obligations came both a deep personal commitment to and sense of moral responsibility toward India, which Butler articulated from the very start of the Indian campaign. In a letter to the editors of the Indian press, which was written jointly with James Stuart and published in the *Sentinel* in May 1887, Butler explained the involvement of the British Committee in Indian repeal in the following terms:

> We, members of the British section of this world-wide Federation, feel that we have a special responsibility and interest in the matter so far as it concerns India. India having become a portion of the British Empire, and the Government of that Empire being professedly Christian, we feel that there is a flagrant inconsistency in the fact that Government has imposed on its Indian subjects a system which is diametrically opposed to the principles and ethics of the religion which we profess. . . . We have an additional responsibility in respect to India . . . namely; that after the fullest investigations of a legal, moral and hygienic kind by the Government of India, under Lord Ripon, [whose] . . . Government reported to the Secretary of State for India, in favour of the complete abolition of the system. . . . Since then the Acts in England have been completely swept away. You will see, therefore in these facts not only our responsibility for the present condition of India, but the ground of our hope and confident expectation that vigorous action . . . will bring about . . . repeal in India.[82]

As her language indicates, Butler's sense of imperial responsibility grew out of Christian feminist principles—principles that had defined and helped sustain the domestic repeal crusade through the first twenty years of agitation. The notion of womanhood as "solidaire" had been at the heart of the domestic repeal campaign and was invoked to bridge what was often a class difference between working-class prostitutes and middle-class reformers. Regulation was considered a leveler, a form of oppression that struck women of all classes equally. "Every woman alive, from the Queen on the throne to the poor girl on the street, is equally degraded" by inspection and registration.[83] In the post-1886 phase the solidarity of female suffering was heralded as the justification for reform on behalf of Indian women. At the first annual meeting of the LNA after victory at home, repeal leaders reminded their fellow workers that "one of the aims of our association . . . [is] to hold the women of the entire world together in one common cause." Anticipating the extension of repeal into the colonies and dependencies, they rejoiced that "the bonds of friendship were more firmly knit together than ever on the basis of a deepening sense of the responsibility of our common womanhood in the future of the world."[84] In Butler's view, this responsibility extended explicitly to "the women of every race and colour."[85] The move from "home" to India and from working-class women to Indian womanhood was facilitated by the dependent posture in which British feminists imagined both their domestic and their colonial female clienteles, as well as by the argument that India was an extension of the reformable domestic space to which responsible British women would turn their attention. It was also made possible by Butler's assumption that the Christian mission of British imperialism was part of the natural order of things. Noting that India had become the main focus of abolitionist activity, Butler told the Friends' Association for the Abolition of State Regulation of Vice that "this is natural, right and necessary because of the great responsibility which England has for India."[86]

From the outset of the Indian campaign Butler's feelings of imperial responsibility centered on the Indian prostitutes in the cantonments, despite the fact that the Contagious Diseases Act in India applied to European prostitutes who trafficked there and that, for many involved in the question of regulation, British soldiers were a primary object of concern. Indeed, for Butler India itself was practically equivalent to the condition of its women. "I cannot feel it possible to work for repeal in India," she declared in 1887, "without grappling more or less with the whole condition of Indian women. Our own responsibility as Christian women presses heavily on my mind."[87] In her writings she describes how their pain was a constant source of agony for her that did not abate even as the crusade for repeal dragged out. As she wrote in 1892, "The sufferings of our Indian sisters are rarely absent from my thoughts."[88] Once again, it was Butler's Christianity that provided the framework of analysis for the plight of Indian prostitutes. In her analysis regulation was an evil because it violated women's privacy and sanctioned organized sexual vice. But at the root of her objection was the fact that regulation perpetuated a double standard for men and women, which she maintained defied evidence in the Old and New Testaments of the equality of the sexes.[89] As in repeal at home, this formula for Christian feminism drove her support for Indian repeal and dictated her concern for the women involved. For not only did she see Indian prostitutes as the victims of regulation, she privileged their suffering as women as the justification for repeal activity. This stemmed from a long-held belief, common to Victorian feminism but especially nurtured over the years in the home repeal movement, that women were more vulnerable to pain and suffering than men. According to Butler in her plea for missionary help in India in 1898, "It is women who are the first and greatest sufferers."[90]

Butler's insistence on the suffering of Indian women also derived from the special bond that she believed to exist among all women. She prefaced several statements pledging herself and the LNA to Indian repeal with some variation on the phrase "we, *as women,* protest in the strongest manner possible."[91] This was no mere formula; it reflected the strong sense of gendered solidarity that Butler experienced with her Indian "sisters" as well as the commitment to international sisterhood that, for many Victorian and especially Edwardian feminists, animated all facets of the women's movement.[92] Especially after the initial legislative success in India in 1888—when, despite repeal of the Indian Contagious Diseases Act, Cantonment Rules continued to require that prostitutes be examined—there were some activists in repeal circles who wanted to shift attention to the condition of the British soldier in India. The British Committee and the LNA both were in contact with the Gospel Purity Association and, in the 1890s, with the Army Purity Association—organizations that targeted the officer and the soldier class with literature and itinerant lecturers promoting the virtues of chastity in military life.[93] They were encouraged by both the military and medical communities, in whose estimation sexual vice was the responsibility of the individual soldier anyway. Although Butler was sympathetic to the plight of the soldier in India, she refused to lose sight of Indian women, whom she always considered to be the real victims of the regulation system. "For us women of the LNA," wrote Butler in 1897, "the question can never be so narrowed down. . . . We feel deeply for the ill-guided and corrupted young soldiers but we feel as deeply for the Indian women. Their cause is our cause, their griefs are our griefs." With the same singularity of conviction she had displayed in the English campaign, Butler insisted that the mistreatment of Indian women must remain the vitally important issue.[94]

Her Christian beliefs, her sense of imperial responsibility, and her commitment to female solidarity combined to make Butler a harsh critic of regulation in India. Her particular brand of Christian imperial feminism also prompted her to see Indian prostitutes as the double victims of oppression against women and of colonization by a foreign power. This condition made Indian prostitutes even more of a special responsibility, as Butler insisted that they were more deserving of repealers' energy—and intervention—because they were a colonized people. In May 1887 she told *Sentinel* readers that "our poor Indian sisters claim our sympathy even more than our own country women who were subjected to the C.D. Acts, for not only are they women oppressed by men, but they are the women of a conquered race oppressed by their conquerors. Their hope of deliverance must seem

to them so very far off."[95] Throughout her writings Butler conceived of
Indian women as more deserving of pity than their English counterparts
who had suffered under the acts at home.[96] As the quotation above indicates, she attributed this in part to the oppression of native customs. When
Butler spoke of Indian women as "oppressed by men," presumably she
meant by those men who ran the British government. She may have also
meant Indian men, though her contact with Indian male social reformers
like Behramji Malabari and the M.P. Dadhabai Naoroji made her less sus-
picious of native males than of Anglo-Indian military officers.[97] What
Butler certainly believed was that Indian women were oppressed by native
religions, which made them less able to resist oppression. Hinduism and
Islam both, she felt, rendered them incapable of even thinking of appealing
to a higher power to assuage their suffering: "They have not even the small
power of resistance which the western woman may have . . . who may have
some clearer knowledge of a just and pitiful God to whom she may make
her mute appeal."[98]

Butler was not as contemptuous of Hinduism or Islam as some other
Victorians could be,[99] and one of her greatest rhetorical themes was the
failure of Christians to live up to the true ethical standards of Christianity.
And yet her own evangelical priorities are unmistakable. While she stopped
short of declaring outright that Christianity was superior, her concern for
the conversion of Indian women underlines her assumption that as a
religion it was more desirable and more salutary than "heathenism" for
Indians. Conversion was not Butler's reform purpose in India, but she did
express concern that regulation, which degraded and enslaved Indian
women, provided little incentive for them to accept the religion of their
conquerors as their own. On these grounds too she rejected the church's
attention to the soldier with this reminder: "But what of the native women
of India . . . to whom we want to bring the gospel?"[100]

If Butler insisted that Indian women were more disadvantaged than their
English sisters because they were a subject race, she did not attribute their
oppression solely to native custom or religious practice. From the outset of
the Indian crusade she was a harsh critic of empire: she consistently blamed
a corrupt British imperial administration and policy for the suffering of
Indian women. Writing to the *Sentinel* in February 1887, Butler expressed
her desire "to engage with all the force I have in the coming crusade,"
adding, "It is an awful thing to take a map of the world and observe in how
many portions of it the abominable system of iniquity has been set up either
under the British flag or through British influence."[101] In the next issue she
was even more vocal in her criticisms:

For myself, I would desire nothing better than to have the honour of being allowed to consecrate my poor remaining powers and days to the service of any heathen subjected races however low in morality, as against their far viler Christian conquerors. I know that it is possible to throw back in our faces the horrors of heathen morality, the sensuality of Mahommedanism, Etc. I would ask, however, which are the more *guilty before God*, the degraded sinners, followers of the false prophet ... or those other sinners, who under the teaching of Christianity, with the light of instruction and education ... go out to these heathen, and while too often adopting their vices, introduce new and unheard of morality, endorsing both alike by law and by ordinance?[102]

This kind of rhetoric was not uncommon for the *Sentinel*, which, under the editorship of Alfred Dyer, hurled a steady stream of vitriolic abuse at the British government for its continuation of state-regulated vice. Articles entitled "Government versus God in India" and phrases like "the Satanic system of licensed lust" were standard fare, and Butler's contributions to the magazine often assumed this anti-imperialist tone.[103]

The Christian standards to which Butler adhered, and against which she measured the British Empire and found it so deficient, led her to question the very morality of conquest. "My own profound conviction has ever been that annexation and conquest are morally wrong," she wrote in the *Sentinel* in March 1887. "In what do they differ from robbery and theft?"[104] Butler further developed this idea in a pamphlet defending independence for Ireland against the arguments of its opponents that Home Rule heralded the dissolution of the British Empire. For the passion of its rhetoric and its unrelenting equation of empire with violence against conquered peoples, it is worth quoting at length:

On what basis does our empire stand? Very largely on that of conquest. Tell me what warrant there is in the teaching of Christianity for the assertion of the righteousness of conquest? Nothing except what is founded in righteousness will stand in these coming days. But you answer, perhaps, "We bring untold blessings to the nations conquered; Christianity is promulgated throughout the world as it would not otherwise be." Is it quite so? Do we bring unmixed blessings? In what manner did we in the first days of conquest or annexation begin to confer a series of blessings on our conquered dependencies? In what manner have we continued to do so? Did we not often begin by aggression, sealed in blood? At the slightest provocation or resistance to our arms, were not resisting races destroyed, their poor huts blown into the air by our guns, and their women and children included in our righteous massacres?[105]

With Butler's diatribe came a vague warning: "Can we gravely imagine that when all these things begin to come to pass, when the powers of heaven and earth shall be shaken, our proud British empire alone shall stand unbroken, unshorne of any of its extensive dominion and power?" In conclusion she reminded readers that all peoples have a right to resistance, hinting that, unless there was cooperation between Britain and Ireland, the Irish would have just cause for invoking that right.[106]

With regard to the Indian Contagious Diseases Acts, Butler did more than hint. In the first memorial presented by the LNA to the government of Indian in 1888 Butler and her supporters declared:

We, as women, desire to protest in the strongest and most solemn manner possible against the wrong done to our sisters and fellow subjects in India. At the same time we venture to warn you of the danger to our Indian rule in thus trifling with the best instincts of the people. We have reason to believe that the seeds of rebellion are being rapidly propagated, especially in the Punjab, the inhabitants of which have hitherto been among the most loyal of our Indian subjects. Nothing so surely produces a spirit of rebellion as trampling on the womanhood of a subject race by its conquerors.[107]

Here and elsewhere during the first ten years of the Indian campaign, Butler called for an end to regulation lest its horrors provoke native revolt. At times her apocalyptic vision made her sound convinced of this eventuality. In 1888 she warned against the government's plans for an imperial federation because she was sure that regulation would become the official norm and that the fate of Indian prostitutes would be sealed. "Then will follow, sooner or later, rebellion and revolution."[108]

Butler also drew ominous parallels between India and other parts of the world where there had recently been political unrest. In an address to the Friends' Association for Abolition entitled "Some Lessons from Contemporary History, Showing the Connections between Revolutionary Movements and State Regulated Vice," she pointed out that the *petroleuses* who had burned sections of Paris during the commune had also been subjected to regulation "just as women are now being enslaved and outraged by decree of the English government in India." Similar events had occurred in Italy, and "by and bye, if we do not take care, this country will also be in revolution, and there will be that element in it."[109] By 1897 she was warning outright that if the government did not do something about regulation in India, Indians would take things into their own hands.[110] This was no doubt intended as a cautionary tale about the dangers of maintaining regulationist practices and, more generally, of deferring colonial reform. It was certainly an indication of Butler's concern that indigenous unrest was not only a menace in and of itself but a threat to the stability of the empire. In Butler's view regulation, because it encouraged vice and turned Indians against the government, "deals a death blow to the whole fabric of our military occupation of India."[111] Of the government's apparent lack of awareness of this threat, Butler wrote, "In vain do they imagine that the wrongs, so far silently borne by conquered Hindus, Chinese, Pacific Islanders, Etc., are matters so far away and conquering races so mean and unimportant that there is no need of serious apprehension for the future." In Butler's eyes this boded ill for the future of the empire, since regulation has "caused our name to be hated by native races."[112] She was not above warning against hubris: "We have too inflated an idea of our Imperial greatness, and in our pride we too easily forget the interests of other nations." But even this critique was motivated by the concern that "pride is the ruin of nations" and that "the sun of our own prosperity may set in clouds and storms."[113] Butler's arguments were predicated on the idea that the real source of British imperial strength lay in the respect its subjects had for it as a just and fair ruler rather than in its military might—an idea that gained currency in the post-Mutiny period.[114] Anything that undermined the premises of moral imperial rule was a threat to empire and unwise as well as dangerous. The council of the London branch of the LNA recognized the stakes involved and warned that Indian regulation "affects not only the poor native women and girls of India . . . but also . . . our character as a nation governing 150 millions of Indian subjects."[115] It was an argument about imperial prestige that bore more than the traces of some Antis' opposition to women's suffrage on the grounds that it would undermine British imperial power in the minds of native subjects.

For all her professed physical frailty and personal modesty, Butler was a shrewd and experienced campaigner. It seems quite likely that this kind of rhetoric was intended as a strategic maneuver to galvanize support for repeal and threaten those in power with popular unrest if regulation were not abolished. The fact that Butler criticized the very principles of empire is misleading, however, for she did not envision an end to empire. Rather, she believed in the possibility of a more ethical imperialism. Although she did not hesitate to condemn regulation and its crimes against Indian women as "this imperially-imposed degradation of their race," it was through a purified imperial attitude that empire become the salvation of Indian women as well: "We have had enough of exultation over our Colonial successes, and our material conquests. Has England not now the heart, as formerly, to aim at some greater and nobler conquests than these? What an opportunity lies before her, of laying her strong imperial hand on a wrong which is crying to heaven for vengeance, and of leading the way among nations in the loudly called for and holy enterprise of giving a death blow to this arch wickedness."[116] Thus empire was not only the cause of but also the solution to social problems in India. Butler's belief in the possibility of an ethical empire made repeal more than just a gross injustice against Indian women: it constituted a monumental obstacle to the future of Britain's imperial greatness.

In this context, the repealers' responsibility was clearly enormous. To them fell the task not just of saving Indian prostitutes but of purifying the British Empire in India as well. Butler saw repeal precisely in these purifying terms: "The sun of our own prosperity may set in clouds and storms, if we do not . . . cleanse our hands from iniquity."[117] The social purity theme had, along with a strong evangelical current, been one of the philosophical mainstays of the domestic repeal campaign. It was readily adapted to empire. In 1893 Butler urged LNA workers not to "give way for one moment our intensity of purpose on the Indian question" because repeal in the cantonments would be "a just and purifying victory for Imperial England."[118] As mentioned above, many repeal workers were equally interested in pursuing social purity reforms (most notably, by working against the white slave trade abroad and in vigilance societies at home), especially as the Indian crusade extended into the 1890s with little evidence of conclusive results.[119] This divergence from regulation and Indian women led Butler to qualify her commitment to purity per se at various points in the 1890s. "The cause for which I have worked is *not* a 'Purity Crusade' nor a morality crusade," she declared in 1896. "It was and is a revolt against [and] an aggressive opposition to a gross and political and illegal tyranny."[120] Butler also sought to distance herself from social purity workers because she disliked the turn that vigilance and rescue work was taking in the 1890s. In her view it was too interventionist, with poor women bearing the brunt of the "external pressure" that reformers brought to bear on prostitutes in "bad" neighborhoods at home.[121] Lady Henry Somerset's defection from the repeal cause in 1897 confirmed Butler's suspicion of social purity groups and their loyalty to the repeal principles.[122] Despite her disassociation from purity reformers, however, Butler continued to support the idea of Indian repeal as a means of cleansing a corrupt empire, although metaphors of purification appeared less frequently in her own writing.[123]

Significantly too for her particular brand of imperial feminism, Butler insisted that it was British *women* who were to be the purifiers of empire. In a very important sense, Butler's attitude was an outgrowth of her radical belief that men, not women, were responsible for vice: it was their uncontrollable sexual desires, rather than any temptation provided by women, that produced organized prostitution. Just as she blamed men for the corruption of prostitutes, so too did she blame men for the corruption of empire: "The Englishman is a powerful agent for evil, as for good. In the best times of our history, my countrymen possessed pre-eminently vigorous minds in vigorous bodies. . . . There is no creature in the world so ready as the Englishman to destroy, to enslave, to dominate and grow fat upon the destruction of weaker human beings whom he has subjected to his bold and iron will."[124]

Women, on the other hand, could be counted on to recognize and redress social evils like regulation. As Butler frequently reminded her audiences, it was women who mounted the antislavery campaigns in both the United States and Britain.[125] Butler continually stressed repeal as women's work after 1886. "The National is dead," she wrote to her friends in 1886, lamenting that its leaders thought that, just because they had lost enthusiasm, the LNA had too. "These *men* have no faith."[126] As noted earlier in this chapter, it was Butler who urged that the LNA remain active after 1886 as a "separate *woman's* organization" committed to securing imperial reform. Thereafter she pleaded with LNA leaders to recruit women workers and encouraged female repealers to stay "to the front" in the repeal cause.[127]

At certain strategic moments in the Indian campaign Butler thought that the pressure of women on the government was crucial and would carry more weight than that of men. She criticized Stuart's version of one repeal petition as too cautious: "Remember this is a *Woman's* Declaration, and we ought not too meekly to accept any man's toning down of it."[128] In 1897 Butler pushed the LNA to seek a memorial signed exclusively by women. "What I *always* like best is the joint action of men and women, but there are occasions . . . when the original women protesters of 1869 and their followers should utter their voice apart as women."[129] Butler's stubbornness on this point led her to distance herself from that enthusiastic repealer Alfred Dyer, whom she felt "always had a tendency not to make women's work as prominent as it ought to have been."[130] In 1887 she had elected not to give Dyer LNA funds because she did not consider him a suitable agent.[131] To her friends the Priestmans she wrote in 1888:

> Dyer is doing a great deal of good work . . . but I daresay you feel as I do that there is one note wanting (and a sad want it is too) and that is the note of compassion for our poor subjected and tormented sisters of India. I cannot discern a trace of pity for them. His expressions are those of disgust and reprobation only, for the poor women, as well as for the men. . . . Dyer calls them "brazen harlots" and all such bad names. But who made them so? . . . They are coerced by our *Imperial* hand. Please dear friends, watch every opportunity of supplying this need in Mr. Dyer's work.[132]

Frustrated, Butler complained too that this compassion was sometimes wanting among her friends in Parliament, "who have not the time to feel as women feel! besides they are men, and *Hindoo* women are far away."[133] The indispensability of women workers to the repeal cause was something Butler championed until her death. In 1905, fearing a new wave of enthusiasm for regulation, she worried that her women's association was flagging. "How is the LNA to be revived? It was the first in the field—and ought to be kept alive."[134]

By emphasizing the role of women as imperial purifiers Butler feminized the imperial ethic of moral improvement and helped to imperialize traditional notions of women's responsibility for the nation-state. In the process she created an imperial feminist possibility on which the whole Indian repeal campaign depended. As with other Victorian feminist writers, national and racial priorities were an integral part of her imperial feminism. With Butler's emphasis on the purifying power of women on empire came an equal insistence on their responsibility as *English* women for reform in India. This national pride was expressed most often with reference to the kinds of constitutional liberties to which Britain as a nation subscribed. The language of national patriotism that was used to justify the privacy of women's bodies and thus to oppose regulation was not new to the post-1886 campaign, though the rhetoric was decidedly more imperial than it had been during the twenty-year domestic repeal struggle. The distinctiveness of English women's abolition work was also used to claim that British repeal organizations had done the pioneering work of international abolitionist reform. Butler was highly conscious of the fact that the LNA had led the way among its European neighbors in the campaign against state-regulated vice, and, indeed, the leadership of Britain in the international world of social reform was a prominent theme among many post-1886 repealers. Repeal polemicists often referred to the regulation system as "foreign" to Britain. Maurice Gregory ascribed its origins to France, where he claimed it had been originated by Napoleon and had persisted unchecked by government much longer than in England.[135] That the British should have repealed the Contagious Diseases Acts first and more successfully than the French was hailed as a sign of the progressive and superior character of English civilization.[136] In fact, although India was considered a possible source of regulation contagion for England, the fear of disease coming via the English Channel ("that narrow hedge") was as great during the heyday of the Indian campaign.[137] One ardent repealer even went so far as to assert that the state regulation of vice was of pagan origins, declaring that "State-pimping was founded by Solon."[138]

The eagerness of repealers to stress the un-Englishness of regulation and the Englishness of the reform impulse reflected racial pride as well. The cry that venereal disease was a threat to the vitality of the Anglo-Saxon race was raised frequently in repeal literature both before and after 1886, but the extension of the crusade to empire did not markedly intensify this rhetoric.[139] What does emerge is a new emphasis on the role of the Anglo-Saxon race as the redeemer of the social problems of the world. Butler had long emphasized that it was Anglo-Saxon women who "have been the first to rise up in rebellion" against slavery, both of black people and of regulation.[140] In spite of her claim that no God-fearing rulers could justify imposing regulation on conquered peoples, Butler still felt that the British were the best exponents of the Christian reform ethic: "It is a happy thing that the Anglo-Saxon race still holds firmly to principles which are derived from the Ethics of Christ, and which will always, so long as they exist, gain the ascendancy."[141] For Butler it was this Christian ethic that explained and ultimately justified Anglo-Saxon supremacy over native races. As her response to the Boer War indicates, she believed that by virtue of their Christian faith, the Anglo-Saxons were the ruling race and as such the designated protectors of native peoples. In her book *Native Races and the War* (1900) she defended British rule in South Africa as a trust from God: "It is my deep conviction that Great Britain will in future be judged, condemned or justified, according to her treatment of those innumerable coloured races, heathen or partly Christianized, over whom her rule extends, or who, beyond the sphere of her rule, claim her sympathy and help as a Christian and civilizing power to whom a great trust has been committed."[142] The perversity of imperial ideology made the fulfillment of imperial rule a duty to the Anglo-Saxon race as much as to the "lower" races; in the wake of the

Boer War national, racial, and imperial stability were believed to depend on the commitment to just such an imperial duty. Quoting Sir Bartle Frere, governor of South Africa, Butler agreed with him that Britain should not shrink from such responsibilities "if we are true lovers of our country and race and of our fellow creatures everywhere."[143]

It could be argued that the limited success of repeal efforts throughout the 1890s, coupled with British failures in South Africa, caused even staunch imperialists like Butler to fear for continued imperial strength and hence to step up rhetoric about the leadership of the Anglo-Saxon women in international reform. But it seems clear that the 1886 victory at home, as well as the whole twenty-year history of the repeal movement, was evidence enough for repealers of British women's moral leadership in the world. Pledging the LNA to the cause of Indian women in 1886, Butler said, "We have a right to remind the public of our past perseverance and success and to take a high tone of Authority about a flagrant injustice which is yet but half-abolished." Their past experience gave British repealers a responsibility to advise, but also the right to lead, since they had initiated the very first movement for reform.[144] For the most part Butler was content to share the leadership with American and even with Swiss women, who had long been active in repeal work. But she was privately resentful of the Germans in the Continental Abolitionist Federation, whom she suspected of being soft on repeal as well as of thwarting her influence on the direction of the repeal movement in the twentieth century.[145]

These were national jealousies underwritten by imperial assumptions and perhaps even imperial insecurities. For Butler, Britain's imperial leadership was based not just on territorial possessions but on the moral example of its people and especially the moral responsibility that its women were prepared to assume. Identification with Britain's national destiny and its imperial greatness gave the repeal movement an international stature and a moral importance without which it might have faltered after the climactic victory of repeal at home. At certain junctures, this identification could be used expressly to drum up support for the imperial campaign, as in May 1908 when Dr. Helen Wilson told the LNA that "the Abolitionists were in the direct line of succession of English Reformers, from the days of Magna Carta downwards, claiming equal justice for weak and strong, for rich and poor." This was followed by a plea for more donations for the imperial crusade.[146] Fueled by the power of Butler's example and her writing, the Indian repeal crusade kept the LNA and its affiliates actively involved in imperial affairs until her death and beyond—though even before her death many repealers were beginning to expand the field beyond simply India and

Indian women. Thus Butler's legacy was twofold. She articulated an imperial Christian feminism and, by institutionalizing it, secured for it an influential place among British feminists and female reformers of the late nineteenth and early twentieth centuries. As the next chapter demonstrates, the twin concepts of a feminized empire and of international female solidarity were crucial to Edwardian suffrage arguments, suggesting that these ideas, which are to be found in feminist domestic reform ideology throughout the nineteenth century, made their way into the twentieth-century suffrage debate partly via the exposure to empire and to the ideology of the white woman's burden that Butler's Indian campaign provided to women working for the suffrage cause.

THE REPEAL CRUSADE AND
IMAGES OF INDIAN WOMEN

Although repealers had little direct contact with Indian women living in and around the military cantonments, they exercised enormous power over how they were represented to the audience of female reformers and feminists at home. As writers for the feminist press were doing in the same period, repeal workers defined Indian women as potential equals while at the same time positioning them in a distinctly subordinate role—that of suffering colonial women in need of saving by their imperial feminist sisters. Indian women emerge from repeal writing as instruments used to further the Indian repeal cause and to provide British women reformers with an imperial identity that legitimized the call for women's work in the colonial field, a call advertised elsewhere (as in the feminist press). Not surprisingly perhaps, information about Indian women in the cantonments was extrapolated into knowledge about the condition—and suffering—of all Indian women. What British feminists at home learned by reading the *Shield*, the *Sentinel*, and other reports of the Indian crusade in the feminist and suffrage press reinforced the contradictions inherent in what they already "knew" about Indian women. Indian women's theoretical equality and their present suffering combined to make them the irresistible objects of British feminist concern as well as the indisputable subjects of their imperial authority.

Equality between British and Indian women was ostensibly the organizing principle behind the repeal crusade for India, the assumption upon which the whole post-1886 movement was predicated. Although to my knowledge she never met an Indian woman, Butler often referred to Indian women as "our Indian fellow subjects," echoing long-standing ideals of imperial citizenship and indicating her belief that Indians and Britons were

all members of equal status in the larger comity of nations. From equality of
status followed equality of treatment: in the context of the repeal campaign
Butler demanded that "the best interests of our poor fellow-women and
fellow-subjects shall never more be placed second to the best interest of our
fellow-subjects of our own race, our soldiers and civilian men in India and
elsewhere."[147] Indian women were not merely "fellow-subjects" or even
"fellow-women." For Butler and other repeal activists they were nothing
less than "our Indian sisters."[148] Sisterhood not only demanded equality of
treatment; it also meant an equal intensity of suffering at the hands of
similar violations. "I can say with truth," Butler wrote in 1898, "that I feel as
deep a pity and indignation on behalf of the Indian women submitted to
this system, as I should do if they were Anglo-Saxon women." And she
assured her audience that "hundreds of English women can say the
same."[149]

In creating Indian women equal, repealers were possibly anticipating the
objection, common enough in the late Victorian period, that Indian women
were racially inferior. More significant perhaps, British feminists defended
the morality of Indian prostitutes against stereotypes of Indian female
licentiousness. Butler's dissatisfaction with Dyer's attitude toward Indian
prostitutes has already been referred to. She objected to his characterizations because he depicted them as brazen harlots rather than as victims of a
foreign system of exploitation and abuse.[150] Butler flatly denied that Indian
women had "no moral sense," citing the testimony of William Gladwin, a
missionary who had lived in India "almost along native lines." Butler had
the story from Maurice Gregory, and she reprinted it as follows:

> He was speaking to me of the chastity of poor Coolie women, so much
> maligned in recent Despatches between the Government of India and
> Lord George Hamilton. Pointing to a group of these, graceful in
> figure and pleasing in features, who were working at the roadside . . .
> digging and carrying earth and stones, he said: "These women could
> get both hands filled with silver at once if they would sell themselves
> to sin; but they choose rather to work at that hard labour, for seven
> days a week, at two pence per day wages." . . . As Mr. Gladwin spoke, [I
> felt] that I was in the presence of really noble women, a moral aristoc-
> racy, far higher than that which a title bestowed by an earthly monarch
> can create.[151]

 As this quotation illustrates, defense of Indian women's morality was one
way of defining Indian women in British feminist terms. Gregory's recom-
mendation of Indian women as "a moral aristocracy" put them on the same

footing as British women, whose own moral superiority was understood to be the justification of their feminist, as well as of their imperialist, reform activity.

Although repeal workers gleaned some of what they knew of Indian conditions from male observers like Gregory and Gladwin, their main source of information on the "morality" of Indian women was from the observations of Elizabeth Andrew and Katharine Bushnell, the two American "lady commissioners" of the LNA and the British Committee. Their "Indian Journal" provides a rare opportunity for examining repealers' attitudes toward contemporary Indian women in situ. Several qualifications need to be made from the outset. They used England as a base for their travels to the East throughout the 1890s. As American temperance reformers, they sympathized with the repeal cause. I have not been able to determine which side of the Butler-Somerset split they supported, but their writings after 1897 stress, as Butler did, the central importance of regulation over other reforms. Like Butler, they were devout Christians whose evangelism informed their perspective on both Indian repeal and empire. The nature of their task did not require any explicit commentary on the British imperial mission, but they shared English repealers' sense of outrage at the state of prostitution as well as the military's indifference to Indian women's fate. Finally, the journal was addressed to the members of the British Committee, which had commissioned their trip to India in late 1891. As noted earlier, it was intended as evidence of the continued operation of regulation throughout India, although the departmental committee before which this evidence was given had not yet been formed when they left for India. The journal is not a diary in the strictest sense of the word, since it was not kept on a daily basis. It was written by hand in India, mainly by Bushnell, who apparently wrote a little every few days about what they had seen as they traveled between military stations. I have chosen to analyze the journal because of the personal contact between repeal women and Indian prostitutes it describes as well as the sense of immediacy and urgency it conveys. In *The Queen's Daughters in India*, which was based on the journal, Bushnell and Andrew devoted as much space to laying out the history of Indian repeal and detailing LNA responses as they did to talking about Indian women.[152] Their book had its own polemical purpose but lacks the intimacy suggested (and intended) by the journal form.

Between their arrival in Calcutta in December 1891 and their return to England in March 1892, Bushnell and Andrew traveled nearly 4,000 miles and visited ten different military stations in India. According to their report, they studied 637 cases of cantonment prostitutes and interviewed 395 persons. Ignorance of the language and unfamiliarity with the intricacies of military rule made their first month useless. Once in Lucknow, they obtained interpreters, whom they described as two female friends "able to talk the Hindustani language." Upon their entrance into the compound they were greeted by a *dhai* (medical attendant) and surrounded by girl prostitutes, who led them into the *chakla* (women's quarters). The *dhai* explained to them that she was paid twelve rupees a months for taking care of the girls. The girls themselves described how they were examined on Tuesdays and Fridays and, "if found diseased," were removed to the lock hospital. Among the people Bushnell and Andrew remarked on in the first *chakla* of their tour was the *mahaldarni*, the matron in charge of procuring prostitutes for the Lancers' regiment, who was "decked out gorgeously with solid gold ornaments, worth hundreds of rupees." They also noticed a two-year-old boy and learned that his father was a British soldier. "He had a beautiful forehead, and plainly showed European blood."[153]

As in all the cantonments, the American repealers tried to give a general description of the physical layout of the Lucknow *chakla*. They described the women's quarters as "a large, pretentious place" with a high wall enclosing a courtyard. The buildings were grim and the windows barred by wood. But what really interested Bushnell and Andrew were the mechanisms of procurement. When a girl was "a candidate for a life of shame," they reported, she went first to the *mahaldarni*, who took her straight to the cantonment magistrate. The girl then paid nine rupees for an application, which was turned over to an inspector. If she was pronounced fit after she was examined for disease, she was returned to the *mahaldarni*, who took her to the *chakla*. The pay scale for services rendered was as follows: one rupee from a sergeant, eight annas from a corporal, and four annas from a private soldier. Elsewhere an officer could be charged up to five rupees. The *mahaldarni* took between one-fourth and one-eighth of the girls' receipts, which, Bushnell and Andrew hinted, explained her gold jewelry.[154]

As they moved from cantonment to cantonment, what they found were variations on the same theme: the government continued to regulate prostitution, either through registration of women, medical inspection, or both.[155] Bushnell and Andrew generally visited lock hospitals first (the one in Meerut was built "like an English bungalow"), where they spoke with the *dhais* and even sometimes with native doctors. At nearly every stop they used interpreters to help them communicate with the people they wanted to interview. Bushnell and Andrew were amazed at how open the doctors were about the fact that their facilities were used for examining women. But it was the *mahaldarnis* who proved the most willing to talk. From them they learned the details of periodic examination and were able to confirm the suspicions of the British Committee that those women who did not submit were expelled from the cantonments.[156] An overseer told them that when a soldier found himself diseased, he went to the hospital officials and told them which woman had infected him. She was then "hunted up" and sent to the lock hospital. One *dhai* boasted that she made a good living, with the government paying them fifteen rupees a month for their work in the hospitals. This would prove fuel for the repeal fire at home, where the immorality of the state's participation was one of the campaigners' most powerful arguments against regulation. In Rawal Pindi several annoyed *mahaldarnis* apparently resented the insinuation of the Americans that they were accepting blood money and defended themselves with the reminder that they were in the employ of the Indian government.[157]

Bushnell and Andrew discovered what they set out to find: evidence that Indian women were still being subjected to examinations in the cantonments and that these examinations were not voluntary, as the statutes dictated, but required if the women wanted to remain within the military station. Their host in one of the stations, a district pleader, informed them that for natives to be thrown out of the cantonments was the equivalent of expatriation. In Meerut they positioned themselves outside the lock hospital on a day when medical inspections were being carried out and watched with horror as the women filed in to be examined, describing the process as "fearfully demoralizing." Much of their testimony was based on conversations with Indian prostitutes, the majority of whom told Bushnell and Andrew that when hospitalized, it had been against their will. One woman explained that she had been detained in a lock hospital because the native doctor in charge "wanted her for the accommodation of his brother-in-law." She managed to escape and found a legal writer to petition the magistrate to take action against the doctor. After Bushnell and Andrew's unsuccessful attempt to intervene with the authorities on her behalf, she was returned to the hospital to wait out the duration of her treatment for disease.[158]

The Indian prostitutes in Bushnell and Andrew's journal are characterized in two ways: as conscious of their shame and as helpless victims of the repeal system—often simultaneously. Bushnell recorded that women often covered their faces when the Americans approached "because the bad women did not wish the good women to see their faces." Several along the route confessed their repentance for their "lives of shame" and, according to the account, begged to be allowed to go to England. Everywhere they visited, Bushnell and Andrew reported that Indian women knew that what they were doing was wrong. Seeking explanations for how these women had ended up where they did, the reformers cited seduction by soldiers and persistent poverty. According to their journal, resistance to regulation was rare and unsuccessful. One prostitute explained the examination process to them "in a passion of indignation," and Bushnell went on to say how the Indian woman's "whole soul revolted in disgust against the indecencies practiced against women." But the helplessness of the prostitutes against their fate was the overall conclusion that Bushnell and Andrew felt compelled to draw from their observations. "Words fail to convey the force and fire and pathos with which this poor untaught woman pleaded the cause of her sisters. It was one voice out of many protesting against this cruel wrong, and representing the undying dignity of a woman's nature, even when forced into deeper abysses than she ever voluntarily chose to enter."[159]

Ironically in terms of Anglo-American reformers' emphasis on their own interventionist capacities, what emerges from the journal is Bushnell and Andrew's own apparent helplessness, especially in cases where they tried to intervene on behalf of individual women. With a Brahmin prostitute in Sitapur, their failure was due to an inability to communicate: the young woman could not understand the Hindustani of their interpreters, and they had to give up helping her get out the lock hospital.[160] Bushnell and Andrew got more involved with the case of another young prostitute named Itwaria. When they first met her in Lucknow, they took to her immediately: "She was attractive in appearance, and did not look like a bad girl; hung her head in shame at meeting good women, and yet was irresistibly drawn to them." She spoke English and eventually confessed to them that she wanted to "leave her life of shame" and go away with them. They were "haunted" by her face. After some discussion they were able to persuade Itwaria to get into their cab with them as they headed for their next cantonment, but at the last minute she leapt out, telling them she had to get permission from the police to leave. The police in turn would not let her leave until she had been examined. Bushnell and Andrew attempted to find her a doctor, but when none could be found, they took her to a magistrate. Evidently under pressure from the Americans, the magistrate told Itwaria she was free to go—but he also told them frankly that he could not guarantee that she would not be molested by soldiers and that if she left she could not come back.[161]

Itwaria ultimately decided to remain, both because the magistrate could not promise her protection and because her mother and sister still resided within the cantonment. Bushnell and Andrew tried to encourage her to take refuge in a mission home, but their attempts were not successful and they left Itwaria behind. They did not comment on her desire to stay with her own kin inside the cantonment and may have even viewed the sisters and mother as part of the problem rather than as part of Itwaria's wider net of local support and female solidarity.[162] As they wrote of another prostitute, "She was held by invisible chains, and we felt that we got only the faintest possible hint of the obstacles in her way."[163] The case of Itwaria is ultimately significant not just because it demonstrates the impact of government legislation on Indian women or even the futility of Bushnell and Andrew's efforts. It testifies both simply and dramatically to the power of regulation over Indian women's lives.

As with emancipationist writers' depiction of Eastern females, Indian prostitutes' apparent helplessness served as a subtle foil to Western women's saving role. Time and again Bushnell described the respect accorded to them by Indian women, who by her account pinned all their hopes on the two visiting reformers: "It was pitiful to us to see them following us from window to window, after we had said good-bye and were walking in the lane outside,—begging us to come again, smiling on us and salaaming, with tender respect."[164]

Itwaria was not the only Indian prostitute who begged the Americans to take her with them. At Meerut, for example, Bushnell reported, "They all said, after we had talked with them awhile, that if they could come and live with us, they would always be good" and that they would follow the repealers back to England if allowed. In these anecdotes Bushnell emphasized the Indian women's sense of identification with herself and Andrew and implied that Indian women recognized them as "good" in comparison with their own "lives of shame." The queen of England was also invoked by Indian women as a model of goodness and as a defender of their rights as women. The same Indian woman who had railed so eloquently against the medical examinations told the Americans that Indian prostitutes knew that it was the commander in chief who demanded inspection, but that the queen did not approve it. Bushnell and Andrew reported that the prostitutes in Peshawar expressed similar sentiments, and this may well be why they titled their book *The Queen's Daughters in India*.[165]

Bushnell and Andrew's findings "sent a thrill of sympathy for our Indian sisters throughout the whole of Great Britain."[166] Before the publication of *The Queen's Daughters in India*, excerpts from their testimony to the departmental committee and from their journal were printed in various repeal and feminist journals, including the *Dawn*, which Butler edited. In these articles Bushnell and Andrew recounted their conversations with Indian prostitutes in the cantonments and reiterated that, contrary to what military officials reported, Indian women were *not* without shame. Of all the Indian prostitutes they interviewed, Andrew boasted, "*not one* ever defended her way of living." As they had in their journal, the Americans again emphasized the helplessness of the women they had encountered for their British reading public. Like Butler, the majority of repealers did not deny that the imported European system of regulation was responsible for the suffering of Indian women. But, unlike Butler, Bushnell and Andrew did not spare what they perceived as the oppression of native custom. "On *every* Oriental woman's head is set a price, she is regarded merely as a *chattel*," lamented Bushnell and Andrew. "She has no rights in herself, and no liberty of choice as to whether she will be pure or not."[167] The extent to which these interpretations were broadcast may be evidenced in the speaking tours Bushnell and Andrew made throughout Britain after their return from India. They addressed large LNA gatherings and traveled to smaller branches, delivering lectures entitled "Social Questions in the Orient" and "The Inextinguishable Sentiment of Dignity in Eastern Womanhood" to a wide variety of female reform and feminist organizations.[168] The British Committee published a pamphlet based on their observations called "Facts Recorded by Eye-Witnesses, and Josephine Butler hailed their work in her own writing and public speeches through the turn of the century.[169]

The sympathy for Indian women generated by Bushnell and Andrew's account intensified the feelings of responsibility that repealers already felt for their "Indian sisters." Between sympathy and responsibility lay the helplessness of Indian women, and it was their dependence on British reformers that moved Butler the most. In an editorial comment in the *Stormbell* of June 1898, Butler lamented that Indian women were "indeed between the upper and nether millstone, helpless, voiceless, hopeless. Their helplessness appeals to the heart, in somewhat the same way in which the helplessness and suffering of a dumb animal does, under the knife of a vivisector. Somewhere, halfway between the Martyr Saints and the tortured 'friend of man,' the noble dog, stand, it seems to me, these pitiful Indian women, girls, children, as many of them are."[170] While this comment tells us something about Butler's sympathy for the antivivisectionist movement— and may well be, as Vron Ware suggests, an attempt to find a "new and more powerfully politically charged language to express her views on the oppression of women"[171]—it is also an unself-conscious disclosure of how she perceived the ordering of a world that she believed to contain imperial and colonial peoples as well as imperial and colonial women. The professed equality of Indian women evaporated in Butler's sympathetic yet thoroughly hierarchical conception of the world of women. Expressing sentiments that neatly parallel the "logic" of Britain's imperial presence in India, Butler hoped that under the tutelage of British female social reformers, Indian women would be led "into a position of greater freedom and light, which will enable them to fight their own battles."[172] In the interim, she viewed India's women as helpless victims and repealers like Bushnell and Andrew as "the mothers of the orphaned girls in India."[173]

Butler's comment reveals the power dynamic operating throughout the depictions of Indian women in the Indian campaign. Given the imperial culture in which the women's movement developed in Victorian Britain, that dynamic is not strictly imperial but more appropriately imperial-feminist. Identifying such an imperial-feminist power dynamic helps to clarify Bushnell's and others' repeated emphasis on Indian prostitutes' recognition of their own shame. At one level, it was part of the repealers' attempts to construct Indian women as equal—not only with English prostitutes but also with the reformers themselves, who also recognized the shame of the prostitute even if they refused to name it as such. More significantly, the fact that Indian women themselves admitted that they were unhappy justified the intervention of repeal workers and in fact made Indian women seem compliant in their own salvation. British repealers were seeking a role for themselves in the Indian crusade that a dependent Indian womanhood provided. The image of an enslaved Indian prostitute in need of rescue by her British feminist sisters furnished repeal women with imperial purpose that structured their commitment to Indian reform. This phenomenon by no means originated with the Indian repeal campaign. It resonated with a long tradition of feminist journalism—by the 1890s, the nineteenth-century women's movement was at least three decades old in Britain. This tradition, evidenced by both pamphlet literature and periodicals like the *Englishwoman's Review*, had depicted Indian women as sad and pathetic prisoners of Eastern custom and prejudice. Butler's crusade made those images even more realistic, and, perhaps most significant, to them she added the weight of her considerable—and, even by the 1880s, her historically feminist—reform authority.

That the instrumentality of Indian women for reinforcing British women's imperial identity did not depend exclusively on Butler herself is especially obvious in her use of Bushnell and Andrew's evidence. For Butler placed an enormous premium on the fact that the Americans' testimony had been based on their personal experience of the cantonments. Theirs was evidence "of what they had seen and known of the Indian women and cantonment life in India," which would "dispel false and misleading statements coming from interested sources." The value of their testimony de-

rived especially from the fact that they were women. From the beginning of
the Indian crusade, Butler believed that the strength of their case lay in the
fact that it was "a woman's argument . . . [about] the wickedness of such
treatment of women."[174] As she wrote ten years later in an 1898 issue of the
Stormbell, Bushnell and Andrew's "intimate personal knowledge of Indian
women gives to the evidence of these friends a rare authority on the subject
of the influence on the native populations of India of the base regulations
of vice established and re-established there by Government. Government
officials know nothing of the minds of Indian women, least of all the
women enslaved and outraged under this system."[175]

The idea that only women could know the true needs of other women
was a long-standing presumption of the repeal movement. As Butler remarked toward the end of her life, "It is perfectly true that women will see
things in connection with our betrayed sisters which men do not so easily
see, and that they will have influence in . . . drawing information from them
which one would not expect men to have in the same way."[176] In the case of
Indian women, Butler equated commonality of gender with knowledge
about Indian women's lives, privileging that female-to-female knowledge
over the empirical evidence of government officials. In her preface to *The
Queen's Daughters in India*, she praised Bushnell and Andrew because they
alone had told "the truth, the terrible truth" about the condition of Indian
women.[177] Books, pamphlets, speeches, and periodical literature connected
to or reporting on the Indian repeal crusade all deployed images of Indian
women to a feminist public and made knowledge about their plight the
possession of hundreds of women reformers in the last decades of the
nineteenth century. This reinforced the general Victorian feminist premise
that there was work for British women in the colonial sphere—that "work"
being Indian women themselves.

Given the fact that the LNA only received such "knowledge" secondhand and that such secondhand knowledge was based mainly on Indian
women designated as or assumed to be prostitutes, the repealers' claim
to have learned "the truth about Indian women" through the accounts
of Bushnell and Andrew is extremely problematic.[178] Yet while English
women reformers sought to exercise power over Indian women, an equally
important site of their struggle for power and legitimacy was the male
political and military establishments. Their task was to prove the viability of
a role for empire, and the cause of Indian women was essential to that
proof. Butler and her followers offered support for the imperial-moral
enterprise by pledging English women's philanthropic activity on behalf of
colonized peoples. To do so was to ally the female reform cause to the

imperial one by making the two mutually dependent. Butler tended to view empire as a field of opportunity for English women, a place for them to exercise their philanthropic skills among deserving natives. "Have you leisure? Have you strength?" If so, she assured of her audience in 1887, "there is a career open, a wide field extending to many parts of the world, a far-off cry of distress waiting for response."[179] As Victorian feminists knew from reading the feminist press, the British Empire and its dominions provided a vast and uncharted workplace for female reform efforts within which British women could prove their imperial worth. Butler's Indian campaign—and the pathos that accompanied its representations to home audiences—gave them even more concrete evidence that Indian women needed feminist intervention and that the imperial space inhabited by colonized women was a fair field for the exercise of British women's imperial authority—no less than of their reform skills. Indeed, in the political culture of late-nineteenth-century British feminism, reform work and imperial authority might be read as practically one in the same.

The success of the Indian cause was, in addition, invaluable to British women in the international reform scene, testifying as it did to the leadership of Anglo-Saxon women. Butler viewed the accounts of Bushnell and Andrew as a showpiece that she recommended be given a prominent place at the Continental Abolitionist Federation's international congress at the Hague in 1893.[180] In the planning of the 1898 congress, which was to be in London, Butler also asked that India be very prominent, declaring that she wanted "to show our foreign friends what an *English* public meeting can be. It will do *much* good, for they really do look to England for inspiration."[181] It would seem that when writing the history of the domestic campaign after repeal at home in 1886, Butler and other repealers stressed the concern of the first repeal activists for India and highlighted the presence of Indians at some of the first meetings. There is no doubt about the participation of these Indians, mainly men, or the import of India in those initial stages. Dadhabai Naoroji had been a member of the British Committee since its foundation, and attending its meeting sporadically in the late 1880s and early 1890s depended largely on whether his parliamentary seat required his presence in London.[182] But that Butler especially should have been so concerned to make Indians appear prominent in her retrospective account of the repeal movement suggests her own recognition of the stature that the imperial phase lent to continued reform and agitation. The LNA's associations with Indian nationalists might have added to the prestige, especially since in this period the Indian National Congress was eager to continue India's association with the Raj.[183] Empire, for all its faults, was supremely desirable and, finally, absolutely necessary to the Victorian British women's movement. Identification with empire and inclusion in it remained critical to Butler's reform objectives throughout the Indian repeal campaign, and, as a result, it became one of the hallmarks of modern British feminist ideology and liberal reformist practice.

THE LAST PHASE (1900–1915) AND THE LIMITS OF IMPERIAL FEMINIST PRACTICE

The decade and a half between the turn of the century and the outbreak of war was one of ongoing work for repeal activists. Despite the push in the late 1890s to suspend regulation once and for all in the Indian cantonments, the examination of Indian prostitutes persisted.[184] So too did the LNA's commitment to the abolition of state-regulated vice in the colonies and dependencies.[185] The deaths of many prominent repeal activists and a decline in subscriptions to the LNA reduced the ranks of the Indian campaign considerably.[186] And yet those who remained were determined to carry on repeal work in the empire. "The old ship, damaged as she is, is not yet gone down," wrote one contributor to the *Shield*. "The doctors are at her, . . . making every effort to keep her afloat."[187] Significantly, at the time of Butler's death in 1906 the British Committee and the LNA both undertook a reevaluation of their goals and principles; they decided that, as long as regulation still operated in the empire, whether officially or unofficially, they would continue to make imperial concerns the focus of their activities. What had begun as an escalation of imperial rhetoric in 1887 was by the twentieth century fully established in the LNA's platform. As the lifelong repealer Helen Wilson phrased it in 1908: "England is still the mother country, and has the mother influence. She has that influence for both good and evil; mistakes she made years ago, though she may have repented them, are apt to be perpetuated in her children beyond the seas."[188]

While reports on the situation in the cantonments continued to appear in the *Shield* and in LNA annual meetings and reports, after 1900 the focus was no longer on India alone. Bushnell and Andrew traveled to Hawaii and Japan as commissioners for the LNA; a British Committee agent, Maurice Gregory, also went to Japan, Hong Kong, and Australia to investigate the operation of the Contagious Diseases Acts.[189] Increasingly too repealers became involved in the problem of the white slave trade, sending delegates to international congresses and working in connection with the National Vigilance Association at home for parliamentary support of age-of-consent bills. And there were changes in the tenor of the Indian campaign as well. Even before Butler's death in 1906, the privileging of colonial women as the focus of repeal attention gave way to concern for the soldier. This took the form of articles in the *Shield* about the importance of soldiers' well-being in the far-flung corners of empire as well as financial support for soldiers' homes in India.[190] Butler herself may have fueled this new direction with her book *Silent Victories*, which dealt with the suffering of British soldiers and the efforts of army purity associations to help them during the Boer War. The condition of Indian women, however, was not completely abandoned. By 1910 the LNA was supporting the creation of rescue homes for Indian women in Northern India—the first material contribution that repealers had made to Indian women's lives since the beginning of the Indian crusade.[191] When the First World War erupted, regulation was still in effect, though British repeal policy now constructed British soldiers and Indian women equally as victims of colonial regulation.[192]

In the final analysis, the contribution of the Indian repeal crusade to the formation of an imperial feminist identity was considerable. Josephine Butler's own Christian feminist imperialism shaped the international commitment of British repeal and her influence cannot be underestimated. As Brian Harrison has written, because of her repeal leadership, antiregulation was practically an article of feminist faith in the Victorian period.[193] And thanks in part to her insistence on Indian women's suffering under the Contagious Diseases Acts, the imperial commitments of British feminist women were a crucial, if not a central, tenet of feminism in the late nineteenth and early twentieth centuries as well. Without the emphasis she placed on Indian women and the pressure she exerted on the LNA to keep to regulation as the central issue, the reform leadership might well have strayed away from empire as well as from repeal. In private Butler described Henry Wilson as "almost brutally English in his views."[194] In contrast, James Stuart said of Butler: "Undoubtedly, of all English people, [she] is the one who is most penetrated with the foreign point of view of our cause."[195] Butler's personal charisma and the enormous respect repeal workers throughout Greater Britain had for her resulted in the incorporation of her imperial feminist philosophy into the very structure of repeal organizations and guaranteed that the imperial direction that she gave to the post-1886 campaign would continue to motivate the repeal program until World War I.

The significance of Butler's imperial reform lies not, finally, in the successes or failures of the Indian repeal movement but rather in its impact on British feminist ideology and feminist-imperial identity in this period. Butler's commitment to India certainly underscored the apparent responsibility

of British feminists for the salvation of Indian women; it also contributed
to the creation of a self-consciously imperial identity for a second, post-
1886 generation of British repeal women, their feminist reform sympathizers, and, in turn, the organizations they oversaw. And it defined some
of the strategic limitations of feminist imperial activism. Readers of this
chapter may be puzzled to find that few if any LNA women went to India
and that the LNA, which generated so much rhetoric about the condition
of Indian women, did little financially or organizationally to improve it.
And yet, given the strategies that operated in Victorian feminist political
culture, this is not entirely unpredictable. Repeal had, since its first phase in
the 1860s, always been a single-issue campaign: it was about the abolition of
regulation, the removal of legal restraints on women's behavior and of
governmental constraints in women's lives. And although repeal at home
gave rise to many related causes, Butler and, because of her, the LNA
remained singularly committed to the work of legislative abolition. This was
no less true in the Indian context than in the pre-1886 campaign. Butler
supported the efforts of missionary women, temperance women, and reform organizations that worked in India and on behalf of Indian women—
and while she might have wished for some overlap between repealers and
social missionaries on the ground in the empire, this never materialized.[196]
Her immediate cause was the repeal of regulation, and she prioritized that
above all other causes—all but one, that is, and the exception is significant:
women's suffrage. She believed, along with many other repeal workers, that
votes for women would make the reinstatement of the Contagious Diseases
Acts and similarly discriminatory legislation impossible and, ultimately,
unthinkable. As she wrote to the editor of the *Auckland Star* in 1895,

> How often, in the course of the long crusade, we in England have
> wished that we had possessed the suffrage. Its possession would have
> saved us from much painful agitation in the past; and in the present, if
> we were voters, we should be much stronger in our vigilant efforts to
> keep out attempts at the re-introduction of these laws, and in the
> gradual but most necessary work of enlightening our legislators on the
> great and vital questions involved in the struggle. We envy the women
> of New Zealand the position they now hold, and it would be a bitter
> grief to us, and a subject of self-abasement as women if it could be said
> throughout the world that the first group of Anglo-Saxon women
> who possessed the vote had failed to use it in this great and purifying
> work.[197]

Butler was not of course the only one to connect repeal with suffrage work in the Victorian period.[198] Such connections were not self-evident, however, and indeed were fraught with difficulty. Many suffrage women, including the later leader of the National Union of Women's Suffrage Societies, Millicent Fawcett, had distanced themselves from repeal in the 1860s and 1870s, and the kinds of associations made between prostitution, venereal disease, and votes for women remained explosive into the early twentieth century, as the furor over Christabel Pankhurst's *The Great Scourge* testifies. The LNA certainly worked hard to insist upon the necessity of votes for women to the repeal cause in the 1890s and after, and I would suggest that it was the Indian-colonial crusade that kept these connections alive for suffrage women down to World War I.[199] The Indian campaign and the imperial rhetoric that Butler and her fellow repealers deployed into the twentieth century helped to cast the Edwardian suffrage movement in an imperial mold. As the next chapter illustrates, there were other strategic reasons for this as well. But there is no doubt that the solidarity on which Butler insisted between Indian prostitutes and British women stemmed from a vision of international sisterhood; suffrage women capitalized on this vision in arguments for votes for women, and its feminist origins were attributed to Butler herself after her death.[200] It was an internationalism premised on the imperial supremacy of British women in the world of women no less than of Britain across the globe; it relied on images of helpless Indian women for its rhetorical force and its cultural and political persuasiveness. As the white woman's—and the white feminist's—burden, Indian women represented not simply a reformable clientele but the colonial subjects in whose name British women's political authority in the imperial nation-state was justified and, in terms of feminist imperial ideology, apparently justifiable.

6

A Girdle round the Earth

BRITISH IMPERIAL SUFFRAGE AND THE

IDEOLOGY OF GLOBAL SISTERHOOD

Although some Victorian feminists distanced themselves from the delicate subject of prostitution in Britain and, consequently, from Butler's pre-1886 repeal campaign on behalf of "fallen women," there was little question in the minds of suffrage workers that the sexual regulation of Indian women was a matter of national and imperial importance.[1] Perhaps even more so than the British prostitutes who were of concern to repealers in the 1860s and 1870s, British feminists viewed the plight of Indian women who were subject to regulation as their special responsibility—thus lending some credence to Millicent Garrett Fawcett's lament that "the philanthropy of the English people, especially of English ladies, is never called into genuine activity unless the people on whose behalf it is invoked are black. . . . The inhabitants of Boorioboolagha can win sympathy and succour where the inhabitants of Whitechapel would find us hard as flints."[2]

Her rueful tone notwithstanding, Fawcett's remarks, as well as the virtually unqualified support of the British women's movement for the LNA's

Indian campaign, reflect the extent to which British feminists depended, especially in the twentieth century, on the cause of Indian women to ratify the political claims they made on the imperial nation-state. What was true of arguments for female emancipation in the most general sense in the nineteenth century could be—and was, emphatically—said about the cause of women's suffrage after 1900: it was believed to be nothing short of a national imperative and an imperial necessity. Indian women, whose status and condition preoccupied suffrage writers in the twentieth century, were crucial to this argument, providing what was considered to be evidence of British women's capacity to shoulder the burdens required of imperial citizens. As they had in other feminist contexts, images of the colonialized Indian woman allowed British suffragists and suffragettes equally to argue that they were already demonstrating their imperial capabilities by virtue of their concern for and involvement in Indian women's lives. "The responsibilities of Empire," wrote the editor of the suffragist organ *Common Cause* in May 1913, "rest on women as well as men. If it were only for the sake of India, women here in Great Britain would be bound to demand the vote."[3] For her as for others, "that vast multitude of silent and too suffering women" signified an imperial feminist burden that ennobled their cause, inspired workers at home, and alerted British women to the kinds of power they might wield in the empire once they got the vote. Suffrage writers often connected women's enfranchisement to the end of the white slave trade and to the dismantling of regulated prostitution in India; this may in fact account for the rapprochement between repealers and suffragists after 1886.[4] Although the so-called plight of Indian women was important in order to prove feminism's imperial commitments to opponents of women's suffrage, it served as an education in imperial duties for women suffragists in Britain as well. Butler's Indian campaign focused what had been decades of British feminist interest in Indian women on the necessity of women's suffrage at home for the sake of "our Indian sisters" in the empire. Knowledge about Indian women—along with understanding, "the first condition of all mutual help"—fitted British feminists for imperial service and made its social and political effectiveness contingent on votes for women in the imperial nation.[5]

If suffrage was marked as an imperialized discourse in the early twentieth century, it remained, as it had been in the Victorian period, egalitarian and international in its rhetoric as well. "Sisterhood" was the watchword of women's suffrage in Britain in much the same way it was in other discourses about female social reform, and it gave feminism a collective and familial basis upon which much of the legitimacy of the quest for female emancipation rested. Regardless of party affiliation or tactical philosophy, women working for the vote shared Josephine Butler's belief that "the womanhood of the world is *solidaire*."[6] The implication was that women the world over were similarly oppressed and therefore equally deserving of enfranchisement—though the how and the when of female emancipation outside of Britain was perhaps less of a priority than developing arguments about women's collective unity on the basis of gender. "No nationality, no political creed, no class distinction, no difference of any sort divides us as women," Annie Kenney told a group of women in Frankfurt in 1907. "We are true to womanhood first of all."[7] As jarring as it may be to late-twentieth-century feminists, Edwardian suffrage workers frequently talked about "Woman" and "Womanhood," claiming these monolithic categories for the "woman movement." According to one suffrage song of the International Woman Suffrage Alliance, "Whatever our race or country be . . . we are one nation/Womanhood."[8] While this was a philosophy shared across suffrage divisions, political commitment to "Everywoman" could also be nuanced by the same terms that defined the militant-constitutionalist divide.[9] Writing for *Votes for Women* in November 1907, Evelyn Sharp reassured her readers that "every woman . . . is by nature a suffragette, whether she has discovered it or not."[10] Even if constitutionalists might contest her claim that women were naturally militant, they generally agreed that the women's movement was international in scope and that from this internationalism it derived much of its strength and its credibility. According to Millicent Garrett Fawcett, it was "the world-wide nature of this movement" that proved the vitality and universalism of claims to female emancipation.[11] The sense of competition exhibited by some British feminists toward their suffrage fellows in other European countries suggests that "internationalism" was not always as equable or as sisterly as its enthusiasts purported.[12] As Ian Tyrrell has written, however, "The *assertions* of feminist leaders concerning the strength of internationalist sentiment must nonetheless be scrutinized as constituent parts of feminist ideology and practice."[13]

There was at times a certain humility among suffrage workers in Britain about their role in advancing the worldwide Cause. Suffrage periodicals regularly featured the work of suffrage women in other lands, especially in the settler dominions of the empire, where the implementation of white women's suffrage was considered a successful experiment in imperial female enfranchisement.[14] Suffrage organizations hosted suffrage women who were either passing through the United Kingdom, attending conferences in London, or taking up extended residence in Britain. Expressions of sympathy with other women's suffrage struggles were not uncommon in executive committee minutes or in the suffrage press; they could even be adopted as formal resolutions—as when members of the Women's Freedom League resolved to recognize "that women are working for freedom all the world over" and that "we are simply one of many societies working for that end."[15] The fact that the headquarters of the International Woman Suffrage Alliance were in London meant that its affiliates had the opportunity to meet a variety of foreign visitors sympathetic to women's rights in the first two decades of the twentieth century. International conferences also provided forums for British feminists to encounter women with similar interests and to get a sense of national differences among women's suffrage movements. "The cause is a world-wide one," wrote Mary Sheepshanks, English secretary for the International Woman Suffrage Alliance, "and every country and every individual gains in inspiration and knowledge by these meetings with women of all countries, all bound together in a common movement for liberty."[16] By 1914—when the war and the question of pacifism shattered some (though by no means all) of British feminism's transnational connections—the ideology of international sisterhood animated virtually every aspect of the Cause.

At the same time, British women active in the suffrage movement believed that Britain was the "storm-centre" of the women's movement—the "home of the rebellion," as Teresa Billington-Greig put it—and that consequently British women would and should lead the way for other feminist movements to follow.[17] Elizabeth Wolstenholme Elmy summarized the sentiments of many of her contemporaries in the pamphlet "Woman's Franchise: The Need of the Hour": "The woman's movement is now in the fullest sense an international one, and whatever is one for women in these islands would therefore speedily be achieved for the women of all civilised nations, and would of necessity lead to the speedy development all the world over of a higher social and political morality. And such a higher social and political morality is vital to the well-being of the race, and essential to its upward and onward progress."[18] Such convictions stemmed from the assumption that Anglo-Saxon racial superiority guaranteed the supremacy of British women's suffrage. This was not simply because Great Britain was "the Mother of Parliaments," though the phrase, evocative of the maternal authority that feminists sought to wield in the empire, was used by more than one suffrage writer.[19] Rather, as Maude Royden claimed, it was "because all representative governments in the world owe something to her traditions and experiences . . . all are the offspring of the one mother—the Parliament of Great Britain."[20] Organizations like the International Woman Suffrage Alliance and the International Council of Women, albeit founded on international cooperation and equality, echoed these sentiments. The president of the IWSA, American suffragist Carrie Chapman Catt, encouraged Britain's imperial leadership; the ICW, headed initially by Fawcett, was called "an Imperial Parliament," made up of "what one might call colonial councils of women."[21] This characterization is more metaphorical than factual, since the membership of both groups was predominantly Western before World War I, but the choice of imperial language is appropriate to describe the top-down manner in which international societies tended to be run.[22] British feminist—and more specifically, Anglo-American suffrage—internationalism was predicated on the assumption that Western women would lead the women of the East to freedom and that American and British suffrage leaders would spearhead the charge. The political enfranchisement of women in New Zealand, in Norway, and in certain Indian municipalities, together with Egyptian women's activism and the fact of constitutional government in Turkey, qualified this triumphalist rhetoric but only partially. Progress toward emancipation elsewhere was alternately hailed and resented, as British suffragists expressed increasing anxiety over the tardiness of women's suffrage in Britain after 1910.[23]

Indian women, whose "suffering" figured centrally in British suffrage rhetoric, were crucial not just to the Cause in Britain but to the ideology of global sisterhood that underwrote the entire British suffrage movement. British suffrage women, like the feminists who wrote for the *Englishwoman's Review*, devoted a considerable amount of space to Indian women in their periodicals. Some favorable characterizations notwithstanding, Indian women were generally depicted by Edwardian suffragists in the same way they had been by Victorian feminist interpreters: as the victims of heathen religious practice and as powerless in their own society. In the context of the suffrage campaign, "the Indian woman" took on additional symbolic meanings. She was thought to be deficient in feminist consciousness *and* she constituted an unrepresented colonial constituency. As members of the imperial nation, British suffrage writers justified "votes for women" partly on the grounds that Indian women needed their political influence and their feminist example—two kinds of patronage, they argued, that only British women could provide. In this sense, Indian women, as represented by suffragists, provided British women with an imperial identity that was linked directly to their demand for the vote. Significantly, imperial identification also allowed British suffragists to join the battle cry of "New Imperialism."[24] This they used to legitimize feminist claims to citizenship and to counter antisuffrage arguments that women did not deserve the vote because they were unfit to govern the British empire.[25] The Edwardian suffrage press, in other words, continued the tradition of Victorian feminist journalism, constructing "the Indian woman" as a means to feminist ends and linking her inextricably to arguments for women's political authority in the public-imperial sphere. It also articulated an international feminist vision whose promise of universal sisterhood came into constant conflict with British feminists' determination to lead the world of women to freedom. Indian women, apparently unrepresented in imperial government, became the grounds on which international sisterhood was imagined and British imperial suffrage was in turn rationalized. The fact that contemporary Indian women showed themselves capable and desirous of effecting their own emancipation made Western women's claims to represent them problematic, though British suffrage workers did not generally acknowledge it as such. For them, women's suffrage was like "a girdle round the earth"[26]—one that encircled and contained as much if not more than it liberated.

SUFFRAGE PERIODICALS AND
FEMINIST IDENTITY

For the advocates of votes for women, suffrage journals were absolutely essential to the Cause, both as publicity and as workshops for suffrage ideas and strategies.[27] The great variety of suffrage periodicals reflects the changing fortunes of the British suffrage movement over time. When Lydia Becker began her *Women's Suffrage Journal* in 1870, it was the first woman's magazine to deal specifically with the suffrage question.[28] This made it as much of a pioneering effort as the petitioning and suffrage agitation of those early societies about which it wrote. In addition to providing an arena for suffrage arguments, the magazine testified to the growing organizational strength of suffrage societies and to the fact that suffrage activity began in Manchester and the north. Only toward the end of the century did it become a London-centered phenomenon.[29] The keen interest that the *Women's Suffrage Journal* took in Indian and other "Oriental" women suggests that imperial concerns and assumptions transcended regional differences that at other times and over other issues could divide rather than unite suffragists.[30]

The absence of any strictly suffrage periodical between Becker's death in 1890 and the publication of the *Woman's Franchise* (National Union of Women's Suffrage Societies) and *Votes for Women* (Women's Social and Political Union) in 1907 reflects the disarray of the constitutional movement in the 1890s and the new direction taken by the whole suffrage cause with the

advent of the Pankhursts. To a large extent government debates and parliamentary possibilities dictated the content of suffrage periodicals. Every year
between 1870 and 1895 the House of Commons tabled a women's suffrage
bill, and every year the periodicals chronicled the raised expectations,
dashed hopes, and renewed determination of suffrage activists. In the
twentieth century the promise of Conciliation Bills from the Liberal government preoccupied both constitutionalists and militants for months at a
time and dominated the pages of all the suffrage journals, until their failure
prompted new strategies and provoked new fissures.[31] Before the production of twentieth-century suffrage periodicals, events pertinent to suffrage
were covered in other feminist journals. The *Englishwoman's Review*, for
example, ran a regular "Events of the Quarter" column that kept track of
parliamentary happenings. Conversely, the suffrage magazines did not exclude nonsuffrage reforms, causes, or personalities. Nonetheless, the pa-
trons and editors of suffrage periodicals conceived of them as traditionally
political organs. Investment in and publication of predominantly suffrage
periodicals was, along with the paraphernalia of suffrage pageantry, the
concrete manifestation of feminists' commitment to the vote as "the most
powerful instrument of usefulness which society in this country pos-
sesses."[32]

With the splintering of individuals and factions from the major suffrage
societies after 1907, suffrage periodicals became concrete evidence of the
strength and vitality of a particular political tack.[33] When Charlotte Despard and Teresa Billington-Greig left the Women's Social and Political
Union in 1907, one of the first things they did was to launch their own
journal, the *Vote*.[34] Although it was not a rival to the WSPU's *Votes for Women*
(it covered all kinds of suffrage news, including Pankhurst activities), it was
certainly a statement in itself of the divergence of suffrage viewpoints
within the movement. In the case of *Votes for Women*, philosophical differences and personal antagonisms directly affected the financial support and
the affiliation of the journal. When the Pethick-Lawrences quit the WSPU
in 1912 over irreconcilable differences with the Pankhurst directorate, they
denied the WSPU access to the journal that they had always funded and
edited in its name. The *Suffragette*, with its overt connotations of militancy,
emerged as the official organ of the WSPU after 1912 and was in large part
"Christabel's own paper."[35]

Discussion of the Pethick-Lawrences' defection (or revolt, depending on
which paper one read) was perfunctory in both publications but significant
nonetheless. Reading about these kinds of rifts in suffrage periodicals was
one of the only ways—aside from word of mouth or by letter—that other

suffrage workers could learn about divisions within the ranks, especially if they did not live in London. Presumably some would have demonstrated their continued allegiance to the Pankhursts by ending their subscription to *Votes for Women* and henceforth buying only the *Suffragette*. Suffrage women's decisions about organized participation could thus be determined as well as changed by journal reading. The act of subscribing to one or the other or both (or neither) was, like the publication of the periodicals themselves, an essential form of feminist practice during this period. And, given the particular political biases that suffrage journals came to embody, a woman's choice of subscription could become the expression of a specific kind of feminist identity because it involved a public identification with certain tactical philosophies within the suffrage movement itself.

In the context of "votes for women," this feminist identity was by definition and by tradition international.[36] Consciousness of a "female world" had enlarged suffragists' imaginative space since the Victorian era, encouraging them to seek connections with foreign women—in part perhaps to compensate for their frustrations with an unforgiving and unrelenting male public. To this end, suffrage periodicals in the early twentieth century provided a forum for uniting women the world over. There is some evidence, for example, that English women living abroad subscribed to *Votes for Women* and that the *Vote* received issues of Indian women's magazines.[37] Temperance organizations in India, which were run by both Anglo-Indians and Indians, had strong personal ties to British suffrage organizations. Frances Hallowes, national president of the World Woman's Christian Temperance Union of India, corresponded with Millicent Garrett Fawcett and was featured in *Common Cause* several times in the 1910s.[38] The Women's Freedom League appears to have had the most personal interaction with Indian women, several of whom participated in the Women's Coronation Procession and were said to be members of the league. Others also participated in an international fair organized by the league in 1912. These activities were all reported in detail, often with photographs, in several suffrage periodicals.[39]

Foreign women's access to British suffrage material was thought by suffrage organizers to be an essential means of spreading the suffrage gospel. Feminists abroad often wrote home, in letters reprinted in the suffrage journals, asking for copies of special issues to share with women friends in foreign parts. Like the women's movement itself, this material was considered a valuable British export, an essential ingredient in the conversion of the world of women to the British feminist cause. The semifictional story "Ajmairee: A Child Mother," from *Common Cause* of February 1914, testifies to the symbolic power with which feminists invested their own suffrage writing. It is the story of an Englishwoman's encounter with the Indian customs of child marriage and early motherhood. When Ajmairee's baby dies, the author, Eva Shaw McLaren (a prominent suffragist and sister of Henrietta Muller), goes to her home to comfort the grieving mother, and this is what she sees:

> Lying on the table was a white pamphlet, with blue lettering, *The Soul of Women's Suffrage*. And instantly, instead of the army of sorrowful children, there came a vision of the Women's Army! Women of every nation, and language, and creed. Women of all classes, and all schools of thought, bound together by the great Over-soul—by the Spirit of God Himself. And the great goal to which they are marching is the freedom of Womanhood. March on! Oh! gallant army of women![40]

Without putting too fine a point on it, the suffrage written word—written in English, with a *white* cover, and discovered in an Indian setting—had the power to conjure up the entire women's movement, at least for the English observer at the scene if not for Ajmairee. According to *Common Cause*, Eva McLaren had found comforting evidence of British women's work in India. As for the readers, they found both evidence of Indian women's dependence on British imperial feminism *and* of the internationalism of their cause.

Like the suffrage pamphlet in the McLaren's story, suffrage periodicals were an object lesson in British women's struggle for the vote as well as a lesson in the significance of the British feminist suffrage victory on behalf of the women of the world. Although no circulation figures are available for the *Women's Suffrage Journal* or *Common Cause*, *Votes for Women* had 50,000 subscribers at its peak and was sold "in the same manner as the popular press of the day," which is to say, to the general public and on the streets.[41] The suffrage audience was thus broader than that of the *Englishwoman's Review* and, in the heated atmosphere of parliamentary debate and feminist street activity, constituted a more politically engaged readership. Suffrage writers endeavored to amplify this enthusiasm by emphasizing both the international and the imperial significance of "votes for women." Throughout the period 1900–15 suffrage workers of all stripes put Indian women to didactic purpose in their periodicals by making them texts from which to read a distinctly imperial role for British women in the international struggle for female emancipation. In doing so, they grounded global sisterhood as well as women's suffrage in imperial ideology—and promised that their inclusion in the imperial nation-state would feminize not just the democratic polity but the empire as well.[42]

FEMALE SUFFRAGE AND INDIAN WOMEN

As the largest single organization working for a government women's suffrage bill during the fifteen years before the war, the National Union of Women's Suffrage Societies generated suffrage propaganda in a variety of printed forms—handbills, posters, pamphlets, and several suffrage magazines.[43] Indian women and other "women of the East" were familiar topics to the readers of the *Women's Franchise* and *Common Cause*, two of the suffrage periodicals supported by the NUWSS during this period.[44] Often treated in the particular—that is, in articles about specific Indian women—they were also generalized as a collectivity (" 'Oriental' or 'Indian' Womanhood") and the extent of their "degradation" was debated with striking frequency in NUWSS publications. Much like the *Women's Suffrage Journal*, these periodicals exhibited an international scope that highlighted the conflict between sisterly solidarity and British suffrage priorities.[45]

Although the NUWSS supported both the *Englishwoman* (1909–21) and the *Women's Franchise* (1907–11) with financial and literary contributions, *Common Cause*, which began in 1909, was always its official organ and was formally adopted as such in April 1910.[46] From the outset *Common Cause* had a "Foreign News" column, which gave notice of women's activities in European countries, with a heavy emphasis on Scandinavia, where women suffragists were making great progress. In the May 12, 1910, issue an article by C. L. Wyllie appeared on a Hindu woman doctor, Dr. Karmarkar, detailing the author's visit to Karmarkar's dispensary in Bombay. Wyllie's description of her encounter with the doctor conveys the sisterly enthusiasm suffragists felt for Indian women on the occasions when they met them personally:

> In the crowd I became separated from my friends, and found myself at one of the tables next to a lady in Hindu dress. I was just noticing her dress, which was elegant, if somewhat less gorgeous than others around, and that the little jewelry she wore was simple and refined, when she turned around, and, smiling, began to talk to me, offering some of the native dishes and explaining their virtues. I felt her personality so strongly that in a moment the crowd of gaily dressed women of many races had melted away, I had forgotten my lost

friends, and was just held by the spell of sympathy. Dr. Karmarkar was telling me of her work.[47]

Intrigued initially by the Indian woman's jewels and clothing, Wyllie ended up feeling connected to Karmarkar because of her professional accomplishments. Karmarkar's medical achievements were meant to bring the reader under the same "spell of sympathy." Wyllie arranged another time to meet, and Karmarkar gave her a personal tour of her facilities. The hospital was primitive, but the doctor was kind and "business-like." Wyllie noted that Mr. Karmarkar was proud and supportive of his wife, concluding, "This busy Eastern woman seems to somewhat disprove the theory that professional work for women is incompatible with the highest privileges and duties of married life—I mean, of course, companionship and sympathy."[48]

The story about Dr. Karmarkar is the most favorable depiction of Indian women to appear in *Common Cause*. In the June 2 issue Olive Chandler wrote a piece entitled "How Women Are Treated in India," which painted quite a different picture of the condition of Hindu women. According to Chandler, "Chivalry in India is unknown." Indian men demand abject submission from their women, and when this is not produced, it is "ruthlessly exacted." "Heathen religions" compel the Indian woman to walk several paces behind her husband, forbid her to have her own opinions, and enslave her as a "domestic drudge" in the home. "Girl babies are never welcome, and in defiance of British law are often strangled, poisoned or starved out of existence." Chandler observed that "thanks to the British Government, the Suttee is practically extinct," but has since been replaced by a "Cold Suttee"—that is, the torturous life of enforced widowhood. She condemned the zenana as "a deliberate waste of brain power and moral force, which, if trained aright, would revolutionize the homes of India."[49] Chandler's diatribe, which is a fairly predictable litany of the horrors of life for women in Eastern societies,[50] finishes rather unexpectedly on this note: "Such are the conditions under which our millions of fellow-subjects live, and it is the point of view exhibited by the men of those countries of which our Anti-Suffragists are so tender when they say that to give English women the vote would be to lose the respect of Indian men."[51] Chandler's article is a condemnation of Indian culture that stereotypes Indian women as totally subjugated and apparently without the capacity or inclination to resist. But ultimately it is intended as a counterweight to antisuffrage arguments and ends up being an apologia for British women's suffrage.

"How Women Are Treated in India" sparked a storm of protest and debate in *Common Cause* through the summer months over the "true" position of Indian women. Letters to the editor rejected Chandler's portrait variously as "unduly pessimistic," a "distorted view," and a "somewhat exaggerated picture." One letter, signed "E.S.," objected strongly to Chandler's characterizations and recommended that she read Annie Besant's writings on the women of India, which emphasized Hindu women as "Queens of the household" and analyzed *purdah* as a sign of social rank. Chandler had not presented the whole story, and the letter warned that "it would be quite as easy to draw as pessimistic a picture of how women are treated in England."[52] Christiana Herringham referred Chandler to a series of lectures recently given by Mrs. Ramsay MacDonald after her visit to India. According to MacDonald, Indian women voted in several municipalities; thus, Herringham argued, "the Anti-Suffrage argument that Indian men would be insubordinate to a Parliament elected by women is invalidated." Herringham also objected to the fact that Chandler had said nothing about Hindu religious laws, which were very favorable to women. In Herringham's estimation, "It is custom more than law which chains and imprisons Indian women."[53] In this same issue the editor, Helena Swanwick, noted that *Common Cause* had received a communication from Dr. A. K. Coomaraswamy protesting Chandler's "sweeping statements" about Indian women.[54] Swanwick quoted from the writings of Manu, "Where women are honoured, the gods are pleased," as evidence of Hindu respect for women. "The fact is," she admonished, "on either side it is quite unsafe to generalise about such matters. Infanticide is, or was, a purely local custom. I should say it is commoner now in Europe than in India."[55]

There were, however, equally ardent defenders of Chandler's view. S. F. Waring wrote to lend credence to the negative picture of Indian women by insisting that the laws of Manu were misogynist and that, having been to India and having talked to Indian women, Waring could testify to the fact that Indian women were considered to be little better than dogs. "What a dog, or a 'pariah,' means in India, you have to go to India to know."[56] Writing in the August 11 issue, "Nydia" agreed with Waring and offered quotations from Manu and Sanskrit texts about the subordination of Indian women. Finally, Helen Hanson, a doctor who had worked in India, wrote to reassure the readers of *Common Cause* that "Miss Chandler does not give at all too dark a picture" of Indian women. Their condition in the *zenanas* was "pitiful," and although there were many things delightful about the Indian home, "to dwell solely on those will not help us to reform the manifold miseries that exist. . . . The condition of the Indian woman is much like that of the English, only more so; and it is with joy that I look forward to the time when, with the effective weapon of the vote in their hands, the women of England, who have themselves learnt so much of suffering, both personal and vicarious . . . shall turn their attention to the women of the East."[57]

The construction and interpretation of Indian women's condition as "good" or "bad" was a common enough tradition in feminist journalism. It had less to do with Indian women per se than with a Western and, in this case, a British feminist standard of evaluation about what "good" treatment of women was. Some of those involved in the Chandler debate were clearly hesitant to be casting the first stone, as Swanwick's comment about infanticide in Europe indicates. Suffragists, whether they saw "the Indian woman" as more or less degraded (even someone as sympathetic as Herringham revealingly described Indian women as "chained" and "imprisoned"), used her as a springboard for arguing about the need for women's suffrage in Britain. And even Herringham, who had pointed out Indian women's voting privileges in Bombay, did not champion that as a victory in and of itself but converted it into yet another reason why British women should get the vote.

Hanson's was the last letter to be published on the subject, but which version of "the Indian woman" won the debate is not clear. It could be argued that the very spirit of debate guaranteed that the negative version advanced by Chandler initially was contested, challenged, and reexamined so that the readers of *Common Cause* could decide for themselves. Perhaps predictably, it was the image of the enslaved Indian woman that reappeared in more general suffrage discussions. In an editorial in January 1914 *Common Cause* readers were informed that suffragists were working for political freedom so that they could "do what is best for motherhood as well as what is best for womanhood." For this very reason,

the work of motherhood will be done when [woman's] claim to full human freedom is conceded. A look at the facts. In Oriental countries, where the limitation of women to the home is most complete, mortality among children is very great. The secluded woman—allowed no interest, and no duty but her children—brings up two or three out of a family of eight or nine. When . . . [this occurs] infant mortality is frightful. It is not too much to say it diminishes in proportion to the freedom, scope, and responsibility given to women.[58]

The debate begun by Chandler and carried on in the pages of *Common Cause* helped to establish the stereotyped view of Indian women as helplessly secluded and pitifully oppressed as a "fact" that could be invoked to support the suffrage position. Whether it overrode more positive portraits like that of Dr. Karmarkar is hard to say. What seems clear is that "the Indian woman" served as an instrument of debate within suffrage circles, where she was used as empirical evidence of the need for votes for British women.

The stereotype of the enslaved Indian woman became a convenient pawn for suffragists, especially in their attempts to refute the arguments of the powerful antisuffrage lobby. In an editorial for *Common Cause* in April 1912, Anti-Suffragists were labeled "orientalists," because, it was argued, their true purpose was to ensure that all women remained slaves. This facile equation of the Orient with female enslavement, which the suffragists themselves promoted elsewhere to justify the vote, was here implied to be the creation of the Antis.[59] The editorial does not deny the negative association, but rather seeks to attribute it solely to the antisuffragists. Indian women are not mentioned specifically, except by innuendo: the mere mention of the harem was perhaps enough to conjure up images of Eastern sexual slavery—images that, if not already evocative of Indian women, recalled the Chandler debate in *Common Cause* the summer before. Here, as in that debate, Indian women are represented as the silent victims of sexual oppression, which the editorial manages to blame on the Anti-Suffragists by attributing to them what was understood as the despotism and backwardness of "orientalism."[60]

But the real priority, as always, was British women's suffrage. *Common Cause* invoked images of non-Western women at this juncture to defend an Irish women's suffrage bill against the objections of the Antis, who were advancing their standard argument that women were not fit to vote in anything but local elections. "Oriental" women functioned not only as a silent specter of what British women were in danger of becoming without the vote, but also of the pernicious antisuffrage argument itself, which equated all women with slaves. For readers of *Common Cause*, the Antis appear as orientalists who want to reduce all women to the status of the Eastern harem slave. That stereotype, so essential to the suffragists' argument, was manipulated to discredit the Antis as primitive, cruel, and vaguely non-English in their attitudes toward women. By contrast, suffragists represented the vote as the guarantee against becoming like "Oriental women," a fate that they insinuated was inescapable for British women at the hands of the Antis.

Slaying the antisuffrage dragon was one of the main activities of suffrage workers from about 1908 onward, at which time women and men opposed to the vote began to organize under the direction of Mrs. Humphrey Ward and Lord Cromer.[61] With Lords Cromer and Curzon both eventually at its head, the anti-suffrage lobby was ferociously nationalist and imperialist, and antisuffrage arguments were bound up in these mentalities. In addition to insisting on separate spheres as divinely ordained and sanctioned by nature, the Antis predicted that suffrage would destroy the family and endanger the progress of the race. This had been a long-standing objection to female emancipation that took on apocalyptic significance in the wake of the Boer War and, in the 1910s, as Germany threatened to overtake Britain as an imperial superpower.[62]

But the mainstay of antisuffragism was the physical force argument, another longtime challenge to the possibility of women's equality that the Antis bolstered with an imperial rationale: as the constitutionally weaker sex, women were not fit to govern an empire which relied upon military might and masculine strength for its preservation. As Goldwin Smith mused rhetorically in 1909, "Imagine the women of England governing India."[63] For some, like Curzon, women were as mentally incapable as they were physically unable to participate in imperial government, lacking as they did the "balance of mind" required for the affairs of empire.[64] Ultimately, however, the imperialists in the antisuffrage leagues emphasized women's physical limitations, steadfastly maintaining that "those persons ought not to make laws who cannot join in enforcing them." Excluded from police duty and the armed forces, women were, in the language of the antisuffragists, "incapacitated from discharging the ultimate obligations of citizenship."[65]

Brian Harrison has argued that the violent tactics of the suffragettes afforded the Antis some much-needed ammunition with which to mount their attacks.[66] From a glance at *Common Cause* between 1909 and 1914, the reverse seems equally true: the growing threat of the Antis, in terms of organization as well as rhetoric, gave the suffragists at least an opportunity to go on the offensive and to develop further their strategic use of Indian women as suffrage propaganda. The Antis also gave suffrage argument the chance to flex its imperial muscle more explicitly than it had previously done. Suffragists refuted the notion that women had no role in the government of the empire and its dependencies. In response to the argument over physical force, they proposed a "new and sane" imperialism that was to be based on feminine values and oriented toward peace rather than war. Throughout the pages of *Common Cause* suffragists demanded the recognition of women as the allies of empire and sought to identify the suffrage movement as the best expression of a great and glorious imperial nation.[67]

Contributors to *Common Cause* tackled the imperial question in a variety of ways. One approach was to challenge the Antis' assumption that men

deserved the responsibilities of imperial rule. A contributor identified as
"E. W.," acknowledging that "the Anglo-Saxon tradition is the finest in the
world, and it must permeate the races of the world," berated male imperialists for failing to do their duty. What men brought to the territories of
empire was sexual appetite, parenting "a race of outcasts." It was the
women of the empire to whom men owed not only the survival of their race
but their civilization as well. This tack led E. W. to a discussion of South
Africa, where, she claimed, "you owe all that is worth having, all the best
British tradition, to the presence of a comparatively few women." White
women's reward for empire-building was to be denied the vote while the
black South African man, "possessing but a veneer of your vaunted civilisation, has the right to control legislation affecting the white woman and her
children." E. W. concluded by lamenting the lack of "adequate protection
for our womanhood black and white" in South Africa; and in doing so
united British feminists, white South African suffragists, and black South
African women against white male power in its imperial and political manifestations. In E. W.'s rendition, imperialism in its current form was revealed
to be masculine, synonymous with self-interest and hypocrisy. To male
imperialists her final retort was, "Call yourself egoist, not Imperialist."[68]

A number of suffragists writing for *Common Cause* developed E. W.'s
theme of imperialism as a distinctly male exercise of power and tried to
replace it with a more "feminine" variety. The author of "The New Imperialism," who was probably *Common Cause* editor Helena Swanwick, agreed
with Lord Milner that imperialism was not "the cheap and tawdry thing it
has come to seem to some of us. We have to redeem the word from its base
uses, and reinterpret it to our ideals." According to Swanwick, suffragists
rejected the "old" imperialist notion that Britain held its empire "at the
point of bayonet." The suffragist imperial ideal was founded "on respect
and mutual self-restraint," on reverence rather than contempt for weakness. Swanwick's editorial emphasized that suffragists reveled in the glory of
empire as much as the Antis did and that they demanded inclusion in it
precisely because they understood Britain's imperial destiny: "It is not
because Suffragists underestimate these responsibilities that they seek a
share in them. Rather it is the consciousness of responsibility that urges us
on. We are the citizens of no mean city. Whether we chose or no, we are
members of an Empire which must leave a mark on human history, from
the sheer size and glory of it. And we are deeply concerned to know what
that mark will be." Swanwick's purpose was to show that British women did
make a contribution to the imperial nation-state—a contribution that was
purifying precisely because it was feminine, because it feminized the brutal

aspects of imperial power. The suffrage ideal of empire she proposed was at once less "masculine" and *more* faithful to the purest imperial values, which in her view had become corrupted by the accretions of time and male prerogative. Restoring the empire to its women was at the core of the suffragists' "new imperialism." In the process of projecting a future British empire run on feminine principles, Swanwick redeemed imperialism as a potentially feminine and feminist ideology.[69]

Indian women receive only brief mention in Swanwick's piece, but they are, significantly, her trump card. "The responsibilities of Empire rest on women as well as men," she wrote, and "if it were only for the sake of India, women here in Great Britain would be bound to demand the vote. The knowledge of that vast multitude of silent and too suffering women weighs on us always and nerves us to the struggle when we ourselves are weary. We know little about them, it is true, but what we know forces us on." As evidence of what she knew about Indian women, Swanwick cited the slow progress of female education, unfavorable medical conditions, and Indian mothers' general superstition and ignorance—by now a standard and familiar feminist catalog for the condition of Indian women. The gist of her argument is that imperial responsibilities compelled British suffragists to demand the vote, not only for themselves but for the sake of their colonial sisters. Empire and suffrage were thus mutually dependent—and the "new imperialism" made votes for women essential to the preservation of imperial rule.[70]

Over the next two years *Common Cause* featured a host of articles on Indian women, many of which took as their point of departure Swanwick's call for a new and more feminized imperialism. In fact, Fawcett promised more articles on India, citing its importance to the women's cause.[71] "England and India," "Lalli: A Mother in India," "Medical Women and India," and "The Education of Indian Women and Girls" are a few representative items. The focus in many of these pieces was ostensibly on improving medical conditions for Indian women through a government training scheme for both English and Indian female doctors, but the imperial value of British women's suffrage was routinely emphasized. In her article on medical women in India, "M. D." reported having met an antisuffrage female doctor in India who claimed that since the British government did not expect its best women to go to India, demands for better pay were unjustified. M. D. made a strong case for equal payment for women, pointing out that their work in India was "indispensable to the welfare of the race." As for the women's antisuffrage bias, M. D. declared, "I need hardly say that Suffragists are more imperially minded."[72]

Proving that women were "imperially minded" was an important project for *Common Cause*. The volume of writing on Indian women during the two years before the war may be interpreted as an attempt on the part of suffragists to demonstrate their knowledge of Indian women's lives and their own usefulness as mediators between England and its colonial peoples, particularly colonial women.[73] For some, "thinking imperially" meant contemplating a life of service in the empire. Hester Gray informed *Common Cause* that women were desperately needed everywhere in Britain's imperial territories. The kinds of women needed were "the most competent women that the feminist movement has put forth." Gray argued that this was another reason for working for "the swift coming of the Suffrage," for "only the passing of an Enfranchising Bill will release for action in the distant places of the Empire, the kind of public servant so urgently needed, so justly demanded by the less privileged women of the East."[74] Gray's appeal to suffragists to work in the empire was testament to the fact that the suffrage movement itself had helped British women to think more "imperially." She explicitly called for "college-trained professional women" rather than missionaries or memsahibs, indicating her belief that the women's movement itself had generated a new kind of imperially minded woman for reform work in the colonial setting.

With the advent of war, thinking imperially became an act of patriotism, and suffragists rose to the occasion. Longtime suffragist Maude Royden, in a 1915 article entitled "The Imperial Idea," contrasted British with Prussian imperialism and found the British version more democratic, more tolerant, more purely "imperial." In contrast to Germany, which imposed its *Kultur* on alien races, Royden argued that Britain prized the individuality of all the peoples and territories in its empire: "We have realized as never before the strength of the links which bind our own empire together just because they are links of respect and freedom instead of coercion and strength."[75] Royden, who began to edit *Common Cause* in the summer of 1913, emerges as an apologist for empire. From this passage it would seem she believes that the British Empire now embodied those "higher" (feminine) imperial values to which Swanwick had earlier aspired. Mary Lowndes wrote a letter to the editor in the next issue precisely to underline these differences and to expand on Royden's critique of the brutality and the sexism of Prussian imperialism.[76] By 1915, *Common Cause* was as concerned with imperial matters as it was with votes for women. This was partly due to the fact that once the war began, suffrage activities were suspended and many suffragists threw themselves into the war effort. But it would be a mistake to interpret Royden's defense of empire merely as the reflex of a patriot during wartime.

As has been shown, identification with and commitment to a "new imperialism" was a well-developed part of the twentieth-century suffrage program.

Suffragists' pride in empire and their imperial ideals rendered notions about global sisterhood problematic. The affiliation of the National Union of Women's Suffrage Societies with the International Woman Suffrage Alliance, an umbrella organization that sought to unite suffragists the world over,[77] exemplified the tensions between British imperial suffragism and British suffragists' commitment to the universal emancipation of women. It was never a question of lack of enthusiasm for the liberation of women in other lands: the concept of womanhood as "solidaire" in all parts of the world was an early feminist idea, voiced most passionately in the Victorian period by Josephine Butler. An editorial in *Common Cause* for June 6, 1913, attributed the international spirit of the women's movement to Butler, calling her "the patron saint" of the international movement because "she taught the unforgettable lesson that the wrongs of every woman are the wrongs of all women, and no woman can be outraged or oppressed, but womanhood itself is the sufferer. She saw, early in her great warfare, that the problem to which she sought solution could never be solved by England alone, but must be linked on to the movement for reform in other countries, and advance made all along the line."[78] For suffragists of the period, the existence of an international movement was one of the most encouraging signs of the future possibility of votes for women. As one contributor to *Common Cause* put it, "Of all the many strong arguments in favour of Women's Suffrage, none is surely stronger than the fact that the movement is world wide."[79] The International Woman Suffrage Alliance was considered to be the instrument of both unity and of women's freedom in global terms. The 1913 congress at Budapest would, readers of *Common Cause* were told, link together "the chain of organisations which now encircle the earth . . . pointing to the certain emancipation of the women of the entire world."[80]

The contradictions inherent in British suffrage ideology stemmed mainly from suffragists' assumption that their own campaign for the vote would be, if not the first to achieve its goals, then at the very least a blueprint for other nations to follow. Participation in the conferences of the International Woman Suffrage Alliance proved to be something of an eye-opening experience for British delegates. At these meetings, held in London in 1909, Stockholm in 1911, and Budapest in 1913, women of many nations sat in congress and heard reports about the progress of the suffrage movement in each country as well as evaluations of the status of women. The experience of such gatherings, which one delegate described as a great "international conversazione," compelled British women to acknowledge the extent of the international women's movement about which they had been rhetoricizing for decades.[81] They came to understand that Britain was not the only country where women were fighting for their rights: by 1911 a total of twenty-four countries were affiliated with the International Woman Suffrage Alliance, including Greece, Turkey, and Japan. The Congress at Budapest hosted 2,800 women.[82] After an IWSA meeting in London in the autumn of 1912, the tone of *Common Cause* was sober, if not somber. Warning against Britain's potential insularity, one editorial reminded, "There are some lessons to be learnt from internationalists after all."[83]

If British suffragists were predisposed to ignore this advice, the president of the IWSA, visiting London after the 1911 conference in Stockholm, pressed the point upon them. Speaking at a banquet given in her honor, Carrie Chapman Catt, the American suffrage leader, praised the British movement as "the most wonderful, powerful, soul-stirring thing." She continued with disarming frankness: "But it [is] not for English women to teach their own methods. Each nationality must have the movement that harmonized with it; the International had not to teach but to inspire. Its work [is] not for women of one race but that womanhood should come into its own."[84] Catt chastised British women for the narrowness of their vision: in its current form it was too British, too "national" to be useful to the cause of international suffragism. What Catt urged on her audience instead was a suffrage philosophy stripped of national character and dedicated to the idea of women as one unified, redemptive race:

> I beg of you to enlarge your ambitions, to look over the great world and forget you are British. Nations will go, but the race remains. We are bringing something new into the world, something not sundering but uniting. Men have always appealed to local patriotism; it remains for women to unite in something greater than nations,—in the motherhood of the world. . . . There are women in Europe as intelligent as you and you are called outside of great Britain to help the women in this larger world. Your work does not end in London. So long as there is one woman living in the world who is taught that she was born an inferior being and so subject to a superior class there is work for you.[85]

Promoting this vision of a single race of mothers was the stated purpose of the IWSA, which viewed itself, an organization comprising women of all nationalities, as evidence of universal sisterhood. Catt rejected "local" (i.e., nation-specific) patriotism as a male phenomenon, making internationalism in turn a feminine impulse. Her message to her British sisters was gentle but firm: national feeling had to be sacrificed for the sake of female solidarity so that the suffrage movement could present a united front to the world.

Significantly, however, Catt did not discourage British suffragists from cultivating their sense of imperial feminist mission. In fact, she claimed that Britain's imperial responsibilities were an asset to the international women's movement. In its "Foreign Notes" column of June 1912, *Common Cause* reprinted a letter Catt wrote to the American *Women's Journal* about the Egyptian women's movement. In it Catt admired the women of Egypt who were "daring to refuse marriage" to demand education and other freedoms. Although Catt discussed the activities of Egyptian women at some length, ultimately it was the influence of England to which she attributed the rise of a women's movement there. "Great Britain has created a new Egypt," she declared. "It has awakened a sleeping race and held before it the dazzling achievements of Western progress."[86] A year later, *Common Cause* reported that Catt, speaking at a reception given in her honor, was intent on emphasizing British suffragists' imperial responsibilities. The British government in India "worked only with men, and could work only with men. Yet it was well known that the recent boycott of British goods [part of the *swadeshi* movement in Bengal] was inspired and kept up by the women. 'Men cannot reach those women,' said Mrs. Catt in a very moving passage; *'you could.'*" *Common Cause* went on to note that "Mrs. Swanwick, moving a vote of thanks to Mrs. Chapman Catt, reminded her hearers that 'if it were only for our responsibilities in India, we women must not rest until we have the vote.'"[87]

Catt's belief in the usefulness of Britain's imperial influence grew out of her ethnocentric view of the world of women. As her comment about the Egyptian women's movement indicates, she believed that the West had lessons to teach the East about not only the appropriate status of women but also about how to operate a successful women's movement. This view was institutionalized in the IWSA, which had been begun by Anglo-American women suffragists at the turn of the century. With a membership that was largely European, the "internationalism" of the IWSA was primarily Western in its makeup. The IWSA leadership, mainly under the direction of Catt, who was its president from 1906 to 1923, took great pride in its efforts to recruit non-Western women for inclusion as "auxiliaries" to the main society. In 1912 Catt and Aletta Jacobs, a Dutch physician, toured India, Egypt, Palestine, Turkey, Persia, Japan, Sumatra, Java, and the Philippines for just this purpose. The account of their travels was the "sensation"

of the Budapest conference in 1913, where Catt revealed to the audience
of international delegates that "there *is* a serious women's movement in
Asia."[88] Contrary to what had previously been thought (and contrary to the
ideas that suffragists had perpetrated themselves), they found compelling
evidence that Eastern women had always rebelled against social and cultural oppression. Catt described the women she met and talked with and
testified to the fact that women in India became doctors and lawyers, and in
some regions were even mounting suffrage campaigns. As a result of her
travels Catt was able to reassure the members of the IWSA and, through
Common Cause, the British suffrage readership that "a movement of extraor-
dinary strength was going on among Eastern women."[89]

Catt's internationalism had the same hierarchical cast as that of British
suffragists. For despite her resistance to the national peculiarities of British
suffragism, she presumed that women of the West would lead the women of
the world toward emancipation. Women of the IWSA occupied "the sum-
mit of international union, where we may observe every manifestation of
this movement in all parts of the world."[90] From this elevated vantage point
Western suffragists could look down on the "armies" of foreign women
crusading for female emancipation. Catt's metaphor is apt, since despite the
considerable rhetoric of sisterhood that she and, under her, the IWSA
generated, she did not view Eastern women on an equal level with Western
suffragists. They were first and foremost colonial women, and, as she told
the Budapest congress, "Any Western nation which tried to rule the East
without taking the women into account was doomed to fail."[91] But if Catt
was concerned with Indian women subverting the colonial order, she saw it
as the task of Western feminists to discourage and perhaps even prevent
them. Her warning, quoted above, that it was India's women who had led
the boycott and that only British women could appeal to them effectively
pledged the international women's suffrage movement to the maintenance
of imperial rule. The East and its women appeared as a new and uncharted
territory for the IWSA in 1913, thanks in the main to Catt's personal tour of
Asian countries. *Common Cause*, assessing the Budapest conference, remarked that "the tone of the Congress has been altogether one of triumph.
Mrs. Chapman Catt, admitting four new societies, declared that we should
soon, like Alexander, have to seek new worlds to conquer. She indicated,
however, that we might find them in the East."[92]

Given Catt's insinuation that Indian women were passively awaiting
conquest and subsequent conversion to the Western feminist creed, it is
necessary at this juncture to remind ourselves about Indian women's reform activities during this period. Women's groups and feminist women

undertook social and political reform in India at the end of the ninete
century, the most prominent among them being Pandita Ramabai, K.
Ranade, Sarojini Naidu, and those associated with the Social Conference of
the Indian National Congress after 1887.[93] Indian reformers worked both
at home and in conjunction with feminists in London to promote not only
the suffrage cause but also improved educational opportunities for Indian
girls and women. As the Indian independence movement gained ground in
the first two decades of the twentieth century, Indian women often found
themselves torn, as have other feminists in colonial contexts past and
present, between the imperatives of national liberation and those of "female emancipation." Indian women were active in the nationalist movement: they involved themselves in the highest-level discussions that male
Indian leaders were having with British government officials, and among
their priorities was female suffrage in provincial legislatures and protective
legislation for girls and women.[94] The Indian Muslim woman Rokeya Hossain wrote a feminist utopian tract in 1905 that anticipated the publication
of Charlotte Gilman's much-touted *Herland*, and individual Indian and
Egyptian women engaged in courageous acts of cultural resistance by
refusing to wear the *burqa*.[95] As Kumari Jayawardena and others have
insisted, feminist consciousness was by no means confined to the "First
World" during the late nineteenth and early twentieth centuries. As in the
West, this period witnessed the emergence of significant autonomous political and social organizations run by women who were often but not exclusively bourgeois elites. Although British feminists and other Western
women promoted the belief that female emancipation was an ideology
foreign to the non-West, it was at the heart of a variety of colonial nationalist ideologies and was used by a variety of reformers in their struggles
against imperialism and capitalism. Nor was it a recent import either, the
product of Western enlightenment: it had a long and indigenous history of
its own outside the West.[96]

There were a number of women active on the London scene with whom
suffrage workers were clearly familiar. In March 1910, the *Vote* reported on
the progress of the Indian women's magazine *Stree Bodhe* and mentioned
that "Indian women in this country are showing their sympathy with the
Suffrage cause; some have become members of the Women's Freedom
League, so that they may evidence it in practical way."[97] These may have
included Mrs. P. L. Roy, Mrs. Nanth, and Mrs. Mukerjea. The Women's
Freedom League organized an International Suffrage Fair at the Chelsea
Town Hall in November 1912; there were booths representing all nations,
including India, where Mrs. Ramdulari Dubé spoke about Indian women's

progress. She was the wife of an Indian barrister named Dubé who contributed an article to the *Vote* in June 1911; she was later described as the secretary to the Indian Women's Congress, an author of papers on Indian women's and children's welfare, and "a member of the Women's Freedom League and of the Lyceum Club, London. By her personality she serves her own country, showing the ability and charm of an Indian woman—and the picturesqueness of her dress."[98] Both Mrs. Roy and Mrs. Mukerjea had been presidents of the London Indian Union Society, and the latter had given lectures on the condition of Indian women. She was also connected with the Indian Female Education Fund and the Women's India Study Association, both of which were London-based groups involved in raising money for the education of Indian women and girls. Roy organized "entertainments" at Caxton Hall, home of myriad suffrage and female reform activities, to fund Indian women's educational training in England; *Common Cause* advertised a similar entertainment held at the Royal Court Theatre in Sloane Square in March 1912. With this kind of publicity and with active suffrage women like Mrs. Cobden Unwin attending Indian Union Society functions, it seems likely that other suffrage workers would have known about and even attended such entertainments.[99] By 1913 the National Union of Women Workers, which was the English affiliate of the International Council of Women, was promoting the Women's India Study Association at its meetings. This, together with the creation of an Indian and Colonial Subcommittee between 1896 and 1898, indicates that connections were made between British suffragists on an organizational as well as on an individual basis.[100] If suffragists were aware of these activities, however, they did not give them much press, and certainly not as much attention as they gave to the "plight" of Indian women in India. Anglo-American suffragists had perhaps too much invested in their own representations of nonwhite women to produce accurate information about either the diversity of the international sisterhood or its indigenous, non-Western feminist traditions. In this sense Catt and the women of the International Woman Suffrage Alliance reproduced Indian women and others as Other and made their internationalist ideologies fundamentally dependent on the notion of a colonized "Oriental" womanhood.

The tension between their vision of international female equality and imperial suffragism does not appear to have struck British suffragists writing for *Common Cause*—partly because convictions of Anglo-American superiority were, by the twentieth century, deeply imbedded in British feminist culture. Organizations like the International Woman Suffrage Alliance and the International Council of Women reinforced these assumptions both rhetorically and structurally.[101] As far as I am able to tell, there was no Indian delegate to the IWSA annual conferences until the poet and feminist activist Sarojini Naidu attended in Geneva in 1920, in spite of the fact that suffragettes knew Sarojini Naidu personally before the war.[102] In April 1914 she spoke at a meeting of the Women Writers' Suffrage League and was touted as a "pioneer of Indian women's education."[103] In the prewar era women of the East and especially Indian women remained, with a few notable exceptions, basically unknown quantities for the majority of British suffragists, whose knowledge of them was mostly gleaned from "thrilling" accounts like Catt's or in *Common Cause* articles. The latter could be more or less flattering, but they always presented "the Indian woman" in terms of her utility to the suffrage argument.

Having typed the Eastern woman as silent and impassive, suffragists were willing to speak for her in the name of universal womanhood; it scarcely occurred to them to do otherwise. In an unusually personal, as opposed to a textual, example of this kind of silencing, an Indian educationalist named Marie Bhor attended an ICW congress session in 1899, but said nothing while the famous Anglo-Indian novelist Flora Annie Steele spoke on her behalf.[104] Bhor, a teacher at the Poona High School for Girls and a student in English literature at Somerville College, stood on the platform with "several other Indian ladies in native dress" while the ICW president invited Steele "to speak for the women of India." Steele exhibited no reticence in doing so. She talked about international sisterhood as one of the purposes of the ICW meeting and finished with the following appeal to British imperial power and longevity: "And so, without the slightest fear, I, representing all those women of the East . . . reach out my hands to the women of the setting sun, knowing that by doing so I shall consolidate that vast Indian Empire which every English man and English woman hopes and prays may last, and hopes and prays that upon it the great sun of righteousness and truth and mercy may never set."[105] As Nancy Paxton has written, Steele's work on behalf of Indian women was almost continually compromised by her elitism and authoritarianism. She believed that colonial subjects' apparent submission to her legitimated her authority, and the above incident suggests that she took Bhor's compliance to signify her own feminist-imperial authority over all Indian women.[106]

It would be a mistake to believe that Steele had the power finally to silence someone like Marie Bhor, who sang at National Indian Association soirees, had her paper on the history of women's education in Bombay published, and was presented to the queen in connection with the ICW festivities.[107] Still, the linkages that British feminists made between their representations of Indian women and imperial stability and prosperity were rarely so baldly stated. Internationalism was touted by active suffragists like Millicent Garrett Fawcett as an ethos that "belongs to no one people" and, more specifically, "binds East and West in a common hope and inspiration that the future shall not be the past, and that women and men together will be a stronger force to combat world-old evils and world-old degradations than men by themselves have ever been."[108] In practice, however, suffrage internationalism commanded the presence of non-Western women as showpieces in a global sisterhood whose existence was seen as proof of the vitality of British women's suffrage itself.[109] Whether it objectified Eastern women as thoroughly degraded or in the process of "awakening" to their own liberation, the international women's movement dictated their silence and subordinated them to Western suffragists in an imaginary as well as in an institutionalized feminist world order.[110]

British suffragists needed Indian women as proof of their imperial role, but they also used them as evidence of universal female solidarity. First on the streets of London and then in the pages of *Common Cause*, they turned them into symbols of both international sisterhood and female colonial compliance. They did this by capitalizing on the pageantry of empire to dramatize a feminist imperial symbolism of their own. Pageantry and processions were in abundance during the first ten years of the new century, some official and others specially orchestrated by the suffragists themselves.[111] In June 1911 the major suffrage societies organized a suffrage procession to complement the King's Coronation Procession in London. *Common Cause* reported that the parade featured "friends from overseas within and without the Empire. . . . This unity in the midst of diversity is the healthiest sign of life. Ours is no sectional demand. It arises from all classes, creeds, and nationalities, parties, and temperaments."[112] Photographs in *Votes for Women* and descriptions in the *Vote* tell us that suffragists put together one section of the procession called the Empire Pageant.[113] According to the program, this section was in the form of "a car emblematical of the Unity of the British Empire," "heralded by the Union Jack, and preceded and followed by groups of women carrying the emblem of *England*—roses." Groups of women representing Scotland and Wales, Australia, and Canada, decked out in costume and "singing their national songs," followed behind.[114]

Several Indian women marched as well, three of whom were identified by the *Vote* as Mrs. Roy, wife of an Indian barrister and "one of the most emancipated of Indian women"; Mrs. Bhola Nanth, honorary secretary of the Indian Women's Educational Fund; and Mrs. Mukerjea, president of the

Indian National Union.[115] *Common Cause* reported that "in the International contingent one was struck ... by the Hindoo women, who called forth from one woman in the crowd the amazed comment, 'Why! Here are some brownies!' And most charming brownies they were too in their Indian costumes."[116] The appearance of Indian women in this procession, and the treatment of their appearance in *Common Cause*, is somewhat at variance with the images of degraded Indian womanhood that readers of the suffrage journal were offered at other times. In spite of the fact that the *Vote* was the only periodical to identify Roy and Nanth by name, these women are, for one thing, contemporary Indian women rather than the faceless types about whom contributors to the Chandler debate were content to generalize. They are also presented, in both the photographs and the commentary, as well dressed, well off, and, in the case of Roy, autonomous and "emancipated." Like the begum of Bhopal, who attended the coronation and was described at length in *Common Cause*'s coverage of the festivities, they were examples of what Indian women were "capable of."[117] Nonetheless, the Indian women represented here remained objects of curiosity. This is especially true of the begum because she traveled in purdah: "The public will see of her no more than a very small lady shrouded in lilac silk and a silver embroidered burka extending almost to her knees, while two slits veiled with gauze will mark the position of her eyes."[118] As for Roy and Nanth, they were "brownies" to be marveled at and are given no context except the imperial one in which they briefly appear and then disappear again—despite their considerable activity in London during this period. That some Indian women living in England experienced this ogling as intrusive and annoying is evident from the diaries of Cornelia Sorabji, a Parsi woman who spent time in Britain in the late 1880s and had connections with the circle of reformers around the National Indian Association. Appearing for the first time in her sari at an At Home, Sorabji recounted how one guest "called out in a loud coarse voice, 'Hallo Connie, and what is this freak?'" Sorabji reported later that she said nothing at the time but "felt inclined to retaliate, 'yes, England makes changes for us all, [does it] not [?]'"[119]

Suffragists in Britain, for their part, were eager to depict "votes for women" as they conceived of it—an international movement in which women of all races and religions stood shoulder to shoulder marching toward universal equality. In events like the suffrage procession, they enlisted Indian women (as they did Welsh and Scottish and Commonwealth women) as participants in a ritualized sisterhood that assumed the empire of Greater Britain as its natural base. This visible solidarity of "imperial women" both white and nonwhite was one way of rejecting the Antis' claims that British women had no role in imperial affairs. In the view of suffrage writers, the whole success of empire required a "free Womanhood" that was understood, as Millicent Garrett Fawcett claimed, to be one of "the western·ideals" which a civilizing Raj brought to India and upon which Britain's continued imperial presence depended.[120] The very existence of colonial women justified the involvement of British feminists, while the mutual regard between Indian women and British suffragists that readers of *Common Cause* appeared to be witnessing embodied the kind of imperial family unity that advocates of empire so strenuously desired. What is most remarkable here is the impression that the organizers of the procession and of other such pageants tried to convey about the participation of Indian women in demonstrations of British suffrage strength. Suffragists paraded Indian women as evidence of British women's imperial connections but also of their claim to speak for women of all races with their consent.[121] In fact, what they got was more like their active participation and their commitment to represent themselves. In the photograph of the India section of the procession reprinted in *Votes for Women*, one of the Indian women looks as if she is holding up the India banner quite firmly and without help from any one else. If the female Other acted as the structural support for British feminists claims to imperial authority, she did so only in the imaginative space they had constructed for her. Twentieth-century Indian feminists clearly manifested their own self-confident and unqualified independence from the constraints of imperial feminism and of its ideological counterpart, global sisterhood.

The impression of consensual suffragism, a suffragism that appeared to contain differences of culture, religion, and race and was manufactured in the pages of periodicals like *Common Cause*, carried with it messages intended for a variety for audiences. It reassured imperialists that women's suffrage, rather than destroying the fabric of empire, would bolster its values, guarantee its maintenance, and contribute to imperial harmony. To suffrage opponents it projected an image of peaceful and unified suffrage activity that implicitly distinguished it from the violent tactics of the militant suffragettes. It may have even served, as Tickner has suggested about suffrage spectacle in general, as a therapeutic substitute for militant activities.[122] Most important, perhaps, it spoke to the suffragists themselves, who were often their own most interested audience.[123] To these it reflected back the kind of image they wished to project to the public at large: that of an international woman's movement spearheaded by British suffragists and subscribed to joyfully by the women of the world.

INDIAN WOMEN AND IMPERIAL
SUFFRAGE IDENTITY

The use of Indian women as a counter in suffrage polemic was not unique either to the moderate suffragists of the National Union of Women's Suffrage Societies or to their periodical literature. *Votes for Women*, the organ of the Pankhursts' Women's Social and Political Union until 1912—and afterward, of a splinter group of suffragettes—featured a number of articles on Indian women and women of the East. Considering the level of domestic suffragette activity in this period—including window-smashing, marching, and the arrest and forcible feeding of many WSPU members—pieces like "The Changing East," "The Awakening of [Indian] Women," "Woman's Place in Hinduism," and a wide variety of articles on Turkish women appeared in *Votes for Women* with considerable regularity.[124] On the one hand, Indian women were still made to service British feminists' ideals of global sisterhood, and British women were not particularly hesitant about associating Indian women's enlightenment with their exposure to Western ideals and with their willingness to embrace "modern thought.[125] On the other hand, militant enthusiasm prompted the suffragettes to construct an "Oriental" woman who was less passive than the suffragists' version of her. In general, Indian women's "awakening" received more attention in *Votes for Women* than in *Common Cause*. In September 1908, for example, it confidently presented a piece entitled "The Last of the Harem," which described a development that Ella Wheeler Wilcox later foreshadowed as the first step in Indian female emancipation.[126] And there were some, like one *Votes for Women* contributor who signed herself "K.D.S.," who saw in a notable Indian women like the begum of Bhopal a real fighting spirit when it came to the exercise of political authority.[127] Little did suffragettes know the effect that their tactics were to have on one particular Indian nationalist, namely M. K. Gandhi. Fresh from the agitation that he had helped to lead on behalf of Indian rights in South Africa, Gandhi visited London in 1906, at which time he was greatly impressed by the courage of women protesting at the House of Commons and of their determination to serve time in prison for their cause. Evidence suggests that he actually might have met some suffragettes, but he followed the news reports of their activities and praised their determination in articles for *Indian Opinion*, though warning that violence in principle was misguided. Ironically, suffrage agitation helped to crystallize for Gandhi the same principle that Indian women signified for British feminists—the justness of the cause of self-representation. For British women this required inclusion in the imperial nation, for Gandhi and India it came eventually to mean secession from the empire.[128]

Despite their internationalist sentiments, British suffragettes, like the moderates of the National Union of Women's Suffrage Societies, exhibited a chauvinism that appears to have been common among nearly all women working for the vote in the early twentieth century. Commenting on the progress of women in the postrevolutionary councils in Turkey, Christabel Pankhurst warned that Eastern women should not expect to be awarded political equality as long as their Western sisters were still denied this fundamental right. British women, she wrote,

> argue that if the men of Turkey and Egypt, with little or no practical knowledge and experience of Parliamentary institutions, are capable of using political rights, the women of this country are more fitted for political liberty. They have nothing to say against the enfranchisement of their fellow creatures in any part of the world, but they feel it hard, being the rightful heirs to the constitutional liberty built up by their foremothers and forefathers, they should have that inheritance withheld, while men of other races are suddenly and almost without preparation leaping into possession of constitutional power.[129]

Pankhurst admitted that Turkish women were fit for the franchise; it was more a question of the inappropriateness of Turks getting the vote before British women.[130] "Shall Britain lead the way?" was a rhetorical question that operated on the presumption that Britain *should* lead the way among the nations in the emancipation of women. Her objections to Turkish suffrage were not finally based on the merits of political experience, but rather on the rightful order of things in a world where Britain was the acknowledged international leader.[131] Pankhurst concluded with the assertion that the ideal of sex equality had after all been created by Great Britain, and therefore to British women emancipation should come first. According to Brian Harrison, Millicent Fawcett shared this conviction.[132] They were both, as we have seen, speaking out of a feminist historical tradition that privileged Anglo-Saxon Britain as the home of equality between the sexes and out of a British feminist political tradition that subscribed to many of the racial and imperial narratives which made that claim seem plausible and, indeed, historically and culturally appropriate.

Pankhurst voiced a sentiment that was expressed by many suffrage workers in the early twentieth century, namely that Britain was the "storm-centre" of the women's movement. This term had been coined by Carrie Chapman Catt at the 1908 meeting of the International Woman Suffrage

Alliance in Amsterdam and was taken up enthusiastically by suffragettes as proof that the advent of militancy had galvanized the movement. Teresa Billington-Greig, a Women's Freedom League member who called herself a nonviolent suffragette, claimed that "the uprising of the women of Great Britain has fixed the attention of the world. From all quarters of the earth people have turned to look upon the latest manifestation of revolutionary progress."[133] *Votes for Women* took up the same cry in 1909, locating the center of the women's movement in Britain because it was the home of the oldest parliamentary system in the world. According to Elizabeth Robins, "Just as truly as the body sitting at St. Stephen's is accounted the Mother of Parliaments—just so truly may the Woman Suffrage agitation in this country be called the Mother of the world-wide New Movement. The late-born corporate spirit among women . . .—this new inspiration lifting up the women East and West—had its birth in England. To England the peoples look for its highest expression."[134] This was by no means a new idea: in 1890, for example, Henrietta Muller, former editor of the *Women's Penny Paper*, told the Marleybone Radical Club that "when English women are free, all other women will follow. England is the centre, the 'Hub' of the world; all other nations take their cue from her."[135] But the storm-center concept did receive a boost by militants after the 1908 IWSA congress, and variations of it were quite common in suffrage writing.[136] It seemed fitting to this generation of feminists that, since England was the Mother of Parliaments and the mother country of the empire, it should be acknowledged as the "mother of the world-wide movement" as well—especially as women in other lands won suffrage victories and began to cast doubt on the primacy of British suffragists' claims to leadership of international feminism.

National pride was at the heart of this conviction and it informed the whole storm-center argument. Suffragettes recognized the role of suffrage periodicals in proving Britain's national leadership in the international women's movement just as their moderate sisters did. Boasting that British suffrage activity was the most fervent of any nation's, Robins pointed to *Votes for Women* to substantiate her claim. "Look down the columns of our paper—at the notices of meetings to be held and of those which have taken place within the week . . . British Suffrage Unions and Societies of every political complexion spread like a network over the three kingdoms."[137] The role of the suffrage press in making manifest this progress and its capacity to unify divisions with the suffrage movement, both to the world and to suffrage workers themselves, is fully articulated here. Such progress was in direct contrast to the apparently retarded development of Indian

women's feminist consciousness. For even when twentieth-century feminists praised the development of Eastern women, they made it clear that
the women's movement in India was moving slowly.[138] *Votes for Women*
reported on the first public meeting for (white) women's suffrage held in
India, led by Frances Hallowes and Eva McLaren. Hallowes indicated that
English women would represent Indian women and claimed that "political
freedom for English women would mean that the women of India, who
formed fully three-fourths of all the women of the Empire, would benefit
thereby. There are all these women needing to have their interests represented in the councils of Empire."[139] The consoling consequence of their
slow progress was that British suffrage women could still claim to be the
most experienced feminists in the world and, on the basis of that experience, could justify Britain's supervision of women's international liberation.
Clearly it was also meant to signify that British women's claims to suffrage
rested partly on their capacity to represent—to speak for, as Flora Annie
Steele and decades of feminist journalism had done—the vast population of
colonized women in the empire.

   In the early twentieth century British suffrage journals were spaces for
showing off feminist colonial possessions and for admiring the effects of
British feminist tutelage of Indian and other Eastern women. During and
after the First World War they began to be forums for beginning to discuss
the self-determination of Indian women in terms of British imperial de-
volution. There is some indication that this was a response to the changing
realities of colonial power on the world scene. In an article called "India,
Comrade and Friend," one anonymous contributor to *Common Cause* in
1915 wrote,

> There is no aspect of the Woman's Movement in which British Suffrag-
> ists take a keener interest than that which concerns their sisters in
> India. They realize that women alone can reach the women of the East,
> and they realize also that towards the women of the East they have a
> special responsibility. This responsibility will only be discharged
> rightly if we appreciate to the full the proud sensitiveness of the Indian
> race, and their deep sense of the age and beauty of their own civiliza-
> tion. India is not, and has never considered herself, a conquered coun-
> try. Recent events [indications that India would pledge itself to the war
> effort] must surely have made the dullest of us realize that she is, and
> must now be treated as "not a dependent but a valued and trusted
> comrade and friend" (*India*, January 22). Our Government recognizes
> this because for the first time it recognizes the INC.[140]

In fact, after the war, British feminists began to take quite a different tone toward Indian women: one of apparent respect and appreciation for their own struggles, at least compared with that of women writing in the prewar period. *Common Cause* featured Indian women's war work, highlighting their loyalty to the national-imperial war effort.[141] And, by 1918, the NUWSS-affiliated *Englishwoman* recognized that there was indeed a women's movement in India, claiming that "the education given to Indian women by European and American teachers has drawn them from that quiet seclusion of spirit in which they dreamed for so many centuries." The author mentioned Pandita Ramabai, Sarojini Naidu, and the Sorabji sisters as pioneers in the Indian women's movement and warned: "India must no longer be looked on as a field for beneficent charity or patronage: she is fast reaching a stage of development in which co-operative work can alone produce the best results; for, though so small a percentage of her women are literate, that percentage wields an enormous influence, and, therefore, presents an appeal ... to our sympathy and friendship."[142] In the interwar period British feminists became well acquainted with Indian women's activities and with their quest for suffrage, chiefly through Eleanor Rathbone's interest in child marriage and related issues of concern to women in India. Although Rathbone was something of a "feminist ally" for Indian women, she was also a missionary for Western feminist attitudes and, in the end, a "maternal imperialist" when it came to sharing with Indian feminists the lessons of the British women's movement. She adopted a distinctively British feminist imperial tone toward a number of prominent Indian women active in social and political reform in the 1930s, and, as Barbara Ramusack indicates, they came to resent her intrusiveness and her "Mother knows best" attitude.[143] As a product of the imperial feminism of the Victorian and Edwardian eras, she acted out of habit and out of the presumption that she *did* know best because of her experiences at the "storm-centre" of the international women's movement.[144]

As British suffrage periodicals amply illustrate, it was not the suffrage experience alone that veterans of the long campaign for the vote felt entitled them to the leadership of the world's women. It was the total experience of being British and the awareness of belonging to the British "world empire," which informed British suffrage internationalism and gave the women's movement its imperial cast. Even suffragettes, who prided themselves on their extraparliamentary methods, never stopped arguing for the vote as their constitutional right, as part of their British heritage.[145] "We are not Hottentots," Emmeline-Pethick-Lawrence reminded the readers of *Votes for Women* in December 1910. "Never let it be said that women of British name and descent were so tamed by brutal handling that they choose submission and humiliation rather than revolt." In Pethick-Lawrence's view, women were militant in part because of their "blood and race": they were British, not aboriginal or subject peoples, and by "choosing revolt" they distinguished between themselves as rightful British citizens and the conquered races of the empire. For her, this was nothing less than a vindication of their British heritage.[146] Charlotte Despard agreed. Of Cromer and Curzon she argued that "both these men have had to do with subject races, have spent a great part of their lifetime in Egypt and India. Do they really think that the women of England are a subject race and can be treated as such? We are out to enlighten them on this point."[147]

Historians have tended to dismiss the rhetoric of Christabel and Emmeline Pankhurst at the outbreak of the war as uncharacteristically nationalistic for the women's movement or as the product of their own peculiar and autocratic temperaments. Brian Harrison seems to suggest moreover that Emmeline Pankhurst's concern for empire was a twentieth-century development and an anomaly in terms of other feminists of her generation.[148] But in light of the nationalist and imperial rhetoric that dominated much of the suffrage movement, at least up to 1915, Christabel Pankhurst's determination that "we will not be Prussianized" seems part of a larger feminist attempt to defend Britain's brand of imperialism as preferable to other European imperial styles.[149] It has more rather than less in common with the nationalist-imperial concerns exhibited by British feminists of all stripes from the 1860s onward. National identity in this period turned on an imperial axis, and British suffragism, for all its internal political divisions, revolved on that same unifying axis. Demands for political suffrage were demands for national subjectivity and imperial citizenship. That these crusades should have produced a nationalist feminist rhetoric is fairly predictable, and it seemed perfectly "natural" and normal to British feminists themselves, who scarcely remarked on it. Indeed they understood it as one of the terms of admission to the imperial nation-state.

Feminists writing for suffrage periodicals relied on the construction of a helpless Indian womanhood to justify "votes for women" not just as a political privilege, but as a right to which they were entitled as citizens of an imperial nation. As represented in suffrage periodicals, "the Indian woman" was at once the site where British feminism's internationalism was exhibited and its imperial structures were revealed.[150] The appropriation of Indian women as a specifically feminist-colonial possession was an effective challenge to the Antis' claims that women were unfit to govern the British Empire. It also affirmed an imperial identity for them in the larger world of women, underscoring the limits of their international feminism. They nonetheless counted heavily on Britain's imperial status, as evidenced by a dependent Indian womanhood, to legitimize them as the arbiters of international sisterhood. In this sense, not simply Indian women but the women of the whole world were the constituency that justified, they argued, their claims to incorporation in the government of a worldwide empire. "One race, one nation/Womanhood" may have been the universal cry of the British suffrage movement, but it gave global sisterhood a "sacral character" and a universalizing tendency that modern Western feminists are still in the process of interrogating.[151]

7

Representation, Empire, and Feminist History

Gayatri Chakravorty Spivak has argued that "it should not be possible to read nineteenth-century British literature without remembering that imperialism, understood as England's social mission, was a crucial part of the cultural representation of England to the English."[1] As this study shows, it is virtually impossible to read the literature of middle-class British feminism in the Victorian and Edwardian periods without being reminded that imperialism was also an essential part of feminists' representation of British feminism to the British. In a cultural climate where claims for women's equality and inclusion were met with repeated hostility, liberal bourgeois feminists involved in various aspects of the women's movement conceived of empire as a legitimate place for exhibiting their fitness for participation in the imperial nation-state. Britain's imperial mission was one that feminists of the period readily embraced: indeed, they claimed it as their own feminist burden and argued that, without female emancipation, Britain's special mission to the world was in peril. Gandhi's comment that "it is no wonder that a people which produces such daughters and mothers should hold the sceptre" is a testament to their persuasive powers.[2] Needless to say, it would have stunned the likes of Cromer and Curzon had they ever heard it. Convincing their opponents that British women had an imperial vision and an imperial role was a critical part of the liberal feminist agenda between 1865 and 1915. Saving Indian women was as much a part of the civilizing mission for feminists as it had been for generations of colonial policymakers who had insisted on the abolition of suttee and, by 1915, for Indian nationalists reworking India's relationship with the British Empire. For British feminists, Indian nationalists, and imperial statesmen, all of whom imagined her variously and for their own purposes, "the Indian woman" was one of the universals upon which their liberal and "liberating" reform projects depended.[3]

The world war brought an end to certain kinds of suffrage activity and to certain kinds of assumptions about the future of traditional imperial relationships. As I suggested in the previous chapter, British feminists' representations of Indian women began to shift away from images of dependency toward a recognition of their independence and their involvement in an indigenous women's movement in India. Clearly Catt's trip to Asia and Indian women's contributions to the war effort affected British feminists' perceptions of what Indian women were "capable of," however belatedly in terms of the actual history of Indian feminism. The war itself meanwhile provided compelling evidence of the sexism of an imperial nation that would take its women's sons and yet deny them citizenship. How much longer, *Common Cause* asked, can it exclude those women who were the very "centre of the Empire?"[4] Not all feminist women supported the war, and in many ways it fragmented what had been the fractured unity of the suffrage movement in the early twentieth century. Nonetheless, given the significance that many British feminists attached to women's war relief work in terms of proving their worthiness and their capabilities for citizenship, it is not surprising that they should have valued similar demonstrations of fitness exhibited by their Indian "sisters."[5]

And yet it would be an exaggeration to conclude that the war radically challenged British feminists' imperial identities with regard to Indian women, or that the representations of the prewar period evaporated after the smoke and fire of the international conflagration had subsided. It is true that after 1918 British feminists had much more personal contact with Indian women, whom they met in their capacity as delegates to IWSA and ICW conferences and with whom they worked on reforms like birth control and legislation affecting women and children. Eleanor Rathbone's work on Indian child marriage is generally the best known of these efforts, but other suffrage women—Edith How-Martyn, for example—who had come up through the feminist ranks in the Victorian and Edwardian periods were also very active on behalf of Indian women.[6] Significantly, M.P. Nancy' Astor's first parliamentary intervention was to urge Indian women's involvement in the Indian political system. And while she was serving as Astor's paid secretary, Ray Strachey campaigned for Indian women's enfranchisement.[7] The lingering effects of Victorian imperial feminism are evident not just in Indian feminists' resentment of British feminists' imperial mannerisms but in the "private doubts" that the most experienced British feminist women expressed about their capacity for citizenship. Like Rathbone, Strachey wondered "what will happen if these very backward women do get the votes."[8] Although she ended with "perhaps nothing worse than the men having it," Strachey's comments reflect decades of Western feminists' belief that colonial women required representation by and through *them* in the colonial state. Enshrined as it had been in the organized British feminist movement, Indian women's incapacity to represent themselves was a conviction that was difficult to give up.

Orientalist references continued to appear in feminists' vocabulary in the postwar period, revealing what remained a generational set of imperial cultural attitudes. Rathbone's often quoted reference to men's "Turk complex" says more about her views of non-Western men, whom she believed to be too proud of their capacity to support women as their dependents to embrace women's equality, than about non-Western women, though she believed they were complicitous in their own oppression.[9] Helena Swanwick's insistence that she would not "commit mental suttee" (by staying home and taking care of her mother once her father had died) and Vera Brittain's equally determined skepticism in 1928 that, despite the pending women's suffrage bill, English women had not "rounded seraglio point," illustrates the persistence with which images of enslaved Oriental womanhood informed feminist discourses well beyond the war.[10] The representations of Indian women upon which liberal British feminist ideology had relied since the 1860s thus continued to circulate as truth, unremarked upon in part because they seemed natural and were understood as references to a set of shared assumptions about the Other woman. They are an example of the way in which ideologies can "harden into objects and so sustain themselves as real presences in the world"—especially given the formal political power that female and feminist M.P.'s now held in the imperial nation-state.[11]

That hard-won parliamentary power was not always easily articulated, as tallies of how often various women M.P.'s spoke in the House in the course of their parliamentary careers suggest.[12] Speaking out on issues of concern to colonial women in the House could also be, as Susan Pedersen has illustrated, a delicate matter.[13] The challenges that talking about African female circumcision on the House floor posed to newly elected women M.P.'s in the 1930s were reminiscent of the conditions under which Butler and her supporters dared to speak the apparently "unspeakable" during the campaign to repeal the Contagious Diseases Acts. British feminists exhibited little unease in taking up *colonial* issues, however, and in articulating their imperial authority in an "imperial voice" in colonial affairs.[14] It was a register in which they had long felt comfortable. Much as they had throughout the half a century before 1915, feminists working for Indian women in the interwar years saw their imperial responsibility as "a one-sided affair." It was a task that Rathbone in particular viewed as "a duty incumbent on the privileged and advanced, an opportunity to spread the achievements of feminism to less fortunate women."[15]

All of which raises important questions about the conditions under which women's citizenship and, more particularly, middle-class British feminist subjectivity, was fashioned in the late Victorian and Edwardian eras. Brian Harrison insists that British feminism "was launched as a political movement in the optimistic mid-Victorian liberal mood of emancipation and free trade." Out of this "optimistic," progressive, and liberal climate emerged not just British feminist campaigns, but also the whole international women's movement.[16] The confidence—and the anxieties—that empire brought cannot be ignored by those seeking to explain the rise of liberal feminism in Britain. Neither can the impact of imperial culture on shaping the ways in which claims for Western women's self-representation were transformed into claims about the authority to be representatives—"those empowered to speak on behalf of their constituency: the authoritative voices of a group."[17] In traditional British political culture, male citizens spoke for British women, children, and colonized peoples. As citizens feminists claimed the right to speak for themselves as women and so therefore to speak for the women and children of Britain. Those same groups in the empire's native populations were, they believed, their natural constituencies as well. In the British context, obtaining self-representation was the equivalent of earning the privilege of conferring salvation. It could not be otherwise in an imperial culture whose self-image depended on the confidence in its own Christian civilizing mission and which viewed representative democracy as the highest form of civilized government. And although some British feminists were sympathetic to Indian nationalists, the discourses they utilized to frame their quest for subjectivity worked to displace the claims that nationalist men were making to represent (and hence to rescue) Indian women. Partha Chatterjee argues that Indian men refused to let Indian women become an issue of negotiation with the colonial state, partly because they wanted to protect them from what they viewed as the corrupting influences of Western materialism.[18] British feminists, in contrast, virtually insisted on making Indian women a major point of negotiation. They did this in large measure because they believed that they were, by virtue of being British women, already identical with the imperial nation and hence both incorruptible and purifying. They did so also, of course, because Indian women appeared to them to be the natural and logical "white woman's burden." It scarcely occurred to them to question the nobility of this cause or the superiorities that justified it.

"Speaking for" Indian women seemed as natural to many liberal middle-class British feminists as did "speaking for" working-class women. The whole concept of "suffrage servants"—women who did the daily secretarial and menial chores of active feminist women—turns on a philosophy of representation that is class marked and has its resonances with the kinds of "services," ideological and otherwise, that Indian women provided to middle-class British feminists. As Agnes, Helena Swanwick's "suffrage servant," told her: "I can't write and speak myself, but I can set you free to write and speak."[19] An important question that follows from this study is the extent to which socialist or working-class women challenged the premises of liberal middle-class feminism and forged different kinds of relationships with empire and Indian women, real or imagined.[20] More work needs to be done too on the impact of feminist support for medical aid to Indian women and of colonial education projects for women in general. And British feminists' attitudes toward the conflicts in the white-settler colonies between votes for white women and black men's suffrage is another dimension of British imperial feminism that requires attention. Both the texts and activities of Western women need to be seen as part of colonial expansion and as part of the maintenance of colonial rule. Women's agency must be acknowledged as operating in opposition to oppressive ideologies and in support of them—sometimes simultaneously.[21] And, finally, empire itself needs to be understood as one of the inspirational causes that British women looked to when seeking a rationale for and a validation of their reform activities in the public sphere. Whether this was as unique to the British as they believed their empire to be remains to be seen. French feminists used the French Revolution as a world-historical inspiration, and, as Karen Offen has also suggested, concerns about depopulation and racial stability dominated feminist rhetoric in the late nineteenth and early twentieth centuries.[22] The extent to which French feminists of the period also relied on North African women to constitute a colonialized female Other would be an interesting point of comparison—although orientalist conventions vary significantly according to cultural context and historical specificity, as Lisa Lowe has admirably demonstrated for the French and British cases.[23] In any event, given its impact on the international women's movement, British feminism's imperial locations are relevant to the national and the international frameworks within which women's movements articulated their claims worldwide during this period. Further excavating the complexities of British imperial feminism will help to reshape the entire field in which the projects of women's history and feminist history are currently conceptualized and undertaken.[24]

This book would not be complete without some critical reflection on the traditions of "speaking for" that Western imperial feminism has left in its historical wake. Anita Levy writes that the project of social historians and historians of women over nearly three decades has been "to adopt the voices . . . of [those] long excluded from history, as they understood it, to restore them to the world of the past, and so to rescue them from obscurity."[25] They have, in other words, been "speaking for" women and other "Others" by (re)producing them as the objects of history. And because feminist theory is so historically grounded, these translations have provided the foundation for much of modern feminist ideology itself. How to produce feminist histories—of women, of men, of social relations, of politics— without either claiming to speak for or doing violence to the ostensible subjects of those projects is at the heart of current feminist epistemological debates.[26] What feminists of color, though not exclusively, have especially claimed is that the process of representing/representation and the process of colonizing can be one in the same, because the creation of an Other has been historically fundamental to the creation of selfhood—that "illegitimate act," as Janaki Nair calls it.[27] The extent to which the vocabulary of "coming to voice," "speaking for," "representing," "recovering," "restoring to history" are both deeply politicized and inscribed equally in contemporary patriarchal and world-imperial relationships is something that all feminist practitioners and historians in general need continually to be aware of. As Laura Donaldson has written, "Empires exist through complex relationships of control, and we can disregard no strategy or micrology of power that disseminates them."[28] That feminisms and their histories have been and are among such strategies suggests that we disregard their historical effects at our peril. It is also a reminder that we must beware of grounding claims about the legitimacy and authority of our work without taking full account of the historical meanings—their situatedness, limitations, and negotiability—attached to the stories we purport to tell.[29]

Notes

ABBREVIATIONS USED IN NOTES

BL   British Library
CC   *Common Cause*
EW   *Englishwoman*
EWJ   *Englishwoman's Journal*
EWR   *Englishwoman's Review*
FL   Fawcett Library
IMR   *Indian Magazine and Review*
IWSA   International Woman Suffrage Alliance
JBALC   Josephine Butler Autograph Letter Collection, Fawcett Library
JBC   Josephine Butler Collection, Fawcett Library
LNA   Ladies' National Association
NUWSS   National Union of Women's Suffrage Societies
OIOC   Oriental and India Office Collections
VFW   *Votes for Women*
WF   *Women's Franchise*
WFL   Women's Freedom League
WH   *Woman's Herald*
WPP   *Women's Penny Paper*
WSJ   *Women's Suffrage Journal*

CHAPTER 1

1. Ware's *Beyond the Pale* devotes one chapter to English women's interest in India, though the book is not concerned with the history of imperial feminism as such. Ferguson's *Subject to Others*, for its part, does not deal with British imperialism per se. And though she does suggest connections to nineteenth-century feminism, Ferguson's emphasis is on female writers as opposed to feminists. See also Rich, "Notes on a Politics of Location," in *Blood, Bread and Poetry*, pp. 210–31; Hewitt, "Sisterhood in International Perspective"; Bulbeck, *One World Women's Movement*; Burton, "The Feminist Quest for Identity"; Rupp, "Conflict in the International Women's Movement"; and Summers, *Angels and Citizens*, pp. 272, 283–85.

2. Woolf, *Three Guineas* and *A Room of One's Own*; Black, "Virginia Woolf and the Women's Movement," in Marcus, ed., *Virginia Woolf*, p. 183; Virginia Woolf, "Mr. Kipling's Notebook," quoted in Marcus, "Pathographies," pp. 818–19.

3. Gillian Beer, "The Island and the Aeroplane: The Case of Virginia Woolf," in Bhabha, ed., *Nation and Narration*, p. 266.

4. Strobel, *European Women*, p. xii. Not even early Indian congressmen wanted an end to the colonial relationship. See Edward C. Moulton, "The Early Congress and the British Radical Connection" in Low, ed., *The Indian National Congress*, pp. 22–23.

5. See, for example, Levy, *Other Women*.

6. Some noteworthy recent exceptions to this tendency are Stanley, "British Feminist Histories"; Marks, "History, the Nation and the Empire"; Hall, *White Male and Middle Class*, esp. chap. 1; and Bayly, *Imperial Meridian*.

7. Amos and Parmar, "Challenging Imperial Feminism."

8. Both Herstein and Levine insist on locating the beginnings of the modern feminist movement in the 1850s as opposed to the 1860s. See *A Mid-Victorian Feminist* and *Feminist Lives in Victorian England*. In a complementary maneuver, Snyder argues that social imperialism in Britain—traditionally considered a late-nineteenth-century phenomenon—can also be located in the 1850s. See his *Myths of Empire*, esp. chap. 5.

9. See Lacey, ed., *Barbara Leigh Smith Bodichon*; Shannon, *The Crisis of Imperialism*, pp. 19–39; and Porter, *The Lion's Share*.

10. Poovey, *Uneven Developments*, pp. 164–98; C. S. Bremner, "Florence Nightingale," *Vote*, May 7, 1915, pp. 597–98; "One of the Great Immortals: Impressive and Far Reaching Commemoration of Florence Nightingale, May 12, 1915," *Vote*, May 21, 1915, pp. 613–14.

11. Butler, *Native Races and the War*; Harrison, *Prudent Revolutionaries*, p. 18; Ann Oakley, "Millicent Garrett Fawcett: Duty and Determination," in Spender, ed., *Feminist Theorists*, pp. 195–96.

12. Sarah S. Amos, "The Woman Suffrage Question," *Contemporary Review* 61 (June 1892): 778.

13. Gorham, " 'The Friendships of Women,' " p. 44.

14. Mohanty, "Feminist Encounters," p. 34. See also Jain, "Can Feminism Be a Global Ideology?"; Kishwar, "Why I Do Not Call Myself a Feminist"; *Feminism and the Critique of Colonial Discourse*, special issue of *Inscriptions* 3–4 (1988); and MacLeod, "Hegemonic Relations and Gender Resistance," p. 537.

15. It is not my intention to exaggerate the actual extent of this decline in 1918 but rather to underline the impact that anxieties about the stability and permanence of empire had on contemporaries. As Samuel notes, although there was a gradual relinquishing of imperial ideals after World War I, Britons still considered Britain to be the mother country, at least down to 1960 if not beyond. See his *Patriotism*, 1:xxii, xxv–xxvii. For the tenacity of beliefs about the nature of British global supremacy after 1945, see Darwin, *The End of Empire*.

16. Ware, *Beyond the Pale*, p. 119.

17. For a discussion of the first generations of British feminists, see Banks, *Becoming a Feminist*.

18. Jacqueline Jenkinson, "The 1919 Race Riots in Britain: A Survey," in Lotz and Pegg, eds., *Under the Imperial Carpet*, pp. 182–207; Fryer, *Staying Power*, esp. chap. 10; Scobie, *Black Britannia*; Fein, *Imperial Crime and Punishment*.

19. Harrison, *Prudent Revolutionaries*, p. 8; Mayhall, " 'Dare to Be Free.' "

20. Emmeline Pethick-Lawrence, report on Albert Hall meeting, *VFW*, April 1908, p. 112.

21. Macmillan, "The Struggle for Political Liberty," lecture given February 16, 1909, p. 15, FL. For discussion of the Woman's Charter, see Claire Hirshfield, "Fractured Faith," p. 192.

22. Harrison, *Prudent Revolutionaries*, pp. 18, 114, 185; Jeffreys, *The Spinster and Her Enemies*, p. 147; Murphy, *The Women's Suffrage Movement*, p. 73.

23. This is the view of Robbins, "Core and Periphery in Modern British History," p. 276. See also Jane Mackay and Pat Thane, "The Englishwoman," in Colls and Dodd, eds., *Englishness*, p. 231.

24. Graham Dawson, "The Blond Bedouin: Lawrence of Arabia, Imperial Adventure and the Imagining of English-British Masculinity," in Roper and Tosh, eds., *Manful Assertions*, p. 139 n. 10. For a discussion of one such conflict between "English" and "British" feminists, see below, Chap. 6.

25. Quoted in Harrison *Prudent Revolutionaries*, p. 179.

26. Stanley, "British Feminist Histories," p. 3.

27. Mackenzie, *Propaganda and Empire*, pp. 1–2.

28. "Empire Day and the Daughters of Empire," *CC*, May 22, 1914, p. 149.

29. Mani, "The Production of an Official Discourse on *Sati*"; Said, *Orientalism*, p. 206; Harper, "Recovering the Other."

30. I am grateful to Barbara Ramusack for emphasizing this axis of comparison.

31. Mrs. Weitbrecht, *The Christian Woman's Ministry*; see also Duff, *Female Education in India.*

32. Nair, "Uncovering the Zenana."

33. Visram, *Ayahs, Lascars, and Princes*; Tharu and Lalita, eds., *Women Writing in India.*

34. Lacquer, "Bodies, Details"; Lawrence, "Just Plain Common Sense."

35. Butler, "Mrs. Butler's Plea," p. 8.

36. Nightingale, "Our Indian Stewardship," p. 330. See also Sen, *Florence Nightingale's Letters*, pp. 16–17; Kaminsky, *The India Office*, p. 160.

37. Carpenter, *Six Months in India*, esp. 2:80–102.

38. Butler, *The New Abolitionists*, pp. 192–94; Carpenter, *The Last Days.* Eleanor Rathbone's family had also hosted Roy during his visit to England. See Ramusack, "Cultural Missionaries" (which also deals with Cousins and Noble), pp. 119–36.

39. Carpenter, *Six Months in India*, 2:83.

40. See, for example, Liddington and Norris, *One Hand Tied Behind Us*; and Dyhouse, *Feminism and the Family.*

41. Levine, *Feminist Lives*, pp. 1–7; Lewis, *Women and Social Action*, p. 282.

42. See Harrison on Teresa Billington-Grieg, *Prudent Revolutionaries*, pp. 45–72; and Strachey on the reluctance of suffrage women to associate with Butler's domestic repeal crusade, *The Cause*, pp. 268–69. Harrison and Dyhouse agree that suffrage was a cause that united women in the twentieth century (*Prudent Revolutionaries*, pp. 1, 310; *Feminism and the Family*, p. 3), though Levine rightly warns against giving suffrage pride of place in the British women's movement (*Feminist Lives*, pp. 1–2). Lewis argues convincingly that national and parliamentary suffrage was divisive among women in the Victorian philanthropic community (*Women and Social Action*, p. 282).

43. National Union of Women Workers, *Official Report of the Central Conference*; Moral Reform Union, *Annual Reports.* See also Adam, *Women in Council.*

44. The NUWW embraced women's suffrage in 1902, but, according to Har-

rison, the ICW moved more slowly; its tardiness was partly responsible for the formation of the International Woman Suffrage Alliance in 1904 (*Prudent Revolutionaries*, p. 6). More significantly, Millicent Fawcett spoke to the NUWW General Committee in October 1897 on the subject of regulated prostitution in India, thus demonstrating the ways in which suffrage women met other female reformers in the cause of Indian womanhood. Fawcett, "New Rules."

45. Holton, *Feminism and Democracy*, pp. 28, 38–52.

46. Carpenter, *Six Months in India*, 2:83.

47. *CC*, May 16, 1913, p. 84.

48. Hester Gray, "The White Woman's Burden," *CC*, November 27, 1914, pp. 565–66.

49. According to Strachey, Fawcett saw the suffrage "as a means to eliminate prostitution, ease divorce constraints upon women, and raise public morals generally." It was a conviction shared by most if not all suffrage women. Quoted in Kent, *Sex and Suffrage*, p. 14.

50. Weitbrecht, *The Christian Woman's Ministry*; Carpenter, *Six Months in India*; Mrs. Bayle Bernard, "The Position of Women in India," *EWR*, July 1868, pp. 471–82.

51. Weitbrecht, *The Christian Woman's Ministry*, p. 6.

52. Henrietta Muller, "A Voice from India," *Shafts*, April 1894, p. 240.

53. Gray, "The White Woman's Burden," pp. 565–66; see also Harrison, *Separate Spheres*, p. 60.

54. Nair, "Uncovering the Zenana," pp. 11–12. I am grateful to Janaki Nair for reiterating this point to me in conversation and in personal correspondence.

55. As Louise Creighton put it, "The act of voting is not, as some would wish to make it, the chief way in which the individual can share in the work of the State for the good of all." "The Appeal versus Female Suffrage," p. 351.

56. Offen, "Defining Feminism"; Cott, *The Grounding of Modern Feminism*, pp. 3–10; Levine, *Feminist Lives*, pp. 1–7.

57. Said, *Orientalism*; Leonore Davidoff, "Class and Gender in Victorian England," in Newton, Ryan, and Walkowitz, eds., *Sex and Class in Women's History*, pp. 19–22; Levy, *Other Women*, esp. pp. 1–19.

58. Harrison, *Prudent Revolutionaries*, p. 304. Kent claims that in the domestic repeal campaign feminists understood the ways in which the whole notion of the respectable middle-class woman depended on a contrast with the "fallen woman" but that they "refused the terms of the contrast"(*Sex and Suffrage*, p. 60). I generally agree, but would qualify it with the caveat that they relied on the pathos of the contrast to help legitimate their own reclamation work.

59. Davidoff and Hall, *Family Fortunes*, pp. 19, 115; Poovey, *Uneven Developments*, p. 9 and chap. 6.

60. Harrison attributes this line of reasoning to both T. B. Macaulay and J. S. Mill (*Prudent Revolutionaries*, p. 305).

61. Levine, " 'The Humanising Influences,' " p. 305.

62. Harrison, *Separate Spheres*, p. 59.

63. Although F. B. Smith has applied the term "Antis" to the anti–C.D. Acts regulationists, the more conventional Victorian application was to the antisuffrag-

ists, and this is how I use it throughout my text. See his "The Contagious Diseases Acts Reconsidered."

64. Goldwin Smith, "Conservatism and Female Suffrage," *National Review*, February 1888, p. 740.

65. Lewis, *Women and Social Action*, p. 247. See also "Ward and the Imperial Franchise," *VFW*, May 22, 1914, p. 526.

66. Quoted in Harrison, *Separate Spheres*, p. 75.

67. Ibid., esp. chaps. 6–9; Tickner, *The Spectacle of Women*, pp. 205 ff.

68. Wright, *The Unexpurgated Case*, pp. 32–33.

69. Leneman, *A Guid Cause*, p. 25.

70. See, for example, the *Punch* cartoon for June 14, 1884, " 'The Angel in the House'; Or, The Result of Female Suffrage (A Troubled Dream of the Future)," reprinted on the cover of Pugh, *Women's Suffrage*.

71. Browne, *The Eighteenth-Century Feminist Mind*, pp. 135–36.

72. "Lord Curzon on Women's Suffrage," *VFW*, May 21, 1909, p. 701.

73. *VFW*, January 7, 1909, p. 246. Harrison mentions both Emmeline Pankhurst and Emmeline Pethick-Lawrence's fatigue over the ridicule and contempt to which women's suffrage workers were subject (*Prudent Revolutionaries*, pp. 31, 305).

74. Hall Caine, "Mother of the Man," *VFW*, November 10, 1911, p. 89.

75. Pfeiffer, "The Suffrage for Women," p. 426.

76. Quoted in Harrison, *Prudent Revolutionaries*, p. 18.

77. Mrs. St. Clair Stobart, "Women and War," *VFW*, February 7, 1913, p. 267.

78. "Women and the Empire" (December 1913), in *NUWSS Pamphlets*, FL.

79. J. Malcolm Mitchell, "Colonial Statesmen and Votes for Women" (London: WFL, ca. 1912), pp. 2–3, FL.

80. For a fuller discussion of imperial suffrage arguments, see Chap. 6.

81. Fawcett, "The Women's Suffrage Bill," p. 555; and her "The Future of Englishwomen"; Pfeiffer, "The Suffrage for Women." See also Goldwin Smith, "The Organization of Democracy," *Contemporary Review* 47 (March 1885): 327–28; and "Female Suffrage," *Macmillan's Magazine* 30 (June 1874): 139–50.

82. "Lord Curzon on Women's Suffrage," p. 701.

83. Mrs. Arthur Lyttleton, quoted in Eva McLaren, National Conference of Delegates of Women's Suffrage Societies in Great Britain and Ireland (Birmingham, 1896), *Women's Suffrage Pamphlets* (1898), p. 10, FL.

84. This was, incidentally, a common presumption among feminists and Antis alike. Lewis, *Women and Social Action*, p. 201. See also below, Chap. 2. I am grateful to Laura Mayhall for suggesting in private correspondence this distinction between "refiguring" and feminization per se.

85. Rogers, *Feminism*, p. 183; Ferguson and Todd, *Mary Wollstonecraft*, p. 65. So cynical was Lady Mary Wortley Montagu about men's capacity to take women seriously as human beings that she lamented, "[In] a Common-wealth of rational Horses . . . it would be an established maxim . . . that a mare could not be taught to pace." Quoted in Rogers, *Feminism*, p. 241.

86. Crosby argues that, for Victorians, women were "the unhistorical other of history" (*The Ends of History*, p. 1).

87. Smith, "Conservatism and Female Suffrage," p. 746.

88. Fawcett, "The Appeal against Female Suffrage," p. 93; Fawcett, "The Women's Suffrage Bill," p. 562; see also her "The Women's Suffrage Movement," in Stanton, ed., *The Woman Question*, p. 6.

89. Frederic Harrison, "The Emancipation of Women," *Fortnightly Review* 56 (October 1891): 451.

90. Monsignor Keller of Youghal called Irish women suffragists "that strange tribe. . . . They are not men, they are not women." Quoted in Owens, *Smashing Times*, p. 68. Lord Cromer, for his part, believed that "there is much more difference, both physically and morally, between an educated European man and woman than there is between a negro and a negress belonging to the same savage Central African tribe." Quoted in Harrison, *Separate Spheres*, p. 60.

91. Berlant, "National Brands/National Body"; Spivak, "Three Women's Texts."

92. Butler, *Gender Trouble*, p. 1; Roper and Tosh, eds., *Manful Assertions*, p. 13; and Hall, "The Economy of Intellectual Prestige," p. 190. Jones argues in the same vein when she claims that historically authority has been implicitly connected with masculinity and that this is "its representational fate." See "The Trouble with Authority," p. 109.

93. According to Hobsbawm, there were in the nineteenth century three criteria for classification as a nation: "historic association with a current state"; a long-established cultural elite "possessing a written national literary and administrative vernacular"; and "a proven capacity for conquest." *Nations and Nationalism*, pp. 37–38.

94. Mills has said the same of Western women's travel writing (*Discourses of Difference*, pp. 1–2). Tyrrell speaks similarly about the WCTU (*Woman's World*, p. 4).

95. Mommsen, *Theories of Imperialism*; Fieldhouse, "Humpty-Dumpty"; Bayly, *Imperial Meridian*, esp. pp. 1–12, 253–56.

96. Callaway, *Gender, Culture and Empire*, p. 5.

97. Mackenzie, *Propaganda and Empire*; Callaway, *Gender, Culture and Empire*; Strobel, *European Women*; Leslie Flemming, ed., *Women's Work for Women*; Claudia Knapman, *White Women in Fiji*. See also Haggis, "Gendering Colonialism or Colonising Gender?" I am grateful to the author for providing me with an early draft of this essay.

98. Hunter, *The Gospel of Gentility*, p. 173.

99. Hyam, "Empire and Sexual Opportunity"; Berger, "Imperialism and Sexual Exploitation"; Hyam, " 'Imperialism and Sexual Exploitation' "; and Hyam, *Empire and Sexuality*.

100. Davidoff and Hall, *Family Fortunes*, pp. 9, 115: Poovey, *Uneven Developments*, pp. 2, 109–10, 194.

101. Stanley, "British Feminist Histories," p. 3; Marks, "History, the Nation and the Empire," pp. 111–19; and Hall, *White, Male and Middle Class*, pp. 20–21.

102. Though perhaps for less than discreet political motives. Sir David Lean's remark in 1980 that "women lost us the empire" is one of the best examples of the transparently political motives behind certain versions of "imperial" history. Quoted in Callaway, *Gender, Culture and Empire*, p. 1.

103. Stanley, "British Feminist Histories," p. 3.

104. Guha, ed., *Subaltern Studies*; Spivak, "Three Women's Texts"; Bayly, *Imperial Meridian*, p. 11.

105. Sangari and Vaid, eds., *Recasting Women*, pp. 1–24.

106. Lata Mani, "Contentious Traditions: The Debate on *Sati* in Colonial India," and Partha Chatterjee, "The Nationalist Resolution of the Women's Question," in Sangari and Vaid, eds., *Recasting Women*, pp. 88–120 and pp. 233–53, respectively; Heimsath, *Indian Nationalism*; and R. Radhakrishnan, "Nationalism, Gender and the Narrative of Identity," in Parker et al., eds., *Nationalisms and Sexualities*, pp. 77–95.

107. Strobel, *European Women*, pp. 50–51.

108. Lewis, *Women and Social Action*, pp. 3, 74, 243, 247.

109. Chandra Mohanty, "Cartographies of Struggle: Third World Women and the Politics of Feminism," in Mohanty, Russo, and Torres, eds., *Third World Women*, p. 33; Linda Gordon, "What's New in Women's History," in de Lauretis, ed., *Feminist Studies*, p. 30. bell hooks articulates a similar concern when she says that "blackness does not mean that we are inherently oppositional." See her "The Politics of Black Subjectivity," in *Yearning*, p. 18.

110. Butler, *Gender Trouble*, p. 2.

111. Marjorie Garber, "The Occidental Tourist: *M. Butterfly* and the Scandal of Transvestism," in Parker et al., eds., *Nationalisms and Sexualities*, pp. 121–46; Dawson, "The Blond Bedouin," pp. 113–44.

112. Gordon, "What's New in Women's History," p. 24. Alarcon argues that "differences may be purposefully constituted for the purpose of domination or exclusion, *especially in oppositional thinking*." "The Theoretical Subject(s)," p. 365; emphasis added.

113. Uma Chakravarti, "Whatever Happened to the Vedic *Dasi*? Orientalism, Nationalism and a Script for the Past," in Sangari and Vaid, eds., *Recasting Women*, pp. 27–87; Kishwar, "Why I Do Not Call Myself a Feminist," pp. 2–9; Parmar, "Other Kinds of Dreams."

114. Strobel accepts "the stance of sympathetic criticism" (*European Women*, p. ix), and Sangari and Vaid reject it (*Recasting Women*, p. 18). Paxton also struggles with these dilemmas in "Complicity and Resistance" and in "Disembodied Subjects: English Women's Autobiography under the Raj," in Smith and Watson, eds., *Decolonizing the Subject*, pp. 387–409.

115. Gordon, "Writing Culture," p. 20.

116. Echols, *Daring to Be Bad*. See also Vogel, "Telling Tales"; Jayawardena, *Feminism and Nationalism*; Hossain, *Sultana's Dreams*; Shaarawi, *Harem Years*; Badran and Cooke, eds., *Opening the Gates*.

117. Davis, *Women, Race and Class*; DuBois, *Feminism and Suffrage*; Terborg-Penn, "Discontented Black Feminists"; Carby, *Reconstructing Womanhood*, esp. pp. 3–34.

118. Amos and Parmar, "Challenging Imperial Feminism."

119. Sandoval, "Feminism and Racism," p. 71.

120. Minh-ha, *Woman, Native, Other*, pp. 41–42.

121. Butler, *Gender Trouble*, pp. 4, 13.

122. Vogel, "Telling Tales," p. 91.

123. Sangari and Vaid, eds., *Recasting Women*, p. 18.

124. Lugones, "Hablando cara a cara," pp. 47–48.

125. Sangari and Vaid, eds., *Recasting Women*, p. 24; hooks, *Yearning*, p. 54.

126. Crosby, *The Ends of History*, p. 151.

127. hooks, *Yearning*, p. 19; Joan Scott, review of *Heroes of Their Own Lives*, by Linda Gordon, *Signs* 15, no. 4 (Summer 1990): 852–53, 859–60.

128. Gordon, "What's New in Women's History," p. 19.

129. Minh-ha, *Woman, Native, Other*, p. 48; Donna Haraway, Panel Discussion 2, *Feminism and the Critique of Colonial Discourse*, special issue of *Inscriptions* 3–4 (1988): 95–96; Sandoval, "Feminism and Racism," p. 66.

130. Minh-ha, *Woman, Native, Other*, p. 48.

131. Mohanty, "Feminist Encounters," p. 39.

132. Eveline Marius, "Let's Make History," in Grewal et al., eds., *Charting the Journey*, p. 315.

133. Moses, "Debating the Present." Gibbon's observation is apt here: the past is not "sealed off, as in a time capsule, but . . . [is] part of an unresolved historical process which engulfs the present." See "Race against Time," p. 106.

134. Nair, "On the Question of 'Agency.' " See also Mira Kamdar, Panel Discussion 1, *Feminism and the Critique of Colonial Discourse*, special issue of *Inscriptions* 3–4 (1988): p. 68.

135. See Crosby, *The Ends of History*, pp. 144–58, where her last chapter is entitled "The High Cost of History."

136. Mohanty, "Feminist Encounters," p. 36.

137. Mills, *Discourses of Difference*, p. 113.

138. For an interesting debate on this question, see Veena Talwar Oldenberg, "Lifestyle as Resistance: The Case of the Courtesans of Lucknow," and Rosalind O'Hanlon, "Issues of Widowhood: Gender and Resistance in Colonial Western India," in Haynes and Prakash, eds., *Contesting Power*, pp. 23–61 and 62–108, respectively.

139. Davis et al., " 'The Public Face of Feminism.' " Thanks to Gary Daily for bringing this essay to my attention.

140. De Lauretis, "Displacing Hegemonic Discourses," p. 132.

141. For discussions about the difficulty of labeling women and men of the past "feminists," see Offen, "Defining Feminism"; Cott, *Grounding*, pp. 13–50; and Sievers, "Six (or More) Feminists," pp. 134–46, and comments that follow by Janet Afary and Asuncion Lavrin, pp. 147–57; and Badran, "Dual Liberation."

142. Paxton, "Complicity and Resistance," pp. 159. Besant was called "a pioneer of the movement for the emancipation of women" and "an important Imperial factor in the welding together of East and West." See Elizabeth Sievers, "Mrs. Annie Besant—President of the Theosophical Society—Her Work for Women" *CC*, July 20, 1911, p. 265.

143. See Ramusack, "Cultural Missionaries," pp. 124–26; Candy, "Margaret Cousins."

144. Manning was one of the first members of the London Suffrage Society in 1866. See Fawcett, "The Women's Suffrage Movement," p. 7; and "Interview: Miss E. A. Manning," *WPP*, August 31, 1889, pp. 1–2.

145. For Fawcett see Rubinstein, *A Different World*, pp. 100–101, 206–7; Fawcett, "Infant Marriage in India"; the *Indian Magazine and Review*, the journal of the National Indian Association, records some of these donations. Frances Power Cobbe, for example, gave £5 to Pandita Ramabai's home, and a Miss Swanwick (possibly Anna) gave £2.2 (November 1886); Arabella Shore donated £1 (February 1888). For support of Rukhmabai by the McLaren-Muller families, see *EWR*, January 15, 1889, and May 18, 1889; *WPP*, April 15, 1889, and June 22, 1889.

146. Tyrrell, *Woman's World*.

147. Ramusack, "Cultural Missionaries," pp. 126–28.

148. Strobel, *European Women*, p. xiii.

149. Kaminsky, *The India Office*, esp. chap. 6. Although policy was not perhaps influenced by public opinion, the India Office was certainly aware of Butler's Indian repeal campaign and had to deal with its supporters lobbying assaults (pp. 198–202).

150. Birkett, *Spinsters Abroad*, pp. 197–99; Lewis, *Women and Social Action*, pp. 196, 220, 250.

151. Lewis, *Women and Social Action*, pp. 288–90.

152. Jayal, ed., *Sidney and Beatrice Webb*, p. 84 n. 2.

153. Harrison, *Prudent Revolutionaries*, p. 320.

154. Fawcett, "New Zealand under Female Franchise"; for her views on suffrage for native men in South Africa, see her "Wanted: A Statesman," speech delivered at Athenaeum Hall, Glasgow, November 22, 1909, FL. See also "Black Peril," *CC*, September 21, 1911, pp. 408–9; "E. W.," "Empire-Building: An Interlude," *CC*, November 29, 1912, p. 585; Irene M. Ashby Macfayden, "Women and the New South African Constitution," *VFW*, August 20, 1909, pp. 1078–79; Emmeline Pethick-Lawrence, "Women or Kaffirs?," *VFW*, July 9, 1909, p. 912.

155. Murphy, *The Women's Suffrage Movement*, pp. 8, 77–78.

156. For a discussion of the national tensions inside the British women's movement, see chap. 6.

157. For a firsthand account of Ramabai's experiences in England, see Shah, ed. *Pandita Ramabai*. Rukhmabai, who came to London to study medicine, was patronized by Eva and Walter McLaren and participated in the Indian age-of-consent debates in Britain in 1890. See, for example, "How to Help Indian Women," *WPP*, April 20, 1889, p. 5; Rukhmabai, "Indian Child Marriages: An Appeal to the British Government," *New Review* 16 (September 1890): 263–69; and Lutzker, *Edith Pechey-Phipson*, esp. pp. 199–209.

158. Ray, "Calcutta Women"; Kishwar, "Gandhi on Women"; Forbes, "The Politics of Respectability," pp. 56–68.

159. Viswanathan, *Masks of Conquest*, p. 12; Alcoff, "The Problem of Speaking for Others."

160. hooks, *Yearning*, p. 57; Mani, "Contentious Traditions," pp. 88–120.

161. See Sinha, "Chathams," p. 109.

162. Vir Bharat Talwar, "Feminist Consciousness in Women's Journals in Hindi: 1910–1920," and Chatterjee, "The Nationalist Resolution," in Sangari and Vaid, eds., *Recasting Women*, pp. 204–32 and 233–53, respectively; Bannerji, "Fashioning a Self"; Forbes, "Caged Tigers"; and Forbes, "Votes for Women."

163. Jayawardena, *Feminism and Nationalism*, pp. 8–13; Forbes, "Caged Tigers." Kishwar points out what she considers a major difference between the emergence of Indian feminism and that of its Western counterparts: it was "characterized by the marked absence of the kinds of hostility from men that women's movements in some other parts of the world had to face" ("Gandhi on Women," p. 58).

164. Ramusack, "Cultural Missionaries," p. 130.

165. "An Indian Woman," "News from India," *WPP*, September 28, 1889, p. 5.

166. Shah, ed., *Pandita Ramabai*; Ramusack, "Catalysts or Helpers?"; Tyrrell, *Woman's World*, p. 102; Ramusack, "Cultural Missionaries," pp. 127–28.

167. Bulbeck, *One World Women's Movement*, p. 103.

168. hooks, *Yearning*, p. 21.

169. Nair, "On the Question of 'Agency,' " p. 18.

170. Aiwha Ong, Panel Discussion 2, *Feminism and the Critique of Colonial Discourse*, special issue of *Inscriptions* 3–4 (1988): 99; Rich, *Your Native Land*, p. 33.

171. Mohanty, "Cartographies of Struggle," p. 34; Jones, "The Trouble with Authority," p. 123; Minh-ha, *Woman, Native, Other*, p. 2.

CHAPTER 2

1. Dorothy Thompson, "Women, Work and Politics in Nineteenth-Century England: The Problem of Authority" in Rendall, ed., *Equal or Different*, pp. 57–58. "The Woman's Suffrage Movement has been, and is, mainly a moral movement, a desire on the part of women to obtain their share of authority in the State in order to cleanse it." See Maud Arncliffe-Sennett, "Women's Suffrage and Parliamentary Morals," in *Manifesto* (Northern Men's Federation for Women's Suffrage, 1916), p. 4, FL. See also Mort, *Dangerous Sexualities*, pp. 92ff.

2. Levine, *Feminist Lives*, esp. pp. 1–7.

3. Despard, "Woman in the Nation," p. 4.

4. Lewis, *Women and Social Action*, chaps. 2, 4, 5.

5. Marks, "History, the Nation and the Empire," p. 111.

6. Samuel, ed., *Patriotism*.

7. The impact of colonial nationalisms on nationalist ideologies "at home" in Europe is practically an unexplored subject, though certainly much of what Indian nationalists in the nineteenth and twentieth centuries were saying about the role of women in Indian society resonates with British feminists' attitudes toward "woman in the nation." Radhakrishnan, "Nationalism, Gender, and the Narrative of Identity"; and Chatterjee, "The Nationalist Resolution."

8. Colley, "Whose Nation?"; Hobsbawm, *Nations and Nationalism*, p. 11.

9. Bayly, *Imperial Meridian*, p. 100.

10. Notable for their attention to the ongoing processes whereby national identities were constituted from the nineteenth century onward in Britain are Robbins, *Nineteenth-Century Britain*, and Colls and Dodd, eds., *Englishness*.

11. Anderson, *Imagined Communities*, p. 102.

12. Marks, "History, the Nation and the Empire," p. 155.

13. Semmel, *Imperialism and Social Reform*, pp. 14–16, 47, and chaps. 2–4; Shan-

non, *The Crisis of Imperialism*. For a discussion of the ways in which English radicals mobilized the nation, see Finn, *After Chartism*, esp. chap. 1.

14. Semmel, *Imperialism and Social Reform*, chaps. 3, 4, esp. pp. 53–54. See also Searle, *The Quest for National Efficiency*, pp. 1–13.

15. Samuel, *Patriotism*, 1:xii.

16. Dawson, "The Blond Bedouin," pp. 118, 139 n. 10.

17. Thane and Mackay, "The Englishwoman," p. 209. Their view is echoed in D. G. Boyce, " 'The Marginal Britons': The Irish," in Colls and Dodd, eds., *Englishness*, p. 231.

18. Save Americans and sometimes Germans, who could be collectively referred to with Britain as "the Anglo-Saxon race."

19. Rich, *Race and Empire*, p. 13. See also Stocking, *Victorian Anthropology*, p. 35.

20. Rich, *Race and Empire*, p. 22.

21. Thane and Mackay, "The Englishwoman," p. 209; Rich, *Race and Empire*, p. 25.

22. As Lord Mayo put it in 1869, "We are determined as long as the sun shines in heaven to hold India. Our national character . . . demand[s] it." Quoted in Pandey, *The Break-Up of British India*, p. 23.

23. Lord Lugard, *Dual Mandate in British Tropical Africa* (1922), quoted in Curtin, ed., *Imperialism*, p. 318. Indirect rule, as Lugard understood it, was "not only . . . a practical and economical method of government, but also . . . an excellent, timely tool of the mission of civilization and trusteeship bestowed on the colonial powers by humanity." Ansprenger, *The Dissolution of Colonial Empires*, p. 64.

24. James Walvin, "Symbols of Moral Superiority: Slavery, Sport and the Changing World Order, 1800–1950," in Walvin and Mangan, eds., *Manliness and Morality*, p. 243.

25. For a discussion of the idea of national morality in Britain, see Newman, *The Rise of English Nationalism*.

26. Walvin, "Symbols of Moral Superiority," p. 243.

27. Benjamin Kidd, *The Control of the Tropics* (1898), quoted in Curtin, ed., *Imperialism*, p. 37.

28. "A Pioneer," "Women in the Mission Field: Should They Assimilate What Is Good in the Great Religions of the East with Christianity?" *Shafts*, June 1896, p. 72.

29. Quoted in Johnston, *Great Britain*, p. 86; see also Morris, *Pax Britannica*, p. 124; Curtin, ed., *Imperialism*, p. 327.

30. Morris, *Pax Britannica*, p. 122.

31. Curtin, ed., *Imperialism*, pp. 329, 331.

32. Semmel, *Imperialism*, pp. 230–31.

33. See Moulton, "The Early Congress."

34. Mackenzie, *Propaganda and Empire*, p. 2.

35. According to Rhodes, "The Empire . . . is a bread and butter question. If you want to avoid civil war, you must become imperialists." Quoted in Lenin, *Imperialism*, p. 79. I am grateful to Emary Aronson for bringing this citation to my attention.

36. Mackenzie, *Propaganda*, p. 3 and chaps. 1, 7–9.

37. Mackenzie, ed., *Imperialism and Popular Culture*; Annie Coombes, "The

Franco-British Exhibition: Packaging Empire in Victorian England," in Beckett and Cherry, eds., *The Edwardian Era*, pp. 152–66.

38. Penny Summerfield, "Patriotism and Empire: Music Hall Entertainment 1870–1914," in Mackenzie, ed., *Imperialism and Popular Culture*, pp. 17–48.

39. Mackenzie, *Propaganda*, p. 254. See also Anderson, *Imagined Communities*, p. 137.

40. Hobsbawm, *Nations*, p. 38.

41. For an excellent discussion of the ways in which empire functioned as a site of imagined collective national unity, see Coombes, "The Franco-British Exhibition."

42. Mackenzie, *Propaganda*, p. 10; emphasis added.

43. Higginbotham, "African-American Women's History," p. 268.

44. Fawcett, "The Emancipation of Women," p. 676.

45. Millicent Garrett Fawcett lauded the reform efforts of unmarried women like Octavia Hill and Florence Nightingale, who, she reminded her readers, had "lived lives filled to the brim with useful work, well and conscientiously done." See her "The Future of Englishwomen," p. 350.

46. See, for example, Butler, ed., *Woman's Work and Woman's Culture*. According to Harrison, "Partnership between men and women had always been the dominant mood within British feminism" (*Prudent Revolutionaries*, p. 306).

47. Frances Power Cobbe was even willing to give up moral superiority in exchange for the recognition of women's moral responsibility. "Granted, let me be physically, intellectually and morally your inferior. So long as you know I possess moral responsibility and sufficient intelligence to know right from wrong . . . I am quite content. It is *only* as a moral and intelligent being that I claim my civil rights." Quoted in Hollis, ed., *Women in Public*, p. 294.

48. Mohanty, "Feminist Encounters," p. 32.

49. See Catherine Hall, "The Early Formation of Victorian Domestic Ideology," in Burman, ed., *Fit Work for Women*, pp. 15–31.

50. Lewis, *Woman's Mission*, pp. 10–12.

51. Ibid., p. 141. Lewis was comparing the treatment of women in Christian countries to their position in pagan Greece and Rome. A reviewer of J. C. Maudley's *Woman outside Christendom* acknowledged that women in some Eastern religions did enjoy freedom, but began the review as follows: "The subject of this book is to prove what we imagine no one contradicts, that the condition of women among barbarous non-Christian nations is almost invariably one of servitude and degradation. Christianity was the first religion which popularly taught . . . the moral equality of men and women. *EWR*, September 15, 1880, p. 338. For echoes of this sentiment, see "X. P." "Women and Theosophy," *WPP*, October 25, 1891, p. 4; *Shafts*, December 10, 1892, p. 84; Blackburn, *Women's Suffrage*, p. 228; and "Paragraphs," *EWR*, January 15, 1877, p. 42.

52. Leslie Flemming, "New Models, New Roles: U.S. Presbyterian Women Missionaries and Social Change in North India, 1870–1910," in Flemming, ed., *Women's Work for Women*, pp 39–40.

53. Milbank, "Josephine Butler." see also Rendall, *The Origins of Modern Feminism*, chap. 7 and esp. p. 232.

54. Vicinus, *Independent Women*, chap. 7.

55. Levine, *Victorian Feminism*, chap. 3.

56. Jessie Boucherett, "Future Plans," *EWR*, January 1870, pp. 1–4.

57. Levine, *Victorian Feminism*, pp. 62–68.

58. Hume, *The National Union of Women's Suffrage Societies*, remains the most detailed study of the NUWSS to date.

59. Doughan and Sanchez, *Feminist Periodicals*, p. 25. *Votes for Women* also ran a column called "The National Campaign." See *VFW*, November 1907, p. 21, and December 1907, p. 37. There was even a National Dress Society. See *EWR*, June 15, 1881, p. 272. For mention of Scottish national suffrage societies, see Leneman, *A Guid Cause*, pp. 2, 61.

60. "Increase of National Strength," *EWR*, July 15, 1881, pp. 289–95; Mrs. Duncan McLaren, "Annual Meeting of the Edinburgh National Society for Women's Suffrage" (1881), in *Women's Suffrage Pamphlets* (1879–83), p. 6, FL.

61. J. E. Howard, "Essay on Woman Suffrage," speech given November 14, 1870, in the Town Hall at Chatham, in support of a resolution for female suffrage, in *Women's Suffrage Pamphlets* (1869–72), p. 16, FL. R. Swiney echoed these sentiments when she wrote that "at present the nation is robbed of the great moral force the enfranchisement of women would bring to bear politically on legislation. . . . The vote is regarded by women as a means toward an end, namely, the advancement of the nobler and purer interests of their country." See her "The Plea of the Disenfranchised Women," *Women's Suffrage Pamphlets* (1898), n.p, FL.

62. Ward et al., "The Appeal against Female Suffrage," p. 783; Lydia Becker and Alice Scatcherd, "Letter to the Ladies on the Isle of Man," from *Fourteenth Annual Report of the Executive Committee of the Manchester National Society for Women's Suffrage* (1881) in *Women's Suffrage Pamphlets* (1879–83), p. 7, FL; and Barbara Leigh Smith Bodichon, "Reasons for and against the Enfranchisement of Women," in Hollis, ed., *Women in Public*, p. 295.

63. Mrs. Bamford Slack, *Twentieth Annual Report of the Central National Society for Women's Suffrage* (1882), in *Women's Suffrage Pamphlets* (1894), p. 18, FL; Helen Blackburn, "Comments on the Opposition to Women's Suffrage," in Lewis, ed., *Before the Vote Was Won*, p. 326.

64. Fawcett, "Degrees for Women at Oxford," p. 356.

65. Walkowitz, "Male Vice and Feminist Virtue," p. 81.

66. Mrs. William Grey, "Is the Exercise of the Suffrage Unfeminine?," in *Women's Suffrage Pamphlets* (1867–82), p. 11, FL.

67. Fawcett, "The Women's Suffrage Bill," p. 556.

68. Samuel, ed., *Patriotism*, 1:xiv.

69. See "The Jolly Girl; or, Some Types in England and Russia," *EWR*, June 15, 1882, pp. 247–51.

70. Euphemia Johnson, "John Bull and His Daughters," *WF*, September 26, 1907, p. 138. A year later the *Women's Franchise* published a page-long poem in which the "turbulent Miss Bull" screamed and shouted and begged to have a voice in public affairs until "John admitted that some day / She might possibly have her way." G. M. George, "The Turbulent Miss Bull," *WF*, October 22, 1908, p. 183. According to Fawcett, "The words Man, Woman, Humanity, etc. send a cold

shudder through the average Briton, but talk to him of John and Elizabeth and he is ready to be interested and, up to his lights, just." Quoted in Stanton, ed., *The Woman Question*, p. 7.

71. See Madge Dresser, "Britannia," in Samuel, ed., *Patriotism*, 3:26–49.

72. For a discussion of female figures as "sacred centers" in cultural politics, see Hunt, *Politics, Culture and Class*, p. 101.

73. Jessie Craigen, "On Woman Suffrage" (1880), in Lewis, ed., *Before the Vote was Won*, p. 372. Craigen went on to say that "the hands of that great clock of the empire move at the bidding of the people . . . and if the North shall say that this claim made tonight by women is set by the true sun of justice, then we shall soon hear 'Big Ben' strike the hour that makes women free citizens of their native land."

74. Lydia Becker, "The Political Disabilities of Women," in Lewis, ed., *Before the Vote*, p. 125; Swiney makes a similar argument in "The Plea of the Disenfranchised Women," n.p.

75. Mrs. Henry David Pochin, "The Right of Women to Exercise the Elective Franchise" (1855; reprint 1873, National Society for Women's Suffrage), in *Women's Suffrage Pamphlets* (1867–82), p. 3, FL.

76. "The Crisis in Our Cause," *WPP*, December 22, 1888, p. 4; "A Wider World" (n.d.), in *NUWSS Pamphlets*, FL.

77. Carpenter, *Six Months in India*, 1:58.

78. Pochin, "The Right of Women," p. 4.

79. "Veritas," "What Is Women's Suffrage? and Why Do Women Want It?," in *Women's Suffrage Pamphlets* (1879–83), p. 9, FL.

80. Mrs. Duncan McLaren, "Are Not Women a Part of the People?," in *Women's Suffrage Pamphlets* (1875–76), n.p, FL. The Scottish suffragist Jenny Taylour articulated much the same idea when she claimed that what women wanted was "to do our proper part in helping on the world's reform." Quoted in Leneman, *Guid Cause*, p. 21.

81. "Increase of National Strength," *EWR*, July 15, 1881, p. 295.

82. See Bland, "The Married Woman," p. 157; and Mariana Valverde's review of *The Sexuality Debates*, ed. Sheila Jeffreys, *Women's Review of Books* 5, no. 4 (January 1988): 6–7. Ware's *Beyond the Pale* (1992) is the first monograph to confront racism in the British women's movement from a historical perspective.

83. See Burton, "The White Woman's Burden." Millicent Fawcett went so far as to assure her opposition that women should not be forced to vote, only that they be given the opportunity to exercise that right if they so choose. Fawcett and Fawcett, *Essays and Lectures*, pp. 226–27.

84. Mona Caird, "Why Do Women Want the Franchise?," speech given at Birmingham, 1892, in *Women's Emancipation Union Pamphlets*, BL, p. 6.

85. Ramusack, "Cultural Missionaries," pp. 119–36.

86. See Burton, "The White Woman's Burden," p. 304; M. Lowndes, "Many Masters," in *NUWSS Pamphlets* (December 1913), FL.

87. Becker, "The Political Disabilities of Women," p. 124.

88. "L.S.," "The Citizenship of Women Socially Considered" (1874), in Lewis, ed., *Before the Vote*, p. 219.

89. Searle, *The Quest for National Efficiency*; Soloway, *Birth Control*, chap. 2; Frank

Mort, "Health and Hygiene: The Edwardian State and Medico-Moral Politics," in Beckett and Cherry, eds., *The Edwardian Era*, p. 26ff.

90. D. T. Steven, "The Eugenic Vote," *CC*, August 31, 1911, p. 356; Mrs. Francis, "Race Suicide," *Vote*, January 21, 1911, pp. 152–53; Mrs. Winthrop Evans, "The Mother as a Factor in Human Progress," *Vote*, September 9, 1911, pp. 248–49.

91. Diver, *The Englishwoman in India*, p. 88.

92. Emmeline Pethick-Lawrence, "Women as Race-Builders," *VFW*, January 21, 1909, p. 280; see also "E. W.," "Empire Building: An Interlude," *CC*, November 29, 1912, p. 585.

93. As Christabel Pankhurst put it, women's suffrage "is not a party question. It is a question for the nation." *VFW*, December 31, 1908, p. 237.

94. Davin, "Imperialism and Motherhood."

95. Mrs. Fabian Ware, "Women's Suffrage and National Responsibilities," *WF*, February 20, 1908, p. 386.

96. Despard, "Woman in the Nation," p. 5.

97. Ibid.; emphasis added.

98. Quoted in Higginbotham, "African-American Women's History," p. 268. See also Anderson, *Imagined Communities*.

99. For an series of expositions on this point, see Offen, Rendall, and Pierson, eds., *Writing Women's History*.

100. This is an application of the idea that disenfranchised groups "have had to appeal to national values precisely to register their claims as political." Parker et al., eds., *Nationalisms and Sexualities*, p. 8.

101. "A.E.G.," "The Manner of Life of Women in England, from the Earliest Historical Period: The Britons," *EWJ*, March 1863, p. 35. Feminist interest in the Anglo-Saxons was not new to the Victorian period. See Smith, *Reason's Disciples*, pp. 142–43.

102. "A.E.G.," "The Manner of Life of Women in England," pp. 38–40.

103. See, for example, Emmeline Pethick-Lawrence, "The ABC of Votes for Women," *VFW*, August 20, 1908, p. 388; Sara Entrican, "Married Women's Property in Ancient Times," *EWR*, October 15, 1896, pp. 229–35; Richard Pankhurst, "Franchise for Women," public meeting in connection with the National Society for Women's Suffrage, in *Women's Suffrage Pamphlets* (1867–82), p. 6, FL. Lydia Becker, "The Rights and Duties of Women in Local Government," in Lewis, ed., *Before the Vote*, pp. 347–53; Mrs. McIlquham, "The Enfranchisement of Women: An Ancient Right, A Modern Need," in *Women's Suffrage Pamphlets* (1894), pp. 5–16, FL; Mrs. Mallet, "Minutes of the Twentieth Annual Report of the National Society for Women's Suffrage," in *Women's Suffrage Pamphlets* (1894), p. 20, FL.

104. Stopes, *British Freewomen*, chaps. 2–7; Blackburn, *Women's Suffrage*, p. 5; Pethick-Lawrence, "The ABC of Votes for Women," p. 388; "Women Agitators in the Past," *WF*, June 27, 1907, p. 2.

105. Becker, "Rights and Duties," p. 348.

106. Helena Normanton, "Magna Carta and Women," *EW*, May 1915, pp. 129–42.

107. "The Magna Carta and the Anglo-Belgian Celebration," *Vote*, June 25, 1915, p. 657.

108. Stopes, *British Freewomen*, p. 1.

109. Blackburn, *Women's Suffrage*, p. 2.

110. Ibid., p. 1.

111. See "Women's Suffrage in the Light of the Second Reading of 1897," in *Women's Suffrage Pamphlets* (1898), pp. 5, 6–17, FL. The anonymous author may have been the source of Blackburn's quotations, or Blackburn may have authored the pamphlet herself.

112. Fawcett, "The Women's Suffrage Question," p. 767.

113. Burton, "The White Woman's Burden," p. 304. Christina Jameson in the Scottish context said, "Will not the men of Shetland now show themselves worthy of their kinship to these free descendants of the old Norse Vikings whom they yearly unite in commemorating?" Quoted in Leneman, *Guid Cause*, p. 93.

114. Boucherett, "Future Plans," p. 3.

115. Stopes, *British Freewomen*; Blackburn, *Women's Suffrage*, preface and chap. 1.

116. Offen, "Women's Memory," pp. 216–23.

117. Tickner, *The Spectacle of Women*, chaps. 3, 4.

118. For a fuller discussion of feminists and theatrical production, see Stowell, *A Stage of Their Own*.

119. *WF*, January 14, 1909, p. 349; see also *WF*, January 21, 1909, p. 360.

120. *CC*, June 29, 1911, p. 217.

121. Leneman, *Guid Cause*, pp. 2, 61, 80–81, 95; Owens, *Smashing Times*, p. 66.

122. Quoted in Caine, *Victorian Feminists*, p. 131.

123. See Butler, *Gender Trouble*; Capo and Hantzis, "(En)Gendered (and Endangered) Subjects"; Mullin, "Representations of History."

124. *CC*, March 7, 1912, p. 824 (review of a Court Theatre performance of Indian women and girls). For more on the relationships between suffrage, actresses, and the theater in Edwardian Britain, see Holledge, *Innocent Flowers*; Hirshfield, "The Actresses' Franchise League"; Stowell, *A Stage of Their Own*; and Gardner and Rutherford, eds., *The New Woman and Her Sisters*.

125. Quoted in Liddington and Norris, *One Hand Tied Behind Us*, p. 221. According to Jessie Boucherett, "The workers in the women's cause are making history," and those writing for the *Englishwoman's Review* were the instruments of that historical process ("Future Plans," p. 3).

126. Parker et al., *Nationalisms and Sexualities*, p. 7.

127. As Paul Fussell so succinctly and aptly put it, the First World War "reversed the Idea of Progress" (*The Great War and Modern Memory*, p. 8).

128. Quoted in Tickner, *The Spectacle of Women*, p. 126.

129. Butterfield, *The Whig Interpretation of History*.

130. "Program of the International Suffrage Fair," November 13–14, 1912 (organized by the WFL), FL; "Women of the Nations, Unite," *Vote*, October 12, 1912, p. 420; October 26, 1912, p. 451; and November 16, 1912, p. 41.

131. "Program of a Pageant of Great Women" (from the Suffrage Shop, ca. 1910), FL. Although this is the historical moment when militant suffragism had emerged (hence the rani's militarism could be read in the context of militant struggle), the Actresses' Franchise League was primarily responsible for the production of the pageant and was "resolutely neutral on tactics," at least in 1909 when

the performance first went up. See Hirshfield, "The Actresses' Franchise League," p. 131.

132. Crosby, *The Ends of History*, pp. 146–47.

133. Stowell, *A Stage of Their Own*, pp. 44–45.

134. "The British Born Woman" was the title of an article in *Vote*, September 15, 1915, pp. 637–38.

135. Kerber, "The Paradox of Women's Citizenship," p. 370.

136. These conflicting stances are reflected in Lydia Becker's claim that women were "the unrepresented half of the nation" and Mrs. Duncan McLaren's complaint that women already constituted, if not represented, the nation. See Becker, "The Political Disabilities of Women," p. 124; and McLaren, "Are Not Women a Part of the People?" Chrystal Macmillan echoed them both when she argued that women's political citizenship went unrecognized. See her "The Struggle for Political Liberty," pp. 1–5.

137. Diver, *The Englishwoman in India*.

138. Hutchins, *The Illusion of Permanence*, p. 137. By the twentieth century Lord Minto considered India to be governed less by force than by "the mere prestige of British authority." Quoted in Hyam, *Britain's Imperial Century*, p. 160.

139. Murphy's observation about Irish suffragists is eminently applicable here (*The Women's Suffrage Movement*, p. 200).

CHAPTER 3

1. The designations Eastern, non-Western, South Asian, Asian, Indian, and Oriental are all politically loaded, not least because of the cultural and historical legacies of British imperialism. The connotations of "Oriental" have been too well documented by Edward Said to rehearse here; as for the rest, they work as geographical descriptors primarily when one's point of reference is Britain or the West. I typically use the term "Eastern" or "non-Western" to refer to those women whom British feminists might have referred to as "Oriental." I use the term "Asian" most often to denote the women of Asia broadly speaking, and the term "Indian" to describe women from the subcontinent regardless of caste or religion.

2. Minh-ha, "Not Like You/Like You," p. 71. For the most sophisticated explication of feminist orientalism to date, see Zonana, "The Sultan and the Slave."

3. See, for example, Fulton, *Votes for Women*; Rover, *Women's Suffrage*; Morgan, *Suffragists and Liberals*; Hume, *The National Union*.

4. Holton, *Feminism and Democracy*, p. 28. Holton emphasizes this claim throughout her second chapter, where she points up the cooperation between the militants and constitutionalists. See pp. 38–52.

5. Lacey, *Bodichon*; Lewis, ed., *Before the Vote Was Won*; and Jeffreys, ed., *The Sexuality Debates*. Some of the pieces in the Jeffreys collection refer to the campaign against the C.D. Acts in India, but this is not evident from any of the titles.

6. Spelman, *Inessential Woman*, p. 122. Spelman's exact formulation is "If the connection between philosophy and racism is not very visible, that invisibility is itself a product of racism."

7. Said, *Orientalism*, p. 69.

8. Nair, "Uncovering the Zenana," p. 14.

9. This is the term Moira Ferguson uses to describe some English feminist writing in the pre-Victorian period. See Ferguson, ed., *First Feminists*, pp. 30–31.

10. The term is Lacquer's. See his "Bodies, Details," p. 200.

11. Ibid., pp. 176–78.

12. For a discussion of Indian women as sites of colonial intervention and domination, see Mani, "The Production of Colonial Discourse."

13. See, for example, *WPP*, June 22, 1889, p. 3, where a Miss Wall reported at length on the position of women in Egypt to the Women's Liberal Federation of Southport. Persian women were featured in "The Persian Parliament Shivers," *Vote*, September 2, 1911, p. 237; C. Despard, "A Woman Apostle in Persia," *Vote*, September 30, 1911, pp. 280–81; and "What Persian Women Are Doing," *Vote*, April 13, 1912, p. 300. See also Saint Nihal Singh, "The Awakening of Asian Women," *EW*, May 1910, pp. 25–31, and "The Persian Woman and the Parting of the Ways," *EW*, February 1911, pp. 173–81.

14. It is worth noting that throughout feminist periodicals the Burmese woman was held up as the most progressive of Eastern females, an anomaly among her "Oriental sisters" because of the freedom she enjoyed and the social equality accorded her. See, for example, Annie T. Barnard, "The Burmese Woman," *EW*, June 1910, pp. 184–95; and E. J. Davy, "Women in Burma," *WF*, September 17, 1908, pp. 122.

15. "Women in Turkey," *EWJ*, September 1860, pp. 46–47. This distinction between the Muslim family and the Turkish husband as the source of Turkish women's oppression persisted into the 1870s. Another author also excused the Turkish husband, claiming that the Turkish woman "has not as a rule much to complain of from personal ill-treatment, the Turk in ordinary life being neither unkind nor cruel to his women." See "Womanliness," *EWR*, March 15, 1877, p. 106.

16. Carpenter, *Six Months in India*, 2:168.

17. Fawcett, "The Women's Suffrage Bill," p. 558.

18. Kabbani, *Europe's Myths of Orient*; Allouella, *The Colonial Harem*.

19. *EWJ*, September 1860, p. 49; "Paragraphs," *EWR*, January 15, 1877, p. 43.

20. Gertrude F. W. Torrey, "Sex Tyranny," *WF*, January 28, 1909, p. 368; see also Pfeiffer, "The Suffrage for Women," p. 422.

21. Bernard, "The Position of Women in India," pp. 471–82.

22. See Rathbone, *Child Marriage*. For a discussion of Rathbone's Indian work, see Ramusack, "Catalysts or Helpers?," pp. 109–50; Forbes, "Women and Modernity"; and Ramusack, "Women's Organizations and Social Change." The *Women's Penny Paper* concerned itself with child marriage throughout the House of Commons debate. See *WPP*, January 19, 1889, p. 3; May 18, 1889, p. 5; August 16, 1890; September 19, 1890, p. 559; February 14, 1891, p. 265; and April 4, 1891, p. 377. Malabari's *An Appeal from the Daughters of India* was cited as evidence of an "Indian Renaissance" in *EWR*, January 1890, pp. 55–57, and his pamphlet discussed in detail in *EWR*, October 1890, pp. 6–12; Edith Pechey Phipson's lecture on the subject was reprinted in *EWR*, January 1891, pp. 15–17. Phipson was a medical doctor who had traveled to India and was active in suffrage circles.

23. Fawcett, "Infant Marriage," pp. 712–20; Rubinstein, *A Different World*, p. 101.

24. See Sidney Smith, "The Enfranchisement of Women the Law of the Land," in *Women's Suffrage Pamphlets* (1871–80), p. 6, FL; "The Hindoo Marriage Law," *EWR*, April 15, 1887, pp. 181–82; and Ethelmer, *Woman Free*, p. 61.

25. Fawcett, "Infant Marriage," p. 720.

26. Schreiber and Mathieson, *Journey towards Freedom*, p. 22. See below, Chap. 6, for a fuller discussion of suffrage "internationalism."

27. Ella Wheeler Wilcox, "The Awakening of Woman," *VFW*, June 9, 1911, p. 591.

28. Lillian Hay-Cooper, "Veil and Lattice," *CC*, April 25, 1913, p. 68.

29. Nair, "Uncovering the Zenana," pp. 9–34.

30. Zonana, "The Sultan and the Slave," pp. 592–617. Writing for *VFW* in 1909, Israel Zangwill objected to Lord Cromer's characterizations of Englishwomen "being dragged from the drawing room. He forgets that Egyptian women are sullied by being dragged *into* the drawing room. They *have* to stay in the harem." See "Old Fogeys and Old Bogeys," *VFW*, June 11, 1909, p. 775.

31. This tradition of rational argumentation claims Mary Wollstonecraft and Millicent Garrett, to name only two. See Spender, ed., *Feminist Theorists*; Browne, *Eighteenth-Century Feminist Mind*, p. 2; Ferguson and Todd, *Mary Wollstonecraft*, p. 124.

32. It has been suggested to me by Deborah Rossum that European depictions of African women may or may not accord with this interpretation. Although no work has been done to date on feminist constructions of "the African woman" by feminists, two important essays on representations of black female sexuality are Gilman, "Black Bodies, White Bodies"; and Joanna de Groot, " 'Sex' and 'Race': The Construction of Language and Imagery in the Nineteenth Century," in Mendus and Rendall, eds., *Sexuality and Subordination*, pp. 89–128.

33. The authorship of this essay has been disputed, as has much of the writing of John Stuart Mill and Harriet Taylor. Gertrude Himmelfarb attributes the original version, which appeared as "Enfranchisement of Women" in an 1851 issue of the *Westminster Review*, to Mill, allowing that subsequent versions "should perhaps more properly be considered a joint work." See her *On Liberty and Liberalism*, p. 170. Contemporary feminists appear to have assumed it was written by Taylor, who was very active in the early suffrage movement, since they reprinted it in her name in 1868. See Taylor, "Enfranchisement of Women," *Women's Suffrage Pamphlets* (1867–82), pp. 1–22, FL. For another early Victorian English woman's ideas on women of the East, see Lady Morgan, *Woman and Her Master* (London: Henry Colburn, 1840), 2:25–58—though this is not necessarily a feminist viewpoint.

34. Taylor, "Enfranchisement of Women," p. 14. For pre-Victorian invocations of women of the East, see Zonana, "The Sultan and the Slave," pp. 603–5.

35. Taylor, "Enfranchisement of Women," pp. 19–20.

36. Millicent Garrett Fawcett, "Mrs. Fawcett on Women's Suffrage," speech delivered in the Town Hall at Birmingham, December 6, 1872, in *Women's Suffrage Publications* (1871–72), p. 5, FL.

37. Mabel Sharman Crawford, "Opinions of Women on Women's Suffrage," issued by the Central Committee of the National Society for Women's Suffrage, in *Women's Suffrage Pamphlets* (1873–97), p. 18, FL.

38. Smith, "Enfranchisement of Women," pp. 6–7.

39. "Women's Suffrage in the Light of the Second Reading of 1897," p. 8.

40. Emily Pfeiffer, "Woman's Claim" (1881), in Lewis, ed., *Before the Vote*, p. 381.

41. Chakravarti, "Whatever Happened to the Vedic *Dasi*?" See also Chatterjee, "The Nationalist Resolution."

42. Storrow actually used "polygamous" incorrectly since it means plural marriage for either spouse and Muslim women did not have multiple husbands (*The Eastern Lily Gathered*, pp. 1, 2, 10, 14–15). Female missionaries tended to agree. According to Mrs. Weitbrecht, "We can only speak, indeed, of Hindu ladies as *prisoners*, for what is the Zenana . . . but a place of confinement, where the ladies of the family are kept strictly and entirely secluded" (*The Christian Woman's Ministry*, p. 4).

43. Storrow, *The Eastern Lily Gathered*, p. iv. Duff, *Female Education in India*, pp. 7, 17. For a detailed examination of Duff, see Viswanathan, *Masks of Conquest*, chap. 2.

44. Barbara Ramusack, private correspondence. See also Marglin, *Wives of the God-King*, esp. pp. 3–8.

45. "Nautches: An Appeal to Educated Hindus," Pice Papers on India Reform, no. 29 (Madras: Christian Literature Society, 1893), BL, pp. 1–12. Thanks to George Robb for bringing this to my attention.

46. J. D. Rees, "Meddling with Hindu Marriages," *Nineteenth Century* 28 (October 1890): 660–75.

47. Max Muller, "The Story of an Indian Child Wife," *Contemporary Review* 60 (August 1891): 184.

48. See Chakravarti, "Whatever happened to the Vedic *Dasi*?"

49. Duff, *Female Education*, p. 19.

50. "A Pioneer," "Will the Legal Status of Women of the East Compare Favorably with That of European Women?," *Shafts*, August 1894, pp. 302–5.

51. In fact, it was Rees's October article entitled "Meddling with Hindu Marriages" in *Nineteenth Century* that partly prompted Fawcett's "Infant Marriage in India."

52. See, for example, a review of Max Muller's *Contemporary Review* article in *WH*, August 22, 1891, p. 693. If the two Mullers were related, I have not been able to find any evidence. See also Chakravarti, "Whatever happened to the Vedic *Dasi*?," pp. 38–46.

53. Fawcett, *What I Remember*, p. 59.

54. Quoted in hooks, *Yearning*, p. 72.

55. Leonard Courtney, "The Women's Suffrage Question, *Contemporary Review* 61 (June 1892): 761–73; Pfeiffer, "The Suffrage for Women," p. 419.

56. Ethelmer, *Woman Free*, note to section 22, p. 80. The identity of Ethelmer is disputed among historians of the British women's movement. Jeffreys claims that Ethelmer was a pen name for Elizabeth Wolstenholme Elmy and attributes *Woman Free* to her (*The Spinster and her Enemies*, pp. 28–32). Lucy Bland thinks the pen name might also have been used by her husband Ben ("The Married Woman," p. 154). Most recently, Levine states unequivocally that Ethelmer *was* Ben Elmy (" 'So Few Prizes and So Many Blanks,' " p. 157 n. 16).

57. Smith, "Woman and Evolution," p. 2.

58. Rendall, *Origins*, p. 76. Rendall is quoting F. A. Cox, *Female Scripture Biography* (London: n.p., 1817), pp. xcvi, 2.

59. Rendall, *Origins*, p. 188.

60. This is not to say that such references are completely absent from eighteenth-century feminist writing. "To preserve personal beauty," Mary Wollstonecraft wrote, Western women's "limbs and faculties are cramped with worse than Chinese bands." See "A Vindication of the Rights of Woman," in Solomon and Berggren, eds., *A Mary Wollstonecraft Reader*, p. 293.

61. Ferguson, "Mary Wollstonecraft." See also her *Subject to Others*.

62. Zonana, "The Sultan and the Slave," pp. 593–94, 600–604.

63. Ibid., p. 600.

64. For an excellent discussion of eighteenth-century orientalisms in the French and British contexts, see Lowe, *Critical Terrains*, chaps. 2, 3. It is worth noting that as late as the 1870s Victorian feminists were concerned with Turkey. Fawcett wrote a pamphlet entitled *The Martyrs of Turkish Misrule*, and contributors to *Women's Suffrage Journal* expressed concerned over the Bulgarian crisis in 1876–77. See Editorial, *WSJ*, October 2, 1876, pp. 133–34.

65. Although she frequently refers to nineteenth-century Western feminists' views of Middle Eastern Muslim women, Ahmed's important book is not very specific when it comes to naming individual feminist women or Western women's groups. See her *Women and Gender in Islam*, esp. chaps. 7–9.

66. Viswanathan, *Masks of Conquest*, pp. 1–22.

67. This interpretation is somewhat at variance with Zonana, "The Sultan and the Slave," pp. 600–604.

68. Rogers, *Feminism*, p. 4. See also Lew, "Lady Mary's Portable Seraglio."

69. Browne mentions in passing that images of Muslim women appeared in feminist writings more at the end of the eighteenth century than at its beginning, which suggests that a shift was taking place as Britain's status as a world power changed over time. See her *Eighteenth-Century Feminist Mind*, p. 176.

70. Ferguson, *Subject to Others*; Midgley, *Women against Slavery*; and Ware, *Beyond the Pale*. See also Davis, *The Problem of Slavery*.

71. For an excellent and much-needed discussion of these connections, see Louis Billington and Rosamund Billington, "'A Burning Zeal for Righteousness': Women in the British Anti-Slavery Movement, 1820–1860," in Rendall, *Equal or Different*, pp. 82–111; and Ware, *Beyond the Pale*, pp. 49–116. Ferguson's *Subject to Others* also devotes several chapters to the political influence of female antislavery writers and activists.

72. For the impact of Butler on later suffrage organizations, see Walkowitz, *Prostitution and Victorian Society*; for that of antislavery on the women's movement, see Billington and Billington, "'A Burning Zeal for Righteousness'"; and Rendall, *Origins*. According to Fawcett, "The disability of sex is as repugnant to true Liberalism as are the disabilities of race and religion" ("Women and Representative Government," p. 285).

73. Taylor, "Enfranchisement of Women," p. 8.

74. Elizabeth Martyn, "The Case of the Helots" (1894), in Lewis, ed., *Before the Vote*, pp. 453–64.

75. See Mort, *Dangerous Sexualities*, esp. chap. 3. The "whiteness" of the white slave trade signified both the non-Britishness of both prostitutes and their procurers as well as its allusive connections with colonial slavery.

76. Marion Holmes, "The ABC of Votes for Women" (London: WFL Pamphlet, ca. 1910–11), p. 1.

77. Yellin, *Women and Sisters*, pp. 29, 31.

78. Arabella Shore, "The Present Aspect of Women's Suffrage Considered," speech delivered at a meeting of the London National Society for Women's Suffrage, May 14, 1877, in Lewis, *Before the Vote*, p. 313.

79. Eva McLaren, "Married Women and the Vote," *WPP*, June 7, 1890, p. 391.

80. At the same time, some feminists of the period saw regulated prostitution in India as the enduring legacy of British slavery. As Lady Henry Somerset told an audience of repealers in 1893, "We prided ourselves in the early days of our rule in India that the weight of our civilisation had forever crushed out the flames of suttee; but I say it calmly, and I say it deliberately, that I believe that the death of the suttee was a chariot of fire carrying women away from the pain, the misery, and the degradation, and ineffably better than the pit of horror to which our English civilisation has condemned these poor women [Indian prostitutes]." See "Progress of Our Cause: Complete Adoption of Our Principles by the Women's Liberal Federation," in *Dawn*, July 1893, p. 22.

81. "What the Vote Means to the Woman as Wife, Part I: Woman's Status in the 19th Century," *VFW*, November 1907, p. 17. For reference to Lady Henry's defection from the repeal camp, see below, Chap. 5.

82. Despard, "Woman in the Nation," p. 5.

83. Ferguson argues that although not all "feminist" writers before 1800 referred to slavery, a significant number did, including Aphra Behn and Mary Wollstonecraft. In fact, Ferguson considers "writings by women opposed to slavery and the slave trade as feminist polemic" in and of themselves, since "opposition to the physical and psychological enslavement of people of color . . . is a necessary condition for the liberation of women of color and, by extension, all women." See her introduction to *First Feminists*, esp. pp. 22, 24, 25, 27, 29–30, 33; her *Subject to Others*; and Smith, *Reason's Disciples*, pp. 75–76.

84. This is how Yellin describes the maneuvers of some white American feminists at certain political moments. See *Women and Sisters*, pp. 25, 76.

85. For an account of the institutionalization of anthropology in the late nineteenth century, see Lorimer, "Theoretical Racism." See also Fee, "Sexual Politics."

86. According to George Stocking, Henry Maine was a great sympathizer with votes for women, viewing women's political privileges as part of the law of progressive development. Contemporary feminists even solicited material and information from him, which may explain their common references to his work. See Stocking, *Victorian Anthropology*, pp. 205–6; see also Fawcett, "The Women's Suffrage Bill," p. 557, and "Infant Marriage in India," p. 712, where she refers to Maine explicitly. Fee takes the opposite tack, arguing that Maine was antifeminist in his formulations ("Sexual Politics," pp. 23–39).

87. Shore, "The Present Aspect of Women's Suffrage Considered," p. 301.

88. Taylor, "Enfranchisement of Women," pp. 7–8.

89. "The Enfranchisement of Women," *EWJ*, July 1, 1864, in Lewis, ed., *Before the Vote*, p. 14. Helen Blackburn was less optimistic. "Brute force," she wrote, "is undoubtedly the substratum of society, for if we analyze civilization, we come in the ultimate residuum to pure physical force. Strip off one by one the motives and the restraints with which civilization has surrounded human life and you find yourself at last reduced to the will of the strongest" ("Comments on the Opposition to Women's Suffrage," p. 327). See also Jane Harrison, "Homo-Sum: Being a Letter from an Anti-Suffragist from an Anthropologist" (London: National Union of Women's Suffrage Societies, ca. 1908–10).

90. Fee, "Sexual Politics," p. 24.

91. Blackburn, "Comments on the Opposition to Women's Suffrage," p. 328.

92. Fawcett, "Mrs. Fawcett on Women's Suffrage," pp. 4–5.

93. John Stuart Mill, "Lecture to the Educational Branch of the National Society for Women's Suffrage, January 12 1871," in *Women's Suffrage Publications* (1871–72), p. 12, FL.

94. Jane Hume Clapperton, "An Evolutionist's Reply to the Appeal against Female Suffrage," *WPP*, August 3, 1889, pp. 4–5. Fawcett echoed this sentiment years later, in 1918, when she spoke of the women's movement as glacierlike: "ceaseless and irresistible." See "War and Reconstruction: Women and Their Use of the Vote," *English Review* 26 (March 1918): 261.

95. "Libra," "Womanhood from the Theosophical Point of View," part 2, *Shafts*, January 7, 1893, pp. 152–53.

96. Harrison, *Prudent Revolutionaries*, p. 19.

97. Despard, "Theosophy and the Women's Movement," pp. 1–2.

98. See Stocking, *Victorian Anthropology*, pp. 18–19; Said, *Orientalism*.

99. Spivak, "The Rani of Sirmur," p. 270.

100. Jane Hume Clapperton introduced her rebuttal of an antisuffrage petition with reference to "the progressive forces of society" ("An Evolutionist's Reply," pp. 4–5). Four years later an editorial in the *Woman's Herald* praised "the forward movements of our time." "Our Policy," *WH*, February 23, 1893, p. 1. In January 1870 and August 1878 the *Englishwoman's Review* measured progress in industrial and feminist terms. Boucherett, "Future Plans," pp. 1–4, and "Three Decades of Progress," *EWR*, August 15, 1878, pp. 337–44. The "progress of the age" was also a common reference; see Helen Taylor, "The Claim of Englishwomen to the Suffrage Constitutionally Considered" (1867), in Lewis, *Before the Vote*, p. 37; and Pfeiffer, "Woman's Claim," p. 386.

101. Bowler, *The Invention of Progress*, p. 3.

102. Lewis, *Woman's Mission*, p. 40.

103. Cobbe, "Duties of Woman," p. 376.

104. Quoted in Lacey, ed., *Bodichon*, p. 464.

105. Frederic Harrison, "Emancipation of Women," p. 449.

106. Henrietta Muller, "A Voice from India," *Shafts*, April 1894, p. 240.

107. Becker and Scatcherd, "Letter to the Ladies on the Isle of Man," p. 7. For another formulation of the same sentiment, see Stopes, *British Freewoman*, p. 194. According to Pfeiffer, "The place of a people on the scale of human development is determined by the condition of its women" ("Woman's Claim," p. 386). See also

"The Family," *WPP*, December 29, 1888, p. 3, where this idea is attributed to Henry Morgan, and *CC*, July 11, 1912, p. 228, where Sir Henry Maine gets the credit.

108. Diver, *The Englishwoman in India*, p. 100; emphasis added.

109. *EWR*, January 15, 1877, p. 42. Mabel Sharman Crawford echoed this sentiment: "At this present day the Turkish empire is crumbling into ruins through the consistently enforced rule of the exclusively domestic sphere of women" ("Opinions of Women," p. 18).

110. McBratney, "Images of Indian Women in Rudyard Kipling," p. 49.

111. In her review of *The Sexuality Debates*, Mariana Valverde takes Sheila Jeffreys to task for failing to make more of the many references to race in feminist discourse ("A Passion for Purity," pp. 6–7).

112. A writer distinguished between the "Moslem and Christian races" in "Paragraphs," *EWR*, January 1877, p. 42. Another author lamented that the white slave traffic could continue to exist after "the final stamping out of slavery in all accessible regions of the earth, largely through the influence and earnestness of the English-speaking race." M. Lowndes, "Slavery," *EW*, September 1913, pp. 241–53.

113. Bland, "The Married Woman," p. 157. Martineau is quoted in Rendall, *Origins*, p. 115; for NUWSS usage, see, for example, "Suffrage or Party?" (London: NUWSS, n.d.), in *NUWSS Pamphlets*, FL.

114. Bland, "The Married Woman," p. 157. It is here that Bland would have us read "human" for "racial."

115. Swiney, *The Awakening of Woman*, p. 121.

116. Ibid., pp. 207–69 passim.

117. For a review that describes it in just this way, see *EWR*, April 17, 1900, pp. 130–31.

118. Mort, *Dangerous Sexualities*, p. 139.

119. For further examination of imperial suffrage rhetoric, see Chap. 6.

120. Muller, "A Voice from India," p. 241.

121. Fawcett, "The Women's Suffrage Bill," p. 565.

122. Despard, "Woman in the Nation," p. 5.

123. Smith, "Woman and Evolution," p. 3.

124. Lady McLaren, "Better and Happier: An Answer from the Ladies' Gallery to the Speeches in Opposition to the Women's Suffrage Bill" (1908), p. 38, FL.

125. Louisa Bigg, "Should the Parliamentary Franchise Be Granted to Women Householders?," paper read at conference in the Council Chamber at Luton, December 11, 1879, in *Women's Suffrage Pamphlets* (1871–80), p. 4, FL. Bigg's pamphlet has also been reprinted in Lewis, ed., *Before the Vote*, pp. 366–70.

126. Mabel Sharman Crawford, " 'Purdah' in the House of Commons," *WPP*, May 24, 1890, p. 363; and *CC*, March 21, 1913, p. 850.

127. Mrs. William Grey, "Is the Exercise of the Suffrage Unfeminine?" (1870), in *Women's Suffrage Pamphlets* (1867–82), p. 6, FL; Smith, *Reason's Disciples*, p. 270.

128. Taylor, "The Claim of Englishwomen" pp. 36–37.

129. Arabella Shore, "What Women Have a Right to" (1879), in Lewis, ed., *Before the Vote*, p. 357; emphasis added.

130. Maud Arncliffe-Sennett, "Why I Want the Vote," *Vote*, February 26, 1910, p. 207.

131. Shore, "The Present Aspect of Women's Suffrage Considered," p. 299.

132. Quoted in Eva McLaren, "National Conference of Delegates of Women's Suffrage Societies in Great Britain and Ireland (Birmingham 1896)," in *Women's Suffrage Pamphlets* (1898), p. 10, FL.

133. Poovey, *Uneven Developments*, p. 43.

134. Shore, "The Present Aspect of Women's Suffrage Considered," p. 307.

135. Stocking, *Victorian Anthropology*, p. 10.

136. Anne Isabella Robertson, "Women's Need of Representation" (1872), in Lewis, ed., *Before the Vote*, pp. 143–44.

137. See, for example, Smith, "Woman and Evolution."

138. "L. S.," "The Citizenship of Women," p. 184.

139. "Woman Suffrage," in *Women's Suffrage Pamphlets* (1869–72), p. 2, FL.

140. "L. S.," "The Citizenship of Women," p. 201.

141. Hilda Smith argues that this ideology was the foundation of seventeenth-century feminism. See *Reason's Disciples*, pp. 4, 192.

142. These are the grounds on which Smith defines "modern" feminism. See ibid., p. 7; Browne, *The Eighteenth-Century Feminist Mind*, p. 22; and Mayhall, "Challenging the State."

143. Barbara Leigh Smith Bodichon, "Objections to the Enfranchisement of Women Considered" (1866), in Lacey, *Bodichon*, p. 114.

144. See Bodichon's "Giving the Suffrage to Qualified Women" (1867), in Lacey, ed., *Bodichon*, pp. 127–28; and "Womanliness," *EWR*, March 15, 1877, pp. 103–11.

145. Shore, "The Present Aspect of Women's Suffrage Considered," p. 293.

146. Bodichon, "Giving the Suffrage to Qualified Women," p. 127.

147. See, for example, Entrican, "Married Women's Property in Ancient Times," pp. 229–35. For a fuller catalog of these kinds of references, see above, Chap. 2. Such concerns were certainly not unique to feminists. For useful sources on the myth of the Norman yoke, see Briggs, *Saxons, Normans and Victorians*; and Levine, *The Amateur and the Professional*, pp. 78–79.

148. See, for example, Pethick-Lawrence, "The ABC of Votes for Women," p. 388; "Homage to the Spirit of Magna Carta" (concerning the celebrations of the anniversary of Magna Carta), *Vote*, June 11, 1915, p. 1; and Macmillan, "The Struggle for Political Liberty," pp. 1–5.

149. Stopes, *British Freewomen*, p. 9 and chap. 1.

150. For a discussion of the cultural components of race, see Bolt, *Victorian Attitudes*, pp. 9ff.

151. See, for example, Mlle Claire de Pratz, "French Women and English Women," *VFW*, February 12, 1908, p. 64; "A French Suffragette," *VFW*, May 14, 1908, p. 161; Mrs. Crawford, "The Women of France," *Young Woman*, 1892–93, pp. 7–9. The *Englishwoman's Review* expressed horror at the creation of the International League of Women against Their Tyrants by the French feminist and communard, Louise Michel. It reported that she proposed to boycott men until women had attained equal political rights. "We cannot help feeling that Englishwomen have been throughout the long course of the movement . . . much more fortunate than their French sisters . . . we must congratulate ourselves that in no case have we in England had to combine ourselves *as women* and men *as men*." For this feminist,

"harmony of purpose" between the sexes working together for feminist ends, as it had always occurred in the British woman's movement, was the most effective means of achieving "national progress." See "An International League of Women," *EWR*, September 15, 1882, pp. 406–7.

152. "The Dangers of the Emancipation of Women: A Criticism," *WH*, November 12, 1892, p. 6.

153. "Albion," "A Reply to Mdlle Adele Crepaz," *WH*, December 10, 1892, p. 7.

154. "Noema," letter to the editor, *Shafts*, March 1894, p. 230.

155. Muller, "A Voice from India," p. 240.

156. "Noema," "Position of Women under Oriental Civilisation," *Shafts*, March 1894, p. 230.

157. Mani, "Contentious Traditions," p. 114.

158. Helen Blackburn, "The Argument of Custom," *EWR*, May 15, 1876, pp. 193–94.

159. Jessie Boucherett, "On the Cause of the Distress Prevalent among Single Women" (1864), in Lacey, *Bodichon*, p. 272.

160. Torrey, "Sex Tyranny," p. 368.

161. Stocking, *Victorian Anthropology*, p. 19.

162. Ong, "Colonialism and Modernity," p. 79.

163. Ibid., p. 86.

164. Mohanty, "Feminist Encounters," p. 30.

165. Lacquer, "Bodies, Details," pp. 197, 200.

166. Chakravorty, "Whatever Happened to the Vedic *Dasi*?," p. 27.

CHAPTER 4

1. The journals I treat in the text of this chapter are the *Englishwoman's Review*, with the *Englishwoman's Journal*, the *Englishwoman*, and the *Women's Penny Paper* mentioned occasionally in the footnotes. Other periodicals that covered Indian women include the suffrage journals (*Common Cause*, the *Vote*, *Votes for Women*, *Women's Franchise*), which are examined in Chapter 6. The *Young Woman* and *Womanhood* also featured stories (or "Paragraphs," as they were sometimes titled) on Indian women, though these latter two were not as consistently or self-consciously "feminist" in orientation as the others. The most up-to-date and comprehensive treatment of British women's periodicals is Doughan and Sanchez, *Feminist Periodicals*.

2. In formulating this argument I am drawing on the work of Mary Poovey, who claims that texts are as constitutive of the reader as they are of meaning, and that hence reading is "an historically and culturally specific activity" (*Uneven Developments*, p. 16).

3. As Levine describes, long-term subscriptions were a problem, and the feminist press faced stiff competition from its mainstream rivals ("The Humanising Influences," pp. 297–98).

4. Ibid., p. 306. See also Burton, "The White Woman's Burden."

5. Cohn, "The Command of Language," p. 276.

6. This is in contrast to the literature on the women's press in the U.S. women's

movement. See, for example, Solomon, *A Voice of Their Own*. The sheer volume of periodicals that Doughan and Sanchez have unearthed in their book *Feminist Periodicals* prevents them from examining in depth the impact of specific journals, though they do emphasize the importance of feminist periodicals as evidence of women's, and especially of feminists', otherwise unheard-of activities. Doughan, "Periodicals by, for and about Women," esp. pp. 266–68, treats some Victorian feminist magazines in more depth. Rendall's excellent treatment of the history of the *Englishwoman's Journal* argues that the journal functions as a history of the politics of the early women's movement "in miniature." See " 'A Moral Engine'? Feminism, Liberalism and the *Englishwoman's Journal*," in Rendall, ed., *Equal or Different*, pp. 112–38.

7. Evelyn March-Philips, "Women's Newspapers," *Fortnightly Review* 62 (November 1894): 670.

8. Quoted in Levine, "The Humanising Influences," p. 299. Smith-Rosenberg's *Disorderly Conduct* was the pioneering scholarly work that examined the idea of women's culture. Although it deals with American women, its value lies in its theoretical approach, and much of her argument is applicable to British women of the same period. For a discussion of a similarly womanist culture in the British setting, see Vicinus, *Independent Women*.

9. Solomon, *A Voice of Their Own*, p. 3; see also Campbell, *Man Cannot Speak for Her*.

10. Solomon, *A Voice of Their Own*, p. 14.

11. For more on global sisterhood, see below, Chap. 6.

12. According to Hilda Martindale, her mother's feminist consciousness originated by reading the *Englishwoman's Journal* and its successor, the *Englishwoman's Review*. See Levine, "The Humanising Influences," p. 296.

13. Solomon, *A Voice of Their Own*, p. 12.

14. Owens, *Smashing Times*, p. 45. Murphy says that the *Irish Citizen* presumed that its readers also read *Votes for Women* and the *Suffragette*, and relied heavily on *Jus Suffragi* for its international news (*The Women's Suffrage Movement*, pp. 31, 56).

15. Doughan and Sanchez, *Feminist Periodicals*, p. 2.

16. Levine, "The Humanising Influences," pp. 293–96; and Rendall, " 'A Moral Engine?' "

17. See Burton, "The White Woman's Burden," p. 301.

18. Quoted in Susan Schultz Huxman, "*The Woman's Journal*, 1870–1890: The Torchbearer for Suffrage," in Solomon, ed., *A Voice of Their Own*, p. 87. For a discussion of the feminist press in the Indian women's movement, see Vir Bharat Talwar, "Feminist Consciousness," Sangari and Vaid, eds., *Recasting Women*, pp. 204–32.

19. Poovey, *Uneven Developments*, p. 16.

20. Bhabha, "The Other Question," p. 27.

21. Tapper, writing on contemporary Western stereotypes about Middle Eastern women, comments that "these stereotypes are important to Western women in a number of ways: their own domestic subordination seems insignificant by contrast, while at the same time their achievements in the public realm seem more significant than perhaps they are. . . . In essence they turn their attention away from the

position of Western women *per se* and indeed they suggest many areas of Middle Eastern life worthy of a reformer's zeal" ("Mysteries of the Harem?," p. 481). The parallels to Victorian and Edwardian feminists are startling.

22. Like Cohn, who has argued that British colonialists took a "textual view of society" ("The Command of Language," p. 276), Mani illustrates how this textualization was applied to the issue of *sati* (widow-burning) in early-nineteenth-century Bengal. The debate over *sati*, as she points out, had less to do with whether it was "good" or "bad" than over how the British government could "manage it" (i.e., abolish it safely and without undue native unrest). Her analysis concludes that, by using Indian scriptural writings to reject *sati* as indigenously "unnatural," the colonial government privileged texts in a way that allowed them to ensure their continued domination over native peoples. If textualization was a mode of colonial domination, Mani insists that "women are the mode through which colonial power is both enforced and contested" ("The Production of an Official Discourse on *Sati*," esp. pp. 114–16).

23. Levine, "The Humanising Influences," p. 298. I am indebted to Janaki Nair for insisting on this set of connections between the *Englishwoman's Review* and British women's reform activities in the "field" of empire.

24. Carpenter, *Six Months in India*, 2:123; Hammerton, *Emigrant Gentlewomen*.

25. Bhabha, "The Other Question," p. 23.

26. Boucherett was the editor from 1866 to 1870, at which time Biggs took over the journal until her death in 1889; it then passed to Helen Blackburn, and in 1895 Antoinette Mackenzie assumed the editorship. See Doughan and Sanchez, *Feminist Periodicals*, p. 3.

27. Bhabha, "The Other Question," p. 18.

28. Rendall, ed., *Equal or Different*, pp. 129–37.

29. Ibid.; Doughan, "Periodicals by, for and about Women," p. 266. "Those of our readers who may remember the *Englishwoman's Journal*," wrote Boucherett in the very first issue, "will perceive that our plan is the same as that of the above periodical. It is, indeed, our intention to follow the plan traced out by those who established the *Englishwoman's Journal* . . . for we believe the favorable change of opinion, and the more respectful tone with regard to women which may be observed in the literature of the present day, to be in no small degree due to the influence of the *Englishwoman's Journal*." "The Work We Have to Do," *EWR*, October 1866, pp. 4–5.

30. Jessie Boucherett, "Caroline Ashurst Biggs," *EWR*, September 14, 1889, p. 388.

31. Rendall, *Equal or Different*, pp. 132–33; Levine, "The Humanising Influences," p. 295.

32. Doughan and Sanchez, *Feminist Periodicals*, p. xiv.

33. Boucherett, "Future Plans," p. 3.

34. Ibid.

35. "Three Decades of Progress," *EWR*, August 15, 1878, pp. 337–38.

36. Boucherett, "Future Plans," p. 4.

37. "Paragraphs: Status of Women in Uncivilised Nations," *EWR*, January 14, 1882, p. 46.

38. "Paragraphs" (on Turkish women), *EWR*, January 15, 1877, pp. 42–44; M. L. Whately, "Woman's Condition in Egypt," *EWR*, September 15, 1884, pp. 395–412; Alicia Bewicke Little, "Lolo and Thibetan Women," *EWR*, April 15, 1893, pp. 83–89.

39. "An Australian Woman," "Openings for Women in the Colonies," *EWR*, January 15, 1888, pp. 6–8. See also "Education of Women in India," *EWR*, June 15, 1877, p. 286, where Mary Carpenter's plan for training English women as teachers for Indian girls' schools is advertised. An item in the *Women's Penny Paper*, under the heading "Women out of Work" and the subheading "Englishwomen for India" promised that "a great field is opening up for women's work in India," especially for teachers and doctors. *WPP*, October 4, 1890, p. 596.

40. "Paragraphs: Women's Rights in Central Africa," *EWR*, September 15, 1883, pp. 431–32.

41. Mani, "Contentious Traditions."

42. "Condition of Women in Mahometan Countries," *EWR*, April 1873, pp. 119–23; "Women in India," *EWR*, August 15, 1876, pp. 366–70.

43. For a discussion of how attributions of "good" and bad" can function similarly in some African American discourse, see hooks, *Yearning*, p. 4.

44. "Condition of Women in Mahometan Countries," pp. 119–20.

45. Review of *Woman Outside Christendom* by J. C. Maudley, *EWR*, September 15, 1880, p. 398. Several years earlier the *Englishwoman's Review* had reprinted with approbation the following extract from a letter to the *Daily News*: "In comparing the forms of Moslemism practised throughout Turkey with any form of Christianity adopted in the same country, there is one great distinction which is . . . amply sufficient to make the lowest form of Christianity superior as a mean of civilisation to the religion of Mahomet . . . and to explain why the Moslems cannot keep pace in prosperity, intelligence and morality with the Christians. This distinction lies in the position assigned to woman. Among all Christian sects she is as nearly the equal of man as she is in Western countries. No Moslem regards her so. To him she is merely an animal." "Paragraphs," *EWR*, January 15, 1877, p. 42.

46. Bernard, "The Position of Women in India," p. 471.

47. Ibid., pp. 474–75.

48. As Huxman says, one of the functions of feminist periodical writing was to change those women "who did not view themselves as an audience" into "persons capable of effecting change" ("*The Woman's Journal*," p. 98).

49. Bernard, "The Position of Women in India," p. 475. This appears to be quite a deliberate paraphrasing of Mary Carpenter's own words: "May many more English women arise, who shall devote themselves to the glorious and blessed work of raising their Eastern sisters, to fill that place in society for which the Creator has destined them" (*Six Months in India*, 2:83).

50. Bernard, "The Position of Women in India," p. 482.

51. In 1880, for example, the *Englishwoman's Review* commented on the widow-marriage movement in Bombay, citing the Indian newspaper *Indu Prakash*. "Foreign Notes and News," *EWR*, February 14, 1880, p. 96. For a brief mention of similar associations in Madras and East Bengal, see *EWR*, May 15, 1882, p. 239. In 1887 the periodical featured a two-page summary of Rukhmabai's case, quoting

from Rukhmabai's letter to the *Times* of April 9 about the hard life of "all Hindoo wives." *EWR*, April 15, 1887, pp. 181–82. Indian male concern for revising Hindu marriage law was considered in "The Indian Renaissance," *EWR*, February 15, 1890, pp. 55–57. See also Engels, "The Limits of Gender Ideology."

52. This is an interpolation of Mani's critique of colonialists' excessive reliance on Indian law as a reflection of Indian society. See "The Production of an Official Discourse on *Sati*," p. 107.

53. See "Condition of Women in Mahometan Countries," *EWR*, April 1873, pp. 119–223; and "The Mahometan Law as Regards Women," *EWR*, February 15, 1881, p. 66.

54. Among the best discussions of the mid-century battles for married women's property are Lewis, *Before the Vote*; Lacey, *Bodichon*; and Holcombe, *Wives and Property*.

55. "The Mahometan Law as Regards Women," *EWR*, February 15, 1881, p. 66.

56. Lutzker, *Edith Pechey Phipson*, pp. 199–209; *WPP*, May 18, 1889, p. 5; "Memorial Addressed to the Rt. Hon. Lord George Hamilton," March 1898, JBC, Box 78A, where Rukhmabai is a signatory. See also Cornelia Sorabji Diaries, December 19, 1889, and February 2, 1890, OIOC, MSS. EUR F165/1.

57. *WPP*, November 10, 1888, p. 5; April 20, 1889, p. 5; May 18, 1889, p. 5; June 22, 1889, p. 10; *EWR*, January 15, 1889, p. 47. See also Fawcett, "Infant Marriage in India," which discusses both Rukhmabai and Pandita Ramabai.

58. "Women in India," *EWR*, August 15, 1876, pp. 366–70; "Education of Women in India," *EWR*, June 15, 1877, pp. 278–80; Annette Ackroyd Beveridge, "The Hindu Mahila Bidyalaya," *EWR*, February 1876, pp. 49–59; "Medical Women for India," *EWR*, November 15, 1883, pp. 512–13; "Present Condition and Future Progress of Medical Women in India," *EWR*, November 1888, pp. 481–87.

59. Mrs. Archibald Little, "A Meeting of Chinese Women," *EWR*, April 15, 1896, pp. 77–85; "A Lady Doctor in Afghanistan," *EWR*, October 15, 1895, pp. 262–65.

60. This was also true of the news of India in the foreign columns. The first two paragraphs of the "India" section of the "Foreign Notes and News" column of the *EWR* for September 1880, for example, were all about European women's educational work in India. In contrast, the "Foreign News and Notes" section of the *Irish Citizen* is where English women's suffrage activities were recounted. See Murphy, *The Women's Suffrage Movement*, p. 59.

61. While remarking that her visits to India made Mary Carpenter a celebrity at home, Manton devotes only one of sixteen chapters to her Indian interests (*Mary Carpenter*, chap. 13). Schupf only mentions Carpenter's Indian connections incidentally ("Single Women and Social Reform," pp. 301, 313). Barbara Ramusack's work is a notable exception: she places Carpenter in a constellation of Victorian and Edwardian feminists interested in Indian women ("Cultural Missionaries," esp. pp. 12–22).

62. "Mary Carpenter," *EWR*, July 15, 1877, p. 296.

63. Bernard, "The Position of Women in India," p. 271.

64. The best source for Victorian women's philanthropic work remains Prochaska, *Women and Philanthropy*.

65. Summers, *Angels and Citizens*, p. 153.

66. Bhaba, "The Other Question," p. 23.

67. Carpenter, *Six Months in India*, 2:16, 42.

68. Ibid., p. 65.

69. See, for example, "Zenana Missions in India," *EWR*, November 15, 1877, p. 502; and "Zenana Societies," *EWR*, May 15, 1882, pp. 231–32.

70. Beveridge, "The Hindu Mahila Bidyalaya," pp. 49–59. This article was based on a paper read to former pupils and friends in the College for Men and Women, January 15, 1876.

71. Lady Anna Gore-Langton was an early feminist who had gone to India with her brother, the governor of Madras. See "The Condition of Hindoo Women: Lecture by Lady Anna Gore-Langton," *WSJ*, March 1, 1877, p. 43.

72. "Education of Women in India," *EWR*, June 15, 1877, p. 279.

73. Quoted in ibid.

74. Callaway, examining the historical and ideological implications of this imperial misogyny, calls it "blaming the women" (*Gender, Culture and Empire*, 3–4). Maud Diver, the well known Anglo-Indian novelist, wrote *The Englishwoman in India* precisely to defend this kind of negative stereotype, insisting that the Anglo-Indian female was "home-loving, home-making, skilled in the love of heart and spirit . . . [and has] done fully as much to establish, strengthen and settled her scattered Empire as shot, steel or the doubtful machinations of diplomacy." Quoted in Greenberger, *The British Image of India*, p. 102. In 1909, the *Englishwoman's Review* recommended Diver's book, "though it passes lightly over the many and perplexing difficulties which underlie her subject." "Reviews," *EWR*, July 15, 1909, p. 219.

75. *EWR*, June 14, 1879, pp. 284–85. A "Lady Granville" was reported distributing prizes at the annual meeting of the London School of Medicine in 1883, and she may have been the same as "Lady Grenville" cited above. *EWR*, June 15, 1883, p. 259.

76. Nupur Chaudhuri, "Shawls, Jewelry, Curry and Rice in Victorian England," in Chaudhuri and Strobel, eds., *Western Women and Imperialism*, pp. 231–46.

77. According to Ray Strachey, Phipson was one of the early British women doctors, as was Frances Hoggan. See Strachey, *The Cause*, pp. 176–78; and Frances Hoggan, "Women in Medicine," in Stanton, *The Woman Question*, pp. 63–86. Phipson's "Address to Hindoos of Bombay on the Subject of Child-Marriage," delivered in Bombay in 1890, indicates some of the connections between English women working for India and feminists at home. I am grateful to Padma Anagol for generously providing me with a full transcription of this speech.

78. See, for example, Mrs. Martindale, "Women in India and the Duty of their English Sisters" (London: Women's Printing Society, 1896). Martindale was a member of the Women's Emancipation Union.

79. Dorothea Beale, "The Marchioness of Dufferin's Report," *EWR*, April 15, 1889, pp. 145–52; and "The Countess Dufferin Fund," *EWR*, January 17, 1894, pp. 40–41.

80. "Medical Education of Women: India, Canada, Europe," *EWR*, September 15, 1883, p. 385.

81. Frances Hoggan, "Medical Work for Women in India, Part I" (read at the Industries Exhibition, Bristol), *EWR*, April 15, 1885, pp. 145, 146.

82. In July 5, 1890, the *Women's Penny Paper* announced that the NIA had founded a number of scholarships for native girls.

83. Frances Hoggan, "Medical Work for Women in India, Part II," *EWR*, May 15, 1885, p. 195.

84. Balfour and Young, *The Work of Medical Women in India*, p. vii. Balfour had been the chief medical officer of the Women's Medical Service in India; Young, in addition to being her assistant, was a lecturer at Lady Hardinge Medical College in Delhi.

85. Hoggan, "Medical Work for Women in India, Part II," pp. 197, 198, 199-200. In an 1889 interview with Mary Scharlieb (whose doctoring in India was a central focus of the article on her), the *Women's Penny Paper* commented with approval that "there is no suspicion of 'professional manner' in Mrs. Scharlieb; it is not needed, for the woman who is a physician *at heart* and *by nature* carries with her unmistakably the mark and seal of her noble calling." "Interview," *WPP*, January 26, 1889, p. 1.

86. Bhownaggree was an Indian M.P. for Finsbury in 1895. See Visram, *Ayahs, Lascars and Princes*, pp. 92-97. His sister Avabai was "one of the few Parsee girls educated on the best English methods." According to the *Women's Penny Paper*, she spent four years in England while her brother was studying for the bar. When he received the C.I.E., she had an interview with the queen and her "intelligent conversation in English much pleased her Majesty." She also studied medicine in England for three years under the auspices of Lady Reay's fund for medical women. See her obituary in *WPP*, January 12, 1889, p. 3. A memorial was made to her at the Nurses Hospital in Bombay at the initiative of Lady Reay. "Colonial and Foreign Notes: India," *EWR*, April 15, 1890, pp. 186-87.

87. "Cama Hospital for Women and Children in Bombay," *EWR*, September 15, 1886, pp. 404-7. The India section of the "Foreign Notes and News" column of January 15, 1884, had first announced the Camas' donation.

88. One early precedent for this can be found in Carpenter, *Six Months in India*, 2:16, where an Indian rani expresses interest in funding a school for girls and asks Carpenter's help. In 1884 the *Englishwoman's Review* reported, via the journal of the NIA, that a Mr. H. Suleiman had offered 20,000 rupees to build a separate dispensary at the Cama Hospital in Bombay. *EWR*, February 15, 1884, p. 96. Information like this was to be found typically in the smaller-print "India" sections of the "Foreign Notes and News" columns. In November of that same year the *Englishwoman's Review*, again thanks to the NIA journal, recognized the pledge of the maharani of Cassim Bazar for 15,000 rupees toward a special female class at the Calcutta Medical College. *EWR*, November 15, 1884, p. 538. Without accusing the *Englishwoman's Review* of deliberately misrepresenting the facts (it did, after all, publish this information, albeit somewhat buried in these columns), I *am* suggesting that the journal tended to give British feminists and social reformers a prominence with regard to these funds that they did not in reality monopolize but rather shared with Indians.

89. Spivak says the same about the rani of Sirmur ("The Rani of Sirmur," p. 270).

90. *EWR*, February 14, 1885, pp. 95-96.

91. For a time the column was designated "Foreign and Colonial Notes"; see, for example, *EWR*, January 15, 1891, p. 65. It remained this way throughout 1891, with "Foreign Notes" at times separate from "Colonial Notes," as in the October issue.

92. *EWR*, October 15, 1878, p. 480.

93. *EWR*, January 15, 1889, p. 47.

94. *EWR*, May 15, 1877, p. 155; February 15, 1885, p. 96.

95. *EWR*, January 15, 1877, p. 40; May 15, 1877, p. 237.

96. See, for example, *EWR*, January 15, 1888, p. 45; June 15, 1889, p. 286. The journal also recognized the current begum of Bhopal when she was made the grand commander of the Star of India by the king in 1910. "The Begums of Bhopal," *EWR*, January 15, 1910, pp. 30–31.

97. See Visram, *Ayahs, Lascars and Princes*, pp. 169–89.

98. Poovey, *Uneven Developments*, pp. 3, 17.

99. Chapman, *Sketches*.

100. "Women's Education in India," *EWR*, November 15, 1882; January 14, 1888, p. 45; September 14, 1889, p. 424.

101. Frances Willard, "Pandita Ramabai," (from the *Union Signal*), *EWR*, October 15, 1888, pp. 451–55.

102. "Review of the Hindu Widows' Home Association, Poona—Ninth Annual Report," *EWR*, July 15, 1905, pp. 212, 215.

103. Carpenter, *Six Months in India*, 2:71.

104. "The Education of Indian Women," *EWR*, January 15, 1904, pp. 14–16.

105. "Womanliness," *EWR*, March 15, 1877, pp. 103–11.

106. Shah, ed., *Pandita Ramabai*. See also Cowan, *The Education of Women in India*, p. 6: "If the book helps the women of the West to realize how critical is the present evolutionary period in the education of the women of India, especially in its relation to constructive Christianity, it will not have failed its purpose."

107. Helen Hanson, "From East to West: Women's Suffrage in Relation to Foreign Missions" (London: Church League for Women's Suffrage, 1913), p. 21.

108. Carpenter, *Six Months in India*, 2:81.

109. In her series for the *Young Woman*, entitled "What-Women-Can-Work-At," Mary Frances Billington recommended mission work for women in India (1894, p. 415). The *Young Woman* also featured an article entitled "London Girls in Persian Harems," May 1897, pp. 281–84, and an interview with Flora Annie Steele, August 1897, pp. 401–4. For the histories of the *Young Woman* and *Womanhood*, see Doughan and Sanchez, *Feminist Periodicals*, pp. 17, 21, where *Womanhood* is described as having "very little feminism."

110. Between September 1909 and August 1910 alone, the *Englishwoman* ran five articles on Indian women: Christiana Herringham, "Travel Sketches of Indian Women," *EW*, September 1909, pp. 199–207; Herringham, "A Visit to a Purdah Hospital," *EW*, February 1910, pp. 101–5; Annie T. Barnard, "The Burmese Woman," *EW*, June 1910, pp. 184–95; Saint Nihal Singh, "The Awakening of Asian Women," *EW*, May 1910, pp. 25–31; and L. F. Waring, "An Indian Poetess," *EW*, August 1910, pp. 61–68. The journal ran monthly. For feminist discussions of imperial questions, see Minna Cowan, "The Education of Indian Women," *EW*, July 1912, pp. 13–18; Eugenia Newmarch, "Women and the Race," *EW*, April

1911, pp. 33–40; Eugenia Newmarch, "The Colour Line," *EW*, September 1911, pp. 293–300; and Moyra Humphries, "Racial Responsibility," *EW*, April 1913, pp. 97–105.

111. Doughan and Sanchez, *Feminist Periodicals*, p. 13.

112. The *Women's Penny Paper* had an erratic "Foreign News" column, where Indian women's achievements were often remarked on. In June 1889 the column carried news of Mrs. Hari Devi, the author of several books, one on the education of children; of a school for Indian girls in Bombay that had been awarded eleven Mary Carpenter scholarships; and of Cornelia Sorabji, the first woman graduate in the Bombay presidency and later an Oxford graduate in law. *WPP* June 8, 1889, p. 5. A later issue also printed an article entitled "News from India" by "An Indian Woman," who might have been either Ramabai or Rukhmabai, both of whom were in England at the time. Dismissing any positive readings of Hindu widows' lives, the author remarked, "If Indian women were to come forward to tell their own story, the world would be sure to hear a totally different account." *WPP*, September 28, 1889, p. 5. Sonderabai Powar, an Indian temperance worker, also contributed an article. See "Widow Life in India," *WPP*, April 27, 1893, p. 156.

113. Mani, "Contentious Traditions," pp. 88ff.; and Radhakrishnan, "Nationalism, Gender, and the Narrative of Identity."

114. The British Committee of the Indian National Congress was founded in 1889, and one of its members, Dadhabai Naoroji (also an M.P. in the 1890s), attended meetings of the British Committee of the international antiregulationist federation. Kaushik, *The Indian National Congress*; Morrow, "The Origins and Early Years of the British Committee"; British, Continental and General Federation for the Abolition of the State Regulation of Vice documents, JBC, Box 80, items 1372, 1410. He also signed a BCG memorial against the reinstitution of the C.D. Acts in India in 1896. See Box 81 (items not numbered); and LNA, *Annual Meetings*, 1886, p. 47; 1891–2, pp. 7, 13; 1893, p. 13, JBC. See also Anagol-McGinn, "The Age of Consent Act."

115. Yegenoglu, "Supplementing the Orientalist Lack," p. 58. See also Lowe, *Critical Terrains*, preface and chap. 1.

116. Balfour and Young, *Work of Medical Women*; Shah, ed., *Pandita Ramabai*, pp. 71–72.

117. Fawcett, *Mary Carpenter*, pp. 4, 15.

118. See, for example, "Infant Marriage in India"; Millicent Garrett Fawcett, Indian Letters, Box 90, FL; and Mathur, *Women's Education in India*, esp. pp. 155–63.

119. Spivak, "The Rani of Sirmur," p. 268; Mani, "Contentious Traditions," p. 118.

120. Fawcett, *Mary Carpenter*, p. 7.

121. Cowan, *The Education of Women in India*, p. 21.

122. Carpenter, *Six Months in India*, 2:218, 83.

123. Mackenzie, *Propaganda and Empire*, chaps. 1, 7–9.

124. Levine, "The Humanising Influences," p. 295.

125. See Huxman, "*The Woman's Journal*," p. 99.

126. Levine, "The Humanising Influences," p. 306.

127. Barbara Leigh Smith Bodichon, "Cleopatra's Daughter, Ste. Marciana, Mama Marabout, and Other Algerian Women," *EWJ*, February 1863, p. 407.

128. Linda Steiner, "Evolving Rhetorical Strategies/Evolving Identities," in Solomon, *A Voice of Their Own*, p. 185.

129. Tickner reiterates the idea that suffrage spectacle was part of the process of self-education for feminists and that they were their own intended audience. According to Emmeline Pethick-Lawrence, it was "our education in that living identification of the self with the corporate whole." Quoted in Tickner, *The Spectacle of Women*, p. 60.

130. The proliferation of academic feminist journals in the past ten years testifies both to the marginalization of women's work in mainstream academic publications (this is changing slowly) and to the power of the feminist press to provide an alternate space for the working out of certain kinds of feminist thinking in public. In terms of mainstream feminism, I am thinking especially of Gloria Steinhem's attempts to keep *Ms.* magazine going as a truly "feminist" journal in the commercial market. For a recent assessment of the feminist press in Britain, see Henegan, "Weathering the Storm."

131. See Klein and Steinberg, eds., *Radical Voices*, advertised as a book that "provides a history of ideas within the women's movement as it has developed over the last ten years."

132. June Purvis, "Editorial," *Women's History Review* 1, no. 1 (1992): 5–8.

133. See especially Amos and Parmar, "Challenging Imperial Feminism"; Barrett and MacIntosh, "Ethnocentrism and Socialist-Feminist Theory," and the responses, Ramazangolu et al., "Feedback"; and, most recently, Mohanty, "'Under Western Eyes.'" I am most indebted to Deb Rossum for these citations. Challenges to feminist imperialism have also occurred in other academic feminist periodicals. See, for example, Ahmed, "Western Ethnocentrism"; and Lugones and Spelman, "Have We Got a Theory for You!" See also *The Past before Us: Twenty Years of Feminism*, special issue of *Feminist Review* 31 (Spring 1989).

CHAPTER 5

1. I am indebted to the comments, insights, and archival contributions that Philippa Levine generously gave me in reading a draft of this chapter. Geraldine Forbes also read a draft version, and I wish to acknowledge her as well. Ware's *Beyond the Pale* was published as I was reworking this material, and I make reference to her treatment of Butler throughout.

2. Carpenter, *Six Months in India*; and Bernard, "The Position of Women in India." Manton treats Carpenter's Indian visits in *Mary Carpenter*, chap. 13. The most thorough treatment of Carpenter and India is Ramusack, "Cultural Missionaries."

3. Balfour and Young, *The Work of Medical Women*, details medical reforms for Indian women in the nineteenth and early twentieth centuries. The *Englishwoman's Review* carried articles and advertisements for organizations like Lady Dufferin's Fund for medical aid to Indian women in the 1880s. See, for example, "Medical

Women for India," *ER*, November 15, 1883, pp. 385–94; and "Present Condition and Future Progress of Medical Women in India," *ER*, November 15, 1888, pp. 481–87.

4. Walkowitz, *Prostitution and Victorian Society*, makes brief mention of the imperial repeal movement but ends with the repeal victory at home in 1886; see also Ware, *Beyond the Pale*, pp. 147–59.

5. Josephine Butler, *Stormbell*, June 1898, p. 59.

6. Walkowitz, *Prostitution*, esp. chaps. 5–7.

7. Ibid., "Epilog," esp. p. 255. See also Kent, *Sex and Suffrage*, chaps. 2, 6.

8. According to the *Shield*, "The origin of the name 'Lock Hospital' is very obscure. One account derives it from a Dr. Lock, who was said to be the founder of the London Lock Hospital—but the official history of that institution does not mention any such person. According to others, the term was initially applied to a Leper Hospital, while others again derive it from an old word meaning rags. Whatever its origin, it is always used to describe hospitals, or wards reserved for patients of either sex suffering from venereal diseases; and it does not necessarily imply (as is commonly supposed) that such places are under lock and key." *Shield*, February 1910, p. 10. For a discussion of the origin and growth of lock hospitals and regulated prostitution in India, see Ballhatchet, *Race, Sex and Class*, chaps. 2, 3. Decisions about when and where to create lock hospitals were governed by statistics (whose reliability is in any case shaky), by politics, and by fiscal considerations (Philippa Levine, private correspondence). See also Butler to Mr. Johnson, October 8, 1887, JBC.

9. Henry J. Wilson, *The History of a Sanitary Failure, Being an Extension of Statements Made at the Conference of the International Federation for the Abolition of State Regulation of Prostitution Held at Berne, 16th–18th September, 1896* (1898), JBC, Box 80.

10. In 1832, for example, the directors of the East India Company doubted the efficiency of the lock hospital system, though the Madras Medical Board disagreed. In 1835 the hospitals in question were shut down by the government. See Wilson, *History*, p. 4.

11. Ibid., pp. 5, 6–18.

12. Butler, *The New Abolitionists*, pp. 192–94. Butler met K. C. Sen personally in her home in Liverpool, according to her recollection of the event thirty years later. According to Ramusack, Sen launched an appeal to English women to get involved in remedying the plight of their Indian "sisters" in 1870, the same year he wrote to Butler ("Cultural Missionaries," pp. 122–23). For a review of the C.D. Acts in India, see also Butler, *Revival and Extension*. The situation in India did not go unremarked during the course of the domestic campaign. A pamphlet issued by the Northern Counties League for Abolishing State Regulation of Vice described how the acts in India and the empire had been "unblushingly established," though no immediate proposal to repeal them there was mentioned. "At Home and Abroad: A Comparison of Certain British and Continental Regulations" (1881), JBC.

13. Butler to the Priestman sisters, May 2, 1886, JBALC. The Priestman sisters, Anna Maria, Mary, and Margaret (later Mrs. Tanner), grew up as Quakers in Bristol and were active in a wide variety of radical political organizations, including the

Ladies' National Association. Margaret went on to become LNA treasurer, and Anna Maria was a member of the Bristol and West of England Society for Women's Suffrage. I am grateful to Philippa Levine for these details.

14. Butler to the Priestman sisters, October 19, 1886, JBALC.

15. H. J. Wilson, *A Rough Record of Events and Incidents Connected with the Repeal of the "Contagious Diseases Acts 1864–69" in the United Kingdom, and the Movement against the State Regulation of Vice in India and the Colonies 1858–1906* (Sheffield: n.p., n.d.), p. 63. The Ladies' National Association became the Ladies' National Association for the Abolition of the State Regulation of Vice and the Promotion of Social Purity in June 1910 and amalgamated formally with the British branch of the British, Continental, and General Federation in October 1915, adopting the name Association for Moral and Social Hygiene. The *Shield*, which had been the organ of the original repeal movement, ceased publication in 1886 but was revived in 1897 as the British Committee's publication, though it routinely covered LNA news. After 1915 it became the official organ of the AMSH.

16. From time to time Butler referred to it as the British *Indian* Committee. See, for example, Butler to Mary Priestman and Mrs. Tanner, June 27, 1894, JBC.

17. Butler, *Revival and Extension*, p. 32.

18. Butler, "Mrs. Butler's Plea." In a letter to Walter McLaren, April 26, 1894, she reminded him, "I am most deeply interested in India, but yet I think that it is important that we should be aware of and try to counteract a poison working very much nearer to us." Similarly in the *Stormbell* for July 1898 she called India "our responsibility" but reminded her readers that repealers had European concerns as well.

19. Minutes of the Executive Meeting, letterbook of the British, Continental, and General Federation, JBC, Box 80, indicates that a committee of the British branch met in December 1887 to discuss the imperial situation, especially with regard to India, but none of the conversations were recorded. See also Wilson, *Rough Record*, p. 65.

20. British Committee letterbooks, JBC, Box 80; LNA, *Annual Reports*, 1886–1906.

21. Josephine Butler, "Current Events—India," *Dawn*, July 1893, p. 1.

22. Stansfeld died in 1898, McLaren in 1913, and Stuart and Wilson in 1914. See Hammond and Hammond, *James Stansfeld*; and Fowler, *Radicalism and Dissent*. Although repeal was not, strictly speaking, a party question (there were Conservatives who were privately supportive of regulation and Gladstone himself fudged the issue), it was generally Liberals who actively and publicly supported abolition.

23. Wilson, *Rough Record*, p. 63.

24. See ibid., pp. 63–71. W. S. Caine, M.P., and Alfred Dyer were among those who provided information for the inquiry.

25. The title of Butler's first Indian repeal publication, *The Revival and Extension of the Abolitionist Crusade*, is one indication of the fact that repeal leaders conceived of India as a second phase. The full title of Wilson's *Rough Record* also clearly separates the domestic crusade from the Indian campaign. Stansfeld, for his part, called India "the second stage of our great drama." LNA, *Annual Report*, 1894–95, p. 19.

26. Wilson, *Rough Record*, p. 67.

27. Cross to Dufferin, May 1888, Viscount Cross Collection, OIOC, MSS. EUR. E 243/18, fols. 92, 24.

28. Dufferin to Cross, June 1, 1888, MSS. EUR. F/130/11A, f. 85; and Dufferin to Cross, March 26, 1888, MSS. EUR. E. 243/24, no fol., Dufferin Collection, OIOC. I am grateful to Philippa Levine for these citations to the Dufferin correspondence.

29. Circular Memorandum No. 21, Addressed to General Officers Commanding Divisions and Districts, June 17, 1886, FL, Box 81.

30. An order issued in 1897 by Sir George White, acknowledging the responsibility of officers for the moral health of their men, ended much of the hostility between London repealers and the Indian army. British Committee, "Some Points Requiring Attention in Reference to Army Reform" (December 1900), FL.

31. Circular Memorandum No. 21.

32. Butler to the LNA, March 16, 1888, JBC. Evidently Stuart told Butler he had access to documents from India that contained evidence that the government had been advised by medical men and officers in northern India to "appoint 'recruiting sergeants' to scour the country in search of young and attractive women to be dragged" into regimental brothels. The Circular Memorandum confirmed this. As Butler wrote to the International Convention of Women in Washington, D.C., in 1888, regulation was the equivalent of providing the army with "selected and superintended healthy women." Josephine Butler, "A Letter to the International Convention of Women at Washington," March 1888, Regulation IX Pamphlets, JBC, pp. 3–4.

33. For a discussion of this imagery in the home campaign, see Walkowitz, *Prostitution and Victorian Society*. While Bushnell and Andrew associated British soldiers with the perpetration of vice in their *Facts Recorded by Eye-Witnesses*, Box 80, item 1425, Butler believed that the officer class was also responsible. See Butler to Henry J. Wilson, April 13, 1891, Box 80, item 1380, where she told him that, with regard to the procurement of women, "I fear such conduct is not so very rare among English officers." See also Butler to Wilson, March 20, 1897, Box 81, item 358, where she reiterated her concern about officers' responsibility for "the present state of things." It is not clear on what basis Butler makes her claims that officers were implicated. The archive is notably silent on the incidence of venereal disease among officers, and Philippa Levine speculates that they either sent out for women (which the regular soldiers could not do) or took up with indigenous women in their own quarters (Levine, private correspondence). This is an area full of scholarly possibility, especially given the common presumption that with the arrival of white women in the empire at the turn of the nineteenth century, relations between officers and "native" women were effectively broken.

34. Butler, *Revival and Extension*, pp. 5–6. Butler blamed bureaucracy, "this secret society, which has sheltered itself behind the visible government of our country and, conscious of its own irresponsibility to the people, has given orders north, south, east and west, throughout the world, for the establishment of this accursed system of regulated vice." Josephine Butler, "A Letter to the Ladies' National

Association, January 1887," in *C.D. Acts Pamphlets*, 5:4, JBC. In "A Letter to the Members of the British, Continental and General Federation for the Abolition of Prostitution" (1895), JBC, Box 80, p. 3, Butler called for "an open and public challenge" to "this gigantic organized wickedness."

35. Wilson, *Rough Record*, p. 71. Although the text does not specify, the council was presumably the governor-general's council at Simla.

36. "Four Remarkable '88s," *Sentinel*, March 1888, p. 33. Dyer had been the chairman of the Working Men's National League, a repeal organization.

37. LNA, *Annual Report*, 1888. See also the report of the LNA Annual Meeting, 1888; and Butler's letter to Mrs. Tanner and the Misses Priestman, June 1888, JBC, Box 80, item 1364.

38. Wilson, *Rough Record*, 73ff. under the heading "Regulation Again Practised in India." For discussion of the Cantonment Rules, see Enloe, *Bananas, Beaches and Bases*, pp. 82–84.

39. Wilson, *Rough Record*, p. 79. Butler recounted how Bushnell and Andrew attended an LNA meeting in 1891 and were drawn to the cause of Indian women. Butler, "The Present Aspect of the Abolitionist Cause in Relation to British India— A Letter to My Friends," JBC, Box 80, item 1428. She urged other repeal workers to meet with Bushnell and Andrew to see for themselves that they were "gentle and quiet, . . . and have deep and strong convictions." Butler to Mrs. Tanner and Mary Priestman, March 9, 1891, JBALC. It would seem from this same letter that Bushnell and Andrew went as delegates expressly because Butler urged them as the representatives of the LNA. "They cannot," she wrote, "fail to make an impression as missionaries for our cause."

40. Wilson, *Rough Record*, p. 113. Before arriving in India, they also visited Cape Colony, Natal, the Orange Free State, and the Transvaal, though *The Queen's Daughters* was chiefly about India. See "Mrs. Andrew and Dr. Kate Bushnell," *Christian*, June 1893, JBC, Box 78A.

41. The observations of Mr. John Hyslop Bell, also an agent for the British Committee, confirmed the reports of Bushnell and Andrew. See his "Special Report to the British Committee," February 20, 1893, JBC, Box 78A.

42. Wilson, *Rough Record*, pp. 83, 85. See also the interview with Lord Roberts, *Christian Commonwealth*, May 11, 1893, JBC, Box 78A.

43. Appendix, Cantonment Rules of 1895, Military Department, Simla, May 3, 1893, Judicial. Fawcett Library Parliamentary Papers, India, 1897–1909, FL.

44. Wilson, *Rough Record*, pp. 90–91, 97.

45. Butler to Miss Forsaith, October 27, 1896, JBALC.

46. LNA, *Annual Meeting*, 1896, p. 64.

47. James Stuart, quoted in LNA, *Annual Meeting*, 1898, p. 58. "We do not believe," declared the British Committee leadership, "in a do-nothing policy." British Committee, "The True Method of Improving the Health and Morals of the Army in India," March 1897, JBC, p. 1.

48. Wilson, *History*, esp. pp. 15–21, which treat the post-1886 disease statistics.

49. *Stormbell*, January 1898, p. 6.

50. LNA, *Annual Meeting*, 1896, p. 87.

51. Ibid.; J. Stuart to Wilson, August 16, 1893, JBALC, Box 80.

52. Reprinted in *Shield*, December 1897, p. 58.

53. Wilson, *Rough Record*, p. 103. Among the protesters against possible reenactment were Eva McLaren, Helen Wilson, Olive Schreiner, Emma Cons, and the Priestman sisters. See Regulation Pamphlets IX, JBC.

54. Wilson, *Rough Record*, p. 103.

55. *Shield*, May 1897, p. 1.

56. Wilson, *Rough Record*, p. 107; *Shield*, August 1897, p. 36.

57. "Memorial Addressed to the Rt. Hon. Lord George Hamilton, Secretary of State of India," March 1898, Henry J. Wilson Files, Box 78A, JBC. I am indebted to Barbara Ramusack for urging me to examine carefully this petition.

58. The examination was to be performed by medical women instead of male doctors. Staunch repealers objected to this scheme because they claimed it was equivalent to complicity with regulation. See *Shield*, May 1899, p. 25.

59. Lady Henry Somerset to the Right Honorable Lord George Hamilton, H.M. Secretary of State for India, April 1897, reprinted from the *Times* by the British Committee, 1897, JBC.

60. Butler, *Truth before Everything*, and Butler to Miss Forsaith, February 18, 1898, H. J. Wilson Regulation File, 1898, JBC. Privately Butler attributed Somerset's position to her ignorance of repeal principles. Butler to the Priestman sisters, June 28, 1897, JBALC.

61. Cited in British Committee, "Reply to Lady Henry Somerset's Scheme for Dealing with the Indian Cantonments" (August 1897), p. 4, FL. See also Tyrrell, *Woman's World*, pp. 204–5.

62. British Committee, "Reply to Lady Henry Somerset's Scheme," p. 11.

63. Butler to Frances Willard, November 29, 1897, JBALC.

64. Sir George White, "Some Points Requiring Attention in Reference to Army Reform" (Chatham: W. and J. Mackay and Co., 1900), p. 1.

65. Wilson, *Rough Record*, 107; "Moral Progress in the Indian Army," *Shield*, April 1913, pp. 35–38; White, "Some Points Requiring Attention," pp. 1–15.

66. Cantonments Acts and Regulations of 1897, reprinted from Fawcett Library Parliamentary Papers, India, 1897–1909, FL.

67. *Stormbell*, February 1898, p. 9.

68. Ibid., May 1898, p. 50.

69. Ware, *Beyond the Pale*, p. 154.

70. Of 1890, the year of her husband's death, she wrote, "I feel so dazed, I do not remember any facts or anything that has happened during the past year." Butler to Miss Priestman, August 29, 1890, JBALC. By the autumn of that year she was feeling "an urging of the heart to be at work again—in a quiet way." Butler to the Priestman sisters, October 18, 1890, JBALC. A little over a year later she told her son Stanley, "I don't want to *come forward* in England again, if I can help, only to *watch*, with the others." Butler to Stanley Butler, February 3, 1891, JBALC. But in 1902 she reassured her repeal colleagues, "I have not ceased to be your fellow-worker, in a certain sense; for though now unable for active work and movement, I am more than ever with our Abolitionist combatants in spirit." Letter to Society of Friends, *Shield*, June 1902, p. 15. For accounts of her life that abbreviate her repeal

work at 1886, see Forster, *Significant Sisters*, pp. 169–202; Petrie, *A Singular Iniquity*, pp. 261–89; Uglow, "Josephine Butler."

71. Butler, *Portrait of Josephine Butler*, esp. chaps. 7, 8, and 9 (which deals briefly with India).

72. Butler to the Priestman sisters, December 21, 1892, JBALC. Her address to the LNA at its annual public meeting in 1896 emphasized the struggle against regulation in Switzerland. "You have heard something of India, you have heard something of our Colonies," she pointed out. "The battle of Geneva was largely reported in the European press . . . but not one of the English press appears to have noticed it. I do not know the reason for this; but because of this silence . . . I am the more anxious to bring home to you . . . the great lesson that these events in Geneva ought to teach us all." Address to the Annual Public Meeting of the Ladies' National Association, London, June 11, 1896, pp. 1–2, JBC.

73. Butler, "Mrs. Butler's Plea," p. 3.

74. Butler to the Priestman sisters, October 19, 1886, JBALC.

75. Between 1887 and 1900 Butler kept up a steady stream of pamphlet writing. In addition to circular letters to the LNA presenting the issue and exhorting the support of its members as well as journal articles and platform speeches, her contributions in the post-1886 phase were *The Extension and Revival of the Abolitionist Cause* (1887); "An Earnest Appeal to Abolitionist Workers" (1893), FL, Box 80, item 1420; "Mrs. Butler's Plea" (1893); "The Present Aspect of the Abolitionist Cause in Relation to British India: A Letter to My Friends" (1893); "A Letter of Earnest Appeal and Warning" (1895); "A Second Letter of Appeal and Warning . . . to the members of the British, Continental and General Federation" (1895); *Truth before Everything* (1897); "A Call to Duty" (1898); and *Silent Victories* (1900).

76. Butler was engaged in a constant effort to keep repeal workers focused on the single cause of prostitution. See Butler to Mrs. Tanner and Miss Priestman, May 29, 1889, JBALC; Butler to Eva McLaren, March 10, 1891, JBC, Box 80, item 1376; Butler, "A Letter to the Members of the British, Continental and General Federation," 1895, JBALC.

77. I am grateful to Philippa Levine for insisting upon this point in private correspondence.

78. By the end of the century, she viewed the *Stormbell* as "my only channel now of speaking to my friends clearly to define our position, and to point out when and how our future path must separate from those who are so ardently after the *new* line of action [vigilance and rescue work]—a good line in itself, but quite *distinct* from direct abolitionism." Butler to H. J. Wilson, July 3, 1899, JBALC. Well after her death, repealers continued to try to toe her strict line, arguing that regulation was the "taproot" of problems like the white slave trade. See *Shield*, April 1913, pp. 25, 31–34.

79. Butler to Mrs. Tanner and Miss Priestman, December 29, 1886, JBALC. See also the flyer issued for the British, Continental, and General Federation on behalf of the English members of its Executive Committee, December 1886, JBC, Box 80, item 1331a; and "Repeal of the C.D. Acts in India and the Colonies," text of report given by J. Stuart at the federation meeting in Copenhagen, August 1888, JBC, Box 80, item 1365b, p. 1. Later India was explicitly prioritized by the British Committee

over Hong Kong. British Committee letterbook, March 15, 1894, JBC, Box 76. In September 1907 the *Shield* differentiated the various parts of the British Empire under regulation as follows: India, "under the India Office"; Gibraltar, Hong Kong, Malta, and the Straits Settlements, "under the Direct Administration of the Colonial Office"; and the Cape of Good Hope, Queensland, New Zealand, and Victoria, "Self-Governing Colonies." British Committee of the Abolitionist Federation, Leaflet No. 116, October 1907, JBC. By the mid-1890s, Butler was urging her friends to consider regulation beyond India, and worried especially about the straits settlements. Butler to J. Stuart, March 25, 1895, JBC, Box 80, item 1509.

80. Butler, *Revival and Extension*, p. 1.

81. Butler to the Priestmans, January 13, 1887, JBALC.

82. *Sentinel*, May 1887, p. 56.

83. Mrs. Fenwick Miller, quoted in LNA, *Annual Meeting*, 1898, p. 47.

84. LNA, *Annual Meeting*, 1887, pp. 10–11, 14.

85. Butler, "Imperial Aspects of the Present Crusade on Behalf of an Equal Standard of Morality," *Stormbell*, April 1900, p. 298.

86. Butler, "Some Lessons from Contemporary History, Showing the Connection between Revolutionary Movements and State Regulated Vice," address at the annual meeting of the Friends' Association for Abolition, May 19, 1898, Regulation Pamphlets IX, p. 3, JBC.

87. Butler, "Our Indian Fellow Subjects," *Sentinel*, September 1887, p. 112.

88. *Dawn*, June 1892, p. 5.

89. See Milbank, "Josephine Butler," p. 157. In 1892 Butler reiterated this central principle: "We must aim at absolute equality for men and women; never forgetting that it is impossible for us to obtain equality in moral matters unless we have a corresponding equality in Legislative matters." *Dawn*, June 1892, p. 5.

90. Butler, "To the Missionary Societies and Christian Ministers of Great Britain," January 1898, Regulation File, 1898, JBC, p. 1.

91. Emphasis added.

92. The ideology of international sisterhood is discussed more fully in Chapter 6.

93. The Gospel Purity Association had been operating in India since the beginning of the campaign, while the Army Purity Association seems to have been a development of the late 1890s. The pledge it required of its members was abstinence "from the sin of fornication." British Committee, "Some Points Requiring Attention in Reference to Army Reform," December 1900, p. 6, JBC. From time to time Butler reported on the Army Purity Association in *Stormbell*. See the issues for August 1899 and March 1900.

94. Quoted in LNA, *Annual Meeting*, 1897, p. 27. However, she was not without sympathy for the European victims of international prostitution rings. See her account of Minna Drescher, a young Austrian girl who fell into the hands of white slave traders, in *Stormbell*, May 1898, p. 53.

95. *Sentinel*, May 1888, p. 55.

96. Remembering the suffering of English women under the C.D. Acts, Butler claimed that the Indian statute "weighs more heavily on the poor Indian woman than on others; she bends under it more hopelessly, more helplessly, a broken reed, trodden down by unholy feet." *Stormbell*, June 1898, pp. 59–60. On the thirtieth

anniversary of the founding of the LNA, Butler exhorted her audience to "cultivate a truly international . . . spirit of sympathy, not only for those of your own race in all our wide dependencies, but with the whole human race, more especially for the native women under the conquering races everywhere. Those women call for the utmost compassion—they so easily, so inevitably fall under the cruel yoke of selfish and oppressive men of the ruling powers." Quoted in LNA, *Annual Report*, 1902, p. 66.

97. In the September 1887 issue of the *Sentinel*, Butler explained the repealers' reliance on sympathetic Indian reformers like Malabari. She expressed similar sentiments in the *Dawn*, which publicized Malabari's work for raising the age of consent in India, saying, "All women owe him a debt of gratitude." *Dawn*, October 1890, p. 12. Naoroji was a member of the Indian National Congress and an M.P. elected on the Liberal ticket in 1892. See Seal, *The Emergence of Indian Nationalism*, p. 285; and Visram, *Ayahs, Lascars, and Princes*, pp. 82–90. Naoroji was also a member of the British Committee and attended meetings off and on in the early 1890s when his parliamentary duties kept him in London. The British Committee notebook (JBC, Box 76) records his attendance at their meetings; LNA, *Annual Meetings*, 1887 and 1889–90, JBC, report his speeches on the Indian situation. Butler urged Priestman to support his canvassing efforts in Somersetshire, telling her, "He is right on every question and such a good man." Butler to Miss Priestman, February 22, 1888, JBALC.

98. *Stormbell*, June 1898, p. 59.

99. Helen Dyer's report "Rescue Work in India," for example, commented that "Hindu worship is inextricably mixed with obscene practices" (JBC, Box 80, items 1366, 1367). She was Dyer's wife and a member of the LNA.

100. Butler is quoted in *Shield*, March 1903, p. 9.

101. "Rise of a Women's Movement in India," *Sentinel*, February 1887, p. 18.

102. *Sentinel*, March 1887, pp. 29–30.

103. *Sentinel*, March 1888 and January 1888, p. 3.

104. Butler, "A Grave Question That Needs Answering by the Churches of Great Britain," *Sentinel*, March 1887, p. 30.

105. Butler, "Our Christianity Tested," BL, p. 28.

106. Ibid., p. 53.

107. LNA Memorial to Lord Salisbury, April 3, 1888, JBC, Box 80.

108. Butler to the LNA, March 16, 1888, JBALC.

109. Butler, "Some Lessons from Contemporary History, Showing the connections between Revolutionary Movements and State Regulated Vice" (London: Friends' Association for the Abolition of State Regulation of Vice, 1898), pp. 9, 10.

110. Butler, *Truth before Everything*, p. 20.

111. Butler, "The Present Aspect," p. 31.

112. Butler, *Revival and Extension*, pp. 51, 5–6.

113. Butler, "Mrs. Butler's Plea," p. 6.

114. By the twentieth century Lord Minto considered India to be governed less by force than by the "mere prestige of British authority." Quoted in Hyam, *Britain's Imperial Century*, p. 160.

115. LNA, *Annual Report*, 1891–92, p. 33.

116. *Stormbell*, February 1899, p. 144.

117. Butler, "Mrs. Butler's Plea," p. 6.

118. Ibid., p. 8. In *Revival and Extension*, p. 3, Butler wrote, "I believe that we are called to take a prominent part in the purifying of our nation's name in distant parts of the world, and in the open and indignant repudiation of her sins."

119. The British Committee tried to make white slave trade reformers realize the importance of abolition by sending delegates to the international conferences and reading memoranda about the details of abolitionist work. See British Committee, "Memorandum Presented to the International Congress on the White Slave Traffic in London, June 21–23, 1899," Regulation Pamphlets IX, JBC.

120. Butler to Stanley Butler [October 1896].

121. Butler wrote, "I have never heartily sympathized with the work of the Vigilance Society, and yet undoubtedly they have done so much good. . . . But there is a constant tendency towards *external* pressure, and inside that a tendency to let pressure fall almost exclusively on women. . . . It is dangerous work, in reference to personal liberty, but few people care for liberty or personal rights now." Butler to Miss Priestman, November 5, 1894, JBALC. She also believed that the cause in Europe was "going quite wrong" because repeal societies there were too concerned with exercising power over prostitutes rather than battling regulation. Butler to the Misses Priestman, April 4, 1895, JBALC. For a brief discussion of the interventionist turn that rescue work took in the 1890s in London, see Walkowitz, "Male Vice and Feminist Virtue," p. 81. See also Tyrrell, *Woman's World*, chap. 9.

122. Butler had suspected Somerset and Willard of too much emphasis on purity several years earlier. "They dwell too much on *general* truths abut 'Social Purity' and do not yet realize the political and aggressive character of our work." Butler to Miss Forsaith, March 30, 1893, JBALC.

123. In the April 1900 issue of the *Stormbell*, Butler approvingly reprinted a large section of Ellice Hopkins's *The Power of Womanhood*, from her chapter on "imperial aspects." In it Hopkins stressed the civilizing nature of the British Empire and its purifying potential for sexual and social life in Britain.

124. Butler, "Social Purity."

125. From the very beginning of the domestic campaign for repeal, Butler equated work against regulation with antislavery. See, for example, *Sursum Corda*; "Letter to the International Convention of Women at Washington," March 1888, JBC; and her account of the repeal campaign, which she entitled *The New Abolitionists*.

126. Butler to Miss Priestman, June 13, 1886, JBALC.

127. Butler to Eva McLaren, March 10, 1891, JBC, Box 80, item 1376.

128. Butler to the Priestman sisters, October 31, 1896, JBALC.

129. Butler to Miss Forsaith, June 3, 1897, JBALC.

130. Butler to Miss Priestman, May 12, 1888, JBALC.

131. Stanley Butler to Miss Priestman, October 13, 1887, JBALC.

132. Josephine Butler to the Priestman sisters, February 27, 1888, JBALC.

133. Ibid. After Stansfeld's death she paid him a compliment that reflects the premium she placed on men with "feminine" characteristics: "I have seldom met

with a man who had so much of the woman's heart in this matter." *Stormbell*, March 1898, p. 22.

134. Butler to Miss Forsaith, April 26, 1905, JBALC.

135. Maurice Gregory, "The Crowning Crime of Christendom" (London: Dyer Brothers, 1896), pp. 3–4, Regulation Pamphlets IX, JBC.

136. Butler called France "the mother of that accursed system." See "Mrs. Butler and the International White Slave Conference," *Shield*, June 1899, p. 35. The English repealer Blanche Leppington declared that regulation in Britain was relatively brief and "so alien to the spirit and traditions of her people . . . that, although it left a mark behind it which is hardly even yet quite obliterated, there was nevertheless not time for it to eat into the substance of our social ideas and institutions to the extent that it must have done had it lasted (as it has in France) for more than three generations instead of less than one." See her pamphlet "Neo-Regulationism: Its Principles, its Practice and its Prospects" (Geneva: Office of the International Federation, 1904), JBC, H. J. Wilson Papers, Box 297, p. 49.

137. Butler, "Mrs. Butler's Plea," p. 6.

138. Scott, *A State Iniquity*, p. 2.

139. Elizabeth Blackwell, "Christian Duty in Regard to Vice," JBC, Box 80, item 1399a.

140. Butler, *Sursum Corda*, p. 20.

141. Butler to Stanley Butler, November 13, 1898, JBALC.

142. Butler, *Native Races*, p. 152.

143. Ibid., pp. 105–6.

144. Butler to the Misses Priestman, December 29, 1886, and January 29, 1887, JBALC.

145. As early as 1895 Butler had expressed concern that in Germany repealers were putting too much emphasis on penal measures against prostitutes and not enough on the abolition of regulation. See Butler, "Letter to the members of the British, Continental and General Federation," 1895, pp. 7–8, JBALC. Throughout 1895 Butler complained about the German's readiness to apply penal measures against prostitutes and railed about the fact the German men in the federation were "insolent." Butler to Mary Priestman, March 2, 1895, JBALC; and to the Priestman sisters, April 4, 1895, JBALC. "They regard me as an inconvenient and unmanageable *intruder* into the Federation, an old woman who sets her own opinion against the whole of German male wisdom. I wish someone would tell them that I *founded* the Federation in 1875!" Butler to the Misses Priestman, May 3, 1895, JBALC. Frustrations with her German colleagues flared up from time to time. "The German element is likely to be difficult to deal with at times," she wrote in the *Shield*, July 1904, p. 48, in anticipation of a congress at Dresden. "They are slow to admit the equality of women with men, and are some of them incorrigible State-worshippers." Of "our dear American friends" Butler wrote, "Their noble characters are marred by a certain self-assertion, and a little jealousy. Even Dr. Bushnell complained to me that there are so few Americans on the Executive Committee [of the Federation] compared with Swiss and English, and [she] could scarcely see how natural that is, since it is in England and Switzerland that our workers have been at

work, for 26 and for 16 years, while, in America, there having been no C.D. Acts to repeal, there have been no repeal workers." Butler to Mary Priestman, October 2, 1895, JBALC.

146. *Shield*, March 1908, p. 14.

147. Butler, *Silent Victories*, p. 82.

148. Or "Sister women," as Butler put it. Butler to Mrs. Tanner and Miss Priestman, December 29, 1886, JBALC. See also Mrs. H. J. Wilson, quoted in LNA, *Annual Report*, 1896, pp. 50–51.

149. Butler, "To the Missionary Societies," p. 1.

150. Dyer described the prostitutes he had seen in Sitapur as "bold-faced" harlots who spoke "saucily." *Sentinel*, March 1888, p. 6.

151. Quoted in Butler, "To the Missionary Societies," p. 2.

152. Andrew and Bushnell, *The Queen's Daughters in India*, esp. pp. 14–15, 24, and chap. 4.

153. Andrew and Bushnell, "Indian Journal," JBC, Box 78A, pp. 1–2, 9–10. They visited Bareilly, Lucknow, Meerut, Lahore, Rawal Pindi, Peshwar, Amritsar, Umballa, Sitapur, and Benares.

154. Ibid., pp. 102, 9–10.

155. Andrew and Bushnell found evidence of registration tickets issued by the government to prostitutes. See *The Queen's Daughters in India*, pp. 93–94.

156. Andrew and Bushnell, "Indian Journal," pp. 45–46.

157. Ibid., pp. 72, 41, 136.

158. Ibid., pp. 75, 57–61.

159. Ibid., pp. 47–48, 10–11, 50.

160. Ibid., pp. 202–3.

161. Ibid., p. 23.

162. Thanks to Philippa Levine for urging me to recognize this possibility.

163. Andrew and Bushnell, "Indian Journal," p. 169.

164. Ibid., p. 5.

165. Ibid., pp. 47–48, 113.

166. Butler, *Silent Victories*, pp. 81–82.

167. Andrew, "Report of the Delegates," pp. 10–11.

168. LNA, *Annual Report*, 1893, 1897. They traveled all over Ireland, Scotland, and England and were sponsored by a diversity of women's organizations, from the YWCA to the Women's Liberal Association. See British Committee letterbooks, meeting of June 28, 1893, JBC, Box 76. *Dawn*, July 1895, pp. 8–12, reprinted in full Andrew's lecture on Indian women's "inextinguishable" dignity. They also gave lectures entitled "Social Questions in the Orient" upon their return to Britain (JBC, Box 80, item 1506); item 346 in the Regulation File, 1898, JBC, cites their appearance at the annual meeting of the York Branch of the LNA in 1898, where they told "from personal knowledge of the sad and baneful effects of the system in India."

169. "Facts Recorded by Eye-Witnesses," JBC, Box 80, item 1425; Butler, *Silent Victories*, pp. 81–82.

170. Butler, *Stormbell*, June 1898, p. 59.

171. Ware, *Beyond the Pale*, p. 157.

172. *Sentinel,* September 1887, p. 113.

173. *Stormbell,* June 1898, p. 60.

174. Butler to the Priestman sisters, October 15, 1888, JBALC.

175. Butler, "The Queen's Daughters in India," *Stormbell,* April 1898, p. 37.

176. Butler to William Coote, reprinted in *Shield,* May 1903, p. 37. This was not only a feminist idea. Sarah Stickney Ellis, author of etiquette books, praised the bond of sisterhood, which she claimed "arises chiefly out of . . . [women's] mutual knowledge of each other's capacity for receiving pain." Quoted in Vicinus, *Independent Women,* p. 34.

177. Butler, preface to *The Queen's Daughters in India,* by Andrew and Bushnell, p. vii.

178. *Stormbell,* January 1898, p. 6.

179. Butler, "Mrs. Butler's Plea," p. 8.

180. "I have said that the wonderful Indian story must have a good place [in the Hague programme]," Butler wrote to H. J. Wilson in August 1893 (JBC, Box 80, item 1446). And on April 20, 1894: "The Continental Friends seem to hail the idea of imbibing some new life in the abolitionist cause, by coming to England, and hearing about our Indian repeal work and meeting friends who are very earnest" (JBALC). Success in India would be "a good thing—a standard—to hold up to our foreign allies at our Conference in July."

181. Butler to H. J. Wilson, February 24, 1898, JBALC.

182. Visram, *Ayahs, Lascars, and Princes,* pp. 82–88; see also LNA, *Annual Meeting,* 1897, p. 27.

183. Moulton, "The Early Congress," pp. 22–23.

184. The Cantonments Code of 1899 permitted brothels to exist, provided certain sanitary standards were maintained. This tended to result in medical examinations. "State Regulation of Vice in the British Empire," *Shield,* September 1907, p. 50.

185. However, the LNA tended to refer practical work on behalf of India to the British Committee. See LNA, *Annual Report,* 1908, p. 9.

186. Subscriptions in 1871 were £1,079.16.8; in 1888, £517.12.5; in 1894, £380.14.7; in 1911, they were down to £213.14.8. See the LNA annual reports for those years.

187. *Shield,* June 1902, p. 25.

188. Dr. Helen Wilson, "The Equal Moral Standard: A Question for Greater Britain," *Shield,* May 1908, p. 19. The *Shield* remained the organ of the British Committee of the Abolitionist Federation and pledged itself to applying repeal principles "in the United Kingdom, in India, and in the British Colonies." When repeal principles were enumerated, the colonies and dependencies were often at the top of the agenda. See *Shield,* June 1910, pp. 41–42.

189. Andrew and Bushnell returned to India in 1899, according to LNA, *Annual Report,* 1899, and traveled to the Far East as well, as they narrated in *Heathen Slaves and Christian Rulers.*

190. Maurice Gregory, "A Great Unsolved Problem," *Shield,* April 1903, pp. 23–24.

191. Money had typically been spent on repeal publications and paid agents. See

"Conditions in India: An Interview with Dr. Agnes McLaren," *Shield,* September 1910, pp. 57–58; "Rescue Homes in North India," *Shield,* November 1910, pp. 76–77; "A Refuge in North India for European Women: The Need to be Met," *Shield,* July 1912, pp. 134–35; and "India: Hopeful Moments," *Shield,* July 1913, pp. 62–63. See also LNA, *Annual Report,* 1911, p. 17.

192. Katherine Dixon, "An Appeal to the Women of the Empire Concerning Present Moral Conditions in Our Cantonments in India" (November 1915), pp. 5–6, FL.

193. Harrison, *Prudent Revolutionaries,* p. 60.

194. Butler to Mr. Johnson, January 24, 1903, JBALC.

195. James Stuart, "Thirtieth Anniversary of the Federation," *Shield,* July 1902, p. 62.

196. In 1887 Butler wrote, "Besides availing ourselves of the existing evangelizing stream, I believe we ought to aim at having our own independent missionaries, men and women going forth to India and our Colonies to do the work which we have done at home. I believe I shall live to see this. I have faith in the spirit of enterprise of our age." *Revival and Extension,* p. 4.

197. Butler to the editor of the *Auckland Star,* May 3, 1895, reprinted in Butler, "A Second Letter of Appeal and Warning," pp. 4–5.

198. See, for example, Elizabeth Wolstenholme Elmy, "The Emancipation of Women" (London: Women's Printing Society, 1888), in which she connects votes for women with preventing the reintroduction of the C.D. Acts in England and the colonies. She was one of many suffrage women involved with the Indian campaign. Suffrage women attended British Committee meetings. See British Committee letterbooks, March and April, 1894, JBC; and LNA, *Annual Report,* 1886–1911; Frances Cobbe et al., "Memorial *re* the Indian Cantonments" (1896), JBC, H. J. Wilson Regulation 3d File, Box 81, file no. 4.

199. See, for example, "The Ladies National Association for the Abolition of the Government Regulation of Vice: Why It Is Still Needed" (1907), FL, Suffragette Fellowship Collection; Martindale, *Under the Surface,* which is addressed to those who see women's suffrage as only about the vote and contains a detailed account of regulation in India; and C. M. Whitehead, "The Suffrage and the C.D. Acts" (London: LNA, 1910).

200. "Solidaire," *CC,* June 6, 1913, pp. 131–32.

CHAPTER 6

1. Fawcett, "New Rules," p. 23. For a discussion of some feminists' reluctance to embrace repeal, see Strachey, *The Cause,* pp. 266–68. As a partial explanation for some feminists' discomfort over the issues raised by Butler's repeal campaign—and by Elizabeth W. Elmy's pregnancy out of wedlock—Harrison's point is a good one: "Ever since being embarrassed by Wollstonecraft's personal life they had been cautious on sexual matters" (*Prudent Revolutionaries,* pp. 22, 313).

2. Fawcett, "The Use of Higher Education to Women," p. 724.

3. [Helena Swanwick], "The New Imperialism," *CC,* May 30, 1913, p. 116.

4. *Common Cause* reported that Frances Hallowes, spokeswoman for the Indian WCTU, spoke to a meeting of the LNA, where she declared that "she considered the agitation for the Suffrage on the part of women as a sacred duty. As long as women have no political importance their agitation against this wrong will have little respect. The white slave trade and the traffic in coloured races should go together. She would like the word 'white' altered to 'women's,' so that all women should be included in the agitation now before the public." *CC*, June 2, 1910, p. 121. See also Hallowes, "Regulation by Authority in Our Indian Army," *CC*, October 19, 1911, p. 487; Emmeline Pethick-Lawrence, "The White Slave Traffic," *VFW*, November 22, 1912, p. 114; Millicent Garrett Fawcett, "England and India," *CC*, September 12, 1913, p. 384; and Tyrrell, *Woman's World*, pp. 217, 221–41.

5. Fawcett, "England and India," p. 384.

6. "Solidaire," *CC*, June 6, 1913, p. 131.

7. Annie Kenney, "To the Women of Germany," *VFW*, October 1907, p. 3. Kenney ended her 1924 memoir with the following hope: "May we pass out of this life having played our part and added our bit to the shining structure of this our illustrious and beloved Empire" (*Memories of a Militant*, p. 308). I am grateful to Lara Kriegel for bringing this quotation to my attention.

8. See Burton, "The White Woman's Burden," p. 307 n. 9.

9. *Votes for Women* actually ran a column under the rubric "Everywoman."

10. Evelyn Sharp, "Woman's Suffrage and the Child," *VFW*, November 1907, p. 16.

11. Millicent Garret Fawcett, speech at Queen's Hall, Langham Place, London, June 2, 1899, in "Speeches at a General Meeting in Support of the Political Enfranchisement of Women," *Women's Suffrage Pamphlets*, 1871–72, vol. 2, FL.

12. "An English Visitor," "A French Suffragette," *VFW*, May 14, 1908, p. 161. It is certainly true that some European suffrage women praised British feminists as the leaders of the international movement. See Thora Daugaard, "Women and the Vote in Denmark," *VFW*, December 27, 1912, p. 196.

13. Tyrrell, *Woman's World*, p. 36; emphasis added.

14. Fawcett, *Women's Suffrage*, pp. 35, 43–44; see also Mitchell, "Colonial Statesmen and Votes for Women"; "Women and the New South African Constitution," *VFW*, August 20, 1909, pp. 1078–79. "Votes for Women in South Africa," *VFW*, November 29, 1912; "Suffragette Travelers from Overseas," *VFW*, January 16, 1914, p. 239; *CC*, February 23, 1911, p. 774.

15. Women's Freedom League, *Report of the Eighth Annual Conference*, (London, March 29, 1913), p. 22.

16. "Notice of the IWSA—Budapest," *CC*, February 13, 1913, p. 770.

17. Teresa Billington-Greig, "The Storm-Centre of the Women's Suffrage Movement," *International*, September 1909, p. 110; see also Burton, "The White Woman's Burden," p. 304.

18. Elizabeth Wolstenholme Elmy, "Woman's Franchise: The Need of the Hour" (1907), p. 13, FL.

19. Burton, "The White Woman's Burden," p. 304. See also Christabel Pankhurst, "Shall This Country Lead the Way?," *VFW*, September 3, 1908, pp. 426–27.

20. Quoted in Adam, *Women in Council*, p. 83.

21. "The International Council of Women," *Fortnightly Review* 72 (December 1899): 154.

22. Tyrrell, *Woman's World*, esp. chap. 3.

23. "Will Britain Lag Behind?," *Vote*, September 21, 1912, p. 366; "Turkey Ahead of England," *Vote*, July 15, 1911, p. 145; "Why Does Britain Lag Behind?," *Vote*, May 18, 1912, pp. 76–77; and *VFW*, June 27, 1913, p. 576.

24. See James Sturgis, "Britain and the New Imperialism," in Eldridge, ed., *British Imperialism*, pp. 85–125.

25. Harrison, *Separate Spheres*. See also Tickner, *The Spectacle of Women*, p. 155.

26. This phrase originated with a suffragette who reported on the conference of the International Woman Suffrage Alliance in 1913. The fuller text reads: "Woman Suffrage is not a question of . . . political tactics, but a great and growing movement that has thrown a girdle round about the earth and is growing, growing, growing." See "Under Freedom's Flag: At Budapest," *VFW*, June 13, 1913, p. 53.

27. For a discussion of feminist periodicals as sites for the production of ideology and for the working out of ideas, see Chap. 4.

28. Doughan and Sanchez, *Feminist Periodicals*, p. 5.

29. Fulford, *Votes for Women*, chaps. 4–7.

30. Nellie M. Hunter, letter to the editor, *CC*, June 29, 1911, p. 217. See also "U.K.," *WF*, January 14, 1909, p. 349; and *WF*, January 21, 1909, p. 360.

31. Morgan, *Suffragists and Liberals*, pp. 64–78. See also Holton, *Feminism and Democracy*, pp. 69–75.

32. Miss Isabella Tod, remarks to the North Ireland branch of the National Society for Women's Suffrage, *WSJ*, March 1, 1875, p. 30.

33. The Women's Social and Political Union was formed in 1903, but until 1907 the NUWSS and the WSPU undertook many cooperative ventures. See Holton, *Feminism and Democracy*, p. 36.

34. Doughan and Sanchez, *Feminist Periodicals*, pp. 24–30.

35. Ibid., p. 34.

36. For a discussion of some of the international concerns of the *WSJ*, see Burton, "The White Woman's Burden," pp. 302–3.

37. *Votes For Women* published a letter in its November 21, 1913, issue, p. 116, indicating that English women in India read the militants' periodical and felt it to be "one of our biggest links with home." The "Votes for Women" Fellowship, orchestrated by Pethick-Lawrence and others who had split with the Pankhursts in 1912, relied on internationalism: "Its boundaries have become world-wide, and its representatives are found in every corner of the English speaking world as well as in every other country where British men and women are to be found." *VFW*, December 5, 1913, p. 143. The *Vote*, which was the organ of the Women's Freedom League, reviewed the Indian reform magazine *Stree Bodhe*, praising it for its attention to Indian widows. See "The 'Stree Bodhe' and Social Progress in India," *Vote*, March 19, 1910; and *VFW*, November 29, 1912.

38. See *Shield*, March 1908, p. 10. Hallowes's work in India centered around Indian women prostitutes and their treatment under the Cantonment Rules. See *CC*, June 2, 1910, p. 121. Hallowes also wrote to Fawcett with information on Indian

women interested in Indian women's education. See her letter from Musoorie, June 17, 1915, in "Millicent Garrett Fawcett's Indian Letters," FL, Box 90.

39. In March 1910 the *Vote* reported on the progress of the Indian women's magazine *Stree Bodhe* and mentioned that "Indian women in this country are showing their sympathy with the Suffrage cause; some have become members of the Women's Freedom League, so that they may evidence it in practical way." These may have included Roy, Nanth, and Mukerjea, cited below. The WFL's International Suffrage Fair at the Chelsea Town Hall in November 1912 had booths representing all nations, including India, where a Mrs. Ramdulari Dube spoke about Indian women's progress. Her husband contributed an article to *Vote*, June 10, 1911, p. 79. See also *Vote*, November 16, 1912, p. 60.

40. Eva McLaren, "Ajmairee: A Child Mother," *CC*, February 20, 1914, p. 882.

41. Doughan and Sanchez, *Feminist Periodicals*, p. xii; Doughan, "Periodicals by, for and about Women," p. 268.

42. Holton, *Feminism and Democracy*, p. 21.

43. Tickner, *The Spectacle of Women*, p. 7. Harrison characterizes the NUWSS as a "broad church for feminists" (*Prudent Revolutionaries*, p. 103).

44. Doughan and Sanchez, *Feminist Periodicals*, pp. 24, 27–28. There was no strictly suffrage periodical between the demise of the *Women's Suffrage Journal* in 1890 and the inception of the *Women's Franchise* in 1907, although journals like the *Woman's Herald* and the *Englishwoman's Review* did cover suffrage activities. The *Englishwoman* received some financial support from the NUWSS, but it was more of a social feminist journal than a suffrage periodical per se. The *Women's Franchise* was divided into sections in which it featured "all major tendencies within the suffrage movement," including the WFL, the Pankhursts, the NUWSS, and the Men's Society for Women's Suffrage. See Doughan and Sanchez, *Feminist Periodicals*, p. 24.

45. Burton, "The White Woman's Burden," pp. 302–5.

46. Doughan and Sanchez, *Feminist Periodicals*, pp. 27–28.

47. C. L. Wyllie, "A Hindu Woman Doctor," *CC*, May 12, 1910, pp. 72–73.

48. Ibid., p. 73.

49. Chapman, *Sketches*.

50. Olive Chandler, "How Women Are Treated in India," *CC*, June 2, 1910, pp. 117–18.

51. Ibid., p. 117.

52. *CC*, June 16, 1910, p. 155.

53. Ibid.

54. Coomaraswamy wrote a piece on Indian womanhood for *Votes for Women* at the same time that the debate was raging in *Common Cause*. See his "The Oriental View of Women," *VFW*, May 13, 1910, p. 531.

55. *CC*, June 16, 1910, p. 155.

56. *CC*, June 23, 1910, p. 172.

57. *CC*, August 11, 1910, p. 298.

58. *CC*, January 23, 1914, p. 791.

59. "The Orientalists," *CC*, April 25, 1912, pp. 36–37.

60. Constance Lytton, quoting the pronouncements of Antis about how de-

graded women were in non-Western countries, indicated that she agreed with their characterizations, arguing that "the contention of woman Suffragists could not be more reasonably presented . . . to meet the Anti-Woman Suffragist argument, it is only necessary to quote their own utterances." *Prisons and Prisoners*, p. 17.

61. Harrison, *Separate Spheres*, pp. 118, 129.

62. According to Cromer, writing in the *Anti-Suffrage Review* in 1910, "The German man is manly, and the German woman is womanly; can we hope to compete with a nation such as this, if we war against nature, and endeavour to invert the natural roles of the sexes? We cannot do so." Quoted in Harrison, *Separate Spheres*, p. 34.

63. Ibid., p. 75.

64. Quoted in Tickner, *The Spectacle of Women*, p. 155. "For the discharge of great responsibilities in the dependencies of the Empire in distant parts," wrote Cromer in 1912, "you want the qualities not of the feminine but of the masculine mind." Quoted in Harrison, *Separate Spheres*, p. 75.

65. Tickner, *The Spectacle of Women*, p. 155.

66. Harrison, *Separate Spheres*, p. 176.

67. Swanwick, "The New Imperialism," p. 115.

68. "E. W.," "Empire Building: An Interlude," *CC*, November 29, 1912, p. 585.

69. Swanwick, "The New Imperialism," p. 116. Doughan and Sanchez identify Swanwick as the first editor of the *Common Cause* (*Feminist Periodicals*, p. 27).

70. Ibid.

71. Fawcett, "England and India," pp. 381–83.

72. "M. D.," "Medical Women in India," *CC*, January 30, 1914, p. 804.

73. Contributions included E. Slater, "Medical Women in India," *CC*, January 11, 1912, p. 689; Fawcett, "England and India," pp. 383–84; Malcolm MacNicol's letter regarding English women in India and Fawcett's response, *CC*, October 10, 1913, p. 461; "Lalli: A Mother in India," *CC*, October 31, 1913, p. 318; "M. D.," "Medical Women in India"; McLaren, "Ajmairee: A Child Mother"; Eleanor McDougall, "The Education of Indian Women and Girls," *CC*, March 27, 1914, pp. 998–99; "Purdah and Its Gradual Abolition," *CC*, June 4, 1914, pp. 214–15; "Women's Education in India," *CC*, October 15, 1915, p. 338.

74. Gray, "The White Woman's Burden," pp. 565–66.

75. Maude Royden, "The Imperial Idea," *CC*, February 19, 1915, p. 723.

76. *CC*, February 26, 1915, p. 733.

77. For an account of the IWSA, see Schreiber and Mathieson, *Journey towards Freedom*.

78. "Solidaire," *CC*, June 6, 1913, p. 131.

79. *CC*, October 13, 1912, p. 507.

80. "Notice of the IWSA—Budapest," *CC*, February 13, 1913, p. 770.

81. Bessie Drysdale, "Report of the Conference of the International Woman Suffrage Alliance," *Vote*, July 15, 1911, pp. 151–52.

82. Schreiber and Mathieson, *Journey towards Freedom*, pp. 10, 15, 24. The 2,800 participants at the Budapest conference included visitors as well as official IWSA members.

83. *CC*, October 13, 1912, p. 507.

84. Quoted in ibid.

85. Ibid.

86. *CC*, June 6, 1912, p. 143.

87. *CC*, May 16, 1913, p. 84.

88. Schreiber and Mathieson, *Journey towards Freedom*, p. 22.

89. Quoted in *CC*, June 20, 1913, p. 171.

90. Catt, "The World Movement for Woman Suffrage," p. 1.

91. Quoted in *CC*, June 20, 1913, p. 171.

92. "A.M.R.," "The International Congress: Impressions," *CC*, June 27, 1913, p. 188. Jacqueline Van Voris argues that over the course of her life, Catt changed from an attitude of "deep suspicion of all foreigners (a regular 'jingoist' she later called herself) to a certainty that the world's people would have to live peacefully together if the species were to survive" (*Carrie Chapman Catt*, p. viii). As Van Voris repeatedly demonstrates, Catt's commitment to peace was framed within an imperial worldview, to which her representations of her trip to the East testify. See also Catt, "The Outgrown Monroe Doctrine," *World Tomorrow*, November 1926, pp. 193–94.

93. Kaur, *Role of Women*; Jayawardena, *Feminism and Nationalism*; Forbes, "The Politics of Respectability," pp. 55–56.

94. Forbes, "Votes for Women"; Ray, "Calcutta Women."

95. Hossain, *Sultana's Dreams*. See also Badran, ed., *Harem Years*.

96. Jayawardena, *Feminism*; Bulbeck, *One World Women's Movement*; Badran and Cooke, eds., *Opening the Gates*; Afary, "On the Origins of Feminism."

97. Louisa Thompson-Price, "Reviews: The 'Stree Bodhe,'" *Vote*, March 19, 1910, p. 249.

98. *Vote*, November 16, 1912, p. 41.

99. The August 1908 issue of the *Indian Magazine and Review*, the journal of the National Indian Association, listed Mrs. P. L. Roy as the president of the London Indian Union Society (p. 223). Mrs. Mukerjea was president in 1911. In that capacity she gave lectures on the condition of Indian women; see, for example, Mukerjea, "Women and the National Movement in India" (read at one of the society's meetings), *IMR*, February 1909, p. 32. The May 1901 issue announced that Roy was organizing an "entertainment" at Caxton Hall, home of myriad suffrage and female reform activities, to fund Indian women's educational training in England. For an advertisement and review, see *CC*, March 7, 1912, p. 824, which described the show as "designed to raise money for the establishment of scholarships for the training of native lady teachers for Indian girls." For Mrs. Cobden Unwin, see *IMR*, May 1911, p. 133.

100. See *IMR*, November 1913, p. 287; International Council of Women, *Report of the Second Quinquennial Meeting*, pp. 108–9; National Union of Women Workers, *Official Report of the Central Conference*, 1893, pp. 145–222; 1898, p. 182.

101. The ICW was an amalgamation of independent National Women's Councils in England and America, and later in Europe. They held their quinquennial meeting in London in 1909. See Adam, *Women in Council*.

102. Schreiber and Mathieson, *Journey towards Freedom*, p. 29; *VFW*, April 24, 1914; *CC*, July 17, 1914, p. 312.

103. *VFW*, April 24, 1914. Naidu had studied in Britain in the 1890s. See Forbes,

"The Politics of Respectability," p. 62; Naidu File, OIOC, EUR. MSS. 95; Navarane, *Sarojini Naidu.*

104. Steele was also president of the Women Writers' Suffrage League. *CC,* December 27, 1912, p. 654; *The Suffrage Annual,* pp. 134–37.

105. ICW, *Report of the Second Quinquennial Meeting,* pp. 71–72. *Transactions of the Educational Section of the International Council of Women* lists a paper from India in the section "Modern Educational Experiments" that was probably given by Marie Bhor. See also "Personal Intelligence," *IMR,* November 1898, p. 308.

106. Paxton, "Complicity and Resistance."

107. *IMR,* August 1899, pp. 221, 225–33. On women's "silence" as resistance, see Audre Lorde, "The Transformation of Language into Silence and Action," *Sister/ Outsider,* pp. 40–44. I am grateful to Darlene Hantzis for helping me to understand Lorde's meanings here.

108. Millicent Garrett Fawcett, "Greeting to Our Guests of the IWSA," *CC,* July 10, 1914, p. 287.

109. After giving her bird's-eye view of the international movement, Carrie Chapman Catt assured the members of the IWSA in 1911 that "Woman Suffrage in Great Britain is inevitable." See Catt, "World Movement for Women's Suffrage," p. 8.

110. Images of degradation are interwoven among articles on Indian women's "progress." See, for example, McLaren, "Ajmairee: A Child Mother," p. 881. For an account of a meeting of Bengali women to protest the treatment of Indians in South Africa, see "A Women's Meeting in India," *CC,* January 9, 1914, p. 745.

111. According to Lisa Tickner, the period 1877–1914 was "the heyday of 'invented traditions'" ("Suffrage Campaigns," p. 102). Coombes, "The Franco British Exhibition," talks about the impact of national and international exhibitions on creating a unified "national culture" by making imperial peoples, in the form of displays or sometimes real/"live natives," accessible to a consumer public.

112. *CC,* June 22, 1911, p. 187.

113. A photograph of the Pageant of Empire car is reprinted in Ticker, *The Spectacle of Women,* p. 127. See also *VFW,* June 30, 1911, p. 641.

114. *Women's Coronation Procession Descriptive Programme,* p. 5.

115. *Vote,* June 17, 1911, p. 95. Mrs. Mukerjea is identified in the *Women's Coronation Procession Descriptive Programme,* p. 6.

116. *CC,* June 22, 1911, p. 190.

117. "A Purdah Queen at the Coronation," *CC,* June 22, 1911, p. 186; see also Burton, "The White Woman's Burden," p. 302.

118. "A Purdah Queen at the Coronation."

119. Cornelia Sorabji Diaries, December 12, 1889, OIOC, EUR. MSS. F165/1.

120. Fawcett, "England and India," p. 383.

121. *VFW,* June 30, 1911, p. 640.

122. Tickner, *A Spectacle of Women,* p. 74.

123. Ibid., p. 60.

124. The first of such articles, entitled "The Last of the Harem," appeared in *VFW,* September 10, 1908, p. 439, and was reprinted from the *Westminster Gazette.* Virtually all of the others were articles written especially for *Votes for Women,*

sometimes by Indians. See Coomaraswamy, "The Oriental View of Women," *VFW*, May 13, 1910, p. 531; Gurmukh Singh Mongla, "Woman's Place in Hinduism," *VFW*, September 20, 1912, p. 531; and Ranee of Sarawak, "East and West," *VFW*, September 20, 1912, p. 50. The bulk, however, was written by British suffrage women—for example, Ella Wheeler Wilcox, "The Awakening of Women," *VFW*, June 11, 1911, p. 591, and Lady Muir Mackenzie, "The Women of India and Modern Thought," *VFW*, September 22, 1911, p. 807. "Women and Turkey," *VFW*, April 12, 1912, p. 444, was excerpted from the *Daily Chronicle*, but again there was no dearth of interest in the subject. See, for example, S. D. Shallard, "Why Turkey Is Beaten," *VFW*, February 21, 1913; "L. H.," "In Search of Western Freedom," *VFW*, February 21, 1913; and "The Turkish Woman's Awakening," *VFW*, April 10, 1914.

125. Mackenzie, "The Women of India," p. 807.

126. "The Last of the Harem," p. 439. See also Wilcox, "The Awakening of Women," p. 591.

127. "K.D.S.," "A Woman Ruler," *VFW*, October 18, 1912, p. 38.

128. Hunt, "Suffragettes and Satyagraha." I am indebted to David Doughan for bringing this paper to my attention. Gandhi's various visits to England shaped him in a variety of important ways. See, for example, Hay, "The Making of a Late-Victorian Hindu."

129. Pankhurst, "Shall This Country Lead the Way?," p. 427.

130. Pankhurst wrote, "It is well known that those of the prosperous classes are highly educated, and are entirely conversant with the affairs of their own and other nations, and since they are capable of this development, there is no reason to doubt that the more humbly placed women are also intelligent and as capable as their menfolk of understanding political questions." Ibid., p. 427.

131. Pankhurst does not specifically cite British *imperial* strength as a justification for British women achieving the vote first, though she does allude to Britain as the most civilized nation.

132. Harrison, *Prudent Revolutionaries*, p. 21.

133. Billington-Greig, "The Storm-Centre," pp. 108–9.

134. Elizabeth Robins, "The Signs of the Times, Part I," *VFW*, March 19, 1909, p. 446.

135. *WPP*, November 22, 1890, p. 75.

136. Robins, "The Signs of the Times," p. 445. See also Israel Zangwill, "Old Fogeys and Old Bogeys," *VFW*, June 11, 1909, p. 774; Adam, *Women in Council*, p. 83. Suffrage writers could wax eloquent about Britain's leading role when discussing subjects apparently unrelated to politics or empire. The author of "Woman's Share in Primitive Culture," for example, extrapolating from a historical discussion of women's role in domestic economy, had this to say about Britain's greatness. "Britain acquired her globe-arching empire under the reign of women . . . Nothing is more natural than that the author of parental government, the founder of tribal kinship, the organiser of industrialism, should have much to say about that form of housekeeping called public economy." *VFW*, August 12, 1910, p. 752.

137. Robins, "The Signs of the Times," p. 445.

138. Fawcett, "England and India," p. 383.

139. *VFW*, September 5, 1913.

140. "India, Comrade and Friend," *CC*, January 29, 1915, p. 674. The journal featured articles by William Wedderburn, an Indian nationalist advocate, and by Lajpat Ral. See William Wedderburn, "India's Loyalty, and Indian Aspiration," *CC*, January 8, 1915, p. 639; "Women's Education in India," *CC*, October 15, 1915, p. 338; Lajpat Ral, "The Position of Indian Women," parts 1 and 2, *CC*, January 29, 1915, pp. 675–76; and February 5, 1915, pp. 693–94.

141. *CC*, February 5, 1915; April 1, 1915, p. 790; January 7, 1916, p. 525.

142. E. I. M. Boyd, "Indications of the Women's Movement in India," *EW*, July 1918, pp. 18–21.

143. Ramusack, "Cultural Missionaries," esp. p. 133.

144. Harrison's evaluation of Rathbone bears some of this out: "To her younger colleagues between the wars she seemed drawn from an earlier generation, a true Victorian who used an old-fashioned vocabulary, wore old-fashioned clothes, and moved about in a rather formal and dignified manner" (*Prudent Revolutionaries*, p. 99).

145. See, for example, Pethick-Lawrence, "The ABC of Votes for Women," p. 388; and Ellis T. Powell, "The Vote for Women as a Constitutional Development," *VFW*, March 19, 1909, p. 447. The commonalities, rather than the differences, between suffragists and militants are also emphasized by Holton in her *Feminism and Democracy*, p. 4. She points out that there were "numerous instances of co-operation between the two wings of the movement during the early years of militancy," when the NUWSS and the WSPU held joint meetings, rallies, and demonstrations; see also pp. 38–52.

146. Emmeline Pethick-Lawrence, "We Are Not Hottentots," *VFW*, December 2, 1910, p. 140.

147. Excerpted from Despard's speech in Hyde Park, reprinted as "Who Are the Antis?," *Vote*, July 30, 1910, pp. 160–61.

148. Harrison, *Prudent Revolutionaries*, pp. 34–35.

149. Christabel Pankhurst, "We Will Not Be Prussianized," *Suffragette*, April 16, 1915, p. 6.

150. The idea of women as contested sites of colonial power is borrowed from Mani, "The Production of an Official Discourse on *Sati*," esp. pp. 114–16.

151. Gorham, "'The Friendships of Women.'" The term "sacral character" is hers.

CHAPTER 7

1. Spivak, "Three Women's Texts," p. 175.

2. Hunt, "Suffragettes and Satyagraha," p. 7. The article in which this quote appeared was written in Gujerati, and in light of Hunt's speculation that it was written for that community, I assume that neither Cromer nor Curzon nor the British public at large would have had access to it.

3. Partha Chatterjee, "Colonialism, Nationalism and the Colonialized Woman"; Mani, "Contentious Traditions," p. 18.

4. "Women and Empire," *CC*, June 11, 1915, pp. 134–35.

5. Wiltsher, *Most Dangerous Women*, esp. pp. 56–81; Florence, Marshall, and Ogden, *Militarism versus Feminism*; Byles, "Women's Experience of World War One"; Vellacott, "Anti-War Suffragists"; Liddington, *The Long Road to Greenham Common*.

6. Ramusack, "Cultural Missionaries." See also Rathbone, *Child Marriage*; and Ramusack, "Embattled Advocates."

7. Harrison, *Prudent Revolutionaries*, p. 174.

8. Ibid.

9. Ibid., p. 109.

10. Ibid.; Helena Swanwick, *I Have Been Young* (London: Gollancz, 1935), quoted in Dyhouse, *Feminism and the Family*, p. 26; Gorham, " 'Have We Really Rounded Seraglio Point?,' " esp. p. 93.

11. Beer, "Representing Women," in Bhabha, ed., *Nation and Narration*, p. 64.

12. Harrison, *Prudent Revolutionaries*, chaps. 4–6.

13. Susan Pedersen, "National Bodies, Unspeakable Acts."

14. The terms "unease" and "voice" are those of Sara Mills. She finds that Victorian travel writers, in contrast to the feminists cited in this study, were not able to adopt an imperial voice with ease. See her *Discourses of Difference*, p. 3.

15. Pedersen, "National Bodies, Unspeakable Acts," p. 679; see also Harrison, *Prudent Revolutionaries*, p. 113.

16. Harrison, *Prudent Revolutionaries*, pp. 125, 193.

17. Beer, "Representing Women," p. 64.

18. Chatterjee, "Colonialism, Nationalism and Colonialized Women," p. 631.

19. Harrison, *Prudent Revolutionaries*, p. 317.

20. One place to begin might be with Margaret Ethel MacDonald. She and her husband, Ramsay MacDonald, made a trip to India before the First World War, and she wrote "Our Indian Sisters" for the *Women's Industrial News*. The piece opens with the following sentence: "The British woman has to change many of her conceptions of life if she would understand in the slightest degree the life of her Indian sisters" (*Women's Industrial News*, April 1910, p. 19). See also her "The New Factory Bill for India," *Women's Industrial News*, July 1910, pp. 19–22, and her husband's account of her life, *Margaret Ethel MacDonald*. His *The Awakening of India* contains two chapters on Indian women written by Margaret.

21. Mills, *Discourses of Difference*, p. 2; and Fox-Genovese, "Placing Women's History in History," p. 29.

22. Offen, "Women's Memory," pp. 216–17; see also Offen, "Depopulation, Nationalism and Feminism"; and Lowe, *Critical Terrains*.

23. For a discussion of French feminist "orientalism" with respect to Algerian women, see Marnia Lazreg on Hubertine Auclert's *Les Femmes Arabes en Algerie* (1900) in her "Feminism and Difference," pp. 333–34. Graham-Brown also discusses Auclert's attitudes toward Algerian women in *Images of Women*, p. 22. I am grateful to Sherifa Zuhur for this reference.

24. Tyrrell, "American Exceptionalism," pp. 1033–38, 1053–54.

25. Levy, *Other Women*, p. 3.

26. Alcoff, "The Problem of Speaking for Others"; Bannerji, "But Who Speaks for Us?"

27. Nair, "On the Question of 'Agency,'" p. 13; see also Alarcon, "The Theoretical Subjects"; and Alcoff, "The Problem of Speaking for Others," p. 6.

28. Donaldson, *Decolonizing Feminisms*, p. 69.

29. See Scott, "The Evidence of Experience," p. 787.

Bibliography

PRIMARY SOURCES

Manuscripts

Fawcett Library, London
  Josephine Butler Autograph Letter Collection
  Josephine Butler Collection
  Millicent Garrett Fawcett Papers
  Parliamentary Papers, India, 1897–1909
  Henry J. Wilson Papers

Oriental and India Office Collections, London
  Cornelia Sorabji Papers

Newspapers and Periodicals

Common Cause, 1910–15
Contemporary Review, 1885–95
Dawn, 1888–96
Englishwoman, 1909–15
Englishwoman's Journal, 1859–63
Englishwoman's Review, 1866–1910
Fortnightly Review, 1889–95
Indian Ladies' Magazine, 1901–12
Indian Magazine and Review (formerly *Journal of the National Indian Association, in Aid of Social Progress and Education in India*), 1885–1916
Jus Suffragi, 1906–14
Macmillan's Magazine, 1875–80
National and English Review, 1885–90
Nineteenth Century, 1878–90
Sentinel, 1885–99
Shafts, 1892–98
Shield, 1897–1915
Stormbell, 1898–1900
Suffragette, 1912–14
Vote, 1909–15
Votes for Women, 1907–15
Womanhood, 1898–1901
Woman's Herald, 1891–93
Women's Franchise, 1907–11
Women's Penny Paper, 1888–90
Women's Suffrage Journal, 1870–88
Women's Suffrage Pamphlets, 1867–98
Young Woman, 1892–1900

Published Primary Sources

Andrew, Elizabeth, and Katherine Bushnell. *Heathen Slaves and Christian Rulers.* Oakland, Calif.: Messiah's Advocate, 1907.

———. *The Queen's Daughters in India.* London: Morgan and Scott, 1898.

Balfour, Margaret, and Ruth Young, *The Work of Medical Women in India.* Oxford: Oxford University Press, 1929.

Blackburn, Helen. *Women's Suffrage: A Record of the Women's Suffrage Movement in the British Isles.* London: Williams and Norgate, 1902.

Butler, Josephine. "Mrs. Butler's Plea for an Interest in the Abolitionist Work on the Continent of Europe." London: British Continental and General Federation, 1893.

———. *Native Races and the War.* London: Gay and Bird, 1900.

———. *The New Abolitionists.* London: Dyer Brothers, 1876.

———. "Our Christianity Tested by the Irish Question." London: n.p., 1887.

———. *The Revival and Extension of the Abolitionist Cause.* London: Dyer Brothers, 1887.

———. *Silent Victories.* London: F. Burfoot, 1900.

———. "Social Purity." Address Given to Students at Cambridge. 2d ed. London: Dyer Brothers, 1881. In *The Sexuality Debates,* edited by Sheila Jeffreys, pp. 170– 89. London: Routledge and Kegan Paul, 1987.

———. "Sursum Corda." Annual Address to the Ladies' National Association. Liverpool, 1871.

———. *Truth before Everything.* London: Dyer Brothers, 1897.

———, ed. *Woman's Work and Woman's Culture.* London: Macmillan and Co., 1869.

Caird, Mona. "Why Do Women Want the Franchise?" Speech given at Birmingham, 1892. *Women's Emancipation Union Pamphlets.*

Carpenter, Mary. *The Last Days in England of the Rajah Rammohun Roy.* Edited by Swapan Majumdar. 1866. Reprint. Calcutta: Riddhi, 1976.

———. *Six Months in India.* 2 vols. London: Longman's, Green and Co., 1868.

Catt, Carrie Chapman. "The World Movement for Woman Suffrage: Being the Presidential Address Delivered at Stockholm to the Sixth Convention of the International Women's Suffrage Alliance on June 13, 1911." British Library.

Central Committee of the National Society for Women's Suffrage. "Opinions of Women on Women's Suffrage." *Women's Suffrage Pamphlets,* 1873–97.

Chadwick, Marion. "The Imperial Aspect of Woman Suffrage." London: Conservative and Unionist Women's Franchise Association, n.d.

Chapman, Mrs. E. F. *Sketches of Some Distinguished Indian Women.* London: Longman's, 1891.

Cowan, Minna. *The Education of Women in India.* London: Oliphant, Anderson and Ferre, 1912.

Creighton, Louise. "The Appeal versus Female Suffrage: A Rejoinder." *Nineteenth Century* 26 (August 1889): 347–54.

Despard, Charlotte. "Theosophy and the Women's Movement." London: Theosophical Publishing Society, 1913.

———. "Woman in the Nation." London: Women's Freedom League, 1910.

Diver, Maude. *The Englishwoman in India.* London: Longman's, 1909.

Dixon, Katherine. "An Appeal to the Women of Empire Concerning Present Moral Conditions in Our Cantonments in India." London: n.p., 1916.

Duff, Reverend Alexander. *Female Education in India.* London: n.p., 1839.

Ethelmer, Ellis. *Woman Free.* Congleton: Women's Emancipation Union, 1893.

Fawcett, Millicent Garrett. "The Appeal against Female Suffrage: A Reply." *Nineteenth Century* 26 (July 1889): 86–96.

———. "Degrees for Women at Oxford." *Contemporary Review* 69 (March 1896): 347–56.

———. "The Emancipation of Women." *Fortnightly Review* 50 (November 1891): 673–85.

———. "The Future of Englishwomen: A Reply." *Nineteenth Century* 6 (August 1878): 347–57.

———. "Infant Marriage in India." *Contemporary Review* 58 (November 1890): 712–20.

———. *The Martyrs of Turkish Misrule.* London: Cassell Peter and Galpin, 1877.

———. *Mary Carpenter.* Some Eminent Women of Our Time Series. London: National Union of Women's Suffrage Societies, 1912.

———. "New Rules for Dealing with the Sanitary Condition of the British Army in India." London: Women's Printing Society, 1897.

———. "New Zealand under Female Franchise." *Contemporary Review* 65 (June 1894): 433–37.

———. "Speeches at a General Meeting in Support of the Political Enfranchisement of Women." *Women's Suffrage Pamphlets,* 1871–72, 2:1–9.

———. "Speech to the General Committee of the National Union of Women Workers (October 1897)." London: Women's Printing Society, 1897.

———. "The Use of Higher Education to Women." *Contemporary Review* 50 (November 1886): 719–27.

———. *What I Remember.* London: T. Fisher Unwin, Ltd., 1924.

———. "Women and Representative Government." *Nineteenth Century* 14 (August 1883): 285–91.

———. *Women's Suffrage: A Short History of a Great Movement.* 1912. Reprint. New York: Source Book Press, 1970.

———. "The Women's Suffrage Bill: I. The Enfranchisement of Women." *Fortnightly Review* 51 (March 1889): 555–62.

———. "The Women's Suffrage Question." *Contemporary Review* 61 (June 1892): 761–68.

Fawcett, Millicent Garrett, and Henry Fawcett. *Essays and Lectures Political and Social.* London: Macmillan and Co., 1872.

Grey, Mrs. William. "Is the Exercise of the Suffrage Unfeminine?" *Women's Suffrage Pamphlets,* 1867–82, pp. 1–12.

Hopkins, Ellice. *The Power of Womanhood; or, Mothers and Sons.* London: n.p., 1899.

Hossain, Rokeya Sakhawat. *Sultana's Dreams and Selections from "The Secluded Ones."* Translated and edited by Roushan Jahan. New York: Feminist Press, 1988.

Howard, J. E. "Essay on Woman Suffrage." *Women's Suffrage Pamphlets,* 1869–72, pp. 1–16.

International Council of Women. *Report of the Second Quinquennial Meeting.* London: n.p., 1899.

Kenney, Annie. *Memories of a Militant*. London: Edward Arnold, 1924.

Ladies' National Association. *Annual Meetings*. London: n.p., 1886–1914.

——. *Annual Reports*. London: n.p., 1886–1914.

Lewis, Sarah. *Woman's Mission*. New York: Wiley and Putnam, 1839.

Lytton, Constance. *Prisoners and Prisons: The Stirring Testimony of a Suffragette*. 1914. Reprint. London: Virago, 1988.

MacDonald, Ramsay. *The Awakening of India*. London: Hodder and Stoughton, 1910.

——. *Margaret Ethel MacDonald*. London: Hodder and Stoughton, 1912.

McIlquham, Mrs. "The Enfranchisement of Women: An Ancient Right, a Modern Need." *Women's Suffrage Pamphlets*, 1894.

McLaren, Mrs. Duncan. "Are Not Women a Part of the People?" *Women's Suffrage Pamphlets*, 1875–76.

Malabari, B. M. *An Appeal from the Daughters of India*. London: Farmer and Sons, 1890.

Martindale, Louisa. *Under the Surface*. 6th ed. London: Macmillan, ca. 1910.

Mill, John Stuart. "Lecture to the Educational Branch of the National Society for Women's Suffrage." *Women's Suffrage Publications*, 1871–72, 2:1–12.

Moral Reform Union. *Annual Reports*. 4 vols. London: n.p., 1882–85.

National Union of Women Workers. *Official Report of the Central Conference*. 6 vols. London: n.p., 1893–98.

Nightingale, Florence. "Our Indian Stewardship." *Nineteenth Century* 14 (August 1883): 329–38.

Pfeiffer, Emily. "The Suffrage for Women." *Contemporary Review* 47 (March 1885): 418–35.

Pochin, Mrs. Henry David. "The Right of Women to Exercise the Elective Franchise." *Women's Suffrage Pamphlets*, 1867–82.

Ramabai, Pandita. *The High-Caste Hindu Woman*. 1888. Reprint. New Delhi: Inter-India Publications, 1984.

Rathbone, Eleanor. *Child Marriage: The Indian Minotaur: An Object-Lesson from the Past to the Future*. London: George Allen Unwin, 1934.

Scott, Benjamin. *A State Iniquity: Its Rise, Extension and Overthrow*. London: Kegan, Paul, Trench, Trubner and Co., Ltd., 1890.

Shah, A. B. *The Letters and Correspondence of Pandita Ramabai*. Bombay: Maharashtra State Board for Literature and Culture, 1977.

Smith, Sidney. "The Enfranchisement of Women the Law of the Land." *Women's Suffrage Pamphlets*, 1871–80.

Smith, Lady Sybil. "Woman and Evolution." London: Women's Freedom League, ca. 1910–14.

Stanton, Theodore, ed. *The Woman Question in Europe*. London: G. P. Putnam and Sons, 1884.

Stopes, Charlotte Carmichael. *British Freewomen: Their Historical Privilege*. London: Swan, 1894.

Storrow, Reverend Edward. *The Eastern Lily Gathered: A Memoir of Bala Shoondore Tagore, with Observations on the Position and Prospects of Hindu Female Society*. London: Sonnenschein and Co., 1852.

Strachey, Ray. *The Cause: A Short History of the Women's Movement in Britain.* 1928. Reprint. London: Virago, 1979.

Suffrage Annual and Women's Who's Who, The. London: Stanley Paul and Co., 1913.

Swiney, Frances. *The Awakening of Woman: Women's Part in Evolution.* 1899. Reprint. London: William Reeves, 1908.

Swiney, R. "The Plea of the Disenfranchised Women." *Women's Suffrage Pamphlets,* 1898.

Transactions of the Educational Section of the International Council of Women. London: International Council of Women, 1899.

"Veritas." "What Is Women's Suffrage? and Why Do Women Want It?" *Women's Suffrage Pamphlets,* 1879–83.

Ward, Mrs. Humphrey, et al. "The Appeal against Female Suffrage." *Nineteenth Century* 26 (June 1889): 782–89.

Weitbrecht, Mrs. *The Christian Woman's Ministry to Her Heathen Sisters.* London: n.p., 1874.

Wilson, Henry J. *The History of a Sanitary Failure: Being an Extension of Statements Made at the Conference of the International Federation for the Abolition of State Regulation of Prostitution Held at Berne, 16th–18th September, 1896.* London: British Committee of the British, Continental and General Federation for the Abolition of the State Regulation of Vice, 1898.

———. *A Rough Record of Events and Incidents Connected with the Repeal of the 'Contagious Diseases Acts 1864–69' in the United Kingdom, and the Movement Against the State Regulation of Vice in India and the Colonies 1858–1906.* Sheffield: n.p., n.d.

Women's Coronation Procession Descriptive Programme. London: Women's Press, 1911.

Woolf, Virginia. *A Room of One's Own.* New York: Harcourt Brace, 1928.

———. *Three Guineas.* New York: Harcourt Brace, 1938.

Wright, Sir Almroth E. *The Unexpurgated Case against Woman Suffrage.* London: Constable and Co., Ltd., 1913.

SECONDARY SOURCES

Adam, H. Pearl. *Women in Council: The Jubilee Book of the National Council of Women of Great Britain.* Oxford: Oxford University Press, 1945.

Afary, Janet. "On the Origins of Feminism in Early Twentieth-Century Iran." *Journal of Women's History* 1, no. 2 (Fall 1989): 65–87.

Ahmed, Leila. "Western Ethnocentrism and Perceptions of the Harem." *Feminist Studies* 8 (Fall 1982): 521–34.

———. *Women and Gender in Islam.* New Haven: Yale University Press, 1992.

Alcaron, Norma. "The Theoretical Subjects of *This Bridge Called My Back* and Anglo-American Feminism." In *Making Face, Making Soul / Haciendo Caras: Creative and Critical Perspectives by Women of Color,* edited by Gloria Anzaldua, pp. 356–69. San Francisco: Aunt Lute Press, 1990.

Alcoff, Linda. "The Problem of Speaking for Others." *Cultural Critique* 17 (Winter 1991): 5–32.

Allouella, Malek. *The Colonial Harem.* Minneapolis: University of Minnesota Press, 1986.

Amos, Valerie, and Parmar, Pratibha. "Challenging Imperial Feminism." *Feminist Review* 17 (July 1984): 3–19.

Anagol-McGinn, Padma. "The Age of Consent Act (1891) Reconsidered: Women's Perspectives and Participation in the Child-Marriage Controversy in India." *South Asia Research* 12, no. 2 (November 1992): 100–118.

Anderson, Benedict. *Imagined Communities: Reflections on the Origin and Spread of Nationalism.* London: Verso, 1983.

Anderson, Nancy Fix. "Annie Besant in India: The Conflict between Anti-Imperialism and Human Rights." Paper delivered at a meeting of the Southeastern Nineteenth-Century Association, Georgetown University, Washington, D.C., April 1988.

Ansprenger, Franz. *The Dissolution of Colonial Empires.* London: Routledge, 1989.

Anzaldua, Gloria, ed. *Making Face, Making Soul / Haciendo Caras: Creative and Critical Perspectives by Women of Color.* San Francisco: Aunt Lute Press, 1990.

———, and Cherrie Moraga, eds. *This Bridge Called My Back: Writings by Radical Women of Color.* New York: Kitchen Table Women of Color Press, 1981.

Badran, Margot. "Dual Liberation: Feminism and Nationalism in Egypt, 1870s–1925." *Feminist Issues* 14 (Spring 1988): 15–34.

———. "The Origins of Feminism in Egypt." In *Current Issues in Women's History,* edited by Arina Angerman et al., pp. 153–70. New York: Routledge, 1989.

———, and Miriam Cooke, eds. *Opening the Gates: A Century of Arab Feminist Writing.* Bloomington: Indiana University Press, 1990.

Balfour, Margaret, and Ruth Young. *The Work of Medical Women in India.* Oxford: Oxford University Press, 1929.

Ballhatchet, Kenneth. *Race, Sex and Class under the Raj: Imperial Attitudes and Policies and Their Critics, 1793–1905.* London: Weidenfeld and Nicholson, 1980.

Banks, Olive. *Becoming a Feminist: The Social Origins of "First Wave" Feminism.* Athens: University of Georgia Press, 1987.

———. *Faces of Feminism: A Study of Feminism as a Social Movement.* New York: St. Martin's Press, 1981.

Bannerji, Himani. "But Who Speaks for Us? Experience and Agency in Conventional Feminist Paradigms." In *Unsettling Relations: The University as a Site of Feminist Struggles,* edited by Himani Bannerji, Linda Carty, Kari Delhi, Susan Heald, and Kate McKenna, pp. 67–108. Boston: South End Press, 1992.

———. "Fashioning a Self: Educational Proposals for and by Women in Popular Magazines in Colonial Bengal." *Economic and Political Weekly,* October 26, 1991, pp. 50–62.

Bannerji, Himani, Linda Carty, Kari Dehli, Susan Heald, and Kate McKenna, eds. *Unsettling Relations: The University as a Site of Feminist Struggle.* Boston: South End Press, 1992.

Barash, Carol. "The Character of Difference: The Creole Woman as Cultural Mediator in Narratives about Jamaica." *Eighteenth-Century Studies* 23, no. 4 (Summer 1990): 406–24.

Barker, Francis, ed. *Europe and Its Others.* Vol. 1. Colchester: University of Essex Press, 1985.

Barrett, Michele. "The Concept of Difference." *Feminist Review* 26 (July 1987): 28–41.

———. *Women's Oppression Today*. London: Verso, 1988.

Barrett, Michele, and Mary MacIntosh. "Ethnocentrism and Socialist-Feminist Theory." *Feminist Review* 20 (Summer 1985): 23–47.

Basu, Aparna, and Bharati Ray. *Women's Struggle: A History of the All India Women's Conference 1927–1990*. New Delhi: Manohar Publications, 1990.

Bayly, C. A. *Imperial Meridian: The British Empire and the World*. London: Longman, 1989.

Beckett, Jane, and Deborah Cherry, eds. *The Edwardian Era*. London: Phaedon Press and the Barbican Art Gallery, 1987.

Belsey, Catherine, and Jane Moore, eds. *The Feminist Reader: Essays in the Politics of Literary Criticism*. New York: Basil Blackwell, 1989.

Berger, Mark. "Imperialism and Sexual Exploitation: A Response to Ronald Hyam's 'Empire and Sexual Opportunity.'" *Journal of Imperial and Commonwealth History* 17, no. 1 (1988): 83–89.

Berlant, Lauren. "National Brands/National Bodies: *Imitation of Life*." In *Comparative American Identities: Race, Sex and Nationality in the Modern Text*, edited by Hortense Spillers, pp. 111–40. New York: Routledge, 1991.

Bhabha, Homi K., ed. *Nation and Narration*. New York: Routledge, 1990.

———. "Of Mimicry and Man: The Ambivalence of Colonial Discourse." *October* 28 (Spring 1984): 125–33.

———. "The Other Question—the Stereotype and Colonial Discourse." *Screen* 24, no. 6 (November–December 1983): 18–36.

Birkett, Dea. *Spinsters Abroad: Victorian Lady Travelers*. Oxford: Basil Blackwell, 1989.

Bland, Lucy. "The Married Woman, the 'New Woman' and the Feminist: Sexual Politics of the 1890s." In *Equal or Different: Women's Politics 1800–1914*, edited by Jane Rendall, pp. 141–64. Oxford: Basil Blackwell, 1987.

Bolt, Christine. *Victorian Attitudes towards Race*. London: Routledge and Kegan Paul, 1971.

Borthwick, Meredith. *The Changing Role of Women in Bengal, 1849–1905*. Princeton, N.J.: Princeton University Press, 1984.

Bowler, Peter J. *The Invention of Progress: The Victorians and the Past*. Oxford: Basil Blackwell, 1989.

Brantlinger, Patrick. *Rule of Darkness: British Literature and Imperialism 1830–1914*. Ithaca, N.Y.: Cornell University Press, 1988.

Bratton, J. S., et al. *Acts of Supremacy: The British Empire and the State, 1790–1930*. Manchester: Manchester University Press, 1991.

Bridenthal, Renate, Claudia Koonz, and Susan Stuard, eds. *Becoming Visible: Women in European History*. Boston: Houghton and Mifflin, 1987.

Briggs, Asa. *Saxons, Normans and Victorians in Sussex*. Sussex: Hastings and Bexhill Branch of the Historical Association, 1966.

Bristow, Edward J. *Vice and Vigilance: Purity Movements in Britain since 1700*. Dublin: Gill and Macmillan, 1977.

Brown, Wendy. "Feminist Hesitations, Postmodern Exposures." *Differences: A Journal of Feminist Critical Studies* 3 (1991): 63–84.

Browne, Alice. *The Eighteenth-Century Feminist Mind.* Sussex: Harvester Press, 1987.

Bulbeck, Chilla. *One World Women's Movement.* London: Pluto Press, 1988.

Burfield, Diana. "Theosophy and Feminism: Some Explorations in Nineteenth-Century Biography." In *Women's Religious Experience: Cross-Cultural Perspectives,* edited by Pat Holden, pp. 28–45. London: Croom and Helm, 1983.

Burman, Sandra, ed. *Fit Work for Women.* New York: St. Martin's Press, 1979.

Burton, Antoinette. "The Feminist Quest for Identity: British Imperial Suffragism and 'Global Sisterhood,' 1900–1915." *Journal of Women's History* 3, no. 2 (Fall 1991): 46–81.

——. " 'History' Is Now: Feminist Theory and the Production of Historical Feminisms." *Women's History Review* 1, no. 1 (1992): 25–38.

——. "The White Woman's Burden: British Feminists and 'The Indian Woman,' 1865–1915." *Women's Studies International Forum* 13, no. 4 (1990): 295–308. Reprinted in *Western Women and Imperialism: Complicity and Resistance,* edited by Nupur Chaudhuri and Margaret Strobel, pp. 137–57. Bloomington: Indiana University Press, 1992.

Butcher, Patricia Smith. *Education for Equality: Women's Rights Periodicals and Women's Higher Education 1849–1920.* New York: Greenwood Press, 1989.

Butler, A. S. G. *Portrait of Josephine Butler.* London: Faber and Faber, 1954.

Butler, Judith. *Gender Trouble: Feminism and the Subversion of Identity.* New York: Routledge, 1990.

Butterfield, Herbert. *The Whig Interpretation of History.* 1931. Reprint. London: G. Bell and Sons, 1963.

Byles, Joan Montgomery. "Women's Experience of World War One: Suffragists, Pacifists and Poets." *Women's Studies International Forum* 8, no. 5 (1985): 473–87.

Caine, Barbara. *Victorian Feminists.* Oxford: Oxford University Press, 1992.

Callaway, Helen. *Gender, Culture and Empire: European Woman in Colonial Nigeria.* London: Macmillan Press, 1987.

Campbell, Karlyn Khors. *Man Cannot Speak for Her.* Vols. 1 and 2. New York: Greenwood Press, 1989.

Candy, Catherine. "Margaret Cousins, Irish Orientalist Feminist in India." *Women's History Review,* forthcoming (November–December 1994).

Capo, Ellen Kay, and Darlene M. Hantzis. "(En)Gendered (and Endangered) Subjects: Writing, Reading, Performing, and Theorizing Feminist Criticism." *Text and Performance Quarterly* 11 (1991): 249–66.

Carby, Hazel V. *Reconstructing Womanhood: The Emergence of the Afro-American Woman Novelist.* New York: Oxford University Press, 1987.

Centre for Contemporary Cultural Studies. *The Empire Strikes Back: Race and Racism in the '70s in Britain.* Birmingham: University of Birmingham, 1976.

Chatterjee, Partha. "Colonialism, Nationalism and the Colonialized Woman: The Contest in India." *American Ethnologist* 16, no. 4 (November 1989): 622–33.

——. "The Nationalist Resolution." In *Recasting Women: Essays in Colonial History,* edited by Kumkum Sangari and Sudesh Vaid, pp. 233–53. New Delhi: Kali for Women, 1989.

———. *Nationalist Thought in the Colonial World: A Derivative Discourse?* Delhi: Oxford University Press, 1986.

Chaudhuri, Nupur. "The Memsahibs and Motherhood in Nineteenth-Century Colonial India." *Victorian Studies* 31 (Summer 1988): 517–35.

Chaudhuri, Nupur, and Margaret Strobel, eds. *Western Women and Imperialism: Complicity and Resistance.* Bloomington: Indiana University Press, 1992.

Clifford, James. Review of *Orientalism* by Edward Said. *History and Theory* 19, no. 2 (1980): 204–23.

Cobbe, Frances Power. "Duties of Woman." In *Barbara Leigh Smith Bodichon and the Langham Place Group*, edited by Candida Lacey. London: Routledge Kegan Paul, 1987.

Cohn, B. S. "The Command of Language and the Language of Command." In *Subaltern Studies IV*, edited by Ranjit Guha, pp. 276–329. New Delhi: Oxford University Press, 1986.

Colley, Linda. *Britons: Forging the Nation, 1707–1837.* New Haven, Conn.: Yale University Press, 1992.

———. "Whose Nation? Class and National Consciousness in Britain, 1750–1830." *Past and Present* 113 (November 1986): 97–117.

Colls, Robert, and Dodd, Philip, eds. *Englishness: Politics and Culture 1880–1920.* London: Croom and Helm, 1986.

Coombes, Annie E. "The Franco-British Exhibition: Packaging Empire in Victorian England." In *The Edwardian Era*, edited by Jane Beckett and Deborah Cherry, pp. 152–67. London: Phaedon Press and the Barbican Art Gallery, 1987.

Corbett, Mary Jean. *Representing Femininity: Middle-Class Subjectivity in Victorian and Edwardian Women's Autobiographies.* New York: Oxford University Press, 1992.

Cott, Nancy. *The Grounding of Modern Feminism.* New Haven, Conn.: Yale University Press, 1987.

Cox, Jeffrey. "Independent Englishwomen in Delhi and Lahore, 1860–1947." In *Religion and Irreligion in Victorian England*, edited by R. W. Davis, pp. 166–84. New York: HarperCollins: 1993.

Cromwell, Adelaide M. *An African Victorian Feminist: The Life and Times of Adelaide Smith Casely Hayford, 1868–1960.* London: Frank Cass, 1986.

Crosby, Christina. *The Ends of History: Victorians and "the Woman Question."* New York: Routledge, 1991.

Curtin, Philip, ed. *Imperialism.* New York: Walker and Company, 1971.

Darwin, John. *The End of Empire: The Historical Debate.* Oxford: Basil Blackwell, 1991.

Davidoff, Leonore, and Catherine Hall. *Family Fortunes: Men and Women of the English Middle Class, 1780–1850.* Chicago: University of Chicago Press, 1987.

Davin, Anna. "Imperialism and Motherhood." *History Workshop Journal* 5 (Spring 1978): 9–65.

Davis, David Brion. *The Problem of Slavery in the Age of Revolution, 1770–1823.* Ithaca, N.Y.: Cornell University Press, 1975.

Davis, Tracy C. *Actresses as Working Women: Their Social Identity in Victorian Culture.* New York: Routledge, 1992.

Davis, Tricia, Martin Durham, Catherine Hall, Mary Langan, and David Sutton.
    " 'The Public Face of Feminism': Early Twentieth-Century Writings on
    Women's Suffrage." In *Making Histories: Studies in history-writing and politics*, edited
    by Richard Johnson, Gregor McLennan, Bill Schwartz, and David Sutton, pp.
    303–24. Minneapolis: University of Minnesota Press, 1982.
De Lauretis, Teresa. "Displacing Hegemonic Discourses: Reflections on Feminist
    Theory in the 1980s." In *Feminism and the Critique of Colonial Discourse*, special is-
    sue of *Inscriptions* 3–4 (1988): 127–44.
———, ed. *Feminist Studies / Critical Studies*. Madison: University of Wisconsin Press,
    1986.
Donaldson, Laura E. *Decolonizing Feminisms: Race, Gender, and Empire Building*.
    Chapel Hill: University of North Carolina Press, 1992.
Doughan, David. "Periodicals by, for and about Women in Britain." *Women's Stud-
    ies International Forum* 10, no. 3 (1987): 261–73.
Doughan, David, and Denise Sanchez, eds. *Feminist Periodicals, 1855–1984: An An-
    notated Bibliography of British, Irish, Commonwealth and International Titles*. Sussex:
    Harvester Press. 1987.
DuBois, Ellen Carol. *Feminism and Suffrage: The Emergence of an Independent Women's
    Movement in America, 1848–1869*. Ithaca, N.Y.: Cornell University Press, 1978.
Dyhouse, Carol. *Feminism and the Family in England, 1880–1939*. Oxford: Basil Black-
    well, 1989.
Eagleton, Terry, Fredric Jameson, and Edward Said. *Nationalism, Colonialism and
    Literature*. Introduction by Seamus Deane. Minneapolis: University of Min-
    nesota Press, 1990.
Echols, Alice. *Daring to Be Bad: Radical Feminism in America, 1967–1975*. Min-
    neapolis: University of Minnesota Press, 1989.
Eldridge, C. C., ed. *British Imperialism in the Nineteenth Century*. New York: St. Mar-
    tin's Press, 1984.
Eley, Geoff. "Defining Social Imperialism: The Use and Abuse of an Idea." *Social
    History* 1 (October 1976): 265–90.
Engels, Dagmar. "The Age of Consent Act of 1891: Colonial Ideology in Ben-
    gal." *South Asia Research* 3 (1983): 107–34.
———. "The Limits of Gender Ideology: Bengali Women, the Colonial State, and
    the Private Sphere, 1890–1930." *Women's Studies International Forum* 12, no. 4
    (1989): 425–37.
Enloe, Cynthia. *Bananas, Beaches and Bases: Making Feminist Sense of International Poli-
    tics*. Berkeley: University of California Press, 1990.
Evans, Richard. *The Feminists: Women's Emancipation Movements in Europe, America
    and Australasia, 1840–1920*. London: Croom-Helm, 1977.
Fee, Elizabeth. "The Sexual Politics of Victorian Anthropology." *Feminist Studies* 1
    (1973): 23–39.
Fein, Helen. *Imperial Crime and Punishment: The Massacre at Jallianwalla Bagh and Brit-
    ish Judgment, 1919–1920*. Honolulu: University of Hawaii Press, 1977.
Ferguson, Moira. "Mary Wollstonecraft and the Problematic of Slavery." *Feminist
    Review* 42 (Autumn 1992): 82–102.

——. *Subject to Others: British Women Writers and Colonial Slavery, 1670–1834.* New York: Routledge, 1992.

——, ed. *First Feminists: British Women Writers, 1578–1799.* Bloomington: Indiana University Press, 1985.

Ferguson, Moira, and Janet Todd. *Mary Wollstonecraft.* Boston: Twayne Publishers, 1984.

Fieldhouse, David. "Can Humpty-Dumpty Be Put Together Again?: Imperial History in the 1980s." *Journal of Imperial and Commonwealth History* 12 (January 1984): 9–23.

Finn, Margot C. *After Chartism: Class and Nation in English Radical Politics, 1848–1874.* Cambridge: Cambridge University Press, 1992.

Flemming, Leslie, ed. *Women's Work for Women: Missionaries and Social Change in Asia.* San Francisco: Westview Press, 1989.

Florence, Mary Sargant, Catherine Marshall, and C. K. Ogden. *Militarism versus Feminism: Writings on Women and War.* Edited by Margaret Kamester and Jo Vellacott. London: Virago, 1987.

Forbes, Geraldine. "Caged Tigers: 'First Wave' Feminists in India." *Women's Studies International Forum* 5, no. 6 (1982): 525–36.

——. "Goddesses or Rebels?: The Women Revolutionaries of Bengal." *Oracle* 2 (1980): 1–15.

——. "In Search of the 'Pure Heathen': Missionary Women in Nineteenth-Century India." *Economic and Political Weekly,* April 26, 1986, pp. 1–7.

——. "The Politics of Respectability: Indian Women and the Indian National Congress." In *The Indian National Congress: Centenary Hindsights,* edited by D. A. Low, pp. 54–97. Delhi: Oxford University Press, 1988.

——. "Votes for Women: The Demand for Women's Franchise in India, 1917–1937." In *Symbols of Power: Studies of the Political Status of Women in India,* edited by Vina Mazumdar, pp. 11–23. Bombay: Allied Publishers, 1979.

——. "Women and Modernity: The Issue of Child Marriage in India." *Women's Studies International Quarterly* 2 (1979): 407–19.

Forster, Margaret. *Significant Sisters: The Grassroots of Active Feminism, 1839–1939.* New York: Alfred Knopf, 1985.

Fowler, W. S. *A Study in Radicalism and Dissent: The Life and Times of Henry Joseph Wilson, 1833–1914.* London: Epworth Press, 1961.

Fox-Genovese, Elizabeth. "Placing Women's History in History." *New Left Review* 133 (May–June 1982): 5–29.

Fryer, Peter. *Staying Power: The History of Black People in Britain.* London: Pluto Press, 1984.

Fulton, Roger. *Votes for Women.* London: Faber and Faber, 1957.

Fussell, Paul. *The Great War and Modern Memory.* Oxford: Oxford University Press, 1976.

Gardner, Vivien, and Susan Rutherford, eds. *The New Woman and Her Sisters: Feminism and Theatre, 1850–1914.* Ann Arbor: University of Michigan Press, 1992.

Gibbon, Luke. "Race against Time: Racial Discourse and Irish History." *Oxford Literary Review* 13 (Spring 1991): 95–117.

Gilman, Sander. "Black Bodies, White Bodies: Toward an Iconography of Female Sexuality in Late-Nineteenth Century Art, Medicine and Literature." *Critical Inquiry* 12 (Autumn 1985): 204–42.

Gordon, Deborah. "Writing Culture, Writing Feminism: The Poetics and Politics of Experimental Ethnography." In *Feminism and the Critique of Colonial Discourse*, special issue of *Inscriptions* 3–4 (1988): 7–26.

Gorham, Deborah. " 'The Friendships of Women': Friendship, Feminism and Achievement in Vera Brittain's Life and Work in the Interwar Decades." *Journal of Women's History* 3, no. 3 (Winter 1992): 44–69.

———. " 'Have We Really Rounded Seraglio Point?': Vera Brittain and Inter-war Feminism." In *British Feminism in the Twentieth Century*, edited by Harold L. Smith, pp. 84–103. Amherst: University of Massachusetts Press, 1990.

Graham-Browne, Sarah. *Images of Women: The Portrayal of Women in Photography of the Middle East, 1860–1950*. New York: Columbia University Press, 1988.

Greenberger, Allen J. *The British Image of India: A Study in the Literature of Imperialism, 1880–1960*. Oxford: Oxford University Press, 1969.

Grewal, Shabnam, Jackie Kay, Liliane Landor, Gail Lewis, and Pratibha Parmar, eds. *Charting the Journey: Writings by Black and Third World Women*. London: Sheba Feminist Publishers, 1988.

Guha, Ranajit, ed. *Subaltern Studies IV*. New Delhi: Oxford University Press, 1986.

Haggis, Jane. "Gendering Colonialism or Colonising Gender? A Review of Recent Women's Studies Approaches to White Women and the History of British Colonialism." *Women's Studies International Forum* 13 (1990): 105–15.

Hall, Catherine. "The Economy of Intellectual Prestige: Thomas Carlyle, John Stuart Mill and the Case of Governor Eyre." *Cultural Critique* 12 (Spring 1989): 167–96.

———. *White, Male and Middle Class: Explorations in Feminism and History*. New York: Routledge, 1992.

Hammerton, James. *Emigrant Gentlewomen: Genteel Poverty and Female Emigration*. London: Croom-Helm, 1979.

Hammond, J. L., and Barbara Hammond. *James Stansfeld: A Victorian Champion of Sex Equality*. London: Longman's, Green and Co., 1932.

Haraway, Donna. "Situated Knowledges: The Science Question in Feminism and the Privilege of Partial Perspective." *Feminist Studies* 14 (Fall 1988): 575–99.

Harcourt, Freda. "Disraeli's Imperialism, 1866–68: A Question of Timing." *Historical Journal* 23, no. 1 (1980): 87–109.

Harper, Mary Jo. "Recovering the Other: Women and the Orient in the Writings of Early Nineteenth-Century France." *Critical Matrix: Princeton Working Papers in Women's Studies* 1, no. 3 (1985): 1–31.

Harrison, Brian. *Prudent Revolutionaries: Portraits of British Feminists between the Wars*. Oxford: Clarendon Press, 1987.

———. *Separate Spheres: The Opposition to Women's Suffrage in Britain*. New York: Holmes and Meier, 1978.

Hay, Stephen. "The Making of a Late-Victorian Hindu: M. K. Gandhi in London, 1888–1891." *Victorian Studies* 33, no. 1 (Autumn 1989): 75–98.

Haynes, Douglas, and Gyan Prakash, eds. *Contesting Power: Resistance and Everyday Social Relations in South Asia.* Berkeley: University of California Press, 1991.

Heimsath, Charles. *Indian Nationalism and Hindu Social Reform.* Princeton: Princeton University Press, 1964.

Henegan, Alison. "Weathering the Storm: New Directions in British Feminist Publishing." *Women's Review of Books* 9, no. 7 (April 1992): 5–7.

Herstein, Sheila. *A Mid-Victorian Feminist: Barbara Leigh Smith Bodichon.* New Haven, Conn.: Yale University Press, 1985.

Hewitt, Nancy. "Sisterhood in International Perspective: Thoughts on Teaching Comparative Women's History." *Women's Studies Quarterly* 1, no. 2 (1988): 22–32.

Higginbotham, Evelyn. "African-American Women's History and the Metalanguage of Race." *Signs* 17 (Winter 1992): 251–74.

Himmelfarb, Gertrude. *On Liberty and Liberalism: The Case of John Stuart Mill.* New York: Alfred Knopf, 1974.

Hirsch, Marianne, and Evelyn Fox Keller, eds. *Conflicts in Feminism.* New York: Routledge, 1990.

Hirshfield, Claire. "The Actresses' Franchise League and the Campaign for Women's Suffrage, 1908–1914." *Theatre Research International* 10, no. 2 (1985): 129–53.

———. "Fractured Faith: Liberal Party Women and the Suffrage Issue in Britain, 1892–1914." *Gender and History* 2, no. 2 (Summer 1990): 173–97.

Hobsbawm, Eric. *The Age of Imperialism.* New York: Pantheon Books, 1987.

———. *Nations and Nationalism since 1780: Programme, Myth, Reality.* Cambridge: Cambridge University Press, 1990.

Hobsbawm, Eric, and Terence Ranger, eds. *The Invention of Tradition.* Cambridge: Cambridge University Press, 1983.

Holcombe, Lee. *Wives and Property: Reform of the Married Women's Property Law in Nineteenth-Century England.* Toronto: University of Toronto Press, 1983.

Holden, Pat, ed. *Women's Religious Experience: Cross Cultural Perspectives.* London: Croom-Helm, 1983.

Holledge, Julie. *Innocent Flowers: Women in the Edwardian Theatre.* London: Virago, 1983.

Hollis, Patricia, ed. *Women in Public: The Women's Movement, 1850–1900.* London: George Allen and Unwin, 1981.

Holt, Thomas C. *The Problem of Freedom: Race, Labor and Politics in Jamaica and Britain, 1832–1938.* Baltimore, Md.: Johns Hopkins University Press, 1992.

Holton, Sandra. *Feminism and Democracy: Women's Suffrage and Reform Politics in Britain, 1900–1918.* Cambridge: Cambridge University Press, 1986.

hooks, bell. *Feminist Theory from Margin to Center.* Boston: South End Press, 1984.

———. "Theory as Liberatory Practice." *Yale Journal of Law and Feminism* 4, no. 1 (1991): 1–12.

———. *Yearning: Race, Gender and Cultural Politics.* Boston: South End Press, 1990.

Hume, Leslie Parker. *The National Union of Women's Suffrage Societies, 1897–1914.* New York: Garland Press, 1982.

Hunt, James D. "Suffragettes and Satyagraha: Gandhi and the British Women's

Suffrage Movement." Paper presented at the annual meeting of the American Academy of Religion, St. Louis, Missouri, October 1976.

Hunt, Lynn. *Politics, Culture and Class in the French Revolution.* Berkeley: University of California Press, 1984.

———, ed. *The New Cultural History.* Berkeley: University of California Press, 1989.

Hunter, Jane. *The Gospel of Gentility: American Women Missionaries in Turn of the Century China.* New Haven, Conn.: Yale University Press, 1984.

Hutchins, Frances. *The Illusion of Permanence.* Princeton, N.J.: Princeton University Press, 1967.

Hyam, Ronald. *Britain's Imperial Century, 1815–1914: A Study of Empire and Expansion.* New York: Barnes and Noble, 1976.

———. *Empire and Sexuality.* Manchester: University of Manchester Press, 1990.

———. "Empire and Sexual Opportunity." *Journal of Imperial and Commonwealth History* 14, no. 2 (1986): 40–75.

———. "'Imperialism and Sexual Exploitation': A Reply." *Journal of Imperial and Commonwealth History* 17, no. 1 (1988): 90–98.

Jain, Devaki. "Can Feminism Be a Global Ideology?" *Quest: A Feminist Quarterly* 4, no. 2 (1978): 9–16.

Jayal, Niraja Gopal, ed. *Sidney and Beatrice Webb: Indian Diary.* London: Oxford University Press, 1990.

Jayawardena, Kumari. *Feminism and Nationalism in the Third World in the Nineteenth and Early Twentieth Centuries.* The Hague: Institute of Social Studies, 1982.

Jeffreys, Sheila. *The Spinster and Her Enemies: Feminism and Sexuality, 1880–1930.* London: Pandora Press, 1985.

———, ed. *The Sexuality Debates.* London: Routledge and Kegan Paul, 1987.

Johnston, W. Ross. *Great Britain, Great Empire: An Evaluation of the British Imperial Experience.* St. Lucia: University of Queensland Press, 1981.

Jones, Kathleen B. "The Trouble with Authority." *Differences: A Feminist Journal of Critical Studies* 3 (1991): 104–27.

Kabbani, Rana. *Europe's Myths of the Orient.* Bloomington: Indiana University Press, 1986.

Kaminsky, Arnold. *The India Office, 1880–1910.* New York: Greenwood Press, 1986.

Kanner, S. Barbara, ed. *The Women of England from Anglo-Saxon Times to the Present: Interpretive Bibliographical Essays.* Hamden, Conn.: Anchor Books, 1979.

Kaur, Manmohan. *Role of Women in the Freedom Movement, 1857–1947.* Delhi: Sterling Publishers, 1968.

Kaushik, Harish. P. *The Indian National Congress in England, 1885–1920.* Delhi, 1972.

Kent, Susan Kingsley. *Sex and Suffrage in Britain, 1860–1914.* Princeton, N.J.: Princeton University Press, 1987.

Kerber, Linda. "The Paradox of Women's Citizenship in the Early Republic." *American Historical Review* 97, no. 2 (April 1992): 349–76.

Kishwar, Madhu. "Gandhi on Women." *Race and Class* 28 (1986): 43–61.

———. "Why I Do Not Call Myself a Feminist." *Manushi: A Journal about Women and Society* 61 (1991): 2–7.

Klein, Renate D., and Deborah Lynn Steinberg, eds. *Radical Voices: A Decade of*

Feminist Resistance from Women's Studies International Forum. New York: Teacher's College Press, 1989.

Knapman, Claudia. *White Women in Fiji, 1835–1930: The Ruin of Empire?* Sydney: Allen and Unwin, 1986.

Krishnamurty, J., ed. *Women in Colonial India: Essays on Survival, Work and the State.* Delhi: Oxford University Press, 1989.

Lacey, Candida, ed. *Barbara Leigh Smith Bodichon and the Langham Place Group.* London: Routledge and Kegan Paul, 1987.

Lacqueur, Thomas W. "Bodies, Details and the Humanitarian Narrative." In *The New Cultural History,* edited by Lynn Hunt, pp. 176–202. Berkeley: University of California Press, 1989.

Lawrence, Errol. "Just Plain Common Sense: The 'Roots' of Racism." In *The Empire Strikes Back,* edited by Centre for Contemporary Studies, pp. 47–75. Birmingham: University of Birmingham Press, 1976.

Lazreg, Marnia. "Feminism and Difference: The Perils of Writing as a Woman on Women in Algeria." In *Conflicts in Feminism,* edited by Marianne Hirsch and Evelyn Fox Keller, pp. 326–48. London: Routledge, 1990.

Leneman, Leah. *A Guid Cause: The Women's Suffrage Movement in Scotland.* Aberdeen: Aberdeen University Press, 1991.

Lenin, V. I. *Imperialism: The Highest Stage of Capitalism.* New York: International Publishers, 1939.

Levine, Philippa. *The Amateur and the Professional: Antiquarians, Historians and Archaeologists in Victorian England, 1838–1886.* Cambridge: Cambridge University Press, 1986.

———. *Feminist Lives in Victorian England: Private Roles and Public Commitment.* Oxford: Basil Blackwell, 1990.

———. " 'The Humanising Influences of Five O'clock Tea': Victorian Feminist Periodicals." *Victorian Studies* 33, no. 2 (Winter 1990): 293–306.

———. " 'So Few Prizes and So Many Blanks': Marriage and Feminism in Later Nineteenth-Century England." *Journal of British Studies* 28, no. 2 (April 1989): 150–74.

———. *Victorian Feminism, 1850–1900.* Tallahassee: Florida State University Press, 1987.

Levy, Anita. *Other Women: The Writing of Class, Race and Gender, 1832–1898.* Princeton, N.J.: Princeton University Press, 1991.

Lew, Joseph W. "Lady Mary's Portable Seraglio." *Eighteenth-Century Studies* 24 (Summer 1991): 432–50.

Lewis, Jane. *Women and Social Action in Victorian and Edwardian England.* Stanford, Calif.: Stanford University Press, 1991.

———, ed. *Before the Vote Was Won.* London: Routledge and Kegan Paul, 1987.

Liddington, Jill. *The Long Road to Greenham Common: Feminism and Anti-Militarism in Britain since 1820.* London: Virago Press, 1989.

———, and Jill Norris. *One Hand Tied behind Us: The Rise of the Women's Suffrage Movement.* London: Virago Press, 1978.

Lorde, Audre. *Sister/Outsider: Essays and Speeches.* New York: Crossing Press, 1984.

Lorimer, Douglas. *Colour, Class and the Victorians.* New York: Holmes and Meier, 1978.

——. "Theoretical Racism in Late Victorian Anthropology, 1870–1890." *Victorian Studies* 31, no. 3 (Spring 1988): 405–30.

Lotz, Rainer, and Ian Pegg, eds. *Under the Imperial Carpet: Essays in Black History, 1780–1950.* Crawley, Eng.: Rabbit Press, 1986.

Low, D. A., ed. *The Indian National Congress: Centenary Hindsights.* Delhi: Oxford University Press, 1988.

Lowe, Lisa. *Critical Terrains: French and British Orientalisms.* Ithaca, N.Y.: Cornell University Press, 1991.

Lugones, Maria C. "Hablando cara a cara/Speaking Face to Face: An Exploration of Ethnocentric Racism." In *Making Face, Making Soul/Haciendo Caras: Creative and Critical Perspectives by Women of Color,* edited by Gloria Anzaldua, pp. 46–54. San Francisco: Aunt Lute Press, 1990.

Lugones, Maria C., and Elizabeth V. Spelman. "Have We Got a Theory for You!: Feminist Theory, Cultural Imperialism and the Demand for 'The Woman's Voice.'" *Women's Studies International Forum* 6, no. 6 (1983): 573–80.

Lutzker, Edythe. *Edith Pechey-Phipson, M.D.: The Story of England's Foremost Pioneering Woman Doctor.* New York: Exposition Press, 1973.

McBratney, John. "Images of Indian Women in Rudyard Kipling: A Case of Doubling Discourse." In *Feminism and the Critique of Colonial Discourse,* special issue of *Inscriptions* 3–4 (1988): 47–57.

McDougall, Hugh A. *Racial Myth in English History: Trojans, Teutons and Anglo-Saxons.* Hanover: University Press of New England, 1982.

Mackenzie, John. *Propaganda and Empire: The Manipulation of British Public Opinion, 1880–1960.* Manchester: Manchester University Press, 1984.

——, ed. *Imperialism and Popular Culture.* Manchester: Manchester University Press, 1986.

MacLeod, Arlene. "Hegemonic Relations and Gender Resistance: The New Veiling as Accommodating Protest in Cairo." *Signs* 17, no. 3 (Spring 1992): 533–57.

McNellie, Andrew, ed. *The Essays of Virginia Woolf.* Vol. 3, *1919–1924.* New York: Harcourt Brace Jovanovich, 1988.

Mangan, J. A. *The Games Ethic and Imperialism: Aspects of the Diffusion of an Ideal.* New York: Viking Press, 1986.

Mani, Lata. "The Production of Colonial Discourse: Sati in Early 19th-Century Bengal." Master's thesis, University of California at Santa Cruz, June 1983.

——. "The Production of an Official Discourse on *Sati* in Early Nineteenth-Century Bengal." In *Europe and Its Others,* edited by Francis Barker, 1:107–27. Colchester: University of Essex, 1979.

Manton, Jo. *Mary Carpenter and the Children of the Streets.* London: Heinemann, 1976.

Marcus, Jane. "Pathographies: The Virginia Woolf Soap Operas." *Signs* 17 (Summer 1992): 809–19.

——, ed. *Virginia Woolf: A Feminist Slant.* Lincoln: University of Nebraska Press, 1983.

Marglin, Frederique Apffel. *Wives of the God-King: The Rituals of the Devadasis of Puri.* Delhi: Oxford University Press, 1985.

Marks, Shula. "History, the Nation and the Empire: Sniping at the Periphery." *History Workshop Journal* 29 (1990): 111–19.

Marshall, P. J. "Empire and Authority in the Later Eighteenth Century." *Journal of Imperial and Commonwealth History* 15, no. 2 (January 1987): 105–22.

Mathur, Y. B. *Women's Education in India, 1813–1966.* Delhi: Asia Publishing House, 1973.

Mayhall, Laura E. Nym. "Challenging the State: The Women's Freedom League and Non-Violent Militance, 1907–1911." Paper presented at a joint meeting of the North American and Pacific Coast Conference on British Studies, Santa Clara, California, March 1991.

——. "'Dare to Be Free': The Women's Freedom League, 1907–1918." Ph.D. diss., Stanford University, 1993.

Mazumdar, Vina, ed. *Symbols of Power: Studies of the Political Status of Women in India.* Bombay: Allied Publishers, 1979.

Melman, Billie. *Women's Orients: English Women and the Middle East, 1718–1918: Sexuality, Religion and Work.* London: Macmillan, 1992.

Mendus, Susan, and Jane Rendall, eds. *Sexuality and Subordination: Interdisciplinary Studies of Gender in the Nineteenth Century.* London: Routledge, 1989.

Mernissi, Fatima. *Beyond the Veil: Male-Female Dynamics in Modern Muslim Society.* Bloomington: Indiana University Press, 1987.

Midgley, Clare. *Women against Slavery: The British Campaigns, 1780–1870.* London: Routledge, 1992.

Milbank, Alison. "Josephine Butler: Christianity, Feminism and Social Action." In *Disciplines of Faith: Studies in Religion, Politics and Patriarchy,* edited by Jim Obelkevich, Lyndal Roper, and Raphael Samuel, pp. 154–64. London: Routledge and Kegan Paul, 1987.

Mills, Sara. *Discourses of Difference: An Analysis of Women's Travel Writing and Colonialism.* New York: Routledge, 1991.

Minault, Gail, ed. *The Extended Family: Women and Political Participation in India and Pakistan.* Columbia, Mo.: South Asia Books, 1981.

Minh-ha, Trin T. "All-Owning Spectatorship." *Quarterly Review of Film and Video* 13 (1991): 189–204.

——. "Not Like You/Like You: Post-Colonial Women and the Interlocking Questions of Identity and Difference." In *Feminism and the Critique of Colonial Discourse,* special issue of *Inscriptions* 3–4 (1988): 71–78.

——. *Woman, Native, Other.* Bloomington: Indiana University Press, 1989.

Mitra, Indrani, and Madhu Mitra. "The Discourse of Liberal Feminism and Third World Women's Texts: Some Issues of Pedagogy." In *Teaching Minority Literatures,* special issue of *College Literature* 18 (October 1991): 55–63.

Mohanty, Chandra. "Feminist Encounters: Locating the Politics of Experience." *Copyright* 1 (Fall 1987): 30–44.

——. "'Under Western Eyes': Feminist Scholarship and Colonial Discourse." *Feminist Review* 30 (Autumn 1988): 61–88.

Mohanty, Chandra, Ann Russo, and Lourdes Torres, eds. *Third World Women and the Politics of Feminism*. Bloomington: Indiana University Press, 1991.

Mommsen, Wolfgang. *Theories of Imperialism*. Chicago: University of Chicago Press, 1977.

Morgan, David. *Suffragists and Liberals: The Politics of Woman Suffrage in England*. Oxford: Basil Blackwell, 1975.

Morris, James. *Pax Britannica: The Climax of an Empire*. New York: Harcourt Brace Jovanovich, 1968.

Morrow, Margot D. "Origin and Early Years of the British Committee of the Indian National Congress, 1885–1907." Ph.D. diss., University of London, 1977.

Mort, Frank. *Dangerous Sexualities: Medico-moral Politics in England since 1830*. London: Routledge, 1987.

Moses, Claire Goldberg. "Debating the Present, Writing the Past: 'Feminism' in French History and Historiography." *Radical History Review* 52 (Winter 1992): 79–94.

Mosse, George. *Nationalism and Sexuality: Middle-Class Morality and Sexual Norms in Modern Europe*. Madison: University of Wisconsin Press, 1985.

Mullin, Molly. "Representations of History, Irish Feminism, and the Politics of Difference." *Feminist Studies* 17 (Spring 1991): 29–50.

Murphy, Cliona. *The Women's Suffrage Movement and Irish Society in the Early Twentieth Century*. Philadelphia, Pa.: Temple University Press, 1989.

Myers, Sylvia Harcstack. *The Bluestocking Circle: Women, Friendship and the Life of the Mind in Eighteenth-Century England*. Oxford: Clarendon Press, 1990.

Nair, Janaki. "On the Question of 'Agency' in Indian Feminist Historiography." Paper presented at the annual meeting of the American Historical Association, Chicago, December 1991.

———. "Uncovering the Zenana: Visions of Indian Womanhood in English-women's Writings, 1813–1940." *Journal of Women's History* 2 (Spring 1990): 8–34.

Navarane, Vishwanath S. *Sarojini Naidu: An Introduction to Her Life, Work, and Poetry*. New Delhi: Orient Longman Ltd., 1980.

Newberry, Jo Vellacott. "Anti-War Suffragists." *History* 62 (October 1977): 411–25.

Newman, Gerald. *The Rise of English Nationalism: A Cultural History, 1740–1830*. New York: St. Martin's Press, 1987.

Newton, Judith L. "Family Fortunes: 'New History' and 'New Historicism.'" *Radical History* 43 (Winter 1989): 5–22.

Newton, Judith L., Mary P. Ryan, and Judith R. Walkowitz, eds. *Sex and Class in Women's History*. London: Routledge and Kegan Paul, 1983.

Obelkevich, Jim, Lyndal Roper, and Raphael Samuel, eds. *Disciplines of Faith: Studies in Religion, Politics and Patriarchy*. London: Routledge and Kegan Paul, 1987.

Offen, Karen. "Defining Feminism: A Comparative Historical Approach." *Signs* 14 (Autumn 1988): 119–57.

———. "Depopulation, Nationalism and Feminism in Fin-de-Siècle France." *American Historical Review* 89 (June 1984): 648–76.

———. "Women's Memory, Women's History, Women's Political Action: The

French Revolution in Retrospect, 1789–1889–1989." *Journal of Women's History* 1, no. 3 (Winter 1990): 211–30.

Offen, Karen, Ruth Roach Pierson, and Jane Rendall, eds. *Writing Women's History: International Perspectives.* Bloomington: Indiana University Press, 1991.

Ong, Aiwha. "Colonialism and Modernity: Feminist Re-presentations of Women in Non-Western Societies." In *Feminism and the Critique of Colonial Discourse*, special issue of *Inscriptions* 3–4 (1988): 79–93.

Owens, Rosemary Cullen. *Smashing Times: A History of the Irish Women's Suffrage Movement, 1889–1922.* Dublin: Attic Press, 1984.

Pandey, B. N. *The Break-up of British India.* London: Macmillan, 1969.

Parker, Andrew, Mary Russo, Doris Sommer, and Patricia Yeager, eds. *Nationalisms and Sexualities.* New York: Routledge, 1992.

Parmar, Pratibha. "Other Kinds of Dreams." *Feminist Review* 31 (Spring 1989): 55–65.

Parry, Benita. *Delusions and Discoveries: Studies on India in the British Imagination, 1880–1972.* London: Macmillan, 1972.

Paxton, Nancy. "Complicity and Resistance in the Writings of Annie Besant and Flora Annie Steele." In *Western Women and Imperialism: Complicity and Resistance*, edited by Nupur Chaudhuri and Margaret Strobel, pp. 158–76. Bloomington: Indiana University Press, 1992.

Pedersen, Susan. "Gender, Welfare and Citizenship in Britain during the Great War." *American Historical Review* 90, no. 4 (October 1990): 983–1006.

———. "National Bodies, Unspeakable Acts: The Sexual Politics of Colonial Policy-making." *Journal of Modern History* 63 (December 1991): 647–80.

Perera, Suvendrini. *Reaches of Empire: The English Novel from Edgeworth to Dickens.* New York: Columbia University Press, 1991.

Petrie, Glen. *A Singular Iniquity: The Campaigns of Josephine Butler.* New York: Viking Press, 1971.

Poovey, Mary. *Uneven Developments: The Ideological Work of Gender in Mid-Victorian Britain.* Chicago: University of Chicago Press, 1988.

Porter, Bernard. *The Lion's Share: A Short History of British Imperialism, 1850–1970.* London: Longman Group, 1975.

Prochaska, F. K. *Women and Philanthropy in Nineteenth Century England.* Oxford: Oxford University Press, 1980.

Pugh, Martin. *Women's Suffrage in Britain, 1867–1928.* London: Historical Association, 1980.

Ramazanoglu, Caroline, et al. "Feedback: Feminism and Racism." *Feminist Review* 22 (February 1986): 82–105.

Ramusack, Barbara. "Catalysts or Helpers?: British Feminists, Indian Women's Rights and Indian Independence." In *The Extended Family: Women and Political Participation in India and Pakistan*, edited by Gail Minault, pp. 109–50. Columbia, Mo.: South Asia Books, 1981.

———. "Cultural Missionaries, Maternal Imperialists, Feminist Allies: British Women Activists in India, 1865–1945." In *Western Women and Imperialism: Complicity and Resistance*, edited by Nupur Chaudhuri and Margaret Strobel, pp. 119–36. Bloomington: Indiana University Press, 1992.

——. "Embattled Advocates: The Debate over Birth Control in India, 1920–1940." *Journal of Women's History* 1, no. 2 (Fall 1989): 34–64.

——. "Women's Organizations and Social Change: The Age-of-Marriage Issue in India." In *Women and World Change: Equity Issues in Development*, edited by Naomi Black and Ann Baker Cottrell, pp. 198–216. Beverly Hills, Calif.: Sage Publications, 1981.

Ray, Bharati. "Calcutta Women in the *Swadeshi* Movement (1903–1910): The Nature and Implications of Participation." In *The Urban Experiment: Calcutta*, edited by P. Sinha, pp. 168–81. Calcutta: n.p., 1987.

Rendall, Jane. *The Origins of Modern Feminism: Women in Britain, France and the United States, 1780–1860*. New York: Macmillan, 1985.

——, ed. *Equal or Different: Women's Politics, 1800–1914*. Oxford: Basil Blackwell, 1987.

Rich, Adrienne. *Blood, Bread and Poetry: Selected Prose, 1979–1985*. New York: W. W. Norton, 1986.

——. *Your Native Land, Your Life: Poems*. New York: W. W. Norton, 1983.

Rich, Paul B. *Race and Empire in British Politics*. Cambridge: Cambridge University Press, 1986.

Ridley, Hugh. *Images of Imperial Rule*. London: Croom-Helm, 1983.

Riley, Denise. *"Am I That Name?": The Category of "Women" in History*. Minneapolis: University of Minnesota Press, 1988.

Robbins, Keith. "Core and Periphery in Modern British History." *Proceedings of the British Academy* 52 (1984): 275–97.

——. *Nineteenth-Century Britain: England, Scotland and Wales: The Making of a Nation*. Oxford: Oxford University Press, 1988.

Rogers, Katherine M. *Feminism in Eighteenth-Century England*. Urbana: University of Illinois Press, 1982.

Roper, John, and Michael Tosh, eds. *Manful Assertions: Masculinities in Britain since 1800*. London: Routledge, 1991.

Rover, Constance. *Women's Suffrage and Party Politics*. London: Routledge and Kegan Paul, 1967.

Rubinstein, David. *A Different World for Women: The Life of Millicent Garrett Fawcett*. Columbus: Ohio State University Press, 1991.

Rupp, Leila J. "Conflict in the International Women's Movement, 1881–1950." Paper presented at the Berkshire Conference of Women Historians, New Brunswick, New Jersey, June 1990.

Ryan, Mary P. *Women in Public: Between Banners and Ballots, 1825–1880*. Baltimore, Md.: Johns Hopkins University Press, 1990.

Said, Edward. *Orientalism*. New York: Vintage Books, 1974.

Samuel, Raphael, ed. *Patriotism: The Making and Unmaking of British National Identity*. 3 vols. London: Routledge, 1989.

Sandoval, Chela. "Feminism and Racism: A Report on the 1981 National Women's Studies Association Conference." In *Making Face/Making Soul*, edited by Gloria Anzaldua, pp. 55–74. San Francisco: Aunt Lute Press, 1990.

Sanford, J. K. *Ladies in the Sun: The Memsahibs in India, 1790–1860*. London: Galley Press, 1962.

Sangari, Kumkum, and Sudesh Vaid, eds. *Recasting Women: Essays in Colonial History*. New Delhi: Kali for Women, 1989.

Sayers, Janet. *Biological Politics: Feminist and Anti-feminist Perspectives*. London: Tavistock Publications, 1982.

Schreiber, Adele, and Margaret Mathieson. *Journey towards Freedom*. Denmark: International Alliance of Women for Suffrage and Equal Citizenship, 1955.

Schupf, Harriet Warm. "Single Women and Social Reform in Mid-Nineteenth-Century England: The Case of Mary Carpenter." *Victorian Studies* 17 (March 1974): 301–17.

Scobie, Edward. *Black Britannia: A History of Blacks in Britain*. Chicago: Johnson Publishing, 1972.

Scott, Joan Wallach. "The Evidence of Experience." *Critical Inquiry* 17 (Summer 1991): 773–97.

———. "French Feminists Claim the Rights of 'Man': Olympe de Gouges in the French Revolution." Paper presented at Washington University, St. Louis, Missouri, April 2, 1990.

———. *Gender and the Politics of History*. New York: Columbia University Press, 1988.

Seal, Anil. *The Emergence of Indian Nationalism*. Cambridge: Cambridge University Press, 1956.

Searle, G. R. *The Quest for National Efficiency*. Berkeley: University of California Press, 1971.

Semmel, Bernard. *Imperialism and Social Reform: English Social-Imperial Thought, 1895–1914*. New York: Anchor Books, 1968.

Sen, P. *Florence Nightingale's Indian Letters*. Calcutta: n.p., 1937.

Sengupta, Padmini. *Sarojini Naidu: A Biography*. London: Asia Publishing House, 1966.

Shaarawi, Huda. *Harem Years: The Memoirs of an Egyptian Feminist*, edited by Margot Badran. New York: Feminist Press, 1986.

Shah, A. B., ed. *The Letters and Correspondence of Pandita Ramabai*. Bombay: Maharashtra State Board for Literature and Culture, 1977.

Shannon, Richard. *The Crisis of Imperialism, 1865–1915*. London: Granada Publishing, 1974.

Sievers, Sharon. "Six (or More) Feminists in Search of an Historian." *Journal of Women's History* 1, no. 2 (Fall 1989): 134–56.

Sinha, Mrinalini. "'Chathams, Pitts and Gladstones in Petticoats': The Politics of Gender and Race in the Ilbert Bill Controversy, 1883–84." In *Western Women and Imperialism: Complicity and Resistance*, edited by Nupur Chaudhuri and Margaret Strobel, pp. 98–118. Bloomington: Indiana University Press, 1992.

Smith, F. B. "The Contagious Diseases Acts Reconsidered." *Social History of Medicine* 3 (1990): 197–215.

Smith, Hilda L. *Reason's Disciples: Seventeenth-Century English Feminists*. Urbana: University of Illinois Press, 1982.

Smith, Sidonie, and Julia Watson, eds. *Decolonizing the Subject: The Politics of Gender in Women's Autobiography*. Minneapolis: University of Minnesota Press, 1992.

Smith-Rosenberg, Carroll. *Disorderly Conduct: Visions of Gender in Victorian America*. Oxford: Oxford University Press, 1985.

Snyder, Jack. *Myths of Empire: Domestic Politics and International Ambition.* Ithaca, N.Y.: Cornell University Press, 1991.

Solomon, Barbara H., and Paula S. Berggren. *A Mary Wollstonecraft Reader.* New York: Mentor Books, 1983.

Solomon, Martha M. *A Voice of Their Own: The Woman Suffrage Press, 1840–1910.* Tuscaloosa: University of Alabama Press, 1991.

Soloway, Richard A. *Birth Control and the Population Question in England, 1877–1930.* Chapel Hill: University of North Carolina Press, 1982.

Spelman, Elizabeth V. *Inessential Woman: Problems of Exclusion in Feminist Thought.* Boston: Beacon Press, 1988.

Spender, Dale, ed. *Feminist Theorists: Three Centuries of Key Women Thinkers.* New York: Pantheon Books, 1983.

Spillers, Hortense, ed. *Comparative American Identities: Race, Sex and Nationality in the Modern Text.* New York: Routledge, 1991.

Spivak, Gayatri Chakravorty. *In Other Worlds: Essays in Cultural Politics.* New York: Metheun, 1987.

———. "The Rani of Sirmur: An Essay in Reading the Archives." *History and Theory* 23 (1985): 247–80.

———. "Three Women's Texts and a Critique of Imperialism." In *The Feminist Reader: Essays in Gender and the Politics of Literary Criticism,* edited by Catherine Belsey and Jane Moore, pp. 175–96. New York: Basil Blackwell, 1989.

Stanley, Liz. "British Feminist Histories: An Editorial Introduction." *Women's Studies International Forum* 13 (1990): 3–7.

———. *Feminist Praxis: Research, Theory and Epistemology in Feminist Sociology.* New York: Routledge, 1990.

Stocking, George. *Victorian Anthropology.* New York: Free Press, 1987.

Stoler, Ann Laura. "Making Empire Respectable: The Politics of Race and Sexual Morality in Twentieth-Century Colonial Cultures." *American Ethnologist* 16, no. 4 (1989): 634–60.

———. "Rethinking Colonial Categories: European Communities and the Boundaries of Rule." *Comparative Studies in History and Society* 31, no. 1 (1989): 134–61.

Stowell, Sheila. *A Stage of Their Own: Feminist Playwrights of the Suffrage Era.* Ann Arbor: University of Michigan Press, 1992.

Strobel, Margaret. *European Women and the Second British Empire.* Bloomington: Indiana University Press, 1991.

———. "Sex and Work in the British Empire." *Radical History Review* 54 (1992): 177–86.

Suleri, Sara. *The Rhetoric of English India.* New Haven, Conn.: Yale University Press, 1992.

Summers, Anne. *Angels and Citizens: British Women as Military Nurses, 1854–1914.* New York: Routledge, 1988.

Tapper, Nancy. "Mysteries of the Harem? An Anthropological Perspective on Recent Studies of Women in the Middle East." *Women's Studies International Quarterly* 2 (1979): 481–87.

Terborg-Penn, Rosalind. "Discontented Black Feminists: Prelude and Postscript to the Passage of the Nineteenth Amendment." In *Women and Power in American*

History: A Reader, edited by Kathryn Kish Sklar and Thomas Dublin, 2:132–45. Englewood Cliffs, N.J.: Prentice-Hall, 1991.

Terry, Jennifer. "Theorizing Deviant Historiography." *Differences: A Feminist Journal of Cultural Studies* 3 (1991): 55–74.

Tharu, Susie, and K. Lalita, eds. *Women Writing in India 600 B.C. to the Present*. Vol. 1, *600 B.C. to the Early Twentieth Century*. New York: Feminist Press, 1991.

——. *Women Writing in India 600 B.C. to the Present*. Vol. 2, *The Twentieth Century*. New York: Feminist Press, 1993.

Thornton, A. P. *The Imperial Idea and Its Enemies*. New York: St. Martin's Press, 1985.

Tickner, Lisa. "The Hysteric, the Militant and the Womanly Woman: Images of Femininity in the Edwardian Women's Suffrage Campaign." *Feminist Art News* 2, no. 5 (1986): 4–5.

——. *The Spectacle of Women: Imagery of the Suffrage Campaign, 1907–1914*. Chicago: University of Chicago Press, 1988.

——. "Suffrage Campaigns: The Political Imagery of the British Women's Suffrage Movement." In *The Edwardian Era*, edited by Jane Beckett and Deborah Cherry, pp. 100–116. London: Phaedon Press and the Barbican Art Gallery, 1987.

Tyrrell, Ian. "American Exceptionalism in an Age of International History." *American Historical Review* 96 (October 1991): 1031–55.

——. *Woman's World, Woman's Empire: The Woman's Christian Temperance Union in International Perspective, 1880–1930*. Chapel Hill: University of North Carolina Press, 1991.

Uglow, Jenny. "Josephine Butler: From Sympathy to Theory." In *Feminist Theorists: Three Centuries of Key Women Thinkers*, edited by Dale Spender, pp. 146–64. New York: Pantheon Books, 1983.

Vaid, Sudesh. "Ideologies of Women in Nineteenth-Century Britain, 1850s–1870." *Economic and Political Weekly*, October 26, 1985, pp. 63–67.

Valverde, Mariana. "A Passion for Purity." Review of *The Sexuality Debates*, edited by Sheila Jeffreys. *Women's Review of Books* 5, no. 4 (January 1988): 6–7.

Van Voris, Jacqueline. *Carrie Chapman Catt: A Public Life*. New York: Feminist Press, 1987.

Vellacott, Jo. "Anti-War Suffragists." *History* 62 (October 1977): 411–25.

Vicinus, Martha. *Independent Women: Work and Community for Single Women, 1850–1920*. London: Virago Press, 1985.

Visram, Rozina. *Ayahs, Lascars, and Princes: Indians in Britain, 1700–1947*. London: Pluto Press, 1986.

Viswanathan, Gauri. *Masks of Conquest: Literary Study and British Rule in India*. New York: Columbia University Press, 1989.

Vogel, Lise. "Telling Tales: Historians of Our Own Lives." *Journal of Women's History* 2, no. 3 (Winter 1991): 89–101.

Walkowitz, Judith R. *City of Dreadful Delight: Narratives of Sexual Danger in Late-Victorian London*. Chicago: University of Chicago Press, 1992.

——. "Male Vice and Feminist Virtue: Feminism and the Politics of Prostitution in Nineteenth-Century Britain." *History Workshop Journal* 13 (Spring 1982): 79–93.

———. *Prostitution and Victorian Society: Women, Class and the State.* Cambridge: Cambridge University Press, 1980.

Walvin, James, and J. A. Mangan, eds. *Manliness and Morality: Middle-Class Masculinity in Britain and America, 1800–1940.* New York: St. Martin's Press, 1987.

Ware, Vron. *Beyond the Pale: White Women, Racism and History.* London: Verso, 1992.

Williams, Patrick. "Colonial Literature and the Notion of Britishness." *Literature, Teaching and Politics* 5 (1986): 92–107.

Wiltsher, Anne. *Most Dangerous Women: Feminist Peace Campaigners of the Great War.* London: Pandora Press, 1985.

Yegenoglu, Meyda. "Supplementing the Orientalist Lack: European Ladies in the Harem." *Inscriptions* 6 (1992): 45–81.

Yellin, Jean Fagan. *Women and Sisters: The Antislavery Feminists in American Culture.* New Haven, Conn.: Yale University Press, 1989.

Zonana, Joyce. "The Sultan and the Slave: Feminist Orientalism and the Structure of *Jane Eyre*." *Signs* 18, no. 3 (1993): 592–617.

Index